Tony Cliff

International Struggle and the Marxist Tradition

Tony Cliff

International Struggle and the Marxist Tradition

SELECTED WRITINGS
VOLUME 1

London and Sydney

Tony Cliff: International Struggle and the Marxist Tradition: Selected Writings Volume 1

First published 2001
Bookmarks Publications Ltd, c/o 1 Bloomsbury Street, London WC1B 3QE, England
Bookmarks, PO Box A338, Sydney South, NSW 2000, Australia

ISBN 1 898876 76 2 (Paperback)
ISBN 1 898876 75 4 (Hardback)

Printed by The Bath Press, Bath
Cover by Ian Goodyer

Bookmarks Publications Ltd is linked to an international grouping of socialist organisations:
Australia: International Socialists, PO Box A338, Sydney South
Austria: Linkswende, Postfach 87, 1108 Wien
Britain: Socialist Workers Party, PO Box 82, London E3 3LH
Canada: International Socialists, PO Box 339, Station E, Toronto, Ontario M6H 4E3
Cyprus: Ergatiki Demokratia, PO Box 7280, Nicosia
Czech Republic: Socialisticka Solidarita, PO Box 1002, 11121 Praha 1
Denmark: Internationale Socialister, PO Box 5113, 8100 Aarhus C
Germany: Linksruck, Postfach 304 183, 20359 Hamburg
Greece: Socialistiko Ergatiko Komma, c/o Workers Solidarity, PO Box 8161, Athens 100 10
Holland: Internationale Socialisten, PO Box 92025, 1090AA Amsterdam
Ireland: Socialist Workers Party, PO Box 1648, Dublin 8
New Zealand: Socialist Workers Organisation, PO Box 13-685, Auckland
Norway: Internasjonale Socialisterr, Postboks 9226 Grønland, 0134 Oslo
Poland: Pracownicza Demokracja, PO Box 12, 01-900 Warszawa 118
Spain: Izquierda Revolucionaria, Apartado 563, 08080 Barcelona
Zimbabwe: International Socialist Organisation, PO Box 6758, Harare

This volume is one of a series devoted to the writings of Tony Cliff (1917-2000). Born in Palestine to a Zionist family, his development as a revolutionary Marxist was shaped by an extraordinary combination of influences. He came to hate all forms of oppression after witnessing the systematic exclusion of Arabs from Zionist society. Opposition to imperialism led to him being jailed by the occupying British power. He came to embrace Trotskyism when Stalin's disastrous international policies helped Hitler become German Chancellor in 1933.

Arriving in post-war Britain from an impoverished colonial country, Cliff was struck by the relative affluence here. This made him question the dogmatic followers of Trotsky who maintained the capitalist economy was collapsing. Above all, Cliff rejected their assertion that Red Army tanks, rather than workers' self-activity, could establish socialism in Eastern Europe. If the Eastern bloc was not socialist, and yet identical to Russia, that country was not socialist either. He concluded it was state capitalist.

This analysis preserved the central Marxist notion that workers' liberation (and therefore humanity's in general) comes from self-activity. This meant that theory and practice must be linked, which helped Cliff avoid the sterile abstractions of much of what passed for Marxism. Such insights guided him and others who formed successively the Socialist Review Group, the International Socialists and the Socialist Workers Party.

A wave of industrial militancy which peaked in the early 1970s enabled the SWP to intervene practically in the class struggle. The focus was in two areas: on rank and file action rather than union bureaucracy; and on the building of a revolutionary party which could offer political leadership in the fight for socialism.

The collapse of Stalinist regimes after 1989 confirmed the state capitalist analysis of 40 years before and cleared the way for the spread of the International Socialist Tendency in many countries.

Across seven decades of revolutionary activism, Cliff was a tireless writer and speaker who always combined theoretical rigour with practical action. We are pleased to be able to republish his writings, not as a monument to the past, but as tools to help build a future where humanity will no longer be threatened by the poverty, oppression, wars and environmental destruction that are inextricably part of capitalism.

Donny Gluckstein

Contents

Revolutions and the international

Introduction

Alex Callinicos

It is appropriate that this collection of Tony Cliff's writings should begin with a volume devoted to his continuous engagement, throughout his career as a revolutionary, with the class struggle in different countries. Marxism as a political and intellectual tradition is defined by its relationship with the class struggle and its development. Cliff's involvement was, of course, practical as well as theoretical: the situations that he sought to understand were those that represented the most urgent political priority for him at the time.

This is most obvious in the first texts, which date from his early years as a revolutionary in his native Palestine. As a revolutionary internationalist for whom the Arab working class was the key to change in the Middle East, Cliff found himself caught between two fires—from the repressive British colonial regime and from the Zionists who would establish the state of Israel in 1948. In his autobiography he describes the difficulties he faced in these conditions in trying to build a tiny Trotskyist group uniting Arab and Jewish workers. He also had to confront, as he did for many decades to come, the identification of Marxism with the Stalinist regime in Russia.[1]

Cliff strove to apply the revolutionary tradition he had inherited from Marx and Engels, Lenin and Trotsky to these circumstances. Already in 1935, at the age of 18, he had written a substantial article on the agrarian question in Egypt. The chapter on Egyptian capitalism included in this volume comes from the manuscript of an unpublished book on the Arab East. Completed in July 1945, it is a substantial work, divided into six parts—'Historical Background', 'Imperialism in the Arab East', 'The Economic Structure of the Arab East', 'The National Movement in the Arab East', 'Zionism', and 'The Working-Class Movement in the Arab East'.

In the chapter reprinted here Cliff went beyond the Trotskyist orthodoxy according to which the dominance of imperialism prevented industrial development in the colonial and semi-colonial countries. Displaying the respect for empirical evidence that is a consistent feature of his writings, he showed that, in the specific conditions of the Great Depression of the 1930s and the Second World War, it proved possible for Egypt to experience significant industrialisation. This led to the rise of a local capitalist class capable of asserting its interests against British imperialism, and also to the emergence of an industrial working class on whose actions the destiny of the Arab East depended.

This analysis anticipated much later discussions of the Newly Industrializing Countries of East Asia and Latin America. It also led Cliff to predict a stormy future for Egyptian society—a prediction amply fulfilled by the struggles that unfolded after 1945, with the fall of the monarchy, the seizure of power by Nasser and the Free Officers' Movement, and the unstable regimes of his successors Sadat and Mubarak. Throughout his life Cliff stressed the centrality of the Egyptian working class to the future of the revolutionary movement in the Middle East.

After his move to Britain Cliff had still to address the question of Palestine, as Israel, relying on massive support from American imperialism, precipitated the Middle East into a series of wars. *The Struggle in the Middle East* first appeared as a pamphlet that Cliff wrote in response to the 1967 Six Day War. Produced at a time when support for Israel was at its zenith on the British left, it shows Cliff utterly uncompromising in his support for the struggle of the Palestinian people.

As an anti-Zionist Jew, Cliff also took a distinctive Marxist stance towards the Nazi Holocaust, in which many of his family perished. He dismissed the predictable attacks on him as a 'self-hating Jew' with uncomprehending contempt. Entirely comfortable in his Jewishness, he was nevertheless an internationalist who fought for the liberation of humankind from all forms of national and racial oppression, rather than preoccupy himself with his own specific 'identity' or 'culture'.

The other texts in this volume show in different ways the interplay between Marxism and the class struggle in Cliff's writings. At the height of the Cold War in the 1950s and early 1960s, he had to confront a situation in which the authentic revolutionary Marxist tradition was completely marginalised. One task in this situation was to preserve this tradition. But, as he says in the late talk on Engels included in this volume, he was never interested in a hagiographic attitude towards the great Marxists. His interest in them always depended on their relevance to the present.

Cliff's little book on Rosa Luxemburg, first published in 1959, is a case in point. It was partly intended to vindicate Luxemburg's greatness at a time when her thought had fallen into neglect or distortion. Ignored by the Stalinists, who found her stress on self-activity inconvenient, she was misused by Cold War social democrats to justify their attempt to identify the entire revolutionary tradition with Stalinism. Cliff's own approach to Luxemburg is by no means uncritical, as is shown by his comments on her theory of capitalist breakdown and her position on the national question. But his interest in her also reflected the fact that her writings allowed him to demonstrate that at the heart of Marxism is the idea of socialism as the self-emancipation of the working class.

At a time when Marxism was identified with what Hal Draper called 'socialism from above'—whether in the form of Stalinist tyranny in the East or social-democratic pragmatism in the West—this was a crucial lesson to draw. It encouraged Cliff to assert that Luxemburg's views on party organisation were more relevant to contemporary socialists than Lenin's. To some extent a similar view informs 'Trotsky on Substitutionism' as well. When the long post-war boom began to falter in the late 1960s, helping to precipitate an explosion of mass struggles throughout the advanced capitalist world, Cliff revised this judgement.

Indeed, perhaps his most important book after *State Capitalism in Russia* was his study of Lenin, published in four volumes between 1975 and 1979. The first volume in particular seeks to demonstrate the centrality of Lenin's political method—firm in principles, strategic in focus, flexible in tactics—to any attempt to build revolutionary socialist organisation. As his views on this question changed, Cliff altered the relevant passage in *Rosa Luxemburg*. The version published here includes both formulations. Cliff's later stress on Lenin's approach to party building did not alter his immense admiration for Luxemburg.[2]

Cliff's turn to Lenin reflected his recognition that the upturn in the class struggle of the late 1960s and early 1970s had created, for the first time since the 1920s, the opportunity for genuine revolutionaries to emerge from the margins and begin to build mass workers' parties.[3] In a series of texts reprinted here Cliff grappled with the interrelations between the dynamics of mass struggle and the tasks of revolutionaries. Even before the upturn exploded, we can see him doing this when he writes about the Belgian general strike of 1960. This article is striking for the care with which Cliff analyses the peculiarities of the Belgian labour movement, for its realism—he refuses to surrender to wishful thinking and treat the strike, coming as it did in the midst of the post-war boom, as a sign of 'a mature revolutionary situation'—and for the clarity with which he outlines both the limitations and the potential of mass strikes.

Cliff's writings on May 1968 in France and the Portuguese Revolution of 1974-75 by contrast represent his response to the struggles that erupted as the long boom came to an end. The French events—the student revolt and general strike of May-June 1968—more than any other of that turbulent era put the authentic Marxist tradition back onto the agenda. David Widgery vividly expressed what they meant for members of the International Socialists: 'It was as if an international political pageant was being acted out—the ideas we had treasured in pamphlets and argued about in tiny pub rooms were now roaming alive, three-dimensional. Marxism had come out of the cold'.[4] *France: The Struggle Goes On*, co-written with Ian Birchall, was Cliff's response: it passionately championed the workers' and students' rising, but also insisted that it had demonstrated the bankruptcy of reformism, represented in this case particularly by the Communist Party, which sought desperately to confine the struggle to a purely economic and electoral battle.

Two specific political concerns run through Cliff's writings on France and Portugal. First of all, in the late 1960s the International Socialists began to transform themselves from a tiny Marxist propaganda group into a small party with some roots in the working class (a change reflected by the adoption of a new name, the Socialist Workers Party, in 1977). Cliff's analyses of France and Portugal served to orient IS activists, many of them freshly won from the student movement of the late 1960s or the strikes of the early 1970s, in a period of struggle unprecedented for a generation. They also sought to show the relevance of the writings of Lenin, Luxemburg and Trotsky—themselves representing the theoretically refined experience of the much greater wave of struggles in the early 20th century—to the problems of contemporary socialists. As one who had rallied to Trotsky and the Fourth International in the early 1930s, Cliff represented for the young revolutionaries of the 1960s and 1970s a connection with that earlier era.

But, secondly, this process of education was directed towards another audience, particularly in the Portuguese case. The far left experienced in continental Europe an even more explosive growth than the IS enjoyed in Britain. The intensity and scale of the struggles of the day—the Italian 'hot autumn' of 1969, the decline of Francoism in Spain, and, most dramatically, the revolutionary process that exploded in Portugal after the overthrow of the dictatorship in April 1974—gave the new revolutionary organisations growing influence over a radicalised minority inside the working class. But these groups drew on theoretical traditions—some version either of Maoism or orthodox Trotskyism—that ill-equipped them to deal with the challenges confronting them.

The gulf that therefore opened up between the potential of the situation and the politics of the left was starkest in Portugal. Here the radicalisation ushered in by the fall of the dictatorship pushed a substantial layer of both workers and soldiers well to the left of both the Communist and Socialist parties. Faced with this enormous opportunity, some sections of the far left found formally democratic reasons for trailing behind the Socialist Party, even when it launched a reactionary offensive against the revolution; meanwhile others sought in an alliance with left-wing army officers a shortcut to socialism.[5] Cliff's writings on Portugal, while making no compromise with reformism, sought with patience and care to demonstrate that only by winning the support of the majority of the working class could the far left hope to open the road to socialist revolution.

Above all, *Portugal at the Crossroads*, translated not merely into Portuguese, but into French, German, Greek, Italian and Spanish, sought to win at least sections of the European far left to the strategic approach of classical Marxism. Portugal proved indeed to be a turning point—though not in the extreme sense that many revolutionaries feared at the time, when they predicted that the only alternative to the working class taking power was fascism. In Portugal, as elsewhere in Western Europe in the mid-1970s, reformism—whether in the form of social democracy or in the shape of the Communist Party, which still exerted a strong hold on many of the most militant workers—acted as a buffer, absorbing and deflecting the impact of the mass radicalisation.[6]

As the revolutionary tide began to recede, most of the far-left organisations in Europe went into crisis and disintegrated.[7] The associated reaction against Marxism went furthest in France, where the so-called *nouveaux philosophes* helped to create the space in which neoliberal ideas could later gain hegemony. Cliff had to grapple with a version of this crisis in Britain in the late 1970s and early 1980s: as the writings included in the second volume of this collection will show, he plotted the course first of the great upsurge in workers' struggles that culminated in the fall of the Heath government in 1974, then of the progressive weakening of the movement under Labour between 1974 and 1979, and finally of the employers' offensive launched by Margaret Thatcher that led to the defeat of the miners' strike of 1984-85.

Cliff's ruthless realism, his insistence on looking unpleasant facts in the face, combined with his unfaltering confidence in the revolutionary Marxist tradition, helped to ensure that the SWP did not collapse in the way that much of the European far left did at the end of the 1970s. But there is a sense in which the kind of strategic analysis that he had developed, notably in his writings on Portugal, went into cold storage. The analysis was not mistaken—indeed the actual outcome largely vindicated it—but problems of revolutionary strategy and tactics were of much less direct relevance at a time when the priority lay in keeping socialist ideas and organisation alive.

This situation began to change in the late 1990s. The East Asian economic crisis of 1997-98 showed how hollow the supposed triumph of capitalism was, even in a region that had experienced spectacular growth for much of the previous two decades. It also helped to precipitate a revolutionary process in Indonesia. The May 1998 rising that overthrew the Suharto regime inaugurated a period of instability very similar to that experienced by Portugal after April 1974, as the ruling class and the masses clashed in a series of confrontations in which political power was constantly at stake. In 'Revolution and Counter-Revolution: Lessons for Indonesia', Cliff applied the strategic understanding that he had shown in his writings of the 1970s to this new case. Translated and circulated widely on the Indonesian left, the text was, once again, an effort to educate a new generation in the classical Marxist tradition.

The Indonesian Revolution was one indication of a more general break in the situation. The great protests at Seattle at the end of November 1999 marked another turning point, as a growing minority around the world began to target capitalism itself, rather than some of its more specific manifestations. Cliff lived to see and to welcome the emergence of this anti-capitalist movement. The writings contained in this volume and its successors will no doubt help to guide many members of this movement as they confront the enemy which Cliff devoted his life to fighting.

Notes

1 T Cliff, *A World to Win* (London, 2000), ch 1.
2 Several key texts on this question will be found in T Cliff, D Hallas, C Harman and L Trotsky, *Party and Class* (London, 1997).
3 See, on this upturn, C Harman, *The Fire Last Time* (rev edn, London, 1998).
4 D Widgery, 'Ten Years for Pandora', *Socialist Review* 2 (May 1978), p9.
5 C Harman, *The Fire Last Time*, ch 13.
6 For an astute near-contemporary analysis, see I Birchall, 'Social Democracy and the Portuguese "Revolution",' *International Socialism* 2:6 (1979).
7 C Harman, 'The Crisis of the European Revolutionary Left', *International Socialism* 2:4 (1979).

Politics in the Middle East

The Palestine question

British policy in Palestine

New International, October 1938

The three principal factors in the political arena in Palestine are British imperialism, the Arab nationalist movement under its present leadership and the Zionist movement. A labour movement as an independent factor exercising influence in political affairs does not yet exist. We shall deal with each of these factors separately.

Palestine represents strategically a highly important colony. It is situated in the vicinity of the Suez Canal, the sea route to India. Across Palestine lies also the air route to the Far East. The greatest airport in the Near East is situated in Palestine. In Haifa the British government is constructing a sea base, naturally at the expense of the Palestine population. The oil of Iraq, of such great importance to British imperialism, flows through a pipeline to Haifa. Palestine likewise serves as an important base of British policy in the Mediterranean. With the strengthening of the Italian air fleet and its Mediterranean base, the strategic significance of Malta for England was considerably reduced. The conquest of Ethiopia weakened England's position in Egypt. Both are important reasons for the fact that Palestine is today of the very greatest significance in the British military set-up. Not for nothing is Haifa called the Singapore of the Near East.

Besides the strategic significance of Palestine for English imperialism it possesses a certain economic significance. British capital is found to be invested in the important industries of Palestine, in the Ruthenberg electrical enterprise, in the Jerusalem station, in the Dead Sea potash works, in the construction of the Haifa Harbour, in the soap and oil factories of Shemen, in the Iraq Petroleum Company and many others. Clearly, however, the principal importance of Palestine for British imperialism lies in the field of strategy and not of economics.

British policy in this country is based on a system of divide and rule, the system of inciting national hatreds between the two peoples in the country in order to assure itself the position of arbitrator. The facts which indicate the extent to which the British provoke national antagonisms are too numerous to recite here. We must content ourselves with a few typical instances.

From the beginning of British rule in Palestine to the present there have been four bloody attacks on the Jews—1920, 1921, 1929 and 1936-38. After the bloody events of 1921 the two leaders of the provocation against the Jews, Emia al Husseini and Aref al Aref, sentenced to 15 years in prison, were quickly released and the former was appointed by the government to the highest Arab office in the country, President of the Supreme Muslim Council, despite the fact that his name was not even included on the Arab list of proposed candidates. The other was promoted to the position of District Commissioner of Beersheba to become the only Arab District Commissioner in the country. This fact alone indicates how far the English government will go to uphold the influence of the feudal elements in their incitement of the Arab masses against the Jews. In 1928 the government began to proclaim the provocative decrees concerning the juridical status of the Wailing Wall (sacred to orthodox Jews) thereby opening the door to the chauvinistic religious propaganda of a gang of effendis and leading to the pogroms of 1929 under the slogan of 'Defend the Holy Places.' Simultaneously the government by this means strengthened the influence of the religious chauvinist element among the Jews (at that time there arose the 'Commissions for the Defence of the Wailing Wall').

The government has systematically prevented all attempts at effecting a reconciliation of the two peoples. An Arab party was organised in Haifa which raised the slogan of 'Peace between the Jews and Arabs' (it was a bourgeois liberal party) and counted among its members even the Arab mayor of the city. The British government together with the feudal Arab leadership and the Zionist organisation were responsible for the defeat of this party in subsequent elections, and brought such pressure to bear on its members that it was dissolved. There used to exist in Palestine an international trade union of railroad workers. The government, however, prohibited membership in this trade union and imported thousands of European labourers to work on the railroads, thus blowing up the union. An attempt was made at one time to establish an organisation called Achwath Poalim (Labour Brotherhood) but the government proscribed it as illegal. Efforts to bring about an understanding between the workers of both peoples were not numerous, but such as they were they encountered the strongest resistance of the English government. In Palestine this policy of divide and rule takes on special characteristics which it does not show in other colonies in the same form.

To draw a clear picture of British policy one must take up two main questions: (a) the British government and its relation to Jewish immigration and settlement, and (b) the British government and the demands of the Arab masses for national self-determination.

Jewish immigration represents a basic factor in the process of accelerating capitalist development. The growth of a Jewish and Arab working class which, considered historically, represent a serious anti-imperialist force is bound up with Jewish immigration into the country. The British government is not interested in fostering any considerable working-class population in Palestine. On the other hand if the Jewish population in the country were to become too strong its dependence on British policy could not be assured even by the threat of strong pogroms. It is therefore plain that the British are not interested in a broad Jewish mass immigration. At the same time the government does not desire to shut off Jewish immigration completely. The government's policy is therefore to open the door to a certain extent and for a limited time, and then to close it. In this way the government heightens the national tensions around the immigration question. The sharp changes in the tempo of immigration lead to sharp conflicts in the relations of Jews and Arabs. The opening of the door arouses a feeling of sympathy for the British among the Jewish masses, and the Arab population receive the impression of a identity of interests between the Jews and British rule, and this fosters the growth of Arab chauvinism. The closing of the doors in turn provokes strong chauvinism in the Jewish population which interprets the immigration restrictions not as a link in the chain of British policy, but merely as the result of an Arab 'victory' and Arab domination over the British government.

The same duplicity characterises the policy of the government in the sphere of colonisation. For many years it professed to protect the interests of the fellaheen (peasants), and from time to time decreed laws for the protection of the Arab tenantry but which gave no genuine relief to the tenant for the simple reason that there was no democratic control. By means of these decrees it also tried to foster chauvinistic tendencies. It was forbidden to evict a leaseholder from the land without assuring him of an equivalent piece of land elsewhere. It was, however, permissible to evict him if he refused to pay higher rents. The purpose of this law is obvious. The government pretended to look after the leaseholder's interests and legislate for his protection, whereas in reality the feudal landowner wasn't affected at all because the effendis whose lands were only partly cultivated could easily evict their tenants on the pretext that they would not work the land that was assigned them. In case the landowner should incidentally have no surplus land he could, according to the law, demand a higher rent and, if the leaseholder were not able to pay, he would be evicted. If these laws were therefore ineffective against the effendis and the speculators then they were effective for the purpose of inciting national antagonisms. The Jewish settlers have no surplus land, and so do not themselves appear to the tenant as lessors who can legally evict him. It is therefore clear that the attitude of the Zionist movement which stands for unlimited purchase of land and against the laws for the protection of leaseholders only sharpens the chauvinistic atmosphere around the whole question of settlement. In any case, the British government did not pass these laws in the interests of the feudal landlords of the Jewish bourgeoisie, nor yet in favour of the Arab fellaheen,but only for the purpose of sharpening national disputes.

From all this it is evident that the British know full well how to exploit the elementary needs of the Jewish worker, namely immigration and colonisation, neither of which contradicts the real necessities of the Arab masses, in order to raise a barrier of hate between the producers of both peoples and to assure itself of the dependence of the Jewish population. This the government achieves principally through pretending to look after the humanitarian interests of the Jews in Palestine.

The government is always declaring its desire to realise the establishment of a Jewish national home. These declarations are intended to win the sympathy of the Jewish population in Palestine as well as the sympathy of the Jews everywhere. The most important of these was the Balfour Declaration. It is important to understand the motives which led England to proclaim the Balfour Declaration. It was at the time when the position of the Entente powers was very unfavourable. Russia stood on the eve of the October Revolution and her rupture with the Allies. England was interested in winning the sympathy of the Russian Jews so that they might strengthen the Russian reaction which wanted to continue the war. The British were also interested in gaining the sympathy of the American Jews so that they could support the united war front of the United States with the Allies, morally and materially. Interestingly enough, the German government at the time, and for similar reasons, proclaimed its own 'Balfour Declaration'. The Balfour Declaration became the means of strengthening the chauvinistic and anti-Jewish tendencies among the Arabs, and strengthened the position of Zionism among the Jews of Palestine and throughout the world, and thereby also the position of British imperialism.

The British at the same time succeeded in canalising the anti-imperialist demands of the Arab masses for national independence. A few facts will suffice to prove this point. In 1929 the High Commissioner of Palestine declared the purpose of the trip he made to England to be the introduction of constitutional reforms in Palestine, and the strengthening of democracy and independence. Directly after the outbreak of 1929 he declared that in consequence of the Arab attacks on the Jews these reforms would no longer be in accord with the real situation. This statement led to the belief of the Arab masses that if there was to be no independence or democracy in the country this was not due to the fact that the British were hostile to these demands but the Jews. The High Commissioner proposed in 1935 to set up a Legislative Council. This British proposal, made in order to obscure the real demands for independent institutions, was anti-democratic insofar as real decisions would remain in the hands of British imperialism. Even today after the British army has demolished Arab villages, blown up hundreds of peasant dwellings, killed villagers and set up concentration camps, the Arab terror is directed not against the British government nor against English soldiers and officials, but against the Jewish population. For the government is always declaring that it undertakes its measures of suppression not to maintain its rule but out of consideration for the Jewish masses, who are the real enemy of the Arabs in their movement for liberation. The Arabs are made to see their national oppressors in the Jews, and the actions of the Arab masses are directed into chauvinist anti-Jewish channels, thus consolidating the role of the feudal leaders who are the real anti-Jewish element.

The Jewish-Arab conflict

New International, November 1938

Arab economy is for the most part feudal. Even its capitalist elements are to a considerable extent tied up with the feudal mode of exploitation (usury) or are feudal in origin, functioning both as landlord and capitalist. Alongside of this development has arisen a new stratum, the intellectuals who are connected with the upper classes (free professions, government officials). For the present it is these upper classes that exercise a dominant influence over the Arab masses. It is capitalist development in Palestine as well as English imperialist oppression of the Arab people which created the conditions for the rise of the Arab nationalist movement under the present leadership of the feudal and semi-capitalist system.

These classes see in the imperialist domination of the country a superfluous and alien guardianship in the political control over the masses. Since, however, there is no fundamental social and economic antagonism between these classes and imperialism, the conflict is not too profound. On the other hand there does exist a conflict between the Arab upper classes and the Jewish population. Not because the latter is an element for the support of British imperialism but because it is a means for the development of Jewish capitalist economy. This conflict arises because the feudal elements among the Arabs fear the modernisation of Palestinian society by the Jews and their own destruction. The Arab capitalist elements take part in this struggle mainly because of their exclusive tendencies and their competition with the Jews.

The Arab ruling classes, aiming to settle the conflict with the Jews in their own favour, are ready to strike a compromise with British imperialism at the expense of the Jews. Thus, for example, Djemal al Husseini, one of the outstanding leaders of the nationalist movement, declared that the Supreme Arab Committee was agreed that Palestine should become a British crown colony, provided that Jewish immigration was halted. Another leader, Hassan Sidky Dajani, wrote in an open letter to the High Commissioner, 'England is mistaken if she believes that we have risen against her...we recognise the power of her troops—a word from you, a word which England will not have to pay for too greatly, would suffice to restore the situation to normal.'

At the same time a basic conflict exists between the interests of the national and social emancipation of the Arab masses and British imperialism. This conflict can only be solved through the abolition of imperialist rule and the establishment of political independence.

Meanwhile there exists, objectively, a conflict between the Arab masses and the Zionist aspirations towards exclusivism and maintenance of British rule. This conflict can only be solved to the extent that Jewish masses in Palestine renounce Zionist exclusivism. While the opposition of the Arab upper classes to the Jews is reactionary, the struggle of the Arab masses against Zionism is absolutely progressive. The upper classes are today successful in diverting the national struggle of the masses into anti-Jewish channels by means of the fact that the predominant majority of the Jewish population is Zionist. The anti-Jewish terror has only increased the influence of Zionism on the Palestinian Jewish masses and diverts their bitterness from the struggle against imperialism. All this leads to a situation where today a great part of the Arab masses believe that through their struggle against the Jews they are furthering their own national liberation, whereas in fact they are only making their struggle more difficult to the extent that they are strengthening the position of imperialism, Zionism and the feudal Arab leadership.

Aspects of Arab nationalism

The entire development of the Arab nationalist movement in Palestine manifests a twofold aspect. On the one hand a feudal semi-bourgeois leadership which leads the movement into anti-Jewish channels without touching imperialism, on the other hand the Arab masses whose will to national liberation becomes increasingly stronger in so far as it crystallises into anti-imperialist hatred. Only an international leadership can resolve this dual aspect. It is interesting and useful to consider the various stages through which Arab nationalism has passed. In the degree that the nationalist movement gained strength, the leaders proceeded to change the slogans, giving them an anti-Jewish twist. In 1921 the main argument of the feudal leaders was that the Jews wanted to gain possession of the holy places, and, secondarily, that the Jews were imparting bolshevism. Definite statements were made that the movement was directed not against England but against Zionism. A couple of years before the pogroms of 1929 religious arguments were used for anti-Jewish agitation.

But with the development of the nationalist movement and the unity of the Arab, Christians and Muslims, the religious argument was soft-pedalled and the question of the influence of Jewish immigration on the economic situation was stressed. The Arab leaders began to carry on propaganda using the slogan, 'The Jews buy land and drive out the Arab peasants; the condition of the Arab peasants is so hard because of Jewish immigration; Arab industry suffers because of the development of Jewish industry; the Jews are to blame for the difficult financial condition of the government treasury; and therefore you must fight the Jewish immigration and settlement.'

The economic exclusivism of the Jews under the influence of Zionism (boycott of Arab workers and goods, etc) enabled this agitation to find a widespread response among the Arab masses. Then came the years of prosperity, 1932-35, in which despite Zionist exclusivism the income and the living standards of the Arab masses arose in consequence of Jewish immigration. The economic arguments of the Arab leaders against the Jews lost their point. The national consciousness among the Arabs gained in step with the capitalist development of the country and of the nationalist liberation movements in the surrounding countries of the Near East. The question of the political set-up became a central problem around which the Arab nationalist movements concentrated. In the same period the Zionist chauvinist tendencies among the Jews became stronger with the decline of the international working-class movement. The chauvinist Zionist slogans among the Jews struck a responsive note with the greater political tension in the Mediterranean and the resulting need of British policy to create a considerable Zionist power in Palestine. Instead of the former slogan of the Zionist organisation, 'Palestine, a bi-national state', Zionist policy came out openly with the slogan of 'The Jewish state'. The Arab feudal and semi-capitalist leaders who were afraid that the nationalist movement would develop along independent and consistently anti-imperialist lines now raised the cry, 'The Jews want to build a Jewish state in Palestine which will oppress the Arab minority while serving as a means of oppression in the hands of English imperialism.'

The present Arab nationalist movement, permeated with an exclusivist spirit in the struggle against the Jews, is fertile soil for chauvinist fascist and particularly anti-Jewish ideas. The fascist powers and propagandists send money to Palestine in order to strengthen this ideological reactionary influence and so gain control of the nationalist movement. In the measure that the Comintern and the Second International play the role more and more of political gendarmes against the movement of liberation in the colonies, and to the extent that the international labour movement finds itself in a state of decline, the influence of chauvinist, anti-Jewish ideologies becomes stronger. Fascism succeeds more and more in making use of Arab nationalism in its own interests.

The Zionist movement

It is our conviction that Zionism is a nationalist reactionary conception because it builds its hopes not on the class struggle of the international working class but on the continuation of world reaction and its consolidation.

The Zionist movement has been fighting for years to realise the slogan '100 percent Jewish labour, 100 percent Jewish production, etc.' Pickets of Jewish workers were organised against Arab workers who held jobs in Jewish enterprises. Among these pickets there were to be found all kinds of people from the right fascist wing of the Zionist movement to representatives of the 'Hashomer Hatzair' (affiliated with the London Bureau). Hashomer Hatzair does not demand 100 percent Jewish labour but Jewish labour only in Jewish enterprise with the exception of localities where the Arab workers have been engaged for many years (only 18 percent of the Arab workers in Jewish enterprise belong to this category). While therefore the Zionist movement generally demands 100 percent Jewish labour the Hashomer Hatzair demands 82 percent Jewish labour. There is still another small Zionist party divided into two wings which is against this picketing—the Left Poale-Zion.

This system of the 'conquest of labour' leads to a situation where only in periods of economic crisis and the decline of wages of the Jewish workers, only in periods of political reaction, can its aim be achieved, the penetration of Jewish workers by the eviction of the Arabs. In periods of the development of the

Jewish and Arab working classes, of increased immigration, of rising living standards, the system of the 'conquest of labour' is thwarted and the Jewish worker leaves the industry which was the bone of contention of the chauvinist struggle. The following table gives the figures for four different periods: (1) September 1933, beginning of prosperity in Palestine; (2) September 1935, high-water mark of prosperity; (3) June 1936, one month after the bloody events and the economic crisis; (4) September 1936, one and a half years after the beginning of the latest sharp crisis. The figures show the number of workers in six of the largest and most important Jewish colonies:

	Jewish workers	Arab workers
September 1933	2,433	1,687
September 1935	1,804	3,009
June 1936	2,739	1,271
September 1936	3,818	896

The business of picketing for Jewish labour only increases the damage which the working class, Jewish as well as Arab, suffers from the unrestricted national competition of the workers of both peoples. The Arab workers, too, begin to set up pickets against Jewish labour, for example in public works. The consequence is that the upper classes gain in influence. The government, too, knows how to exploit the situation. It plays the role of arbitrator and declares picketing illegal when it is on account of race, religion or language. This enables Jewish employers to avail themselves in any real conflict of Arab strikebreakers and likewise gives the Arab employer his chance to use Jewish strikebreakers. The system of the 'conquest of labour' with its picketing weakens the working class and strengthens the position of both employers and British imperialism.

We should like to touch on the question of the relation of Zionism to imperialism. The Zionist movement is against the independence of Palestine and against every form of democracy ('as long as the Jews are a minority'). The extreme right wing of Zionism, the Revisionists, who have their separate organisation, have for years been demanding the establishment of the Jewish state on the basis of 'an understanding between the Jewish legions and the strategic interests of British imperialism'. Other sections of the Zionist bourgeoisie headed by Dr Weizmann once declared that 'Palestine will remain as Jewish as England is English'. Later they declared that Palestine would be 'bi-national' and that the mandate must be upheld at all costs. Today they support the partition plan and the setting up of a Jewish state as an ally of British imperialism. The Zionist reformist party (Mapei) calls for cooperation with the government and for the most part supports the idea of partition. Hashomer Hatzair calls for the struggle to preserve the mandate. The Poale-Zion party is for an anti-imperialist struggle but does not indicate what form of political regime is its immediate aim, so that its slogans remain empty. Like the other Zionist parties it is against the democratisation of the political system in the country. In consequence of its opposition to the immediate independence of Palestine a section of its supporters have rallied to the partition plan.

The whole Zionist movement with all its wings, therefore, supports British rule in Palestine in one form or another.

The Jews and British imperialism

There are two opinions about the relation between the Jews in Palestine and British imperialism. The one views them as an integral part of the imperialist camp (this is the idea of the extreme Arab nationalists and their lackeys in the camp of the Stalinists); the second looks upon the Jews as an integral part of the Palestinian population and as such anti-imperialist. Neither of these views is correct. The former is wrong because the Jews are no thin, privileged stratum representing the exploiting interests of the Motherland. Simple comparison between the whites in South Africa and of the Jews in Palestine shows how wrong this view is.

The reformist leaders of the Jewish labour movement have drawn this comparison as an argument against the international organisation of workers in Palestine. The Communist Party of Palestine (Stalinist) has naturally seized on this analogy in order to expose the 'imperialist' role of the Jews. In the first place, however, the Jewish working population makes up more than half of the entire working class of Palestine, whereas in South Africa the whites are only one fifth of the working population. The South African white workers are for the most part the skilled element, and the natives are common labourers. In Palestine categories of all kinds of labour are represented in both the Jewish and Arab sections. The South African whites are a thin 'aristocratic' upper crust, who get about five times the pay of the natives. In Palestine the Jewish workers constitute not a thin crust, but a class. In South Africa the whites enjoy ample political rights (democratic legislation, progressive labour legislation, etc) whereas the Negroes are suppressed colonial slaves. In Palestine both Jews and Arabs are oppressed by an alien government and are deprived of any kind of democratic rights.

Furthermore, take the fact that in Palestine there are two cities of mixed population where the Jews are in the majority, Jerusalem and Haifa. In both places, nevertheless, in accordance with the decrees and appointments of the government, the mayors are Arab. The Jews are as little privileged in the matter of budget expenditures as of municipal administration. The Jews contribute 63 percent of the government income, whereas in return they receive merely 14 percent (1934-35) of the government expenditure on education, only 34 percent of the public works expenditures, etc. Nor are they privileged in the matter of labour legislation.

If the Jews were an integral part of the imperialist camp, if their existence depended upon the exploitation and oppression of the Arab masses, it would be the duty of every revolutionary socialist to fight against the growth of the

Jewish population. But the position is quite otherwise. On the other hand, the view that compares Jewish immigration into Palestine with Jewish immigration in America is equally unreal. The Jews in America are a part of the general economic system and entertain no chauvinist aspirations such as the boycott of foreign goods and labour or the establishment of a national state. The Jewish population in Palestine does strive to become a majority and determines its political road in accordance with this perspective, building up a relatively closed national economy, and boycotting Arab labour and goods. Influenced by imperialism and Zionism both, this population is against every attempt to obtain the democratisation and independence of the country. If the Jewish population were an integral part of the Palestinian, it would be the duty of the revolutionary socialist to support the increase of this population element in all its forms as part of the anti-imperialist struggle. But to support all forms of the extension of the Jewish element (eg to be against democratisation for fear that it would hold up the growth of the Jews) would be to sharpen the Jewish-Arab conflict, diminish the class differences inside the Arab population, and strengthen the Zionist tendency among the Jews.

The Jewish-Arab conflict

What are the causes of this conflict? Two answers are advanced in Palestine. The Zionist groups say that the conflict is simply the collision of feudalism and reaction with the progressive forces of capitalism. The Arab nationalists and their Stalinist supporters claim that the collision is between the Arab liberation movement and Zionism.

But the first explanation is wrong because the fact of the conflict between feudalism and capitalism does not explain the Arab national movement in Palestine. There are parallel manifestations of nationalism in the adjacent countries (Syria, Egypt). Moreover it does not explain how a clique of effendis succeeded in getting control over a militant national movement of hundreds of thousands. It is clear that the basis of the antagonism of the Arab masses to the Jewish population does not arise from the fact that the latter have brought in a higher standard of living and have created a modern labour movement. Their principal opposition arises from the fact that they see in the Jewish population the bearers of Zionism, that political system based upon national exclusivism, and hostility to the aspirations of the Arab masses to independence and democratisation of the political regime.

The second view, the claim of the Arab nationalists, is likewise erroneous. It does not take into consideration that there really is a conflict between feudalism and capitalist development, secondly, that inside the nationalist movement there is an Arab bourgeoisie which in competition with the closed Jewish economy develops exclusivist Arab tendencies, and thirdly, that the Jewish population is no integral part of the imperialist camp.

What follows therefore is that the collision in the Arab-Jewish conflict is between two national exclusivist movements (between Zionism and the feudal, semi-bourgeois Arab leadership on the one hand, and on the other the struggle of the Arab masses against Zionism). The consistent struggle for the easing up of this conflict is therefore only possible on the basis of the struggle against Zionism, against Arab national exclusivism and anti-Jewish actions, against imperialism, for the democratisation of the country and its political independence.

Class politics in Palestine

New International, June 1939

The political situation in Palestine is highly complicated. Many factors are jumbled together in a large chequered knot. Hence it is very hard to establish an internationalist class policy for the Palestine proletariat; hence also the great confusion in the circles of the revolutionary left with regard to the problems of this country. The fact that in Palestine itself there does not yet exist a large revolutionary force, which might illuminate the international labour movement in this darkness, has also contributed to an increase in the confusion.

The political problem of Palestine must be considered from two main points: first, a definition of the essence of the Arabian national movement, and, second, the role played by Jewish immigration and settlement. Only an exact Marxian analysis of these two questions can lead us on the correct revolutionary socialist road in the country.

The Zionists and the Arab movement

All wings of the Zionist movement hold firmly to the theory that no anti-imperialist liberation movement exists in Palestine and that the existing Arab movement is the product of the propaganda of the Arab feudalists, and the agents of German and Italian fascism. This is said not only by the fascist Zionists and the liberal bourgeoisie, but also by the reformists and even the members of the London Bureau—'Poale Zion and Marxist Circle' and the 'Hashomer Hatzair'. As grounds for this view they use three arguments: (1) at the head of the Arabian movement stand feudalists for the most part, hence the movement is reactionary; (2) a movement that practises terrorism against the Jewish population, and is mainly against Jewish workers, is nothing but a pogrom movement; (3) a movement supported by Hitler and Mussolini is necessarily reactionary and fascistic. These arguments are wrong from the ground up and distort the reality, inasmuch as they are calculated to cover up more or less Zionist aspirations and an alliance with oppressive British imperialism.

Have not many national movements been led by feudalists (eg Abd-el Krim in Morocco, the Syrian and Egyptian national movements in their inception, etc)? Were not national liberation movements at the beginning of their development, when they were under feudal leadership, often directed against members of other nationalities in their land (Ireland, formerly also India, the Boxer uprising in China, etc)? And are not national liberation movements exploited largely by other imperialist forces which are hostile to the imperialism against which the movement is directed? There is no doubt that the Arab national movement in Palestine, like its parallels in other colonial countries, is historically essentially an anti-imperialist movement.

This premise is accepted not only by Marxists, but also by Stalinists. The latter, however, draw therefrom absolutely opportunistic conclusions. They attempt to maintain the unity of the national movement and so prevent a class differentiation. The lessons of the national liberation movements and especially the lessons of the Chinese Revolution clearly demonstrate the correctness of the view of Lenin and Trotsky, namely that the only path to national liberation lies through deepening the social conquests of the masses and extending the class struggle among the nationally-oppressed people.

This view obviously applies to Palestine too; and especially here for another reason: Palestine cannot emancipate itself from the imperialist yoke unless a unification of the Arab and Jewish masses takes place, for the latter represent a third of the population, the Jewish workers are half of the Palestine working class, and Jewish economy is decisive in many branches of industry. The Jewish toiling masses will not, however, support the anti-imperialist movement if no class differentiation takes place in the Arabian national movement. What is so terrible in the situation in Palestine is that, on the one hand, there is a strong national differentiation between Jews and Arabs and, on the other, the national unity in the Arab camp is very firm.

There is, therefore, a grave error in the article reprinted in the *New International* (February 1939) from the *Spark*, in which the author speaks with great satisfaction and enthusiasm of the Arabian national unity which has been displayed in the last two and a half years.

The revolutionary Marxists are duty-bound to support the national liberation movement with all their strength even if the bourgeoisie or the feudalists stand for the time being at its head. At the same time, however, they must preserve their independence by showing the proletarian road to national emancipation, for only proletarian hegemony and class differentiation in the national movement can assure the complete and stable emancipation of the colonial people.

Zionism utilises the national and social oppression of the Jewish masses of the world to direct their embitteredness towards national unity, not towards international class struggle. Zionism creates reactionary illusions among the masses with regard to the road to the solution of its problems. Having grown stronger by the decline of the labour movement and the growth of chauvinistic tendencies, Zionism is also necessarily exclusivist and tries to repress the Arabian inhabitants of the country, to gain a Jewish majority, a Jewish state, under any conditions, and to boycott the Arab worker and Arab products. This basic tendency has become increasingly strong in recent years which were years of the alliance with British imperialism.

The Jewish population and Zionism

Yet from the negation of Zionism does not yet follow the negation of the right to existence and extension of the Jewish population in Palestine. This would only be justified if an objectively necessary identity existed between this population and Zionism, and if the Jewish population were necessarily an outpost of British imperialism and nothing more. Those who consider the Jewish population and Zionism to be identical are the Arabian feudalists, the Zionist Jewish leaders and the English imperialists. The Arabian feudalists need this conception in order to recruit the Arab masses to a chauvinistic anti-Jewish struggle, by saying, 'Smash the Jews, for they are Zionist conquerors!' The Jewish leaders assert that this identity exists in order to anchor the Zionist ideology among the Jewish masses, by saying, 'You are Jews, you must therefore necessarily be Zionists as well!' British imperialism employs these arguments, for they offer it a magnificent basis for national antagonisms. We wish therefore to examine whether the Jewish camp is really an integral part of the imperialist camp and whether anti-imperialist struggle also demands struggle against this population, or whether, on the contrary, we can and must win its majority, namely the toiling Jewish masses, for the anti-imperialist struggle.

The Stalinists in Palestine regard the Jewish population as an integral part of the imperialist camp and thus arrive at slogans like these: 'Block Jewish immigration! Prohibit the sale of land to Jews! Expropriate the land of the Jews and arm the Arabs!' The CPP preens itself before the Arab population with anti-Jewish terrorist actions. These slogans of the Stalinists are based upon their view of the *objectively* pro-imperialist role of the Jewish population and Jewish immigrants. In order to motivate these views they often use the simple analogy between the position of the Jewish toilers and the position of the whites in South Africa. It is especially dangerous that such a perverted analogy should take root among the Marxists of South Africa. Unfortunately, there were various mistakes in the article from the *Spark* which are based upon this analogy. On the side of the reformist leaders of the Jewish labour movement in Palestine, too, the attempt has been made to compare the position of the Jews in the country with that of the whites in South Africa. This analogy was drawn in order to show that the Jewish worker must not unite with the Arab, as an argument against the international organisation of the workers in Palestine. The analogy was then of course seized upon by the CPP in order to show the 'imperialistic character' of the Jews in Palestine. We wish to test this analogy in order to show clearly that the Jewish worker in Palestine is not an integral part of the imperialist camp and that his objective interests will lead him to unification with the Arab worker.

In the first place, it is to be noted that the Jewish workers make up more than half of the total working class, whereas in South Africa (according to the figures of 1922-25) the white workers were only one fifth of the working class. The white workers of South Africa are craftsmen for the most part, and the Negroes are employed only at hard labour. In Palestine there are workers of all categories both among the Jewish and the Arab working class. A large part of the white workers in South Africa are thrown some crumbs from the table of the English big bourgeoisie which exploits the Negro worker. The result is that the wage of the white worker is from five to six times as large as the wage of the black worker. That is, the white workers in South Africa represent a thin aristocratic layer. In Palestine the Jewish workers are not a layer, but a class in which, although there are aristocratic layers, there are still more simple workers. The whites in South Africa have wide political rights (democratic legislation, advanced labour laws, etc), whereas the Negroes are oppressed colonial slaves. In Palestine both the Jews and the Arabs are oppressed by a foreign power without having any democratic rights at all.

Britain's attitude towards the Jews

To show more clearly that the Jewish population in Palestine is not given preference over the Arabian by the British government, we wish to present some outstanding facts. There are two large cities in which Jews are in the majority—Haifa and Jerusalem. In both of them, according to the ordinances and appointments of the government, the mayors are Arabs. Other democratic institutions there are none. (Even these institutions, the municipalities, are 'democratic' only in quotation marks. In comparison with the other governmental institutions, however, they are the ideal of democracy.) In the field of municipalities, therefore, the Jews are not given preference. The Jews defray 63 percent of the government income, while expenditures are alloted to them as follows (1934-35): 14 percent to education; 34 percent to public works, etc. Labour legislation too gives no preference to the Jewish worker as against the Arab. The Jewish workers in Palestine, therefore, represent, by their objective interests, an integral part of the general working class and are not given preference by the British government.

On the other hand, that view would also be wrong which saw no chauvinistic-exclusivist, pro-imperialist tendencies at all in the Jewish population. It is a fact that it maintains a relatively closed economy against the Arab economy and raises slogans like '100 percent Jewish products', etc; and as a result of the influence of the Zionist leaders, most of the population demands a Jewish majority in Palestine and a Jewish state.

The Jewish population in Palestine therefore has objectively a dual character. Corresponding to its class differentiation, it contains on the one hand a Jewish working class and accelerates the rise of an Arab working class, that is, forces which are objectively anti-imperialist, and on the other hand, to the extent that it is permeated by Zionist exclusivist tendencies, that is, submitted to bourgeois influence, it strengthens the positions of imperialism and of reaction in the country. On this premise the revolutionary socialist policy and its attitude towards Jewish immigration must be built up.

Since the World War, two hostile camps face each other in Palestine, an Arab and a Jewish. The former demands the stopping of Jewish immigration and identifies this demand with the struggle against Zionism. The latter demands the opening of the doors of the country to immigrants and sees therein the essence of Zionism.

Against both these camps there appeared directly after the World War a section of the Comintern which for a number of years adopted an independent internationalist position. The members of the Comintern in Palestine, up to the great turn in the colonial question at the time of the Chinese Revolution, while absolutely opposed to Zionism (against the national boycott, against slogans like the Jewish majority and the Jewish state, alliance with England, etc), declared at the same time that the Jewish population is not to be identified with Zionism and hence demanded the maximum freedom of movement for Jewish immigration into Palestine. Not only this, but they demanded from the government also material aid for the establishment of the Jewish immigrants in the country. They declared plainly that the struggle of the Arab national movement against Zionism, the Jewish majority, does not require the demand of stopping Jewish immigration, and they justified the unconditional maintenance of the Arab majority. They declared that the struggle against Jewish immigration shifted the anti-imperialist struggle to anti-Jewish rails, and that this was profitable only to English imperialism. They declared plainly that any struggle against Jewish immigration would only strengthen Zionist chauvinism among the Jewish masses.

With the turn to the right in the colonial policy of the Comintern, however, which was also manifested in Palestine, the Communist Party of Palestine, submissive to Stalinism, began the struggle against Jewish immigration, asserting that it was an immigration of conquest, and that the struggle of the Arab national movement was a defensive struggle. But is the correct answer to Jewish aggressive chauvinism, Arabian defensive chauvinism? Unfortunately, there is a similar error in the article from the *Spark*: the struggle of the Arabs against Jewish immigration is a defensive struggle against the conquering Zionist movement, and therefore, even though we are, as socialists, generally in favour of free immigration, it is not necessary in Palestine. The 'Hashomer Hatzair', of the London Bureau, argues similarly: the struggle we are conducting against the political independence of Palestine is a defensive struggle against the aggressive Arab national movement and therefore, even though we are, as socialists, generally in favour of the independence of the colonies, it is not necessary in Palestine.

Without taking a clear internationalist position on the question of Jewish immigration, without a sharp struggle against any oppression of the Arab population by imperialism and Zionism, without a sharp struggle against attempts to suppress Jewish immigration, the establishment of a broad anti-imperialist front is impossible.

Two views on settlement

In the question of Jewish settlement, two main views are prevalent. One, that of the Zionist movement, demands complete free settlement and land purchase, without protecting the tenant from being dispossessed; the other, that of the feudal leadership of the Arab national movement, which hides under the cloak of 'tenant protection', demands the prohibition of land sale to Jews.

Before 1926-27, the Comintern in Palestine was for tenant protection and the recognition of his right to the land, but at the same time demanded that Jewish settlement on uncultivated land be made possible; it repeatedly declared that there are still large areas of land in the hands of the government and the Arabian effendis which are cultivable but uncultivated. This attitude was genuinely internationalist.

But since Stalinism has completely dominated the Comintern, its supporters in Palestine began the struggle against the right of Jewish settlement. Thus there is not today any internationalist force in Palestine: the Comintern people let themselves be taken in tow by the Arab feudal leaders, and the Socintern and London Bureau people make up an integral part of the Zionist movement. Unfortunately there are certain deviations and not internationalist views on this question in the article from the *Spark*.

If we are to set down our attitude towards Jewish immigration, we must keep the following two fundamental views in mind: (1) the Zionist movement sees in immigration the basis for paradise in the country; (2) the feudal leadership of the Arabian national movement sees in Jewish immigration the basis for hell in the country. Both views are false. Marxists cannot be for immigration or against it, just as they cannot be for or against immigration from country to city. Marxists must only record that in the capitalist order it is necessary to fight for free migration, without falling into illusions about the 'liberating role' and the 'creation of happiness' attributed to this migration, without adopting a chauvinistic attitude towards this migration ('Jewish majority', 'Jewish products', 'Jewish labour', etc). The same view must be adopted by the Marxists with respect to settlement.

It is correct that the Arab national movement must be supported in its struggle against imperialism. But this is not at all the same thing as saying that we must support the actions of the feudal leadership of this movement which are calculated to turn the movement from anti-imperialist to anti-Jewish paths. A little illustration will plainly show how the struggle against Jewish immigration distorts the anti-imperialist struggle: a short time ago rumours spread in Palestine that the government was on the verge of stopping Jewish immigration; whereupon the Arabs organised joyous demonstrations in which they cried: 'Long live Chamberlain!' 'Long live England!' 'The government is with us!'

The reader may say, 'Between the struggle for the right of existence and free immigration of the Jews, and the struggle for the independence of the country, there is an unbridgeable gulf, and we must therefore choose one of the two.' The complete victory of the movement for independence in Palestine is, however, impossible without the support of the Jewish toilers, who hold important positions in Palestine's political and economic life. The liberation movement will not receive this support so long as the anti-Jewish terror exists and so long as the Arabian toiling masses will struggle against Jewish immigration. On the other hand, the existence of the Jewish population will not be assured, and there will be no immigration without terrible suffering for the Jewish masses, without the support of the Arabian toiling masses who are the majority of the country's population; and the Arabian masses will not give this support so long as the Jewish masses are against the independence of the country and remain a tool in the hands of England for the suppression of the Arab masses. Only an internationalist labour movement can be the leading force in the consistent anti-imperialist struggle. So long as such a force does not yet play an important role in the country, the Jewish masses and the Arab national movement will remain in a difficult and distressed position.

A revolutionary socialist policy

The revolutionary socialist policy in Palestine must be built up on the following foundations:

(1) The Jewish question can only be solved by the socialist world revolution. Zionism is a factor that weakens the class struggle of the Jewish masses, and strengthens the reaction outside of Palestine as well as the reactionary forces in Palestine.

(2) Jewish immigration into Palestine, which is mainly an immigration of workers, strengthens, on the one side, the power and weight of the working class in the country, the power which, regarded historically, is the most extreme anti-imperialist factor and, on the other hand, in so far as it is Zionist, it strengthens the exclusivist positions and the forces of imperialism in Palestine.

(3) The Arab national movement expresses, on the one hand, the aspirations of the Arab masses for national and social emancipation, but, on the other hand, in so far as it is under feudal and semi-bourgeois leadership, it strengthens the exclusivist tendencies in the country, thereby weakening and narrowing down the anti-imperialist range by leaving the Jewish population to the influence of imperialism and of Zionism

(4) Internationalist socialism in Palestine is the only force that can lead the anti-imperialist struggle consistently to the very end, eliminate Jewish and Arabian antagonism, and link the national liberation movement of the Arabs with the struggle of the Jewish masses for the right to their existence in the country and their growth through immigration.

These are the foundations on which the programme of the Bolshevik-Leninist movement in Palestine must be built. Here is not the place to occupy ourselves with the details of this programme and we wish, therefore, only to indicate the essential main paragraphs:

For what must revolutionary socialists fight in Palestine?

The maximum programme of the revolutionary socialists is the proletarian dictatorship, as transitional stage to socialism. To attain this maximum programme, the revolutionary socialists fight for the following minimum demands:

As the immediate political task: abolition of the rule of imperialistic, absolutist bureaucracy and the establishment in its place of a republic on the basis of a democratic constitution, which is guaranteed by the following points:

(1) The concentration of the ruling power of the state in the hands of a legislative assembly composed of representatives of the people.

(2) General, secret, direct, and equal proportional elections for the legislative assembly and for all local governmental institutions.

(3) Inviolability of the person and domicile of citizens.

(4) Unrestricted freedom of conscience, of speech, of press, of assembly, right to strike and organisation.

(5) Separation of religious institutions from the state and the schools.

(6) General compulsory education, support of poor schools by the state.

In order to attain complete equality of rights of the toilers of both peoples and to abolish all national exclusiveness, regardless of what side it may come from:

(1) Establishment of a joint organisation of the workers and struggle against the 'conquest of labour'.

(2) Struggle against all boycotts of one people against the products of another people and the acceptance of members into all existing co-operatives without distinction of nationality.

(3) Distribution of the governmental and municipal budget in accordance with the needs of the masses, without regard to nationality.

(4) Struggle against the national terror and against Zionism, against all exclusivist tendencies and aspirations for creating national majorities or for suppressing national minorities.

(5) In case of settlement, participation of the peasant already occupying the land in the action of the colonisation, ie to grant him the same facilities that are used by the settlers.

(6) Complete equality of rights for both peoples to increase by means of immigration. Right of immigration for the Jews from Europe and other continents as well as for Arabs from surrounding countries.

In order to democratise the Palestinian state economy:

(1) Direct taxes instead of indirect. Progressive income tax.

(2) Salary reductions for the high officials.

(3) Reduction of the budget for the army, police and prisons.

(4) Fundamental increase of the budget for education, health and agriculture.

(5) Distribution of the budget according to the needs of the masses without regard for nationality.

In order to abolish feudalism, the following demands:

(1) Transfer of the lands of the big landowners, the government and the religious institutions to those who till them without regard for religion or nationality.

(2) General annulment of the debts of the fellaheen and the distribution of cheap credit to the fellaheen.

To protect the working class and to strengthen its struggle and its liberating power:

(1) Eight-hour working day and six-hour working day for youth.
(2) One rest-day in the week.
(3) Prohibition of night work, except for branches in which it is technically necessary.
(4) Prohibition of child labour.
(5) Prohibition of the labour of women in such work as is injurious to them.
(6) Minimum wage for all branches of industry.
(7) Social insurance.
(8) Old-age pensions for workers.
(9) Government inspection, with participation of representatives of the workers, to control the carrying out of labour laws.

To attain the immediate political and economic aims, the revolutionary socialist movement must support all oppositional movements directed against the existing social and political order in Palestine, while always retaining its own independence.

The completely consistent and lasting realisation even of this minimum programme is possible only through the overthrow of imperialism, and the establishment of the rule of workers' and peasants' councils.

Industry and banking in Egypt

Part Three, Chapter Eight, *Imperialism and the Arab East*
(Unpublished, Palestine, 1946)

The industry that developed in Egypt is mainly an import from abroad. Not only were the machines imported, but also the capital, and just as the technique of Egyptian industry is the last word in ultra-modernity, so too is its organisation ultra-modern. The concentration of the enterprises and the tightening of the ties of mutual dependence between them, the rule of finance capital (the merging of industrial with banking capital under the hegemony of the latter), the merging of finance capital with the state—all these are fundamental features of Egyptian industry. And this ultra-modernity is based on an agrarian, barbaric economy, from which it draws its strength and weakness alike.

Foreign capital

There is almost no country in the world where the weight of foreign capital compared with local capital is as great as in Egypt. According to an estimate made by French circles, foreign capital in 1937 amounted to £450 million, the entire wealth of the country being estimated at £963 million, which means that foreigners owned 47 percent of it.[1]

According to another estimate, capital investment, besides land, in the same year amounted to £550 million.[2] Seeing that the price of land is estimated at £500 to £600 million (or according to another estimate £670 million), the total property of Egypt amounts to between £1,000 and £1,100 million. According to another estimate of 1937 based on English calculations, foreign capital invested in Egypt amounted to £500 million. Thus the property of foreigners constitutes 40 to 50 percent of Egypt's total property, which sum does not differ from that arrived at by the French experts.

There are no exact figures for the distribution of foreign capital among the foreigners of the different countries. According to the above estimate made by the French, three fifths of all the foreign capital invested in Egypt belongs to Frenchmen, ie about £270 million, England has £100 to £120 million, ie 22 to 28 percent. The rest belongs to Belgians, Greeks and Italians. We shall follow a less arbitrary method of calculation, and shall take the share of the different foreign companies in the paid-up capital of all the foreign companies, besides the Suez Co, active in Egypt (1933):

Country	Number of companies	Capital (£E)	%
France	16	38,763,000	47.6
England	45	31,900,000	39.2
Belgium	18	6,651,000	8.2
Italy	11	1,923,000	2.4
Switzerland	8	1,379,000	1.7
Others	11	749,000	0.9
Total	109	81,365,000	100.0

In Suez shares France's portion is also a little greater than England's. If the proportions in the table are correct as far as the total foreign capital is concerned, we may assume (if the above French estimate of the total foreign capital in Egypt is correct) that French capital invested in Egypt amounts to between £200 and £225 million, and English to between £170 and £180 million. If the total capital amounts to £500 million (according to the English calculation) the French capital amounts to between £230 and £240 million.

Of course we must take into account the fact that there is capital not organised in companies, mainly Egyptian capital, which is also active in these spheres. The portion of foreign capital is therefore less than appears in the figures given, but not much less. At any rate it is clear that, besides landed property, less than a quarter of other property belongs to Egyptians.

Foreign capital has a far-reaching influence in all spheres of the economy. In its hands are the key positions of all the branches—transport, electricity, water, industry, agricultural mortgage, etc. It is also the most concentrated capital, and it draws into its orbit local Egyptian capital too. As it takes a great part of the surplus value created by the fellaheen and workers, it retards the accumulation of capital in Egypt, shrinks the purchasing power of the masses, and by these two actions prevents the materialisation of the two basic conditions for any energetic industrialisation—the accumulation of capital and the widening of markets. Being bound up with great landed property, it constitutes an important support of the existing relations of land property, of the feudal system.

Finance capital

According to the words of Marx written about 80 years ago, the banking system 'presents indeed the form of universal book-keeping and of distribution of means of production on a social scale, but only the form.'[3] According to its form, banking is social, but according to its content it is private, subjugated to the interests of big private capital. By the power over the financial operation of the economy as a whole the bank transforms itself from a simple book-keeping institution into a controller and determining factor of the destiny of the economy as a whole. This process reached its maturity in Europe and the US at the beginning of the present century when the industrial capitalism of free competition gave place to monopolist capitalism. The same system in an ultra-modern form was imported to Egypt.

In a country such as Egypt the banking system, besides being an institution for the distribution of means of production on a social scale, is, and to a decisive degree is, an institution built upon the basis of the wringing of surplus value from the toilers who produce by pre-capitalist, primitive methods, and is therefore an institution which *disturbs* the accumulation and distribution of means of production on a social scale. In any case, if the banking system has a social form as regards the first function, which is a manifestation of the growing social character of production (even though this is subordinated to the needs of big capital), then as regards the second function of the bank—as a superstructure on primitive agrarian economy—it is in its entirety retrogressive.

Here we shall deal with the general organisation of the banking system and also with its function as regards industry, transport, communications, etc, only touching on its connections with agriculture.

The most important banks whose centres are in Egypt are: The National Bank of Egypt, Crédit Foncier Egyptien, Banque Misr, Crédit Agricole d'Egypte, Land Bank of Egypt and Banque Belge et Internationale en Egypte. These banks in 1942 together had assets amounting to £E162.2 million, while the assets of all the other banks did not go above £E10 million. Thus the concentration of the banking system in Egypt is very high. This would be shown even more clearly if the fact were taken into account that many small banks are in reality branches of the big banks.

Many arteries connect these banks with one another: the participation of one bank in the capital of another, the purchase of shares by one from another, or the exchange of shares among one another, the giving of credit by one to the other, etc. Unfortunately the statistical material is much too scarce for us to be able to show the degree of intertwining of the six banks. We shall be compelled to be satisfied with illustrating the connections between them through the directorships. In the following illustration every square signifies the assets of the banks and every line connecting them signifies a director sitting on the boards of both banks:

Assets of the six big banks in Egypt and the connections among them through directors

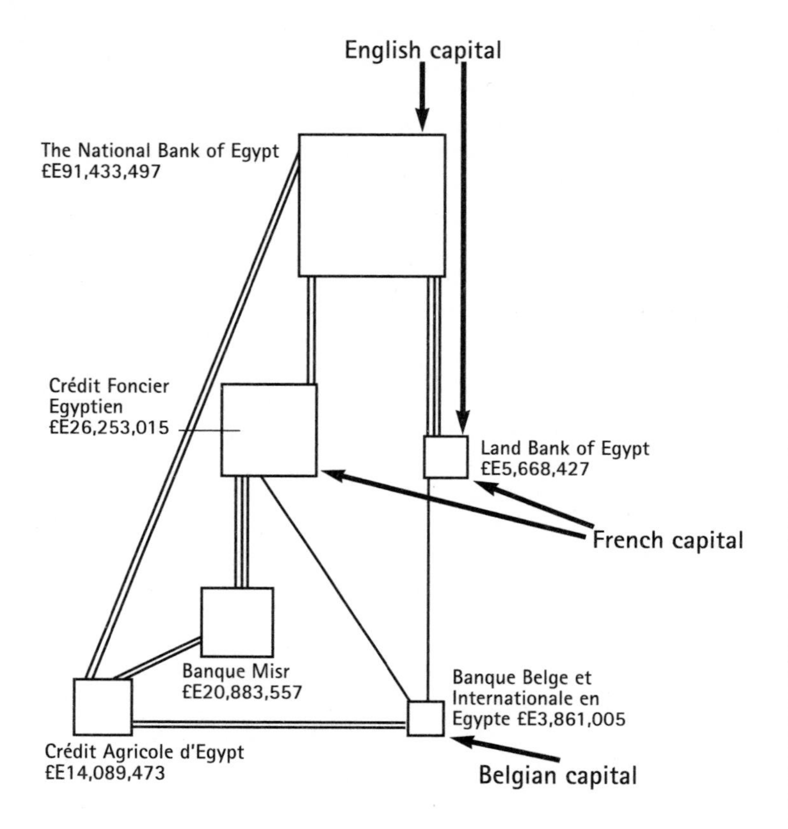

The following figures include only those people who have five or more directorships (1943):

	Number of people	Total number of directorships in their hands
5 to 9 directorships	43	278
10 to 14 directorships	14	158
15 and more directorships	9	185
Total	66	621

Thus of a total number of directorships of 1,620 in 441 companies, 621 are concentrated in the hands of 66 people.

In the main the same men have interests in and sit on the boards of directors of enterprises belonging to entirely different branches of the economy, as the following table shows:

	Total	Banking	Industry	Transport	Trade	Insurance	Film/Theatre	Finance	Electricity	Land	Hotels
Abdel Maksud Ahmed	23	3	11	5	2	1	1	-	-	-	-
Aboul Kheir, Abdel Razzak	12	2	6	1	2	1	-	-	-	-	-
Afifi, Hafez	32	2	15	6	4	1	1	2	1	-	-
Cattaui, Aslan	15	-	6	1	2	2	-	2	-	2	-
Farghaly, Mohamed Ahmed	21	2	11	1	1	1	-	4	-	1	-
Khalil, Mohamed Mahmoud	17	2	6	1	2	1	1	1	-	3	-
Rolo, R J	10	1	6	-	-	2	-	-	-	1	-
Rolo, R S	10	2	1	2	-	2	-	1	-	2	-
Sidky, Ismail	19	1	8	4	1	-	-	1	-	3	1
Yeghen, Ahmed Midhat	19	-	10	5	1	1	1	1	-	-	-
Yehia, Aly Emine	21	1	9	2	4	2	-	1	-	2	-

Thus all the enterprises of industry, transport, commerce, etc, are connected to one another by a close network of canals and by another network to the big banks, all enterprises in this way making up one economic unit subjugated to a handful of banks which constitute one gigantic monopolistic concern.

The merging of finance capital with the state

The industrial capitalist of the 18th and first half of the 19th century was liberal. He did not want the intervention of the state in economic life except in the interests of the protection of private capitalist property from 'anarchy'. By liberty he meant his defence from the arbitrariness of the state bureaucracy and the nobility. The colossal capitalist of the 20th century has no cause to fear the state bureaucracy. His strength is sufficient for him to negotiate with the ministers as the representative of a power on an equal footing with the state. More than this, he even desires the state's increasing intervention in foreign affairs—by a policy of imperialist expansion, wars, etc, and also in domestic affairs—having a 'strong hand' against the proletariat. If during the period of industrial capital, therefore, no class connection existed between the bureaucracy or the capitalist state and the individual capitalist; now, in the period of imperialism, finance capital grows into the state. In face of the close connection between the different enterprises in Egypt and the high degree of merging of industrial with banking capital, it is readily understood that the relation of big capitalists to the state is not like the relation of the bourgeoisie toward the states in the Europe of the 18th and first half of the 19th century, but rather like that of the bourgeoisie in the developed capitalist states of the 20th century. The dependence of the state on an imperialist power increases even more the tendency of the growing of finance capital into the state. This tendency is revealed in many forms—the dependence of the state finances on the subscription of its securities by the big banks, the dependence of industry on government orders and subventions, and on the customs policy, etc. It takes on its most open form in the personal ties between the directorships of the different companies and the bureaucracy of the state.

Thus among the 696 directors of all the companies holding 1,620 directorships there were (1943):[4]

	Number of people	Number of directorships
Former Prime Ministers	3	34
Former Ministers	25	95
Senators	20	111
Members of the Chamber of Deputies	9	28
High officials	14	36
Total	71	304

The increased industrialisation of Egypt

Egypt is still to a decisive degree an agrarian country. According to the 1937 census the whole of Egyptian industry together with building employed 609,733 persons, without building 478,199. Those working in industry therefore make up 6.4 percent of the total earning population. If we exclude from the calculation those whose employment is not known, the percentage employed in industry comes up to 7.8 percent. (Actually it may safely be assumed that a considerable portion of the 'unknowns' are really handicraft workers for petty industry, so that the percentage is slightly higher.)

Things do not stand still. And precisely those contradictions which strangled the industries of Europe and the US gave a great push forward to the industrial development of Egypt: the decline of world capitalism which received its clearest expression in the serious 1929 crisis and which increased the competition between the imperialist powers; and the economic 'revival' which was caused mainly by the preparation for war and which increased the aggressiveness of the 'have not' imperialist powers—Germany, Italy and Japan—crisis and prosperity alike weakened the position of Britain in Egypt. Britain was therefore compelled to make concessions in favour of the industrial development of Egypt, especially by raising the customs duties. For a very long period lasting up to 1930, customs duties had been very low, and fixed according to the value of each article, the average for all goods not exceeding 8 percent of the value of the imports plus 2 percent consumption tax. In 1930 the government introduced a system of special tariffs, and from then on the customs duties rose by leaps and bounds till they reached 20 percent of the value of imports in 1931, 23 percent in 1932, and eventually far exceeded even this percentage, being on an average 40.5 percent in the years 1936-41.

This raising of the customs duties is the result of the pressure of the Egyptian national movement and also of the fact that, even if today, as in the past, English capitalism is not interested in the industrial development of the colonial countries which is liable in the course of time to compete with its own industry, this does not prevent it from collaborating in this development in the interests of the export of capital which finds no profitable field in the home country, and is drawn to the colonies because of their cheap labour and inexpensive raw materials. Strategic reasons (preparation for coming wars) also increase the tolerance of imperialism towards a certain industrial development in its colonies.

Besides increasing customs duties for defence of industry in Egypt, the government took some other measures: it began to give preference to home products in its purchases. The municipalities followed suit. The government also gave financial aid, giving credit on relatively easy terms to different industrial enterprises. A number of exemplary government factories and workshops were also set up under the protection of the Ministry of Industry and Commerce, which served both as laboratories and experimental stations, and also as centres for the training of skilled workers.

But besides the government intervention which facilitated the development of industry, and intervention enmeshed in contradictions as the result of the general decline of the capitalist world, Egyptian industry found another not less important fountain of life—the severe agrarian crisis which cut down wages and the price of raw materials.

And indeed the general decline of world capitalism together with the barbarian relations in Egyptian agriculture alone explain the speed of the industrialisation of the country, and at the same time the narrow limits which frame it in.

In certain fields foreign competition has been almost entirely done away with: building materials (cement, marble, ceramic products, etc), metal bedsteads, metal and wooden furniture, shoes and other leather products, cotton blankets and coverlets, flour, alimentary pastes, carpets, tarbushes.

In other fields where foreign competition was not entirely done away with, local industry nevertheless rapidly pushed it aside to a great extent: cotton yarn, cotton piece goods, soap (common), glass and glassware, matches. Of great importance is the pushing aside of foreign cotton goods from Egypt's markets. Over about ten years Egypt's cotton industry managed to get almost complete control over the local market, as the following table shows:

COTTON PIECE GOODS, CONSUMPTION, PRODUCTION AND IMPORT
(1,000 square metres)

Year	Imported	% of total consumption	Locally manufactured*	% of total consumption	Total consumption
1930	180,000	96.8	6,000	3.2	186,000
1936	169,500	75.5	55,000	24.5	224,500
1939	74,000	31.7	159,500	68.3	233,500
1941	57,000	22.2	200,000	77.8	237,000

*Not including production by handlooms

Nevertheless, notwithstanding the great tempo of the industrialisation of Egypt in the last decade or so, the level the industrialisation has reached is very low. This will become clear from the percentage of those occupied in industry, and also from a comparison of the capital invested in industry and commerce (there are no separate figures for industry and commerce) per capita of the earning population in Egypt, with the same in other countries. As regards the latter, figures for Egypt are for 1937 and for other countries for 1913 (in International Units[5]): Egypt 147, USA 1,560, Canada 1,630, Australia 965, Britain 1,658. The fact that the figures for Egypt are for a much later year than those for the other countries to some extent blurs over the backwardness of Egypt as compared with other countries. This backwardness can also be seen in the consumption of electricity. While the annual consumption of electricity per capita in Egypt in 1937 was 18 kwh, it was in the USSR 215, in the United Kingdom (1938) 608, in USA (1929) 1,160.

The concentration of capital in industry

Even if only a tiny minority of the Egyptian population is occupied in industry and the industrialisation is very backward, the existing industrial enterprises nevertheless show a high degree of concentration: they are ultra-modern enterprises.

Unfortunately, owing to the poverty of the statistics, it is impossible to calculate the degree of concentration according to the quantity of products, number of workers or motor power. The only calculation that can be made, and then not very accurately, is that of the concentration of capital in industry.

Seeing that there are no exact figures of the total quantity of capital in the enterprises of the different sizes except for the 250 largest, but there are data of the number of enterprises sorted according to the quantity of capital invested in them. I have made use of these figures, taking the maximum figures for the capital of the small enterprises (thus, for instance, if 3,089 enterprises have £50 to £99 per enterprise, I have assumed that altogether they have £3,089 times 100). This method of calculation does not overestimate the concentration of capital in industry but, on the contrary, underestimates it:

[Editor's note: the next three pages are missing. They include sections on: rationalisation, productivity of labour and the rate of exploitation in industry; the rate of profit in industry; and the conditions of life of the urban workers.]

...up the electric poles, steal, seek food or rags among the garbage, and 'hide their crimes behind a screen of polishing shoes or selling lottery tickets'. 'The homeless children of today are the criminals of tomorrow.' The speakers at the conference also gave the reason for this: '80 percent of the crimes are the fruit of poverty'.[6]

Two incidents which were reported in the papers bear witness to the extent of poverty in Egyptian towns: in September 1943 four people were trampled to death when alms were being distributed, and in March 1944 an Egyptian woman sold her daughter to a merchant immediately after birth—for £20.

Even the representatives of the Egyptian bourgeoisie are forced to admit the direness of the situation. One of the members of the Chamber of Deputies said in March 1943:

> The war has brought about a concentration of capital in the hands of a few hundreds. The wealth of the rich has risen while the poor have been forced down into more dire poverty; the abyss between the classes has deepened. The social system is shaken and grave dangers threaten it. A good future cannot be prophesied for the country.

The narrowness of local markets hampers industrialisation of Egypt

According to a reliable calculation made before the war the consumption of industrial products in Egypt was nearly £90 million per annum, £5.5 per capita. The production of local industry was £65 to £70 million or £4 per capita. Thus already before the war local industry satisfied nearly three quarters of the industrial consumption of the country. During the war Egyptian industry continued to develop, so that it is nearing the stage of satisfying all the needs of the Egyptian population with means of consumption as they are today.

This fact is not at all surprising, as the power of consumption of the masses is very low indeed. Cleland makes the following calculation:

	£E	£E
Clothing	from 2.870	to 5.040
Bedding, blankets	from 1.000	to 1.250
Other items of consumption	from 1.060	to 1.240
Total	from 4.930	to 7.530
Average	6.230	and per capita 1.250

If we compare these figures with those given in the chapter 'The Agrarian Question in Egypt', we see that Cleland's figures are somewhat too high. But even following Cleland's figures, we see that the agricultural population of about 10 million does not need industrial products of more than £E12 million.

According to a calculation of Cleland, in 1936 there were 232,000 people whose income was above the minimum necessary, their average income amounting to £E420, or taking the total, £E97,440,000. (Of course among these there are a handful of millionaires, and masses of middle and petty bourgeoisie whose position is comfortable compared with the masses of workers and simple fellaheen, but who are far from being well-to-do.) Excluding this layer, there are yet 16 million other inhabitants of Egypt (according to 1937 census figures). If we deduct the agriculturists, there remain about 6 million people—workers and their families, domestic servants, petty officials, etc. The average income of the workers and officials in industry (according to a partial census) is £E40.3 per annum, or if we include their families, about £E10 per person The major portion of such a low income goes for food. We should not be underestimating the figures if we assumed that at most a quarter of the expenditure of a worker and petty official goes towards the purchase of industrial products, ie two and a half Egyptian pounds per person. According to this estimate, all workers, domestic servants, petty officials and their families buy a total of £E15 million worth of industrial products. Thus the masses of poor and middle peasantry and of workers buy industrial products to at most the value of £E27 million.

While the buying of industrial products by the masses of people is limited by the low purchasing power their small incomes afford them, the buying of industrial products by the wealthy is limited firstly because of the fact that a part of them are foreign capitalists living in other countries and buying the products of those countries, and secondly because of the fundamental law of capitalist accumulation—the tendency of the capitalist to increase his savings as against his consumption.

The urgent problem confronting Egyptian industry of extending its markets can therefore not be solved except by raising the power of the masses of agriculturists to buy means of consumption and means of production, which means the emancipation of the fellaheen from their feudal burdens, and the rapid advance of the forces of production in agriculture. The extension of markets for Egyptian industry demands also the abolition of the monopolistic position of foreign capital in the national economy. Thus the widening of internal markets demands a struggle against feudalism and imperialism.

But Egyptian capitalists who are junior partners of foreign capital or its agents, and whose ties with the feudal lords are strong, of course do not dare to conduct this struggle with all the necessary vigour. They are also put off from the struggle by the constantly growing fear that every anti-imperialist and anti-feudal liberatory struggle is liable to deepen and turn into a struggle also against the local bourgeoisie. And so, instead of a revolutionary struggle, Egyptian industrial circles find other ways.

The president of the Egyptian Federation of Industries, Ismail Sidky Pasha, now Prime Minister, writes, 'It is through the medium of export alone that our industry can realise considerable progress and great compass'.[7]

It is easy to say 'export', but how to do it? Is a really serious increase of the export of Egyptian industry possible at all?

Even in the markets of neighbouring countries Egypt did not manage to establish herself against the competition of the advanced industries of Europe and the efforts of the imperialist powers. The total annual export of Egypt to neighbouring countries was on an average £E1,742,000 for the years 1933-38, or about 5 percent of the total export of Egypt.

With world capitalism not rising, but in decline, with world markets shrinking and the struggle for them becoming fiercer and fiercer, with a world cut into pieces by high customs walls, currency restriction, etc, the outlet for young and weak Egyptian industry is—export! Can there be anything more fantastic?

Egyptian industry during the war

The war was an important turning point for Egyptian industry. The army encamped in Egypt became a huge market for the products of Egyptian industry. Industries which had closed down before the war came to life again, and factories and sometimes whole branches sprouted and bloomed rapidly. In the war period there arose in Egypt a chemical industry (producing acids, ammonium salts, copper sulphate, aluminium, magnesium, borax, lead oxide and zinc, lacquer), a medical industry (with 25 enterprises), a large paper industry, and also glass, pipes and machine parts, starch and rice husking industries. Since the beginning of the war the amount of cotton manufactured by Egyptian industry has risen by 65 percent and the production of cloth by more than 100 percent.

The industries made tremendous profits. For most of the companies we have figures of the net profit only up to 1942.[8] Since then profits must certainly have increased, but the tendency of their development is shown clearly enough from the figures for 1938 or 1939 and 1942 relating to a few companies chosen at random:

	1938 (£E)	1942 (£E)	% increase
Eastern Co (tobacco)	105,558	625,004	592
The Egyptian Salt and Soda Co Ltd	53,776	179,311	333
Crown Breweries	17,366	258,799	1,490
Filature Nationale d'Egypte	115,779	279,709	241
Soc Anon des Bières Bomonti et Pyramides	9,555	107,885	1,129
Soc Egypte de Ciment Portland, Tourah	65,198	164,083	252
Soc Gen des Sucreries et de la Raffinerie d'Egypte	277,663	848,739	306
Soc Misr pour la Filature et le Tissage	83,003	485,954	509
Soc Misr de la soie	(1939) 31,437	152,839	409
Soc Viticole et Vinicole d'Egypte	261	63,081	24,169
Soc Financière et Industrielle d'Egypte	7,406	77,049	1,040
Kafr-el-Zayat Cotton Co Ltd	26,537	77,108	291
Soc Misr pour le lin	(1939) 3,206	52,961	1,652
Helwan Portland Cement Co	33,312	91,605	275
Industrie Fibres Textiles	501	27,995	5,588

When reading the above table we must remember that companies tend to minimise their profits as much as possible (by putting large sums into hidden reserves, etc). But nevertheless one thing is sure—that the big companies in Egypt made excellent profit out of the war. During the war the number of millionaires (mainly foreign) in Egypt rose from 50 to 400. This tremendous enrichment was not accompanied by any rise whatsoever in the living standard of the workers but by a decline (as has already been shown above).

How foreign and Egyptian capital prepare for the period after the war and the 'reconstruction'

With the cessation of war orders, the building of camps, etc (which until now have continued on a large scale), the contradictions in Egyptian capitalism will reach their climax. The 500,000 workers employed by the army will be discharged and the authorities' buying of Egyptian products to the extent of tens of millions of pounds will cease. On the other hand there are already insurmountable difficulties in the conversion of the large surpluses of frozen accounts, amounting to £400 million which accumulated in England to Egypt's credit, into means of production so badly needed by Egyptian industry whose machines and buildings were largely amortised during the war. In the not too distant future another difficulty will arise—the danger of the flooding of the markets by overseas products.

How does foreign capital visualise the future?

La Bourse Egyptienne and *Great Britain and the East* warn against the industrialisation of Egypt. The British Chamber of Commerce is not satisfied with general declarations and speaks at length about the situation of Egypt after the war. They express fear of the aggressiveness of the Egyptian bourgeoisie, which, having gained much wealth during the war, will want to defend its positions during peacetime too by a constant increase of the customs duties. The British capitalists try to turn the bitter pill to their advantage.

> Since it is certain that a large number of Egyptian industries have come to stay, and that the Egyptian authorities are likely to do all in their power to protect them, it is desirable that United Kingdom firms should participate with Egyptians in their promotion. We consider that, in some industries at least, there may well be a fruitful field for Anglo-Egyptian collaboration by the provision of equipment and finance from the United Kingdom. Such collaboration has in the past already been advocated by His Majesty's Government and been most successful in many of the existing industries... Alternatively British firms should consider the desirability of manufacturing their products in Egypt as it may be better for the United Kingdom to derive invisible exports from this development than to cease taking an interest in those branches of industry where local production would be likely to supplant visible exports from the United Kingdom.[9]

But there is a danger that the Egyptian government may go too far. Then 'should this occur, His Majesty's Government may have to intervene in order to restrain excessive protectionism', and this intervention will be particularly necessary if something further happens and the fear of foreign capital comes true 'that the [Egyptian] government may introduce legislation of a nature to limit or to acquire before the date of the termination of the concession public utility and concessionary companies which for the most part have been formed by foreign enterprises and capital'.

As far as the payment of Britain's war debt to Egypt is concerned, capitalist and government circles in Britain think only of payment bit by bit in the form of goods, with very limited possibilities of converting this debt into a basis for acquiring international credit (ie dollars).

The different sections of the Egyptian bourgeoisie did not delay in putting forward their demands. The late head of the Egyptian government, Ahmed Maher Pasha, remarked:

> Free trade is the best economic system which the world has known and which history has proved to be the most beneficial to mankind. It will harm Egypt intensely

> if she does not adopt free trade as soon as conditions permit. Trade protection was only adopted by countries in exceptional circumstances and maintained until conditions came back to normal. Egypt should return to free trade as soon as possible. I demand freedom of commerce in the same way I demand political freedom.[10]

This representative of the stock exchange and the comprador bourgeoisie connected with the landowners is much more interested in trade with overseas than in the development of Egyptian industry.

On the other hand, Ismail Sidky Pasha, President of the Egyptian Federation of Industries, said:

> The throne speech's reference to the suppression of protection tariffs had caused concern in industrial quarters. Also disconcerting was the announcement of the possibility of abandoning the policy of national self-sufficiency in favour of international specialisation in industry and agriculture. This meant that Egypt could not rely on protection for its growing industries and had to concentrate on developing its agriculture. But in the same breath the Government said it would make every effort to encourage local industries and provide them with every assistance. It would be interesting to see what aid the Government can give Egyptian industry when it proposes to remove the slight protection given in 1930, which had to save it from an early death in face of overwhelming competition.

The stand of a large section of the bourgeoisie towards the payment of the British debt to Egypt created during the war was not less assertive. Thus at the session of the Senate on 20 February 1945 Senator Ahmed Ramzi Bey said that the currency restrictions meant that Egypt could not get dollars and buy in America, but only in England, and this was a serious handicap. He proposed that England should supply dollars or even hand over to Egypt some of her shares in companies in Egypt, such as the Suez Co, Anglo-Egyptian Co, etc. He also mentioned the decline in practice, if not in theory, of the value of the Egyptian pound compared with the pound sterling. The paper *Al-Ahram* of 19 April 1944 states that the United Kingdom's debt to Egypt is the debt of the strong to the weak, and of course it was dependent on the will of the strong whether and how to pay. A week later the same paper quotes Senator Mohamed Barakat Pasha as stating that the United Kingdom would not be able to pay her debts, and advising Egypt to leave the sterling bloc. The same theme of leaving the sterling bloc and transferring Suez and other shares to Egyptian hands repeats itself over and over again in the Egyptian press.

In addition to the pressure on Britain the capitalists have in mind another more important measure—the increase of pressure on the workers. In this sphere there is no dispute among the different sections of the Egyptian bourgeoisie, all of them seeing this as their main task. Fouad Saraj ed-Din, a large landowner who was Minister of Agriculture, Internal Affairs and Social Welfare, says that in order that Egyptian cotton be able to compete with Indian, Chinese and Brazilian cotton, with artificial silk and nylon, the rise of wages in agriculture must be stopped. Hafez Afifi, Director of Banque Misr, also states that the rise of wages deprives Egyptian industry of the possibility to compete with foreign products. The paper *Al-Ahram* of 19 July 1943 states that workers get a high wage which accustoms them to luxuries—sic!

In short, the conclusion of the Egyptian bourgeoisie is a struggle against British imperialism in order that some concessions be wrung from it or in order to come under the wing of the US, and drastic cuts in the starvation wages of the workers. Seeing that they are very hesitant on the one front of their struggle, and they fear strong and revolutionary opposition on the other, they are seized with fear when they look into the future, a fear which was expressed in *Al-Ahram* (4 April 1944) in these words: 'God save us from the peace!'

If the war deepened the abyss of social contradictions and changed the country into a volcano liable to erupt any minute, now with the peace which is accompanied by the efforts of the bourgeoisie of the 'mother' country to cast the results of the war and the burden of the crisis onto the shoulders of the colonial masses, and with the increasing tendency of the local bourgeoisie to use a heavy hand against the workers, the volcano is sure to erupt. The first smoke heralding this has already been seen in the upheavals of the last few months.[11]

Notes

1 *L'Egypte Indépendante par le Groupe d'Études de l'Islam* (Paris, 1938), pp144-145.
2 A Bonne, *The Economic Development of the Middle East* (Jerusalem, 1943), p73.
3 K Marx, *Capital*, vol III, p712.
4 The calculation is made according to the *Stock Exchange Yearbook of Egypt*, 1943. As many directors are not listed as senators, state officials, etc, although they are, the concentration of directorships is greater than is shown in the table.
5 An International Unit equals approximately one US dollar. This unit was introduced by Colin Clark for the purpose of international comparisons.
6 *Al-Ahram*, 23 February 1944.
7 *La Revue d'Egypte Economique et Financière*, April 1940.
8 From the *Stock Exchange Yearbook of Egypt*, 1943.
9 Quoted in 'British Trade Prospects In Egypt', *Egyptian Gazette*, 12 January 1945.
10 *British Chamber of Commerce of Egypt Journal*, March 1945.
11 See chapter 'The Trade Unions in the Arab East'. [Editor's note: this is a reference to a later chapter in Cliff's unpublished manuscript, *Imperialism and the Arab East* (Palestine, 1946).]

The struggle in the Middle East

First published as a pamphlet in 1967,
edited and reprinted in *Socialist Worker Review*, October 1990

Oil is the key feature of imperialism in the Middle East.

Middle East oil exploitation is fantastically profitable. The cost of producing one barrel of crude oil in the Middle East is only 15 cents, as against $1.63 in the US. The official rate of profit on Middle East oil averaged 67 percent between 1948 and 1960, as against 21 percent in Venezuela and 10.8 percent in the US.

Before the Second World War Britain controlled 100 percent of Iranian oil and 47.5 percent of Iraqi oil; the US interest was only 23.75 percent in Iraq (equal to France's). Since then the situation has changed radically; in 1959 the US share of all Middle East oil rose to 50 percent, while that of Britain declined to 18 percent (France had 5 percent, the Netherlands 3 percent, others, including local Arab governments, 24 percent).

Oil has had very little beneficial impact on the development of the countries of the Middle East. The distortion of their economic, social and political development caused by feudalism and imperialism has been accentuated further.

Employment in oil is very small: in Iran only 1 percent of the employed population earn their livelihood in the industry; in Iraq 1 percent; in Saudi Arabia 2 percent. Altogether the total employment in oil in the Middle East is less than the employment in textiles in Egypt alone.

The richest oil resources are in countries with the most archaic social regimes. The boundaries between states were imposed by imperial powers to run between the main population centres—by far the most socially and politically advanced—and the main natural resources of the Arab region.

Zionism

A series of human tragedies brought the Jews to Palestine—pogroms in Tsarist Russia, persecution in Eastern Europe and the Holocaust of Nazism. When they reached Palestine they found it was inhabited by Arabs. Whatever the motivation that brought the Jews in, an increasing conflict between Zionist settlers and the Arabs was unavoidable.

The Arab peasant offered labour and produce at a very low price. How could a European worker find a job under such conditions? The only way was to block the employment of any Arab workers by Jewish employers. In Tel Aviv, which on the eve of the founding of the state of Israel had barely 300,000 inhabitants, there was not one Arab worker nor one Arab inhabitant.

The Zionists prevented the fellahs [peasants] from selling their produce in the Jewish market. And when, under pressure of hunger, a fellah dared to break the boycott, he was beaten.

Every member of the Zionist trade union federation, the Histadrut, had to pay two special compulsory levies: (1) 'For Jewish Labour'—funds for organising pickets, etc, against the employment of Arab workers—and (2) 'For Jewish Produce', for organising the boycott of Arab produce. Not one Zionist party, not even the most extreme 'left' of Hashomer Hatzair, now Mapam, opposed the boycott of the Arab workers and peasants.

The boycott of the Arabs was inherent in Zionism: without the boycott no European worker or farmer would have survived economically.

In opposing the local Arab population, Zionism had to try and serve the ruling imperialist power. Theodore Herzl, the founder of political Zionism, courted mainly the Turkish Sultan and the German Kaiser. After the First World War, Zionism was orientated towards British imperialism. After the Second World War, Zionism switched its attachment to US imperialism.

The Haganah, the main military Zionist organisation in the 1920s and the 1930s, worked hand in glove with the British Army of Occupation and the police.

The Auxiliary Police Force was established in the spring of 1936. An important part of the Haganah as well as some members of Etzei (the other Zionist military organisation) became a legal armed force. In the spring of 1939 this force numbered some 21,000 men. Of course not one Arab was allowed into it. The present Israeli army is the natural continuation of the old British-controlled Auxiliary Police Force.

Are the people of Israel a colonial nation? The Israeli economy is not a backward economy suffering from exploitation by Western imperialism. Altogether between 1949 and 1964 nearly $6,000 million came to Israel via German reparations, economic aid from the US government, and from Jews in the US and elsewhere. This sum comes to some $3,000 per head, or more than £1,000. Even at the height of empire net profit per average Briton from investments in the empire did not come to £10 per head per year!

Is Israel interested in radical land reform? Of course not. Zionism got rid of the Arab fellahs. Agrarian revolution—the restoration of the land to its original cultivators—is the last thing Israel would wish for.

Does Israel have an interest in the unity of the Arab countries into one state? Of course not. Israel is not a colony suppressed by imperialism, but a *colon*, a settler's citadel, a launching pad of imperialism. It is a tragedy that some of the very people who had been persecuted and massacred in such bestial fashion should themselves be driven into a chauvinistic, militaristic fervour, and become the blind tool of imperialism in subjugating the Arab masses.

In the same way that the existing social order is to be blamed for the calamity of the Jews, so it is to be blamed for the exploitation of their catastrophe for reactionary, oppressive aims. Zionism does not redeem Jewry from suffering. On the contrary, it imperils them with a new danger, that of being a buffer between imperialism and the national and social liberation struggle of the Arab masses.

The Jewish population in Israel *is* divided into classes and a class struggle rends the country. But this in itself does not mean that any significant number of Israeli workers are ready to join forces, or will be ready to join forces, with the Arab anti-imperialist struggle.

The white workers of South Africa have gone on strike many times. One need only remember the 1922 white miners' strike which was suppressed only after Smuts used planes to bombard the strikers. But the white workers never joined the black workers in struggle against their oppression!

In Algeria many of the 1 million European settlers supported the Communist Party in 1945.

But all this changed with the Arab national rebellion. One account records:

> ...the further down one went in the social scale, among Algeria's Europeans, the greater the fear of the Muslim masses, ready to step into unskilled jobs and deprive even the poorest Europeans of their living.[1]

While the Jews were the underdogs of Europe, in the Middle East the Arabs are the underdogs, and the Israelis the privileged and oppressors, the allies of imperialism.

The Arab national movement

The rulers of the Arab countries are divided, by and large, into two separate groups: first, the feudal kings and sheikhs—King Feisal of Saudi Arabia, King Hussein of Jordan, the Sheikh of Kuwait and other rulers of Persian Gulf dukedoms. They, together with the state of Iran, are reliable allies of imperialism.

The Arab countries with relatively more progressive social and political regimes are Egypt, Syria, Algeria and Iraq.

Of course no Chinese wall separates the regimes of the two groups of countries, but there is a significant difference between them. The first group can get (together with Israel) arms from the United States and Britain. The second does not.

It is not an accident that Adeni workers, probably the most advanced section of the Arab working class, do not keep pictures of King Feisal or the Imam of Yemen in their homes, but of Nasser. (Of course it would have been far better if they had pictures of Marx, Lenin and Trotsky.)

However inconsistently and haltingly, Nasser has carried out some measures against imperialism and feudalism. Nasser nationalised the Suez Canal in 1956. Bank Misr and the National Bank of Egypt were nationalised in February 1960.

In June 1960 the press was nationalised, and the Cairo bus services were municipalised. All banks and insurance companies were nationalised, and about

300 industrial and trading establishments were taken over either wholly or partly by the state.

Between October 1961 and February 1962 the property of 600 of Egypt's wealthiest families was sequestered by the state.

In August 1963 there was a further series of nationalisations. About 300 concerns were affected, including the Dutch-British Lever Brothers, 14 partly nationalised shipping companies and 29 land transport companies. In April 1964 the Shell-BP interests were nationalised.

In 1958 a maximum land holding of 300 acres was decreed for a single family. This was further reduced to 100 acres in June 1961. The result was that, while peasants who had less than five acres owned 33.2 percent of all cultivated land in 1943, in 1964 their share rose to 54.7 percent. However, the land reform—although it eliminated the very big landlords—was far from being radical enough.

Two million peasant families remained with less than one acre each, while many landlords remained with 100 acres (some even found loopholes to get round this upper limit). The number of landless agriculturists had not decreased at all, but has increased since 1952.

In Syria the Ba'ath regime has been more radical than Nasser's regime in the field of land reform. But neither Nasser nor the Ba'ath can ever become revolutionary, or grow beyond their middle-class social basis. Their social base is the army officers, civil servants and teachers, sons of merchants and prosperous artisans, better-off peasants and small-scale landowners.

This section of Arab society stands between the feudal lords and the big bourgeoisie on the one hand, and the workers and peasants on the other. The lower middle class is as far from the latter as from the former. A breakdown of urban class division in 1958 is shown in the table below.

Strata	% of total population	Relative per capita income (industrial workers = 100)
Bourgeoisie and aristocracy	3	1,391
Lower strata of the middle class		
(A) Middle officials, professions	8	220
(B) Artisans (employees)	9	202
(C) Low grade officials	14	174
Proletariat		
(A) Industrial and transport workers	10	100
(B) Craftsmen	5	66
Lumpen proletariat		
(A) Permanently-employed unskilled	2	44
(B) Domestic servants	12	35
(C) Permanently unemployed	37	–

The characteristics of 'Arab socialism' spring from this equivocal position.

Nasser and the Ba'ath accept a criticism of feudalism, imperialism and monopoly capitalism. They reject bourgeois parliamentary democracy as a fraud. They accept the need for radical change in order to break the power of the landlords and the big capitalists.

They advocate the transfer of key parts of the economy to state ownership and are enthusiasts of planning. But Nasser rejects the agency of the working class, so his state ownership and planning have nothing to do with socialism.

The attitude of the middle class to state enterprise and planning is very ambivalent indeed. As part of the state bureaucracy, they are interested in a rapid advance of state enterprise. However, as sons, brothers and cousins of small property owners they are quite willing to let the private sector milk the state sector. Hence the Egyptian economy suffers from both the bureaucratic inertia of state capitalism and the speculative working of private capitalism.

The social position of Nasser has prevented him getting rid of the old bureaucracy inherited from the Farouk period prior to the coup by Nasser's Free Officers. On top of this bureaucracy a new expanded one had risen.

These shallow roots in the masses make Nasserism very brittle, very prone to factionalism—hence the break-up of the UAR in 1961 (this short-lived attempt at unity between Egypt and Syria fell apart when the Syrians objected to their second class status within the union), the bitter conflicts with Qasim's Iraq, and so on.

Because of its social base Nasserism vacillates between republicanism and the obscene embrace of 'our Arab brothers' King Hussein in Jordan or King Feisal of Saudi Arabia. Nasserism also vacillates between an attack on the 'Muslim Brotherhood', including the execution of their leadership, and Islamic fervour.

One of the main lessons from the collapse of Ben Bella in Algeria and Qasim in Iraq is that the Bonapartist regimes in backward countries, trying to balance between the working class and the peasantry on the one hand and imperialism on the other, are extremely unstable.

For a really successful anti-imperialist revolutionary struggle, Nasserism is found wanting: it is too far removed from the self-initiative of the masses. For such a struggle it is necessary for the national revolution to be intertwined with the social revolution, for the workers to take over the oilfields and factories, and for the peasants to carry out a revolutionary land reform.

The Communist Parties

One of the shabbiest roles in the situation in the Middle East has been played by the Communist Parties. Instead of keeping independent from the Bonapartist regimes of Nasser, the Ba'ath and previously of Qasim, they completely capitulated to them.

The Communist Parties—following the Moscow guidelines—accepted the peaceful transition to socialism in the 'Third World', rejecting the Marxist-Leninist analysis about the need to smash the bourgeois state machine. The

Communist Parties followed the line of 'national unity', the line separating the national struggle against imperialism from the struggle for social emancipation.

Khaled Bakdash, the General Secretary of the Communist Parry of Syria, has for decades been by far the most important Communist leader in the Middle East.

In a key guideline on the general policy of Arab Communists, he stated in 1944:

> It is evident that the problem of national liberation is a problem of the nation as a whole and it is therefore possible without discussion to get the compliance of the whole nation around this great slogan for the realisation of full national unity. National liberation is in the interests of the national landowners; it is in the interests of small and big merchants alike.

And:

> Our appreciation and honour of the national capitalist who struggles faithfully for national liberation is not less than our appreciation and honour of the national workers who struggle faithfully for national liberation.

And without any shame he said:

> He who reads our National Programme, the programme which was adopted by the congress of the Syrian and Lebanese Communist Parties, will find that it does not mention socialism. There is not one expression or demand with a socialist colouring.

In accordance with this line, the Communist Parties in Syria and Lebanon have long since done away with the Red Flag and the Internationale as their anthem, and adopted the national flags and anthems.

Bakdash reassured the landowners:

> We do not demand and will not demand in parliament the confiscation of their estates and lands, but on the contrary we want to help them in demanding the construction of large-scale irrigation enterprises, the facilitation of the import of fertiliser and modern machinery... All we demand in exchange for this is pity on the fellah, that he be taken out of his poverty and illiteracy, and that knowledge and health spread in the village... These are our economic, or if you can say so, our social demands. They are democratic and very modest.
>
> All we demand...is the introduction of some democratic reforms that all speak about and all agree are necessary. Our demand is not, nor will be and it is not on our programme, to confiscate national capital and national factories. We promise national capital and the national factory owner that we will not look with envy or hate at his national factory, but on the contrary we desire his progress and flourishing. All that we demand is the amelioration of the lot of the national workers and the realisation of a democratic labour legislation which will regulate the relation between the employers and the workers on the basis of justice and national solidarity.

This line has led the Syrian Communist Party to cringe before the Ba'ath in Syria. It led the Iraqi 'Communist' leaders to support General Qasim uncritically until he suppressed them in 1959, and his heir, General Aref, massacred many of them, and imprisoned and tortured many others.

The same opportunist policy led the Egyptian Communists to splits and vacillations, and at last to the dissolution of the most important of the Communist splinters which joined Nasser's 'Socialist Union'.

The 1967 war

The recent war between Israel and its Arab neighbours followed an illuminating sequence of events. The anti-imperialist struggle in Aden has been rising.

This, together with the revolutionary struggle against the Imam of Yemen, threatened Feisal, the King of neighbouring Saudi Arabia. In addition, a dispute blew up between Syria and the Iraq Petroleum Company [a cartel of Western oil companies covering much of the Middle East].

After the nationalisation of the oilfields in Syria itself in December 1964, the IPC suffered a further blow at the end of 1966. The Syrians demanded (and obtained) a 46 percent increase in charges paid by the IPC for use of the pipeline crossing their territory.

In addition, Syria wanted to raise the loading tax from 1s 1d to two shillings per ton. IPC was only willing to agree to 1s 7d. Everything seemed close to agreement. Syria also claimed that payments on the basis of the former agreement of 1955 had been wrongly calculated and that it had lost 110 million Syrian pounds.

In the course of the negotiation the Syrian authorities reduced their demands to £40 million for the years 1956-65. IPC, however, apparently agreed to change its calculations for the future but adamantly refused to discuss the payment of arrears. As a result, the Syrian government stopped the flow of oil.

In reply, the US and Britain poured arms into Saudi Arabia. An Islamic League was formed on 15 May by Iran, Saudi Arabia, Kuwait and Jordan. The Prime Minister of Israel announced that if raids on Israel continued the Israeli army would march on Damascus.

The next steps followed suit in terrible tragedy. The Egyptian army concentrated in Sinai, and a 'Jihad' (holy war) of all Arab states—republican and monarchist alike—was declared. The rest is history.

Who benefited from the Israeli victory? Above all, Western imperialism.

The *Daily Telegraph*, in an editorial entitled 'Israel's Triumph', made it clear why the West benefited from the defeat of the Arab states:

> As a result of Israel's amazing victory, the whole balance of power in the Middle East has decisively changed... On the whole the West must be profoundly grateful to Israel... President Nasser had long been a danger to the West and to world peace. He may not be so much longer.

Peregrine Worsthorne of the *Sunday Telegraph* really waxed poetic in an article entitled 'Triumph of the Civilised':

> Last week a tiny Western community, surrounded by immensely superior numbers of the underdeveloped peoples, has shown itself able to impose its will on the Arabs today almost as effortlessly as the first whites were able to do on the Afro-Asian native in the imperial heyday.

And the City reacted in consonance: sterling has been stronger than for a long time. The *Economist* put it well: 'The brilliant speed of the Israeli advance saved the pound.'

The way ahead

Only people who wholeheartedly support a colonial people in rebellion against imperialism are justified in being severe critics of their leaders' policies and tactics. It is right to be very severe in criticism of the Arab national movement as led by Nasser.

The strength of any anti-imperialist liberation movement is in the masses of workers and peasants mobilised, in their self-activity on the one hand, and the correct choice of the weakest link in the imperialist chain, on the other. Hence the National Liberation Front (NLF) in Vietnam is absolutely right in relying on mass guerilla bands and armies, and harassing the US army and its hangers-on.

The potential strength of the Arab anti-imperialist movement lies in the mass of workers and peasants. The targets of attack should be the oilfields, the oil pipelines and refineries. The peasants should carry out revolutionary land reform, thus creating the base for a guerilla war. Nasser's military confrontation with Israel is exactly the opposite of the policy and tactics of the NLF.

Israel, being modern and privileged, is an even stronger bastion of imperialism than Saigon. Furthermore, an anti-Israeli campaign quite easily degenerates into a 'Jihad', in which the most reactionary regimes save themselves by channelling the struggle into racial channels.

Nasser of Egypt and the Ba'ath of Syria are incapable of following the policies of the NLF in Vietnam, not to speak of the Bolsheviks in Russia.

Hence no guerilla war or workers' attack on the oilfields can be led by the Nasserites.

The Russian leaders are hardly good friends for a mass colonial liberatory movement. Their tanks, planes, missiles and technicians supplied to Nasser were no help at all to the Arab national movement, but an impediment, helping the Nasserite military caste to divert the movement to a wrong path.

The Arab workers and the peasants who suffered oppression over a long period of time need both social and national revolutionary policies.

National emancipation and social emancipation are inseparable. The theory of Nasser, Khaled Bakdash and their ilk about stages separating the one from the other is completely reactionary and utopian.

Only when the workers take the key industries and the peasants take into their hands the land can a really victorious struggle against imperialism and its hangers-on be carried out, however long, bloody and tortuous this struggle may be.

The only possible solution to the needs of the Middle East is the workers' and peasants' revolution aimed at the establishment of a socialist republic, with full rights for Jews, Kurds and all national minorities.

Notes

1 E Behr, *The Algerian Problem* (1961), p214.

The Jews, Israel and the Holocaust

Socialist Review, May 1998

The birth of Zionism

The French Revolution liberated Jewry. Between 1789 and the unification of Germany and Italy nearly a century later, the physical, economic and intellectual ghetto disappeared. Mendelssohn, Heine and Marx, all Jews, were prominent personalities in German culture. Widespread anti-Semitism, and even pogroms, did take place, but this happened in Tsarist Russia, where the yoke of feudalism still bore down and where modern capitalism had barely a foothold. When capitalism became old and decrepit, especially after the Great Depression of the 1930s, it turned on all the democratic achievements of its youth. Now the Jews were not simply pushed into the ghetto, but beyond—into the gas chambers.

In between these two periods a terrible case of anti-Semitism broke out in France. In 1895 a Jewish army officer, Dreyfus, was accused of being a German spy. A witch-hunt trial led to mob hysteria against Jews. This wave of anti-Semitism was the by-product of the battle between rising French imperialism and German imperialism. In Paris at the time was a well-established Viennese journalist, Theodor Herzl. Herzl drew the conclusion from the furore that anti-Semitism was natural and inevitable. He wrote in June 1895:

> In Paris, as I have said, I achieved a freer attitude toward anti-Semitism, which I now began to understand historically and to pardon. Above all, I recognised the emptiness and futility of trying to 'combat' anti-Semitism.

Herzl criticised Emile Zola and other French people, mainly socialists, who came to the defence of Dreyfus. He complained that the Jews:

> ...seek protection from the socialists and the destroyers of the present civil order... Truly they are not Jews any more. To be sure, they are no Frenchmen either. They will probably become the leaders of European anarchism.

He argued that the answer to anti-Semitism lay in the Jews leaving the countries where they were not wanted and establishing their own state. In this effort, he declared, 'the anti-Semites will be our most dependable friends...our allies.' Hence he went to meet the Tsarist minister of the interior, Plevhe, the man who had organised the Kishinev pogrom of 1903. He dangled the bait before him that taking the Jews out of Russia would weaken the revolutionary movement, Plevhe's enemy.

If antagonism between Jews and Gentiles was supposedly natural and inevitable then of course it followed that antagonism between Jews and Arabs in Palestine was natural and inevitable. To start with, Herzl defined Zionism as 'giving to a people without a country a country without people'. When his attention was drawn to the fact that there were Arabs in Palestine, Herzl took it for granted that the job was simply to get rid of them. On 12 June 1895 he wrote, 'We shall try to spirit the penniless population across the border by procuring employment for it in the transit countries, while denying it any employment in our own country.' What an outrageous expression of ethnic cleansing intent!

Closed Zionist economy

The Zionists who emigrated to Palestine from the end of the 19th century did not want to establish an economy similar to that of the whites in South Africa. There the whites were the capitalists while the blacks were the workers. The Zionists wanted the whole population to be Jewish. With the very low standard of living of the Arabs compared to Europeans, and with both very widespread open and hidden unemployment, the only way of achieving this aim was by closing the Jewish labour market to Arabs. There were a number of methods used to achieve this. First, the Jewish National Fund, owner of a big proportion of the land owned by Jews, including, for instance, a large chunk of Tel Aviv, had a statute that insisted that only Jews could be employed on this land.

In addition, the Zionist trade union federation, the Histadrut (General Federation of Hebrew Labour), imposed on all its members two levies: one for the defence of Hebrew labour, and one for the defence of the Hebrew product. The Histadrut organised pickets against orchard owners who employed Arab workers, forcing the owners to sack them. It was also common to see young men walking in the Jewish market among the women selling vegetables or eggs, and if they found one who happened be an Arab, they poured paraffin on the vegetables and smashed the eggs.

I remember in 1945 a cafe in Tel Aviv was attacked and almost entirely broken up because of a rumour that there was an Arab working in the kitchen washing the dishes. I also remember, when I was in the Hebrew University in Jerusalem between 1936 and 1939, repeated demonstrations against the vice-chancellor of the university, Dr Magnus. He was a rich American Jew and a liberal, and his crime was that he was a tenant of an Arab landlord.

Dependence on imperialism

Knowing that they would face resistance from the Palestinians, the Zionists were always clear that they needed the help of the imperialist power that had the major influence in Palestine at the time.

On 19 October 1898 Herzl went to Constantinople to have an audience with Kaiser Wilhelm. At that time Palestine was in the Ottoman Empire, which was a junior partner of Germany. Herzl told the Kaiser that a Zionist settlement in Israel would increase German influence as the centre of Zionism was in Austria, which was a partner of the German Empire. He also dangled another carrot: 'I explained that we were taking the Jews away from the revolutionary parties.'

Towards the end of the First World War, when it was clear Britain was going to take over Palestine, the leader of the Zionists at the time, Chaim Weizmann, contacted the British foreign secretary, Arthur Balfour, getting from him, on 2 November 1917, a declaration promising the Jews a homeland in Palestine. Sir Ronald Storrs, the first British military governor of Jerusalem, explained that the Zionist 'enterprise was one that blessed him, that gave as well as him that took, by forming for England "a little loyal Jewish Ulster" in a sea of potentially hostile Arabism'. The Zionists would be the Orangemen of Palestine.

With the Second World War it became clear that the main power in the Middle East would cease to be Britain and would be the United States. Ben Gurion, the Zionist leader at the time, therefore rushed to Washington to cement deals with the United States. Israel is now the most reliable satellite of the United States. It is not for nothing that Israel gets more economic aid from the United States than any other country, even though it is so tiny. It also gets more military aid than any other country in the world.

The Holocaust

Understanding the barbarity of Nazism, Trotsky foresaw the annihilation of the Jews. On 22 December 1938 he wrote:

> It is possible to imagine without difficulty what awaits the Jews at the mere outbreak of the future war. But even without war the next development of world reaction signifies with certainty the *physical extermination of the Jews*... Only audacious mobilisation of the workers against reaction, creation of workers' militia, direct physical resistance to the fascist gangs, increasing self-confidence, activity and audacity on the part of all the oppressed can provoke a change in the relations of forces, stop the world wave of fascism, and open a new chapter in the history of mankind.

Until the Second World War the overwhelming majority of Jews in the world, especially working class Jews, were not supporters of Zionism. Thus in Poland, where the biggest community of Jews in Europe existed at the time, council elections took place in December 1938 and January 1939 in Warsaw, Lodz,

Krakow, Lvov, Vilna and other cities. The Bund, the Jewish socialist workers' anti-Zionist organisation, received 70 percent of the votes in the Jewish districts. The Bund won 17 out of 20 seats in Warsaw, while the Zionists held only one.

All this was changed radically by the Holocaust. There is hardly a Jew in Europe who did not lose members of his or her family in it. I remember a short time before it an aunt of mine from Danzig came to visit us in Palestine. I did not meet the rest of her family, but she, together with all the rest, disappeared in the Holocaust. A cousin of mine, whom I knew very well, moved to Europe with her husband and child of five just before the war, and they were also murdered in the gas chambers.

Today the overwhelming majority of Jews are Zionists, and this is very understandable.

The catastrophe

This is the term used by the Palestinians to refer to the establishment of the state of Israel in 1948. Since then, in the three wars between Israel and the Arabs in 1948, 1967 and 1973, there has been a massive ethnic cleansing of the Palestinians. Today there are 3.4 million Palestinian refugees, far more than the number of Palestinians remaining in the areas they lived in before. Figures of land ownership testify to their elimination: in 1917 the Jews owned 2.5 percent of the land in the country. In 1948 it rose to 5.7 percent, and today it is about 95 percent in the pre-1967 borders, while the Arabs own only 5 percent.

It is one of the most tragic cases in history that an oppressed nation like the Jews, who suffered from the barbarity of the Nazis, have imposed oppression and barbarism on another nation—the Palestinians, a nation which was in no way involved in bringing about the Holocaust.

The solution

The Palestinians have not the strength to liberate themselves. They do not even have the strength to achieve any serious reforms. They are not like blacks in South Africa, who have achieved very important reforms. They got rid of apartheid, they won the right to vote and they elected a black president. It is true that economic apartheid is still in place. Wealth is still concentrated in the hands of a tiny group of white people, now alongside a tiny number of rich blacks. The overwhelming majority of blacks are still in abject poverty. The blacks in South Africa are incomparably stronger than the Palestinians. First of all, there are five to six times more blacks than whites in South Africa, while the number of Palestinians is more or less the same as the number of Israelis (the majority of Palestinians are refugees). Secondly, black workers are at the heart of the South African economy, while the Palestinians are very marginal to the economy. The South African trade union COSATU is a massive trade union which played a crucial role in the smashing of apartheid. The Palestinians have no comparable trade union organisation.

If there is a situation where Trotsky's theory of permanent revolution applies perfectly, it is that of the Palestinians. His theory argues that no democratic demands, no national liberation can be achieved without the proletarian revolution. The key to the fate of the Palestinians and everyone else in the Middle East is in the hands of the Arab working class, whose main centres of power are in Egypt, and less so in Syria, Iraq, Lebanon and other countries. Tragically the potential of the Arab working class has not become actuality because of the damaging effect of Stalinism. which dominated the left in the Middle East for a long time. It was the Stalinists who opened the door to the Ba'ath Party and Saddam Hussein in Iraq, who brought Assad and the Syrian Ba'ath to power, who opened the door to Nasser and the subsequent Islamists in Egypt.

A revolution of the Arab working class would put an end to imperialism and Zionism. It is simple hypocrisy to claim that this will menace the Jews of the area. When the apartheid regime dominated South Africa the supporters of the regime claimed that the ANC stood for the butchery of the whites. Nothing of the sort has taken place.

Thinkers in the revolutionary tradition

Rosa Luxemburg

First published as a pamphlet in 1959,
reprinted 1968, 1969 and 1980

Foreword

On 15 January 1919 a soldier's rifle butt smashed the skull of Rosa Luxemburg, revolutionary genius, fighter and thinker. A personification of the unity of theory and practice, Rosa Luxemburg's life and work require a description of her activities as well as her thoughts—they are inseparable. In the framework of a pamphlet, however, one cannot hope to do justice to both. In trying to avoid falling between two stools, this pamphlet concentrates mainly on Rosa Luxemburg's ideas, as they contain her main permanent contribution to the international socialist movement.

Little of her writing has been translated into English. It is, therefore, useful to give as varied a selection from her work (largely translated from the original German) as possible.

A scientific socialist, whose motto was 'doubt all', Rosa Luxemburg could have wished for nothing better than a critical evaluation of her own work. The present essay is written in a spirit of admiration and criticism of its subject.

Biographical sketch

Rosa Luxemburg was born in the small Polish town of Zamosc on 5 March 1871. From early youth she was active in the socialist movement. She joined a revolutionary party called Proletariat, founded in 1882, some 21 years before the Russian Social Democratic Party (Bolsheviks and Mensheviks) came into being. From the beginning Proletariat was, in principles and programme, many steps ahead of the revolutionary movement in Russia. While the Russian revolutionary movement was still restricted to acts of individual terrorism carried out by a few heroic intellectuals, Proletariat was organising and leading thousands of workers on strike. In 1886, however, Proletariat was practically decapitated by the execution of four of its leaders, the imprisonment of 23 others for long terms of hard labour, and the banishment of about 200 more. Only small circles were saved from the wreck, and it was one of these that Rosa Luxemburg joined at the age of 16. By 1889 the police had caught up with her, and she had to leave Poland, her comrades thinking she could do more useful work abroad than in prison. She went to Switzerland, to Zurich, which was the most important centre of Polish and Russian emigration. There she entered the university where she studied natural sciences, mathematics and economics. She took an active part in the local labour movement and in the intense intellectual life of the revolutionary emigrants.

Hardly more than a couple of years later Rosa Luxemburg was already recognised as the theoretical leader of the revolutionary socialist party of Poland. She became the main contributor to the party paper, *Sprawa Rabotnicza*, published in Paris. In 1894 the name of the party, Proletariat, was changed to become the Social Democratic Party of the Kingdom of Poland; shortly afterwards Lithuania was added to the title. Rosa continued to be the theoretical leader of the party (the SDKPL) till the end of her life.

In August 1893 she represented the party at the Congress of the Socialist International. There, a young woman of 22, she had to contend with well-known veterans of another Polish party, the Polish Socialist Party (PPS), whose main plank was the independence of Poland and which claimed the recognition of all the experienced elders of international socialism. Support for the national movement in Poland had the weight of long tradition behind it: Marx and Engels, too, had made it an important plank in their policies. Undaunted by all this, Rosa Luxemburg struck out at the PPS, accusing it of clear nationalistic tendencies and a proneness to diverting the workers from the path of class struggle; and she dared to take a different position to the old masters and oppose the slogan of independence for Poland. (For elaboration on this, see 'Rosa Luxemburg and the national question' below.) Her adversaries heaped abuse on her, some of them, like the veteran disciple and friend of Marx and Engels, Wilhelm Liebknecht, going so far as to accuse her of being an agent of the Tsarist secret police. But she stuck to her point.

Intellectually she grew by leaps and bounds. She was drawn irresistibly to the centre of the international labour movement, Germany, where she made her way in 1898.

She started writing assiduously, and after a time became one of the main contributors to the most important Marxist theoretical journal of the time, *Die Neue Zeit*. Invariably independent in judgment and criticism, even the tremendous prestige of Karl Kautsky, its editor, 'the Pope of Marxism' as he used to be called, did not deflect her from her considered opinions once she had become convinced.

Rosa Luxemburg entered heart and soul into the labour movement in Germany. She was a regular contributor to a number of socialist papers—in some cases their editor—she addressed many mass meetings and took part energetically in all the tasks the movement called upon her to perform. Throughout, her speeches and articles were original creative works, in which she appealed to reason rather than emotion, and in which she always opened up to her readers a wider and grander horizon than they had known before.

At that time the movement in Germany was split into two main trends, one reformist and the other revolutionary, with the former growing in strength. Germany had enjoyed continuous prosperity since the slump of 1873. The workers' standard of living had improved uninterruptedly, if slowly; trade unions and co-operatives grew stronger.

Against this background, the bureaucracy of these movements, together with the increasing parliamentary representation of the Social Democratic Party, moved away from revolution and lent great strength to those who were already proclaiming gradualism or reformism as their principle. The main spokesman of this trend was Eduard Bernstein, a disciple of Engels. Between 1896 and 1898 he wrote a series of articles in *Die Neue Zeit* on 'Problems of Socialism', more and more openly attacking the principles of Marxism. A long and bitter discussion broke out. Rosa Luxemburg, who had just entered the German labour movement, immediately sprang to the defence of Marxism. Brilliantly and with magnificent drive, she attacked the spreading cancer of reformism in her booklet, *Social Reform or Social Revolution*. (For an elaboration of her criticism of reformism see 'Reform or Revolution' below.)

Soon afterwards, in 1899, the French 'Socialist' Millerand entered a coalition government with a capitalist party. Rosa Luxemburg followed this experiment closely and analysed it in a series of brilliant articles dealing with the situation in the French labour movement in general, and the question of coalition governments in particular (see 'Reform or Revolution' below). After the fiasco of MacDonald in Britain, of the Weimar Republic in Germany, of the Popular Front in France in the 1930s and the post-Second World War coalition governments in the same country, it is clear that the lessons drawn by Rosa Luxemburg are not of historical interest alone.

In 1903-04 Rosa Luxemburg indulged in a polemic with Lenin, with whom she disagreed on the national question (see the section on the national question below), and on the conception of party structure, and the relation between the party and the activity of the masses (see 'Party and class' below).

In 1904 after 'insulting the Kaiser' she was sentenced to three months imprisonment, of which she served a month.

In 1905, with the outbreak of the first Russian Revolution, she wrote a series of articles and pamphlets for the Polish party, in which she developed the idea of the permanent revolution, which had been independently developed by Trotsky and Parvus but was held by few Marxists of the time. While both the Mensheviks and Bolsheviks, despite the deep cleavage between them, believed that the Russian Revolution was to be a bourgeois democratic one, Rosa argued that it would develop beyond the stage of bourgeois democracy and would either end in workers' power or complete defeat. Her slogan was 'revolutionary dictatorship of the proletariat based on the peasantry.' (It was not for nothing that Stalin denounced Luxemburg posthumously in 1931 as a Trotskyist.[1])

However, to think, write and speak about the revolution was not enough for Rosa Luxemburg. The motto of her life was, 'At the beginning was the deed.' And although she was in bad health at the time, she smuggled herself into

Russian Poland as soon as she was able to do so (in December 1905). The zenith of the revolution had by then passed. The masses were still active, but were now hesitant while reaction was raising its head. All meetings were forbidden, but the workers still held meetings in their strongholds, the factories. All workers' papers were suppressed, but Rosa Luxemburg's party paper continued to appear daily, although printed clandestinely. On 4 March 1906 she was arrested and kept for four months, first in prison, then in a fortress. Thereafter she was freed, on the grounds of ill health and her German nationality, and expelled from the country.

The Russian Revolution of 1905 gave flesh and blood to an idea Rosa Luxemburg had conceived some years earlier: that mass strikes—political and economic—constitute a cardinal element in the revolutionary workers' struggle for power, distinguishing socialist from all previous revolutions. Now she elaborated the idea on the basis of a new historical experience (see 'Mass strikes and revolution' below).

Speaking to this effect at a public meeting, she was accused of 'inciting to violence' and spent another two months in prison, this time in Germany.

In 1907 she participated in the Congress of the Socialist International held in Stuttgart. She spoke in the name of the Russian and Polish parties, developing a consistent revolutionary attitude to imperialist war and militarism (see 'The fight against imperialism and war' below).

Between 1905 and 1910 the split widened between Rosa Luxemburg and the centrist leadership of the SPD, of which Kautsky was the theoretical mouthpiece. Already in 1907 Rosa Luxemburg had expressed her fear that the party leaders, notwithstanding their profession of Marxism, would flinch before a situation in which decisive action was called for. The climax came in 1910, with a complete break between Rosa Luxemburg and Karl Kautsky on the question of the workers' road to power. From now on the SPD was split into three separate tendencies: the reformists, who progressively adopted an imperialist policy; the so-called Marxist centre, led by Kautsky (now nicknamed by Luxemburg the 'leader of the swamp') which kept its verbal radicalism but confined itself more and more to parliamentary methods of struggle; and the revolutionary wing, of which Rosa Luxemburg was the main inspiration.

In 1913 Rosa Luxemburg published her most important theoretical work, *The Accumulation of Capital: A Contribution to the Economic Explanation of Imperialism*. This is, without doubt, one of the most original contributions to Marxist economic doctrine since *Capital*. In its wealth of knowledge, brilliance of style, trenchancy of analysis and intellectual independence, this book, as Mehring, Marx's biographer, stated, was the nearest to *Capital* of any Marxist work. The central problem it studies is of tremendous theoretical and political importance: namely, what effects the extension of capitalism into new, backward territories has on the internal contradictions rending capitalism and on the stability of the system (for an analysis of this work, see 'The Accumulation of Capital' below).

On 20 February 1914 Rosa Luxemburg was arrested for inciting soldiers to mutiny. The basis of the charge was a speech in which she declared, 'If they expect us to murder our French or other foreign brothers, then let us tell them, "No, under no circumstances".' In court she turned from defendant into prosecutor, and her speech, published later under the title *Militarism, War and the Working Class*, is one of the most inspiring revolutionary socialist condemnations of imperialism. She was sentenced to a year's imprisonment but was not detained on the spot. On leaving the courtroom she immediately went to a mass meeting at which she repeated her revolutionary anti-war propaganda.

When the First World War broke out, practically all the leaders of the Socialist Party [SPD] were swept into the patriotic tide. On 3 August 1914 the parliamentary group of German Social Democracy decided to vote in favour of war credits for the Kaiser's government. Of the 111 deputies only 15 showed any desire to vote against. However, after their request for permission to do so had been rejected, they submitted to party discipline, and on 4 August the whole Social Democratic group unanimously voted in favour of the credits. A few months later, on 2 December, Karl Liebknecht flouted party discipline to vote with his conscience. His was the sole vote against war credits.

This decision of the party leadership was a cruel blow to Rosa Luxemburg. However, she did not give way to despair. On the same day, 4 August, on which the Social Democratic deputies rallied to the Kaiser's banner, a small group of socialists met in her apartment and decided to take up the struggle against the war. This group, led by Luxemburg, Karl Liebknecht, Franz Mehring and Clara Zetkin, ultimately became the Spartakus League. For four years, mainly from prison, Rosa continued to lead, inspire and organise the revolutionaries, keeping high the banner of international socialism (for further details of her anti-war policy, see 'The fight against imperialism and war' below).

The outbreak of the war cut Rosa Luxemburg off from the Polish labour movement, but she must have gained deep satisfaction from the fact that her own Polish party remained loyal throughout to the ideas of international socialism.

The revolution in Russia of February 1917 was a realisation of Rosa Luxemburg's policy of revolutionary opposition to the war and struggle for the overthrow of imperialist governments. Feverishly she followed the events from prison, studying them closely in order to draw lessons for the future. Unhesitatingly she stated that the February victory was not the end of the struggle but only its beginning, that only workers' power could assure peace. From prison she issued call after call to the German workers and soldiers to emulate their Russian brethren, overthrow the Junkers and capitalists and thus, while serving the Russian Revolution, at the same time prevent themselves from bleeding to death under the ruins of capitalist barbarism.

When the October Revolution broke out, Rosa Luxemburg welcomed it enthusiastically, praising it in the highest terms. At the same time she did not believe that uncritical acceptance of everything the Bolsheviks did would be of service to the labour movement. She clearly foresaw that if the Russian Revolution remained in isolation a number of distortions would cripple its development; and quite early in the development of Soviet Russia she pointed out such distortions, particularly on the question of democracy (see 'Rosa Luxemburg's criticism of the Bolsheviks in power' below).

On 8 November 1918 the German Revolution freed Rosa Luxemburg from prison. With all her energy and enthusiasm she threw herself into the revolution. Unfortunately the forces of reaction were strong. Right-wing Social Democratic leaders and generals of the old Kaiser's army joined forces to suppress the revolutionary working class. Thousands of workers were murdered; on 15 January 1919 Karl Liebknecht was killed; on the same day a soldier's rifle butt smashed into Rosa Luxemburg's skull.

With her death the international workers' movement lost one of its noblest souls. 'The finest brain amongst the scientific successors of Marx and Engels', as Mehring said, was no more. In her life, as in her death, she gave everything for the liberation of humanity.

Reform or revolution

Running through Rosa Luxemburg's entire work was the struggle against reformism, which narrowed down the aims of the labour movement to tinkering with capitalism instead of overthrowing it by revolutionary means. The most prominent spokesman of reformism (or revisionism, as it was known then) against whom Rosa first took up arms was Eduard Bernstein. She refuted his views with special incisiveness in her pamphlet *Social Reform or Social Revolution*, which was made up of two series of articles published in the *Leipziger Volkszeitung*, the first in September 1898 as an answer to Bernstein's articles in *Die Neue Zeit*, the second in April 1899 in answer to his book *The Preconditions of Socialism and the Tasks of Social Democracy*.

Bernstein redefined the fundamental character of the labour movement as a 'democratic socialist reform party' and not a party of social revolution. Opposing Marx, he argued that the contradictions in capitalism do not get sharper, but are continually being alleviated; capitalism is steadily being tamed, steadily becoming more adaptable. Cartels, trusts and credit institutions gradually regularise the anarchic nature of the system, so that, instead of recurring slumps as visualised by Marx, there is a tendency towards permanent prosperity. Social contradictions are also weakened, according to Bernstein, by the viability of the middle class and the more democratic distribution of capital ownership through stock companies. The adaptability of the system to the needs of the time is shown also in the improvement of the economic, social and political condition of the working class as a result of the activities of the trade unions and co-operatives.

From this analysis Bernstein concluded that the socialist party must devote itself to bettering gradually the conditions of the working class, and not to the revolutionary conquest of political power.

In opposition to Bernstein, Rosa Luxemburg argued that capitalist monopoly organisations (cartels and trusts) and credit institutions tend to deepen the antagonisms in capitalism and not to mitigate them. She describes their function:

> In a general way, cartels...appear...as a determined phase of capitalist development, which in the last analysis aggravates the anarchy of the capitalist world and expresses and ripens its internal contradictions. Cartels aggravate the antagonism existing between the mode of production and exchange by sharpening the struggle between the producer and consumer... They aggravate, furthermore, the antagonism existing between the mode of production and the mode of appropriation by opposing, in the most brutal fashion, to the working class the superior force of organised capital, and thus increasing the antagonism between Capital and Labour.
>
> Finally, capitalist combinations aggravate the contradiction existing between the international character of the capitalist world economy and the national character of the State—insofar as they are always accompanied by a general tariff war, which sharpens the differences among the capitalist States. We must add to this the decidedly revolutionary influence exercised by cartels on the concentration of production, technical progress, etc.
>
> In other words, when evaluated from the angle of their final effect on capitalist economy, cartels and trusts fail as 'means of adaptation'. They fail to attenuate the contradictions of capitalism. On the contrary, they appear to be an instrument of greater anarchy. They encourage the further development of the internal contradictions of capitalism. They accelerate the coming of a general decline of capitalism.[2]

Credit, too, said Rosa Luxemburg, far from circumventing the capitalist crisis, actually deepened it. The two most important functions of credit are to expand production and facilitate exchange, both of which functions aggravate the instability of the system. Capitalist economic crises develop as a result of the contradictions between production's permanent tendency to expand and the limited consumption capacity of the capitalist market. Credit, by encouraging production on the one hand, encourages the tendency towards overproduction, and, being itself subject to grave instability in adverse circumstances, tends to shake the economy more and deepen the crisis. The role of credit in encouraging speculation is another factor increasing the instability of the capitalist mode of production.

Bernstein's trump card in support of his argument that the contradictions of capitalism were decreasing was that for two decades, since 1873, capitalism had not suffered a major slump. But, in Rosa Luxemburg's words:

> Hardly had Bernstein rejected, in 1898, Marx's theory of crises, when a profound general crisis broke out in 1900, while seven years later, a new crisis, beginning in the United States, hit the world market. Facts proved the theory of 'adaptation' to be false. They showed at the same time that the people who abandoned Marx's theory of crisis only because no crisis occurred within a certain space of time merely confused the essence of this theory with one of its secondary exterior aspects—the ten-year cycle. The description of the cycle of modern capitalist industry as a ten-year period was to Marx and Engels, in 1860 and 1870, only a simple statement of facts. It was not based on a natural law but on a series of given historic circumstances that were connected with the rapidly spreading activity of young capitalism.[3]

In fact:

> Crises may repeat themselves every five or ten years, or even every eight or 20 years… The belief that capitalist production could 'adapt' itself to exchange presupposes one of two things: either the world market can spread unlimitedly or, on the contrary, the development of the productive forces is so fettered that it cannot pass beyond the bounds of the market. The first hypothesis constitutes a material impossibility. The second is rendered just as impossible by the constant technical progress that daily creates new productive forces in all branches.[4]

As a matter of fact, Rosa Luxemburg argued, what is basic to Marxism is that the contradictions in capitalism—between the rising productive forces and the relations of production—are becoming progressively aggravated. But that these contradictions should express themselves in a catastrophic general crisis 'is of secondary importance' only.[5] The form of expression of the fundamental contradiction is not as important as its content. (By the way, Rosa Luxemburg would in all probability not dispute the idea that one form in which the basic contradictions can express themselves is in the permanent war economy with its tremendous wastage of the productive forces.)

Rosa Luxemburg argued that when Bernstein denied the deepening contradictions within capitalism he cut away the basis of the struggle for socialism. Socialism thus became transformed from an economic necessity into a hoped-for ideal, a Utopia. Bernstein complained, 'Why represent socialism as the consequence of economic compulsion? … Why degrade man's understanding, his feeling for justice, his will?'[6] Rosa Luxemburg commented:

> Bernstein's superlatively just distribution is to be attained thanks to man's free will, man's will acting not because of economic necessity, since this will itself is only an instrument, but because of man's comprehension of justice, because of man's idea of justice.
>
> We thus quite happily return to the principle of justice, to the old war horse on which the reformers of the earth have rocked for ages for the lack of surer means of historic transportation. We return to that lamentable Rosinante on which the Don Quixotes of history have galloped towards the great reform of the earth, always to come home with their eyes blackened.[7]

Abstracted from the contradictions of capitalism, the urge towards socialism becomes merely an idealistic chimera.

Eduard Bernstein (and many after him) looked upon the trade unions as a weapon weakening capitalism. Rosa Luxemburg, in contradistinction, argued that, while trade unions can somewhat affect the level of wages, they cannot by themselves overthrow the wages system and the basic objective economic factors determining the wage level:

> Trade unions are nothing more than the organised defence of labour power against the attacks of profit. They express the resistance offered by the working class to the oppression of capitalist economy.
>
> …trade unions have the function of influencing the situation in the labour-power market. But this influence is being constantly overcome by the proletarianisation of the middle layers of our society, a process which continually brings

> new merchandise on the labour market. The second function of the trade unions is to ameliorate the condition of the workers. That is, they attempt to increase the share of the social wealth going to the working class. This share, however, is being reduced with the fatality of a natural process, by the growth of the productivity of labour...
>
> In other words, the objective conditions of capitalist society transform the two economic functions of the trade unions into a sort of labour of Sisyphus,[8] which is, nevertheless, indispensable. For, as a result of the activity of his trade unions, the worker succeeds in obtaining for himself the rate of wages due to him in accordance with the situation of the labour-power market. As a result of trade union activity, the capitalist law of wages is applied and the effect of the depressing tendency of economic development is paralysed, or, to be more exact, is attenuated.[9]

A labour of Sisyphus! This expression enraged the German trade union bureaucrats. They could not admit that the trade union struggle, however useful in protecting the workers from the immanent tendency of capitalism to depress their standards progressively, is not a substitute for the liberation of the working class.

While for Bernstein the trade unions (and co-operatives) were the main economic levers for achieving socialism, parliamentary democracy was the political lever for this transition. According to him, parliament was the embodiment of society's will, in other words, it was an above-class institution.

Rosa Luxemburg, however, argues: '...the present State is not "society" representing the "rising working class". It is itself the representative of capitalist society. It is a class State'.[10] 'All in all, parliamentarism is not a directly socialist element impregnating gradually the whole capitalist society. It is, on the contrary, a specific form of the bourgeois class State'.[11]

At the time that the dispute about the parliamentary road to socialism was at its height in Germany, what they believed to be the conquest of political power through parliament was achieved for the first time by French socialists. In June 1899 Alexandre Millerand entered the Radical government of Waldeck-Rousseau, sitting side by side with General Galliffet, butcher in chief of the Paris Commune. This action was acclaimed by the French socialist leader Jaurès and the right-wing reformists as a great tactical turning point: political power was now wielded no more by the bourgeoisie alone, but jointly by the bourgeoisie and the working class, which situation, according to them, was a political expression of the transition from capitalism to socialism.

Rosa followed this first experiment in coalition government between capitalist and socialist parties with close attention, making an extremely thorough investigation of it. She pointed out that this coalition, by binding the working class hand and foot to the government, prevented the workers from showing their real power. And in fact what the opportunists called 'arid opposition' was a much more useful and practical policy: '...far from rendering real, immediate, and tangible reforms of a progressive character impossible, an oppositional policy is the only way in which minority parties in general and socialist minority parties in particular can obtain practical successes'.[12] The socialist party should take only those positions which give scope for anti-capitalist struggle:

> Of course, in order to be effective, Social Democracy must take all the positions she can in the present State and invade everywhere. However, the prerequisite for this is that these positions make it possible to wage the class struggle from them, the struggle against the bourgeoisie and its State.[13]

And she concluded: 'In the bourgeois society the role of Social Democracy is that of *opposition party*. As a *ruling party* it is allowed to rise only on the ruins of the bourgeois State'.[14]

The final dangers inherent in the coalition experiment were pointed to: 'Jaurès, the tireless defender of the republic, is preparing the way for Caesarism. It sounds like a bad joke, but the course of history is strewn with such jokes'.[15]

How prophetic! The fiasco of MacDonald in Britain, the replacement of the Weimar republic by Hitler, the bankruptcy of the Popular Front in the 1930s and the coalition governments in France after the Second World War, leading to de Gaulle, are some of the final fruits of the policy of coalition government.

To the reformists, who believed that parliamentarism and bourgeois legality meant the end of violence as a factor in historical development, Rosa countered:

> What is actually the whole function of bourgeois legality? If one 'free citizen' is taken by another against his will and confined in close and uncomfortable quarters for a while, everyone realises immediately that an act of violence has been committed. However, as soon as the process takes place in accordance with the book known as the penal code, and the quarters in question are in prison, then the whole affair immediately becomes peaceable and legal. If one man is compelled by another to kill his fellow men, then that is obviously an act of violence. However, as soon as the process is called 'military service', the good citizen is consoled with the idea that everything is perfectly legal and in order. If one citizen is deprived against his will by another of some part of his property or earnings it is obvious that an act of violence has been committed, but immediately the process is called 'indirect taxation', then everything is quite all right.
>
> In other words, what presents itself to us in the cloak of bourgeois legality is nothing but the expression of class violence raised to an obligatory norm by the ruling class. Once the individual act of violence has been raised in this way to an obligatory norm the process is reflected in the mind of the bourgeois lawyer (and no less in the mind of the socialist opportunist) not as it really is, but upside down: the legal process appears as an independent creation of abstract 'Justice', and State compulsion appears as a consequence, as a mere 'sanctioning' of the law. In reality the truth is exactly the opposite: bourgeois legality (and parliamentarism as the legislature in process of development) is nothing but the particular social form in which the political violence of the bourgeoisie, developing its given economic basis, expresses itself.[16]

Hence the idea of superceding capitalism by means of the legal forms established by capitalism itself, which, at bottom, are nothing but the expression of bourgeois violence, is absurd. In the final analysis, for the overthrow of capitalism, revolutionary violence is necessary:

> The use of violence will always remain the *ultima ratio* for the working class, the supreme law of the class struggle, always present, sometimes in a latent, sometimes in an active form. And when we try to revolutionise minds by parliamentary and other activity, it is only in order that at need the revolution may move not only the mind but also the hand.[17]

How prophetic now, after the demise of the Weimar Republic to be followed by the Nazis, were the following words of Rosa Luxemburg written in 1902: 'If Social Democracy were to accept the opportunist standpoint, renounce the use of violence, and pledge the working class never to diverge from the path of bourgeois legalism, then its whole parliamentary and other activity would sooner or later collapse miserably and leave the field to the untrammelled dominance of reactionary violence'.[18]

But though Rosa Luxemburg knew that the workers were compelled to resort to revolutionary violence against exploitation and oppression, she suffered keenly the pain of every drop of blood shed. She wrote during the middle of the German Revolution:

> Rivers of blood streamed during the four years of imperialist murder of nations [the First World War]. Now we must be sure to preserve every drop of this precious liquid with honour and in crystal glasses. Uncurbed revolutionary energy and wide human feeling—this is the real breath of socialism. It is true a whole world has to be overturned, but any tear that could have been avoided is an accusation; a man who hastens to perform an important deed and unthinkingly treads upon a worm on his way is committing a crime.[19]

Among reformists as well as some who claim to be revolutionaries the theory is prevalent that only hunger may cause workers to follow a revolutionary path: the better-off workers of Central and Western Europe, argued the reformists, could therefore learn very little from the hungry and downtrodden Russian workers. Rosa Luxemburg made a big point of correcting this wrong conception, writing in 1906:

> ...the notion that under the Tsarist regime prior to the revolution the working class standard of living was that of paupers is much exaggerated. On the contrary the layer of workers in large industries and big cities which was most effective and active in the economic and political struggle enjoyed a standard of living hardly lower than the corresponding layer of the German proletariat; indeed, in some trades the same, or here and there, an even higher wage, obtained in Russia than in Germany. Also in regard to working hours the difference between large industrial concerns in the two countries is scarcely significant. Hence the conception that assumes that the Russian working class has the material and cultural conditions of helots is invented out of thin air. This conception contradicts the facts of the revolution itself and the prominent role of the proletariat in it. Revolutions of this political and spiritual maturity are not made by paupers; the industrial worker in the vanguard of the struggle at Petersburg, Warsaw, Moscow, Odessa, is much closer culturally and spiritually to the West European type than is imagined by those who think that the only and indispensable school for the proletariat is bourgeois parliamentarism and 'correct' union practice.[20]

Incidentally, empty stomachs, besides encouraging rebellion, lead also to submission.

Basing herself on the class struggle of the working class, whether latent or open, whether aimed at winning concessions from the capitalist class or at its overthrow, Rosa Luxemburg supported the struggle for social reforms as well as social revolution, considering the former above all a school for the latter, whose greater historical import she made clear in analysing the mutual relations of the two:

> Legislative reform and revolution are not different methods of historic development that can be picked out at pleasure from the counter of history, just as one chooses hot or cold sausages. Legislative reform and revolution are different factors in the development of class society. They condition and complement each other, and are at the same time reciprocally exclusive, as are the north and south poles, the bourgeoisie and the proletariat.
>
> Every legal constitution is the product of a revolution. In the history of classes, revolution is the act of political creation, while legislation is the political expression of the life of a society that has already come into being. Work for reform does not contain its own force, independent from revolution. During every historic period, work of reforms is carried on only in the direction given to it by the impetus of the last revolution, and continues as long as the impulsion of the last revolution continues to make itself felt. Or, to put it more concretely, in each historic period work for reforms is carried on only in the framework of the social form created by the last revolution. Here is the kernel of the problem.
>
> It is contrary to history to represent work for reforms as a long drawn-out revolution and revolution as a condensed series of reforms. A social transformation and a legislative reform do not differ according to their duration but according to their content. The secret of historic change through the utilisation of political power resides precisely in the transformation of simple quantitative modification into a new quality, or, to speak more concretely, in the passage of an historic period from one given form of society to another.
>
> That is why people who pronounce themselves in favour of the method of legislative reform in place of and in contradistinction to the conquest of political power and social revolution do not really choose a more tranquil, calmer and slower road to the same goal, but a different goal. Instead of a stand for the establishment of a new society they take a stand for surface modifications of the old society. If we follow the political conceptions of revisionism, we arrive at the same conclusion that is reached when we follow the economic theories of revisionism. Our programme becomes not the realisation of socialism, but the reform of capitalism; not the suppression of the system of wage labour, but the diminution of exploitation, that is, the suppression of the abuses of capitalism instead of the suppression of capitalism itself.[21]

Mass strikes and revolution

In May 1891 a mass strike of some 125,000 Belgian workers demanded changes in the electoral system. In April 1893 another strike, embracing about a quarter of a million workers, broke out for a similar demand. The outcome was universal, but unequal, franchise, the votes of the rich and 'cultured' counting for two or three times those of workers and peasants. The workers, dissatisfied, carried out another mass strike nine years later, demanding a complete revision of the Constitution. These mass political strikes made a great impression on Rosa Luxemburg. Two articles devoted to the subject—'The Belgian Experiment',[22] and 'Yet a Third Time on the Belgian Experiment'[23]—point out the revolutionary nature of the mass political strike as the specific working-class weapon of struggle. For Rosa Luxemburg the mass strikes, political and economic, constitute a central factor in the revolutionary struggle for workers' power.

Rosa Luxemburg's enthusiasm for this method and incisive understanding of it reach a new height with the Russian Revolution of 1905:

> In former bourgeois revolutions where, on the one hand, the political education and leadership of the revolutionary masses was undertaken by the bourgeois parties, and, on the other hand, the revolutionary task was limited to the overthrow of the government, the short battle on the barricades was the appropriate form of revolutionary struggle. Today, at a time that the working class must educate, organise and lead itself in the course of the revolutionary struggle, when the revolution itself is directed not only against the established State power but also against capitalist exploitation, mass strikes appear as the natural method to mobilise the broadest proletarian layers into action, to revolutionise and organise them. Simultaneously it is a method by means of which to undermine and overthrow the established State power as well as to curb capitalist exploitation... In order that the working class may participate *en masse* in any direct political action, it must first organise itself, which above all means that it must obliterate the boundaries between factories and workshops, mines and foundries, it must overcome the split between workshops which the daily yoke of capitalism condemns it to. Therefore the mass strike is the first natural spontaneous form of every great revolutionary proletarian action. The more industry becomes the prevalent form of the economy, the more prominent the role of the working class, and the more developed the conflict between labour and capital, the more powerful and decisive become the mass strikes. The earlier main form of bourgeois revolutions, the battle on the barricades, the open encounter with the armed State power, is a peripheral aspect of the revolution today, only one moment in the whole process of the mass struggle of the proletariat.[24]

Budapest, 1956!

Contrary to all reformists who see a Chinese wall between partial struggles for economic reform and the political struggle for revolution, Rosa Luxemburg pointed out that in a revolutionary period the economic struggle grows into a political one, and vice versa:

> The movement does not go only in one direction, from an economic to a political struggle, but also in the opposite direction. Every important political mass action, after reaching its peak, results in a series of economic mass strikes. And this rule applies not only to the individual mass strike, but to the revolution as a whole. With the spread, clarification and intensification of the political struggle not only does the economic struggle not recede, but on the contrary it spreads and at the same time becomes more organised and intensified. There exists a reciprocal influence between the two struggles. Every fresh attack and victory of the political struggle has a powerful impact on the economic struggle, in that at the same time as it widens the scope for the workers to improve their conditions and strengthens their impulse to do so, it enhances their fighting spirit. After every soaring wave of political action, there remains a fertile sediment from which sprout a thousand economic struggles. And the reverse also applies. The workers' constant economic struggle against capital sustains them at every pause in the political battle. The economic struggle constitutes, so to speak, the permanent reservoir of working class strength from which political struggles always imbibe new strength. The untiring economic fight of the proletariat leads every moment to sharp isolated conflicts here and there from which explode unforeseen political struggles on an immense scale.
>
> In a word, the economic struggle is the factor that advances the movement from one political focal point to another. The political struggle periodically fertilises the ground for the economic struggle. Cause and effect interchange every second. Thus we find that the two elements, the economic and political, do not incline to separate themselves from one another during the period of the mass strikes in Russia, not to speak of negating one another, as pedantic schemes would suggest.[25]

The logical and necessary climax of the mass strike is the 'open uprising which can only be realised as the culmination of a series of partial uprisings which prepare the ground, and therefore are liable to end for a time in what looks like partial "defeats", each of which may seem to be "premature".'[26]

And what a rise in class consciousness results from the mass strikes:

> The most precious thing, because it is the most enduring, in the sharp ebb and flow of the revolutionary wave, is the proletariat's spiritual growth. The advance by leaps and bounds of the intellectual stature of the proletariat affords an inviolable guarantee of its further progress in the inevitable economic and political struggles ahead.[27]

And what idealism workers rise to! They put aside thoughts of whether they have the wherewithal to support themselves and their families during the struggle. They do not ask whether all the preliminary technical preparations have been made:

> Once a really serious period of mass strikes opens up, all such 'costing operations' are something like an attempt to measure the ocean with a bucket. And it is an ocean, a sea of terrible troubles and privations for the proletariat—that is the invariable cost of every revolution. The solution which a revolutionary period brings with it for this apparently insoluble problem of providing material support for the strikers, is to generate such a tremendous volume of idealism among the masses that they appear to become almost immune to the most terrible privations.[28]

It was this glimpse of the magnificent revolutionary initiative and self-sacrifice that the workers rise to during a revolution that justified Rosa's faith.

The fight against imperialism and war

During the two decades preceding the outbreak of the First World War support for imperialism grew steadily, within the Socialist International.

The Stuttgart Congress of the International in 1907 showed this clearly. The colonial question was placed on the agenda because at this time the jostling of imperialist powers in Africa and Asia was becoming fierce. The socialist parties did indeed speak out against the rapacity of their own governments, but as the discussion at the Stuttgart Congress showed, a consistent anti-colonialist position was far from the thoughts of many leaders of the International. The Congress appointed a Colonial Commission, the majority of which drafted a report stating that colonialism had some positive aspects. Its draft resolution stated, '[The Congress] does not reject on principle and for all time every colonial policy.' Socialists should condemn the excesses of colonialism, but should not renounce it altogether. Instead:

> ...they are to advocate reforms, to improve the lot of the natives...and they are to educate them for independence by all possible means.
>
> To this purpose the representatives of the socialist parties should propose to their governments to conclude an international treaty, to create a Colonial Law, which shall protect the rights of the natives and which would be guaranteed by all the signatory States.

This draft resolution was in fact defeated, but by a rather slim majority—127 against 108. Thus practically half the Congress sided openly with imperialism.

When the First World War, which was essentially a fight between the imperialist powers for the division of the colonies, broke out in 1914, its support by the majority leaders of the Socialist International did not come out of the blue.

At the Stuttgart Congress Rosa Luxemburg came out clearly against imperialism, proposing a resolution which outlined the policy necessary to meet the threat of imperialist war:

> In the event of a threat of war it is the duty of the workers and their parliamentary representatives in the countries involved to do everything possible to prevent the outbreak of war by taking suitable measures, which can of course change or be intensified in accordance with the intensification of the class struggle and the general political situation.
>
> In the event of war breaking out nevertheless, it is their duty to take measures to bring it to an end as quickly as possible, and to utilise the economic and political crisis brought about by the war to arouse the masses of the people and accelerate the overthrow of capitalist class rule.

This resolution made it clear that socialists should oppose imperialism and its war, and that the only way to put an end to both is through the overthrow of capitalism, of which both are the outgrowth.

This resolution was passed, but even so it was becoming more and more evident that, of those leaders who were not openly supporting colonialism, many did not conceive of the fight against imperialism in revolutionary terms.

These leaders, whose main spokesman was Kautsky, adopted the view that imperialism was not a necessary outgrowth of capitalism, but an abscess which the capitalist class as a whole would more and more wish to get rid of. Kautsky's theory was that imperialism was a method of expansion supported by certain small but powerful capitalist groups (the banks and the armament kings), which was contrary to the needs of the capitalist class as a whole, as expenditure on armaments reduced available capital for investment in the country and abroad, and therefore affected the majority of the capitalist class which would progressively increase its opposition to the policy of armed imperialist expansion. Echoing the same ideas, Bernstein, as late as 1911, argued confidently that the desire for peace was becoming universal and that it was out of the question that war should break out. The armaments race, according to the Kautsky-led 'Marxist Centre', was an anomaly that could be overcome by general disarmament agreements, international arbitration courts, peace alliances, and the formation of the United States of Europe. In short, the 'Marxist Centre' relied on the powers-that-be to bring peace on earth.

Rosa Luxemburg brilliantly tore to shreds this capitalist pacifism:

> ...the belief that capitalism is possible without expansion, is the theoretical formula for a certain definite tactical tendency. This conception tends to regard the phase of imperialism not as a historical necessity, not as the final bout between capitalism and socialism, but rather as the malicious invention of a group of interested parties. It tries to persuade the bourgeoisie that imperialism and militarism are deleterious even from the standpoint of bourgeois interests, in the hope that it will then be able to isolate the alleged handful of interested parties and so form a block between the proletariat and the majority of the bourgeoisie with a view to 'curbing' imperialism, starving it out by 'partial disarmament', and 'removing its sting'. Just as a bourgeois Liberalism in its period of decay appealed from the 'ignorant' monarchs to the 'enlightened' monarchs, now the 'Marxist Centre' proposes to appeal from the 'unreasonable' bourgeoisie to the 'reasonable' bourgeoisie with a view to dissuading it from a policy of imperialism with all its catastrophic results to a policy of international disarmament treaties; from an armed struggle for world dominance to a peaceable federation of democratic national States. The general settling of accounts between the proletariat and capitalism, the solution of the great contradiction between them, resolves itself into an idyllic compromise for the 'mitigation of imperialist contradictions between the capitalist States'.[29]

How apt these words are, not only for the bourgeois pacifism of Kautsky and Bernstein, but for all those who adhered to the League of Nations, the United Nations, 'collective security', or Summit talks!

Rosa Luxemburg showed that imperialism and imperialist war could not be overcome within the framework of capitalism, as they grow out of the vital interests of capitalist society.

The *Guiding Principles* of the Spartakus League drawn up by Rosa Luxemburg stated:

> Imperialism, the last phase and highest development of the political rule of capitalism, is the deadly enemy of the workers of all countries… The struggle against imperialism is at the same time the struggle of the proletariat for political power, the decisive conflict between Capitalism and Socialism. The final aim of Socialism can be achieved only if the international proletariat fights uncompromisingly against imperialism as a whole, and takes the slogan 'war against war' as a practical guide to action, summoning up all its strength and all its capacity for self-sacrifice.[30]

Thus the central theme of Rosa Luxemburg's anti-imperialist policy was that the fight against war is inseparable from the fight for socialism.

With great passion Rosa Luxemburg ends her most important anti-war pamphlet, *The Crisis of Social Democracy* (better known as the 'Junius Brochure', as she wrote under the pseudonym Junius):

> Imperialist bestiality has been let loose to devastate the fields of Europe, and there is one incidental accompaniment for which the 'cultured world' has neither the heart nor conscience—the mass slaughter of the European proletariat… It is our hope, our flesh and blood, which is falling in swathes like corn under the sickle. The finest, the most intelligent, the best-trained forces of international Socialism, the bearers of the heroic traditions of the modern working-class movement, the advanced guard of the world proletariat, the workers of Great Britain, France, Germany and Russia, are being slaughtered in masses. That is a greater crime by far than the brutish sack of Louvain or the destruction of Rheims Cathedral. It is a deadly blow against the power which holds the whole future of humanity, the only power which can save the values of the past and carry them on into a newer and better human society. Capitalism has revealed its true features; it betrays to the world that it has lost its historical justification, that its continued existence can no longer be reconciled with the progress of mankind…
>
> Deutschland, Deutschland Uber Alles! Long live Democracy! Long live the Tsar and Slavdom! Ten thousand blankets, guaranteed in perfect condition! A hundred thousand kilos of bacon, coffee substitutes—immediate delivery! Dividends rise and proletarians fall. And with each one sinks a fighter for the future, a soldier of the Revolution, a liberator of humanity from the yoke of capitalism, and finds a nameless grave.
>
> The madness will cease and the bloody product of hell come to an end only when the workers of Germany and France, of Great Britain and Russia, awaken from their frenzy, extend to each other the hand of friendship, and drown the bestial chorus of imperialist hyenas with the thunderous battle cry of the modern working-class movement: 'Workers of the World Unite![31]

With visionary power Rosa Luxemburg states:

Bourgeois society faces a dilemma; either a transition to Socialism, or a return to barbarism...we face the choice: either the victory of imperialism and the decline of all culture, as in ancient Rome—annihilation, devastation, degeneration, a yawning graveyard; or the victory of Socialism—the victory of the international working class consciously assaulting imperialism and its method: war. This is the dilemma of world history, either—or; the die will be cast by the class-conscious proletariat.[32]

And we who live in the shadow of the H-bomb...

Party and class

Rosa Luxemburg has been accused of mechanical materialism, a conception of historical development in which objective economic forces are independent of human will. This accusation is totally unfounded. Hardly any of the great Marxists has laid greater stress on human activity as the determinant of human destiny. She wrote:

Men do not make history of their own free will, but they do make their own history. The proletariat is dependent in its action on the given degree of maturity in social development existing at the time, but social development does not proceed independently of and apart from the proletariat, and the proletariat is as much its cause and mainspring as it is its product and consequence. The action of the proletariat is a determining factor in history, and although we can no more jump over stages of historical development than a man can jump over his own shadow, still, we can accelerate or retard that development. The victory of the Socialist proletariat will be the result of iron historical laws, and it would depend upon a thousand steps in previous, laborious and all-too-slow development. However, it will never be fulfilled unless the material conditions brought together by the historical process are vitalised with the life-giving spark of conscious will power generated in the great masses of the people.[33]

Following the line of thought propounded by Marx and Engels, Rosa Luxemburg believed that consciousness of the aims of socialism on the part of the mass of workers is a *necessary prerequisite* for achieving socialism. *The Communist Manifesto* states:

All previous historical movements were movements of minorities or in the interests of minorities. The proletarian movement is the self-conscious independent movement of the immense majority, in the interest of the immense majority.'

Again Engels wrote:

The time of revolutions carried through by small conscious minorities at the head of unconscious masses is past. Where it is a question of a complete transformation of the social organisation, the masses themselves must also be in it, must themselves already have grasped what is at stake, what they are going in for with body and soul.[34]

Rosa Luxemburg wrote in similar vein, 'Without the conscious will and the conscious action of the majority of the proletariat there can be no Socialism'.[35]

Again, the *Programme of the Communist Party of Germany (Spartakus)*, drafted by Rosa, states:

> (1) The Spartakus League is not a party that wishes to succeed to power either over the working class or by means of it. The Spartakus League is merely that part of the working class most convinced of its object; it is the part that directs the broad labour movement to its historical function at every step; at every single stage of the revolution it represents the final socialist aim and in all national questions the interests of the proletarian world revolution.
>
> (2) The Spartakus League will never assume governmental authority except through the clear unambiguous will of the vast majority of the German working class; in no other way except through its conscious concurrence with the views, aims and fighting tactics of the Spartakus League.
>
> The proletarian revolution can only achieve clarity and maturity going step by step along the hard path of suffering, bitter experience, through defeats and triumphs.
>
> The victory of the Spartakus League is not at the beginning but at the end of the revolution; it is identical with the victory of the many-millioned mass of the socialist proletariat.[36]

While the working class as a class must be conscious of the aims of socialism and the methods of achieving it, it still needs a revolutionary party to lead it. In every factory, on every dock and on every building site, there are more advanced workers—that is, workers more experienced in the class struggle, more independent of the influence of the capitalist class—and less advanced workers. It is up to the former to organise into a revolutionary party, and try to influence and lead the latter. As Rosa Luxemburg said, 'This mass movement of the proletariat needs the lead of an organised principled force'.[37]

The revolutionary party, while conscious of its leading role, must beware of slipping into a way of thinking that the party is the fount of all correct thoughts and deeds, while the working class remains an inert mass without initiative.

> Of course through the theoretical analysis of the social conditions of struggle, Social Democracy has introduced the element of consciousness into the proletarian class struggle to an unprecedented degree; it gave the class struggle its clarity of aim; it created, for the first time, a permanent mass workers' organisation, and thus built a firm backbone for the class struggle. However, it would be catastrophically wrong for us to assume that from now on all the historical initiative of the people has passed to the hands of the Social Democratic organisation alone, and that the unorganised mass of the proletariat has turned into a formless thing, into the deadweight of history. On the contrary, the popular masses continue to be the living matter of world history, even in the presence of Social Democracy; and only if there is blood circulation between the organised nucleus and the popular masses, only if one heartbeat vitalises the two, can Social Democracy prove that it is capable of great historical deeds.[38]

The party, in consequence, should not invent tactics out of thin air, but put it as its first duty to *learn* from the experience of the mass movement and then generalise from it. The great events of working-class history have shown the correctness of this emphasis beyond all measure of doubt. The workers of Paris in 1871 established a new form of state—a state without a standing army and bureaucracy, where all officials received the average worker's salary and were subject to recall, before Marx began to generalise about the nature and structure of a workers' state. Again the workers of Petrograd, in 1905, established a Soviet (workers' council) independently of the Bolshevik Party, actually in opposition to the local Bolshevik leadership and in face of at least suspicion, if not animosity, on the part of Lenin himself. Therefore one cannot but agree with Rosa Luxemburg when she wrote in 1904:

> The main characteristics of the tactics of struggle of Social Democracy are not 'invented', but are the result of a continuous series of great creative acts of the elementary class struggle. Here also the unconscious precedes the conscious, the logic of the objective historical process comes before the subjective logic of its bearer.[39]

It is not through didactic teaching by the party leaders that the workers learn. As Rosa Luxemburg countered to Kautsky and company:

> They think that to educate the proletarian masses in a socialist spirit means the following: to lecture to them, distribute leaflets and pamphlets among them. But no! The Socialist proletarian school does not need all this. Activity itself educates the masses.[40]

Finally, Rosa Luxemburg comes to this conclusion: 'Mistakes committed by a genuine revolutionary labour movement are much more fruitful and worthwhile historically than the infallibility of the very best Central Committee.[41]

Placing such emphasis (and quite rightly) on the creative power of the working class, Rosa Luxemburg nonetheless inclined to underestimate the retarding, damaging effect that a conservative organisation may have on the mass struggle. She believed that the upsurge of the masses would sweep aside such a leadership without the movement itself suffering serious damage. She wrote in 1906:

> If, at any time and under any circumstances, Germany were to experience big political struggles, an era of tremendous economic struggles would at the same time open up. Events would not stop for a second in order to ask the union leaders whether they had given their blessing to the movement or not. If they stood aside from the movement or opposed it, the result of such behaviour would be only this: the union or Party leaders would be swept away by the wave of events, and the economic as well as the political struggles would be fought to a conclusion without them.[42]

And it was this theme that Rosa Luxemburg reiterated again and again.

To understand the roots of Rosa Luxemburg's possible underestimation of the role of organisation and possible overestimation of the role of spontaneity, one must look at the situation in which she worked. First of all she had to fight the opportunist leadership of the German Social Democratic Party. This leadership emphasised the factor of organisation out of all proportion, and made little of the spontaneity of the masses. Even where they accepted the possibility of a mass strike, for instance, the reformist leadership reasoned as follows: the conditions in which the mass political strike will be launched and the appropriate time—as, for instance, when the union treasuries were full—would be determined by the party and trade union leadership alone, and the date fixed by them. It was their task also to determinate the aims of the strike, which, according to Bebel, Kautsky, Hilferding, Bernstein and others, were to achieve the franchise or defend parliament. Above all, this precept must remain inviolable: that nothing is done by the workers except by order of the party and its leadership. It was with this idea, of the mighty party leadership and the puny masses, that Rosa Luxemburg joined battle. But in doing so she may have bent the stick a little too far.

Another wing of the labour movement with which Rosa Luxemburg had to contend was the Polish Socialist Party (PPS). The PPS was a chauvinistic organisation, its avowed aim the national independence of Poland. But there was no mass social basis for its struggle: the landlords and bourgeoisie stood aside from the national struggle while the Polish working class (looking upon the Russian workers as their allies) had no desire to fight for a national state (see below, 'Rosa Luxemburg and the national question'). Under these conditions the PPS adopted adventuristic activities such as the organisation of terrorist groups, and so on. Action was based not on the working class as a whole, but only on the party organisations. Here too the social process counted for little, the decision of the leadership for everything. Here too (in her long struggle against PPS voluntarism) Rosa Luxemburg stressed the factor of spontaneity.

A third trend in the labour movement with which Rosa battled was syndicalism, a mixture of anarchism (without its individualism and with a much-exaggerated emphasis on organisation) with the trade unions. The main base of this tendency was in France where it spread its roots in the soil of industrial backwardness and lack of concentration. It gained strength after the series of defeats suffered by the French labour movement in 1848 and 1871, and the betrayal of Millerand and the Jaurès party, which developed suspicion among the workers of all political activities and organisations. Syndicalism identified the general strike with social revolution, rather than looking upon it as only one important element of modern revolution. It believed that the general strike could be touched off by an order, and the overthrow of bourgeois rule would follow. It thus again emphasised and oversimplified the revolutionary factor; that is, that the voluntary and free will of the leaders, independent of the compulsion of a mass upsurge, could initiate decisive action. While renouncing this voluntarism, German reformists developed a similar trend. Where the French syndicalists painted a caricature of the mass strike and revolution, the German opportunists, in making a laughing stock of it, threw out the whole idea of mass strikes and revolutions. At the same time as Rosa battled against the German brand of voluntarism, she fought the

French edition in its syndicalist form, showing it to be essentially a bureaucratic denial of workers' initiative and self-mobilisation.

The main reason for Rosa Luxemburg's overestimation of the factor of spontaneity and underestimation of the factor of organisation probably lies in the need, in the *immediate* struggle against reformism, for emphasis on spontaneity as the *first* step in all revolutions. From this one stage in the struggle of the working class, she generalised too widely to embrace the struggle as a whole.

Revolutions do indeed *start* as spontaneous acts without the leadership of a party. The French Revolution started with the storming of the Bastille. Nobody organised this. Was there a party at the head of the people in rebellion? No. Even the future leaders of the Jacobins, for instance Robespierre, did not yet oppose the monarchy, and were not yet organised into a party. The revolution of 14 July 1789 was a spontaneous act of the masses. The same was true of the Russian Revolutions of 1905 and February 1917. The 1905 Revolution started through a bloody clash between the Tsar's army and police on the one hand, and the mass of workers, men, women and children, on the other, led by the priest Gapon (who was actually an agent provocateur of the Tsar). Were the workers organised by a clear decisive leadership with a socialist policy of its own? Certainly not. Carrying icons, they came begging their beloved 'little Father'—the Tsar—to help them against their exploiters. This was the first step in a great revolution. Twelve years later, in February 1917, the masses, this time more experienced, and among whom there were a greater number of socialists than in the previous revolution, again rose spontaneously. No historian has been able to point a finger at the organiser of the February Revolution, for it was simply not organised.

However, after being triggered off by a spontaneous uprising, revolutions move forward in a different manner. In France the transition from the semi-republican government of the Gironde to the revolutionary one, which completely annihilated feudal property relations, was not carried out by unorganised masses without any party leadership, but under the decisive leadership of the Jacobin party. Without such a party at the helm, this important step, which demanded an all-out fight against the Girondists, would have been impossible. The people of Paris could spontaneously, leaderlessly, rise up against the king after decades of oppression. But the majority of them were too conservative, too lacking in historical experience and knowledge, to distinguish, after only two or three years of revolution, between those who wanted to drive the revolution as far as it would go and those who aimed at some compromise. The historical situation required a struggle to the bitter end against the party of compromise, the allies of yesterday. The conscious leadership of this great undertaking was supplied by the Jacobin party, which fixed the date and organised the overthrow of the Gironde on 10 August 1792 down to the last detail. Similarly the October Revolution was not a spontaneous act but was organised in practically all its important particulars, including the date, by the Bolsheviks. During the zigzags of the revolution between February and October—the June demonstration, the July days and subsequent orderly retreat, the rebuff of the rightist

Kornilov putsch—the workers and soldiers came more closely under the influence and guidance of the Bolshevik Party. And such a party was essential to raise the revolution from its initial stages to its final victory.

While accepting that perhaps Rosa Luxemburg underestimated the importance of such a party, one should not say too little of the really great historical merit of Rosa Luxemburg, who in the face of prevailing reformism emphasised the most important power that could break the conservative crust—that of workers' spontaneity. Her enduring strength lay in her complete confidence in the workers' historical initiative.

While pointing out some of the deficiencies in Rosa Luxemburg's position regarding the link between spontaneity and leadership in the revolution, one should be wary of concluding that her critics in the revolutionary movement, above all Lenin, were at every point nearer a correct, balanced, Marxist analysis than she was.

Whereas Rosa Luxemburg had worked in an environment in which the main enemy of revolutionary socialism had been bureaucratic centralism, with the result that she had constantly stressed the elementary activity of the masses, Lenin had had to contend with the amorphousness of the labour movement in Russia, where the greatest danger lay in an underestimation of the element of organisation. Just as one cannot understand Rosa Luxemburg's views outside the conditions of the countries and labour movements in which she worked, so it is difficult to understand Lenin's position without due reference to the concrete historical conditions of the labour movement in Russia.

Lenin's conceptions of the relation between spontaneity and organisation were put forward in two main works: *What is to be Done?* (1902) and *One Step Forward, Two Steps Backward* (1904). At the time they were written, the Russian labour movement could not be compared in strength with that of Western Europe, especially Germany. It was made up of isolated, small, more or less autonomous groups without any commonly-agreed policies, and only marginally under the influence of the leading Marxists abroad, Plekhanov, Lenin, Martov and Trotsky. In these groups, because of weakness and isolation, sights were set low. While the Russian workers were rising to a high level of militancy in mass strikes and demonstrations the socialist groups propounded no more than immediately realisable economic demands; this so-called 'economist' tendency was predominant in the socialist groups. Lenin's *What is to be Done?* was a merciless attack on 'economism' or pure trade unionism. He argued that the spontaneity of the masses' struggle—everywhere so obvious in Russia at the time—must be supplemented by the consciousness and organisation of a party. A national party with a central newspaper of its own must be created in order to unify the local groupings and infuse the labour movement with *political* consciousness. Socialist theory must be brought to the working class from the outside; this was the only way the labour movement could move directly to the struggle for socialism. The projected party would be made up largely of professional revolutionaries, working under an extremely centralised leadership. The political leadership of the party should be the editorial board of the central newspaper. This should have the power to organise or reorganise party branches inside the country, admit or expel members and appoint local committees. Criticising the Mensheviks, Lenin wrote in 1904:

> The basic idea of comrade Martov...is precisely false 'democratism', the idea of the construction of the Party from the bottom to the top. My idea, on the contrary, is 'bureaucratic' in the sense that the Party should be constructed from above down to the bottom, from the Congress to the individual Party organisation.[43]

How often have Stalinists, and many so-called non-Stalinists, the many who came after Lenin, quoted *What is to be Done?* and *One Step Forward, Two Steps Backward*, as being applicable *in toto*, in all countries and movements, whatever the stage of development!

Lenin was far from these so-called Leninists. As early as 1903, at the Second Congress of the Russian Social Democratic Party, he pointed out some exaggerations of the formulations in *What is to be Done?*: 'The economists bent the stick to one side. In order to straighten it out again, it had to be bent towards the other side and that is what I did'.[44] Two years later, in a draft resolution written for the Third Congress, Lenin emphasised that his organisational views were not universally applicable: 'Under free political conditions our party can and will be built up entirely upon the principle of electibility. Under absolutism this is unrealisable.' During the 1905 Revolution, with the tremendous increase in party membership, Lenin ceased to talk of professional revolutionaries. The party was no more to be an elite organisation:

> At the Third Congress I expressed the wish that in the party committees there should be two intellectuals for every eight workers. How obsolete is this wish. Now it would be desirable that in the new party organisations, for every intellectual belonging to the Social Democracy, there should be a few hundred Social-Democratic workers.

Whereas in *What is to be Done?* Lenin wrote that the workers through their own efforts could only reach trade union consciousness, now he wrote, 'The working class is instinctively, spontaneously Social Democratic'.[45] 'The special condition of the proletariat in capitalistic society leads to a striving of workers for socialism; a union of them with the Socialist Party bursts forth with spontaneous force in the very early stages of the movement.' Where, in 1902, Lenin wanted the party to be a tight, closely-knit, small group with very exclusive standards of membership, in 1905 he wrote that workers should be incorporated 'into the ranks of the Party organisations by the hundreds of thousands'. Again in 1907, in a foreword to the collection *Twelve Years*, Lenin said:

> The basic mistake of those who polemicise against *What is to be Done?* today is that they tear this work out of the context of a definite historical milieu, a definite, now already long past period of development of our Party... *What is to be Done?* polemically corrected Economism, and it is false to consider the contents of the pamphlet outside of its connection with this task.[46]

Unwilling for *What is to be Done?* to be misused, Lenin did not relish its proposed translation in 1921 into non-Russian languages. He told Max Levien, 'that is not desirable; the translation must at least be issued with good commentaries which would have to be written by a Russian comrade very well acquainted with the history of the Communist Party of Russia in order to avoid false application'.[47]

When the Communist International was discussing its statutes, Lenin argued against those that were being proposed because, he said, they were 'too Russian' and overemphasised centralisation, even though these statutes did provide for freedom of criticism within the parties and for the control of the party leadership from below. Overcentralisation, Lenin argued, did not suit the conditions of Western Europe. (It is true that in Lenin's own party at the time the organisation was highly centralised, even semi-military, but this form was forced upon it by the dire conditions of the civil war.)

Lenin's views on organisation, his bending of the stick too far over to centralism, must be considered against the background of conditions in Russia.

In backward Tsarist Russia, where the working class was a small minority, the idea that the working class alone can liberate itself could easily be passed over. The more easily still, since Russia had quite a long tradition of minority organisations trying to substitute for elementary mass activity. In France it was the people who overthrew the monarchy and feudalism; in Russia, Decembrists and Narodnik terrorists took it upon themselves to do this.[48]

Marx's statement about the democratic nature of the socialist movement, quoted previously, and Lenin's, that revolutionary Social Democracy represents 'the Jacobins indissolubly connected with the *organisation* of the proletariat', are definitely contradictory. A conscious, organised minority at the head of an unorganised mass of the people suits the bourgeois revolution, which is, after all, a revolution in the interests of the minority. But the separation of conscious minority from unconscious majority, the separation of mental and manual labour, the existence of manager and foreman on the one hand and a mass of obedient labourers on the other, may be grafted on to 'socialism' only by killing the very essence of socialism, which is the collective control of the workers over their destiny.

It is only by juxtaposing Luxemburg's and Lenin's conceptions that one can attempt to assess the historical limitations of each which were, inevitably, fashioned by the special environment in which each worked.

Emphatic as she was that the liberation of the working class can be carried out only by the working class itself, Rosa Luxemburg was impatient of all sectarian tendencies, which expressed themselves in breakaways from the mass movement and mass organisations.

Although for years at loggerheads with the majority leadership of the German Social Democratic Party, she continued to insist that it was the duty of revolutionary socialists to remain in this organisation. Even after the SPD rallied to the side of the imperialist war, after Karl Liebknecht's expulsion from the SPD parliamentary group (12 January 1916), she and Liebknecht continued to adhere to the party on the grounds that breaking away would turn a revolutionary group into a sect. She held to this viewpoint not only when she was the leader of a tiny, insignificant revolutionary group. On the contrary, she persevered with this view when the Spartakus League gained influence and was becoming a recognisable force as the war dragged on.

As we have seen, on 2 December 1914 only one deputy, Liebknecht, voted against the war credits. In March 1915 a second, Otto Rühle, joined him. In June 1915 1,000 party office-bearers signed a manifesto opposing the class collaboration policies, and in December 1915 as many as 20 deputies voted against the war credits in the Reichstag. In March 1916 the SPD parliamentary group expelled the growing opposition from its midst, although it did not have the power to expel it from the party.

What happened in parliament was a reflection of what was taking place outside, in the factories, the streets, the party branches and the Socialist Youth organisation.

The anti-war journal *Die Internationale*, edited by Rosa Luxemburg and Franz Mehring, distributed 5,000 of its one and only issue in one day (it was immediately suppressed by the police).[49] The Socialist Youth, at a secret conference at Easter 1916, declared itself overwhelmingly behind Spartakus. On May Day 1916 some 10,000 workers assembled on the Potsdamer Platz in Berlin in an anti-war demonstration. In other towns—Dresden, Jena, Hanau—anti-war demonstrations also took place. On 28 June 1916, the day on which Liebknecht was sentenced to two and a half years hard labour, 55,000 workers went on strike in Berlin munitions factories in solidarity with him. Demonstrations and strikes took place the same day in Stuttgart, Bremen, Braunschweig and other cities. Under the influence of the Russian Revolution, in April 1917 a huge wave of munitions strikes spread throughout the country: 300,000 workers were out in Berlin alone. Another wave of strikes of munitions workers in January/February 1918 engulfed as many as 1.5 million workers.

These strikes were largely political in nature. The Berlin strike of some half a million workers demanded immediate peace without annexations and reparations, and the right of self-determination of nations; it raised as its central slogan the revolutionary cry, 'Peace, freedom, bread.' Six workers were killed during the strike, and many wounded. Thousands of strikers were conscripted into the army.

Against this background Rosa Luxemburg continued to argue for remaining in the SPD right up to April 1917, when the Centre, led by Kautsky, Bernstein and Haase, split from the Right and formed a new party—the Independent Social Democratic Party (USPD). The USPD was a purely parliamentary party which did not want to stir the workers up into mass strikes and demonstrations against the war, but aimed to put pressure on the governments of the belligerent countries to negotiate peace. The Spartakus League, formed in January 1916 as a faction inside the SPD, now attached itself loosely to the USPD, keeping its separate organisation and its right of independent action. Only after the outbreak of the German Revolution on 29 December 1918 did the League finally sever its connections with the USPD and establish an independent party—the Communist Party of Germany (Spartakus).

There had been constant pressure from the ranks of the revolutionaries to leave the SPD and later the USPD. But Rosa Luxemburg resisted this. There had been a precedent for breaking away in 1891, when quite a large group of revolutionaries split from the SPD, accusing it of reformism, and founded an Independent Socialist Party. This had enjoyed a very short life before completely disappearing.

On 6 January 1917 Rosa Luxemburg put the case against those revolutionaries who wished to split from the SPD:

> However commendable and comprehensible the impatience and bitterness which leads so many of the best elements to leave the party today, a flight remains a flight. It is a betrayal of the masses, who, sold to the bourgeoisie, writhe and choke from the stranglehold of Scheidemann and Legien. One may withdraw from small sects when they do not suit one any longer in order to found new sects. It is nothing more than immature fantasy to want to liberate the mass of the proletariat from this heavy and terrible yoke of the bourgeoisie by a simple withdrawal, and thus set a brave example. The discarding of membership cards as an illusion of liberation is nothing but the illusion, stood on its head, that power is inherent in a membership card. Both are different poles of organisational cretinism, the constitutional sickness of old German Social Democracy. The collapse of German Social Democracy is an historical process of immense dimensions, a general struggle between the working class and the bourgeoisie, and one should not run from this battlefield in order to breathe purer air behind a protective bush. This battle of giants should be fought to the end. The fight against the deadly stranglehold of official Social Democracy, and the official Free Trade Unions, which was imposed by the ruling class upon the neck of the misled and betrayed working class, should be fought with all force to the end. We should stand by the masses to the end, even in the most terrible struggle. The liquidation of this 'heap of organised corruption', which today calls itself Social Democracy, is not the private affair of the few, or of a few groups... The decisive fate of the class struggle in Germany for decades is the fight against the authorities of Social Democracy and the trade unions, and therefore these words apply to each of us to the very end: 'Here I stand, I can do nothing else'.[50]

Rosa Luxemburg's opposition to leaving the mass workers' party did not cover any concession to reformism. Thus at a conference of Spartakus on 7 January 1917 the following resolution inspired by her was passed: 'The Opposition stays in the Party in order to thwart and fight the policy of the majority at every step, to defend the masses from an imperialist policy covered over with the mantle of Social Democracy, and to use the Party as a field of recruitment for the proletarian, anti-militarist class struggle'.[51]

Rosa Luxemburg's reluctance to form an independent revolutionary party followed her slowness to react to changed circumstances. It was a central factor in the belatedness of building a revolutionary party in Germany. In this, however, she was not alone. Lenin was no quicker to break with Kautsky than Rosa. There is no ground to the Stalinist story according to which Lenin was opposed to the revolutionary Left's adherence to the SPD and continuing association with Kautsky.[52] Actually Rosa Luxemburg made a clearer assessment of Kautsky and Co, and broke with them long before Lenin did. For some two decades Lenin looked upon Kautsky as the greatest living Marxist. A few instances: *What is to be Done?* quotes Kautsky as the main authority for its central theme, and praises the German Social Democratic Party as a model for the Russian movement. In December 1906 Lenin wrote, 'The vanguard of the Russian working class knows Karl Kautsky for some time now as its writer'; he described Kautsky as 'the leader of the German revolutionary Social Democrats'.[53] In August 1908 he cited Kautsky as his authority on questions of war and militarism.[54] In 1910, at the time of Rosa Luxemburg's debate with Kautsky on the question of the path to power, Lenin sided with him against her. And as late as February 1914 Lenin invoked Kautsky as a Marxist authority in his dispute with Rosa Luxemburg on the national question. Only the outbreak of the war and the betrayal of internationalism by Kautsky shattered Lenin's illusions in him. Then he admitted, 'Rosa Luxemburg was right; she realised long ago that Kautsky was a time-serving theorist, serving the majority of the Party, in short, serving opportunism'.[55]

The form of organisation of the socialist workers' movement everywhere and at every stage of development of the struggle for power has an important influence on the moulding of workers' power itself. Hence a debate on the form of organisation of the revolutionary party has an importance that goes beyond the stage in which a certain accepted form of organisation is being applied. In no country did the debate on organisational problems assume as sharp a tone as in the Russian labour movement. Much of this was due to the vast distance between the final aim of the movement and the autocratic semi-feudal reality in which it arose, a reality that prevented a free organisation of workers.

Where Rosa Luxemburg's position regarding the relation between spontaneity and organisation was a reflection of the immediate needs facing revolutionaries in a labour movement controlled by a conservative bureaucracy, Lenin's original position—that of 1902-04—was a reflection of the amorphousness of a vital, fighting revolutionary movement at the first stage of its development under a backward, semi-feudal and autocratic regime.

However, whatever the historical circumstances moulding Rosa's thoughts regarding organisation, these thoughts showed a great weakness in the German Revolution of 1918-19.

Rosa Luxemburg and the national question

Rosa Luxemburg, as leader of a workers' party in Poland, a country divided among three empires—Russian, German and Austrian—had necessarily to take a definite position on the national question. She held to this position from its formulation in 1896 in her first scientific research work, *The Industrial*

Development of Poland, till the end of her life, despite sharp conflicts with Lenin on the subject.

Her attitude was both a continuation of and diversion from the teachings of Marx and Engels on the national question, and in order to understand it properly it is necessary to glance—even if cursorily—at their attitude to the question.

Marx and Engels lived during the rise of capitalism in Europe, a period of bourgeois democratic revolutions. The framework of a bourgeois democracy was the national state, and the duty of socialists, according to them, was to fight 'in alliance with the bourgeoisie against absolute monarchy, against feudal land ownership and the petty bourgeoisie'.[56] The greatest enemy of all democratic revolutions, they stated in 1848, was Tsarist Russia, and, second only to it, Hapsburg Austria. Russia, the enslaver of Poland, was the chief butcher of the Kossuth democratic revolution in Hungary (1849); Russia and Austria together, through direct and indirect intervention in the internal affairs of the Germans and Italians, prevented the complete unification of these nations. Marx and Engels consequently supported all national movements which were directed against the Tsars and Hapsburgs. At the same time, using the same criterion, they opposed national movements which objectively played into the hands of the Tsars or the Hapsburgs.

The independence of Poland would have had tremendous revolutionary repercussions, argued Marx and Engels. Firstly, a wall would be created between democratic revolutionary Western and Central Europe and the 'gendarme of Europe', Russia. Secondly, the Hapsburg Empire, shaken as it would be by a national uprising of the Poles, would collapse following national uprisings of other nations; all the nations of this empire would then be free, and the Austrian Germans would be able to unite with the rest of Germany; this would constitute the most consistent democratic revolutionary solution to the German question. Thirdly, the independence of Poland would strike a sharp blow against the Prussian Junkers, thus further strengthening democratic revolutionary tendencies in Germany as a whole.

Marx and Engels called on all democratic movements in Europe to wage war on Tsarist Russia, the chief enemy of all progress. Specifically they called on revolutionary Germany to take up arms for the emancipation of Poland. A democratic war against Tsarism would safeguard the national independence of Poland and Germany, hasten the downfall of absolutism in Russia and give a fillip to the revolutionary forces throughout Europe.

Marx and Engels, while supporting the Polish and Hungarian (Magyar) national movements, did not support others. Thus, for instance, during the 1848 revolution, they condemned the national movements of the South Slavs—Croats, Serbs and Czechs. They did this because they thought that these movements objectively aided the main enemy: Croatian troops, who hated the Magyars more than they did the Hapsburg Empire, helped the Tsar's troops as they marched into Hungary; Czech troops helped to suppress revolutionary Vienna.

In all wars in which Tsarist Russia was involved, Marx and Engels did not adopt a position of neutrality or opposition to both contending camps, but one of militant opposition to Russia alone. Thus they criticised the British and French governments during the Crimean War for not waging war consistently to the bitter end against Russia. In the Russo-Turkish War that broke out in 1877, Marx again supported 'the gallant Turks'.[57] To the end of their lives Tsarist Russia represented for Marx and Engels the main bastion of reaction, and war against her was a revolutionary duty.

Because of the criterion they used to judge national movements—their effect on the bourgeois democratic revolution in West and Central Europe—Marx and Engels naturally limited their conclusions regarding national questions to Europe (and North America) where capitalist development was more or less advanced. They did not, justifiably at that time, attribute the concept of revolutionary bourgeois nationalism to Asian, African or South American countries. Thus, for instance, Engels wrote, 'In my opinion the colonies proper, ie the countries occupied by a European population, Canada, the Cape, Australia, will all become independent; on the other hand the countries inhabited by a native population, which are simply subjugated, India, Algiers, and the Dutch, Portuguese and Spanish possessions, must be taken over for the time being by the proletariat and led as rapidly as possible towards independence'.[58] Engels thought it possible that India might emancipate itself through a revolution, but such an event would have only secondary importance for Europe. If India should liberate itself, 'this will have to be given full scope...as the proletariat emancipating itself cannot conduct any colonial wars'. But the idea that the emancipation of the colonies could precede the socialist revolutions in Europe, or even aid them considerably, was completely foreign to Engels (as to Marx). If India, Algeria or Egypt should free themselves, then this:

> ...would certainly be the best thing for us. We shall have enough to do at home. Once Europe is reorganised, and North America, that will furnish such colossal power and such an example that the semi-civilised countries will follow in their wake of their own accord.[59]

Rosa Luxemburg, in the footsteps of Marx and Engels, considered the national movement mainly European, attributing only small importance to the Asian and African national movements. Like Marx and Engels, she also rejected any absolute criterion for judging struggles for national independence. She was, however, no follower who merely repeated the words of the founders of scientific socialism.

Quite early in her political life she pointed out that the situation in Europe in general, and Russia in particular, had changed so much towards the end of the 19th century that the position of Marx and Engels towards national movements in Europe had become untenable.

In Western and Central Europe the period of bourgeois democratic revolutions had passed. The Prussian Junkers had managed to establish their rule so firmly that they were no more in need of aid from the Tsar. At the same time Tsarist rule ceased to be the impregnable bastion of reaction, deep cracks beginning to cleave its walls: the mass strikes of workers in Warsaw, Lodz, Petrograd,

Moscow and elsewhere in the Russian Empire; the rebellious awakening of the peasants. Actually, whereas at the time of Marx and Engels the centre of revolution was in Western and Central Europe, now, towards the end of the 19th century and at the beginning of the 20th, it had passed east to Russia. Whereas at the time of Marx Tsarism was the main gendarme suppressing revolutionary uprisings elsewhere, now Tsarism itself came to need the help (mainly financial) of the Western capitalist powers. Instead of Russian bullets and roubles going westwards, now German, French, British and Belgian munitions and marks, francs and pounds flowed in a widening stream to Russia. Rosa Luxemburg pointed out further that basic changes had taken place as regards the national aspirations of her motherland, Poland. Whereas at the time of Marx and Engels the Polish nobles were leaders of the national movement, now, with the increasing capitalist developments of the country, they were losing ground socially and turning to Tsarism as an ally in the suppression of progressive movements in Poland. The result was that the Polish nobility cooled to aspirations toward national independence. The Polish bourgeoisie also became antagonistic to the desire for national independence, as it found the main markets for its industry in Russia. 'Poland is bound to Russia with chains of gold,' Rosa Luxemburg said. 'Not the national state but the state of rapine corresponds to capitalist development'.[60] The Polish working class too, according to Rosa Luxemburg, was not interested in the separation of Poland from Russia, as it saw in Moscow and Petrograd the allies of Warsaw and Lodz. Hence there were no social forces of any weight in Poland interested in fighting for national independence. Only the intelligentsia still cherished the idea, but they by themselves represented a small social force. Rosa Luxemburg concluded her analysis of the social forces in Poland and their attitude to the national question with the following words: 'The recognisable direction of social development has made it clear to me that there is no social class in Poland that has at one and the same time both an interest in and ability to achieve the restoration of Poland'.[61]

From this analysis she came to the conclusion that under capitalism the slogan of national independence had no progressive value, and could not be realised by the internal forces of the Polish nation; only the intervention of one or another imperialist power could bring it into being. Under socialism, argued Rosa Luxemburg, there would not be any place for the slogan of national independence, as national oppression would be no more and the international unity of humanity will have been realised. Thus under capitalism the real independence of Poland could not be realised, and any steps in that direction would not have any progressive value, while under socialism there would be no need for such a slogan. Hence the working class had no need for the struggle for national self-determination of Poland, and this struggle was in fact reactionary. The national slogans of the working class should be limited to the demand for national autonomy in cultural life.

In taking this position, Rosa Luxemburg and her party, the SDKPL, came into bitter conflict with the right-wing members of the Polish Socialist Party (PPS) led by Pilsudski (the future military dictator of Poland). These were nationalists who paid lip service to socialism. Lacking a mass basis for their nationalism, they contrived adventures, plotting with foreign powers to the extent even of relying on a future world war as the midwife of national independence. In Galicia, the stronghold of the right-wing PPS, the Poles, under Austrian rule, received better treatment than those in the Russian Empire, mainly because the rulers of the Hapsburg Empire, a medley of nationalities, had to rely on the Polish ruling class to fortify their imperial rule. Hence the PPS leaders inclined to prefer the Hapsburg Empire to the Russian, and during the First World War they acted as recruiting agents for Vienna and Berlin. Earlier, during the 1905 Revolution, Daszynski, the leader of the PPS in Galicia, had gone so far as to condemn the mass strikes of Polish workers, because, according to him, they tended to identify the struggle of the Polish workers with that of the Russian, and thus undermine the national unity of the Poles. It is only when one has a clear view of Rosa Luxemburg's opponents in the Polish labour movement that one can properly understand her position on the Polish national question.

The struggle that Rosa had to wage against the chauvinistic PPS coloured her entire attitude to the national question in general. In opposing the nationalism of the PPS she bent so far backwards that she opposed all reference to the right of self-determination in the programme of the party. It is because of this that her party, the SDKPL, split as early as 1903 from the Russian Social Democratic Party, and never subsequently joined the Bolsheviks organisationally.

Lenin agreed with Rosa Luxemburg in her opposition to the PPS, and, with her, argued that the duty of the Polish socialists was not to fight for national independence or secession from Russia, but for international unity of the Polish and Russian workers. However, as a member of an oppressing nation, Lenin, rightly, was wary lest a nihilistic attitude to the national question should bring grist to the mill of Great Russian chauvinism. Hence, while the Polish workers could, and should, avoid demanding the establishment of the national state, Russian socialists should fight for the right of the Poles to have their separate state if they so wished:

> The great historical merit of our comrades, the Polish Social Democrats, is that they have advanced the slogan of internationalism, that they have said: 'we treasure the fraternal alliance of the proletariat of all countries more than anything else and we shall never go to war for the liberation of Poland.' This is their great merit, and this is why we have always regarded only these Social-Democratic comrades in Poland as Socialists. The others are patriots, Polish Plekhanovs. But this unique situation, in which in order to safeguard socialism, it was found necessary to fight against rabid, morbid nationalism, has been productive of a strange phenomenon: comrades come to us and say that we must renounce the freedom of Poland, its right to secession.
>
> Why should we, Great Russians, who have been oppressing a greater number of nations than any other people, why should we repudiate the right of secession for Poland, the Ukraine, Finland? ...the Polish Social Democrats argue that precisely because they find the union with the Russian workers advantageous, they are opposed to Poland's secession. They have a perfect right to do so. But these

> people do not wish to understand that in order to strengthen internationalism there is no need to reiterate the same words; what we in Russia do is to stress the right of secession for the subject nations, while in Poland we must stress the right of such nations to unite. The right to unite implies the right to secede. We Russians must emphasise the right to secede, while the Poles must emphasise the right to unite.[62]

The difference between Lenin and Luxemburg on the national question may be summarised as follows: while Rosa Luxemburg, proceeding from the struggle against Polish nationalism, inclined to a nihilistic attitude to the national question, Lenin saw realistically that, the positions of oppressed and oppressor nations being different, their attitude to the same question must be different. Thus, starting from different and opposing situations, they proceed in opposite directions to reach the same point of international workers' unity. Secondly, while Rosa Luxemburg disposed of the question of national self-determination as incompatible with the class struggle, Lenin subordinated it to the class struggle (in the same way as he took advantage of all other democratic strivings as weapons in the general revolutionary struggle). The fount of Lenin's approach to the national question, missing in Rosa Luxemburg, is the dialectic: he saw the unity of opposites in national oppression, and the subordination of the part—the struggle for national independence—to the whole—the international struggle for socialism.

Rosa Luxemburg's strength regarding the national question lies, as elsewhere, in her complete devotion to internationalism and her independence of thought. This led her, via Marx's method, to see how the position of Poland had changed *vis-à-vis* Russia between Marx's time and her own. It caused her, contrary to Marx, to oppose the national struggle of Poland, but at the same time, and again contrary to Marx and Engels, led her to *support* the national movement of the South Slavs against Turkey. Marx and Engels had argued that to halt the advance of Tsarism the unity of the Turkish Empire had to be defended; and the national movements of the South Slavs, which were engulfed in Pan-Slavic ideas, and were blind weapons in the hands of Tsarism, had to be opposed. Rosa Luxemburg made an excellent analysis of the new conditions in the Balkans since the time of Marx. She concluded first that the liberation of the Balkan nations suppressed by the Turks would rouse the nations of the Austro-Hungarian Empire. The end of the Turkish Empire in Europe would also mean the end of the Hapsburg Empire. Secondly, she argued that since Marx's time the national movement of the Balkans had come under the dominion of the bourgeoisie, and hence any continuation of Russian influence was due only to suppression by Turkey. The liberation of the Balkan peoples from the Turkish yoke would not enhance the influence of Tsarism, but would weaken it, as these peoples would be under the leadership of a young and progressive bourgeoisie which would clash more and more with reactionary Tsarism. Thus, in the case of the Balkan nations, Rosa Luxemburg's attitude to their national strivings differed greatly from her attitude to Poland.

Rosa's lively independence of thought was tempered nevertheless by the weakness that lay, as we have seen in some of the questions already dealt with, in her tendency to generalise too readily from her immediate experiences to the labour movement elsewhere.

Rosa Luxemburg's criticism of the Bolsheviks in power

During September and October 1918, while in Breslau prison, Rosa Luxemburg wrote a pamphlet on the Russian Revolution. As a basis, she used not only the German but also the Russian press of the time that was smuggled by her friends into her prison cell. She never finished or polished the work, for the beginning of the German Revolution opened the doors of her prison.

The first edition of this pamphlet was published in 1922, after Rosa Luxemburg's death, by her comrade-in-arms Paul Levi. This edition, however, was not complete, and in 1928 a new edition was published on the basis of a newly-found manuscript.

Rosa Luxemburg was a most enthusiastic supporter of the October Revolution and the Bolshevik Party, and she made this clear in her pamphlet, writing:

> Whatever a party could offer of courage, revolutionary far-sightedness and consistency in an historic hour, Lenin, Trotsky and the other comrades have given in good measure. All the revolutionary honour and capacity which Western Social Democracy lacked was represented by the Bolsheviks. Their October uprising was not only the actual salvation of the Russian Revolution; it was also the salvation of the honour of international socialism.[63]

Again she wrote:

> It is not a matter of this or that secondary question of tactics, but of the capacity for action of the proletariat, the strength to act, the will to power of Socialism as such. In this, Lenin and Trotsky and their friends were the *first*, those who went ahead as an example to the proletariat of the world; they are still the only ones up to now who can cry with Hutten: 'I have dared!
>
> This is the essential and *enduring* in Bolshevik policy. In *this* sense theirs is the immortal historical service of having marched at the head of the international proletariat with the conquest of political power and the practical placing of the problems of the realisation of Socialism, and of having advanced mightily the settlement of the score between Capital and Labour in the entire world... And in this sense, the future everywhere belongs to 'Bolshevism'.[64]

Although praising the October Revolution in the highest terms, Rosa Luxemburg believed that an uncritical acceptance of everything the Bolsheviks did would not be of service to the labour movement. The Marxist method of analysis, according to her, was to accept nothing that had not been submitted first to revolutionary criticism.

It was clear to her that the conditions of isolation of the Russian Revolution caused by the betrayal of Western Social Democracy must lead to distortions in its development. Without international revolutionary support, 'even the greatest energy and the greatest sacrifices of the proletariat in a single country must inevitably become tangled in a maze of contradictions and blunders'.[65]

After pointing out some of these contradictions and blunders, she clearly uncovers their causes, saying:

> Everything that happens in Russia is comprehensible and represents an inevitable chain of causes and effects, the starting point and end term of which are: the failure of the German proletariat and the occupation of Russia by German imperialism. It would be demanding something superhuman from Lenin and his comrades if we should expect from them that under such circumstances they should conjure forth the finest democracy, the most exemplary dictatorship of the proletariat, and a flourishing socialist economy. By their determined revolutionary stand, their exemplary strength in action and their unbreakable loyalty to international socialism, they have contributed whatever could possibly be contributed under such devilishly hard conditions.[66]

While objective factors may lead revolutions to blunder, *subjective factors* in the leadership may make these blunders dangerous. They contain a special hazard when they are turned into virtues: 'The danger begins only when they make a virtue of necessity and want to freeze into a complete theoretical system all the tactics forced upon them by these fatal circumstances, and want to recommend them to the international proletariat as a model of socialist tactics'.[67]

But it was precisely this dangerous idea that was swallowed lock, stock and barrel by the Stalinist parties (and, alas, also by some who call themselves anti-Stalinist).

Rosa Luxemburg criticised the Bolsheviks in power for what she considered their wrong policies with regard to the following:

(1) the land question;
(2) the nationalities question;
(3) the Constituent Assembly;
(4) the democratic rights of workers.

We shall deal with each problem separately.

A socialist land policy, argued Rosa Luxemburg, must aim to encourage the socialisation of agricultural production:

> ...only the nationalisation of the large landed estates, as the technically most advanced and most concentrated means and methods of agrarian production, can serve as the point of departure for the socialist mode of production on the land. Of course, it is not necessary to take away from the small peasant his parcel of land, and we can with confidence leave him to be won over voluntarily by the superior advantages of social production and to be persuaded of the advantages first of union in co-operatives and then finally of inclusion in the general socialised economy as a whole. Still, every socialist economic reform on the land must obviously begin with large and medium land ownership. Here the property right must first of all be turned over to the nation, or to the State, which, with a socialist government, amounts to the same thing; for it is this alone which affords the possibility of organising agricultural production in accord with the requirements of interrelated, large-scale social production.[68]

However, Bolshevik policy was quite contrary to this: '...the slogan launched by the Bolsheviks, immediate seizure and distribution of the land by the peasants...not only is...not a socialist measure; it even cuts off the way to such measures; it piles up insurmountable obstacles to the socialist transformation of agrarian relations'.[69]

And Rosa Luxemburg, rightly and, as life proved, prophetically, pointed out that the distribution of the landed estates among the peasants would strengthen the power of private property in the countryside, and thus would heap added difficulties in the path of the socialisation of agriculture in the future:

> Formerly there was only a small caste of noble and capitalist landed proprietors and a small minority of rich village bourgeoisie to oppose a socialist reform on the land. And their expropriation by a revolutionary mass movement of the people is mere child's play. But now, after the 'seizure', as an opponent of any attempt at socialisation of agrarian production, there is an enormous, newly-developed and powerful mass of owning peasants who will defend their newly-won property with tooth and nail against every socialist attack.[70]

And how important this fact—the isolation of a small working class in a sea of antagonistic, backward, petty capitalist peasants—proved to be in the rise of Stalin!

However, Lenin and Trotsky had no alternative. It is true that the Bolshevik Party programme provided for nationalisation of all landed estates. And for many years Lenin had argued heatedly against the Social Revolutionaries who were in favour of distributing the landlords' land among the peasants. However, in 1917, when the land problem demanded an immediate solution, he straight away adopted the slogans of the much-condemned Social Revolutionaries, or rather of the spontaneous peasant movement. If the Bolsheviks had not done this, they, and the urban working class they led, would have been isolated from the countryside, and the revolution would have been stillborn, or at most short-lived (as was the Hungarian Revolution of 1919).

By no stretch of strategy or tactics could the Bolsheviks overcome a basic contradiction in the Russian Revolution, the fact that it was carried out by two different contradictory classes, the working class and the peasantry, the former collectivist, the latter individualist. As early as in 1906 Trotsky had postulated the prospect that the future revolution, in which the working class would lead the peasants, would end with the latter so bitterly opposing the former that only the spreading of the revolution could save the workers' power from being overthrown:

> The Russian proletariat...will meet with organised hostility on the part of world reaction and with readiness on the part of the world proletariat to lend the revolution organised assistance. Left to itself, the working class of Russia will inevitably be crushed by the counter-revolution at the moment when the peasantry turns its back upon the proletariat. Nothing will be left to the workers but to link the fate of their own political rule, and consequently the fate of the whole Russian Revolution, with that of the socialist revolution in Europe.[71]

Rosa Luxemburg's estimate of the Bolshevik land policy shows much true insight into the situation in the Russian Revolution, and points out the frequent dangers inherent in the Bolshevik policies. But the situation did not allow the Bolsheviks any other revolutionary land policy besides the one they implemented: acceding to the democratic, spontaneous wish of the peasants to distribute the land expropriated from the landlords.

Rosa Luxemburg was no less critical of the Bolshevik policy on the question of nationalities, warning of the gravest dangers to the revolution:

> The Bolsheviks are in part responsible for the fact that the military defeat was transformed into the collapse and breakdown of Russia. Moreover, the Bolsheviks themselves have, to a great extent, sharpened the objective difficulties of this situation by a slogan which they placed in the foreground of their policies: the so-called right of self-determination of peoples, or—something which was really implicit in this slogan—the disintegration of Russia.[72]

Instead of the slogan of self-determination she proposed the policy of 'working for the most compact union of the revolutionary forces throughout the area of the Empire...of defending tooth and nail the integrity of the Russian Empire as an area of revolution and opposing to all forms of separatism the solidarity and inseparability of the proletarians in all lands within the sphere of the Russian Revolution as the highest command of politics'.[73]

How wrong Rosa Luxemburg was on this question!

If the Bolsheviks had followed her advice on this issue the ruling classes of the formerly oppressed nations would have managed more and more to rally the popular masses around them and so enhance the isolation of the Soviet power. Only by the formerly oppressing nation putting forward the slogan of self-determination could they gain the revolutionary unity of all peoples. It was in this way that the Bolsheviks did manage to rally at least part of the territory lost in the world war and the beginning of the civil war—Ukraine, for instance. It was because of a deviation from this policy of self-determination for all peoples that the Red Army was first repulsed at the gate of Warsaw, and then brought upon themselves the hatred of the Georgians by marching into and occupying Georgia in a most bureaucratic, anti-democratic fashion.[74]

In the case of the national question, as well as the land question, Rosa Luxemburg erred because she departed from the principle of popular decision, a principle so central to her thoughts and actions in general.

One of the criticisms Rosa Luxemburg levelled at the Bolsheviks concerned their dispersal of the Constituent Assembly. She wrote:

> It is a fact that Lenin and his comrades were stormily demanding the calling of a Constituent Assembly up to the time of their October victory, and that the policy of dragging out this matter on the part of the Kerensky government constituted an article in the indictment of that government by the Bolsheviks and was the basis of some of their most violent attacks upon it.
>
> Indeed, Trotsky says in his interesting pamphlet, *From October to Brest-Litovsk*, that the October Revolution represented 'the salvation of the Constituent

Assembly' as well as the revolution as a whole. 'And when we said', he continues, 'that the entrance to the Constituent Assembly could not be reached through the Preliminary Parliament of Zeretelli, but only through the seizure of power by the Soviets, we were entirely right'.

After thus calling for the Constituent Assembly, the same leaders dispersed it on 6 January 1918.

What Rosa Luxemburg proposed in her pamphlet was the idea of Soviets plus Constituent Assembly. But life itself showed quite clearly that this would have led to a dual power, which would have threatened the organ of workers' power, the Soviets. The Bolshevik leaders justified the dispersal of the Constituent Assembly in the first place on the grounds that the elections had been held under an obsolete law, which gave undue weight to the rich minority of the peasants who, at the one and only session of the Assembly, refused to ratify the decrees on land, peace and the transfer of power to the Soviets. Rosa Luxemburg countered this by arguing that the Bolsheviks could simply have held new elections which did not suffer from past distortions.

But the real reason for the dispersal lay deeper than this.

It was first of all a result of the fact that, while the Soviets were largely working-class organisations, the Constituent Assembly was based mainly on the votes of the peasants. It was therefore no accident that the Bolsheviks, who had the overwhelming majority in the Second Congress of the Soviets (8 November 1917) which were elected by some 20 million people, did not command the support of more than a quarter of the Constituent Assembly elected by all the people of Russia. The peasant, devoted to private property, could not identify himself with Bolshevism, even if he was happy to have Bolshevik support for land distribution and the fight for peace. The Soviets were therefore a much more reliable support for workers' rule than the Constituent Assembly ever could be.

But there is an even more basic reason—one that has nothing to do with the peasant predominance in the Russian population—for not having a Constituent Assembly (or Parliament) side by side with Soviets. Soviets are the *specific* form of rule of the working class, in the same way as parliament was the specific form of domination of the bourgeoisie.

Actually, in the German Revolution Rosa Luxemburg radically altered her standpoint and vigorously opposed the slogan of the USPD: 'Workers' Councils *and* a National Assembly'. Thus on 20 November 1918 she wrote:

> Whoever pleads for a National Assembly is consciously or unconsciously depressing the revolution to the historical level of a *bourgeois* revolution; he is a camouflaged agent of the *bourgeoisie* or an unconscious representative of the petty bourgeoisie…
>
> The alternatives before us today are not democracy and dictatorship. They are *bourgeois* democracy and socialist democracy. The dictatorship of the proletariat is democracy in a socialist sense.[75]

Rosa's chief criticism of the Bolsheviks was that they were responsible for restricting and undermining workers' democracy. And on this issue the whole tragic history of Russia proves that she was, prophetically, absolutely correct.

The heart of Rosa Luxemburg's pamphlet on the Russian Revolution, as of all she wrote and said, was a belief in the workers, the conviction that they, and they alone, are capable of overcoming the crisis facing humanity. She fervently believed that workers' democracy is inseparable from proletarian revolution and socialism. She wrote:

> ...socialist democracy is not something which begins only in the promised land after the foundations of socialist economy are created; it does not come as some sort of Christmas present for the worthy people who, in the interim, have loyally supported a handful of socialist dictators. Socialist democracy begins simultaneously with the beginnings of the destruction of class rule and of the construction of socialism. It begins at the very moment of the seizure of power by the socialist party. It is the same thing as the dictatorship of the proletariat.
>
> Yes, dictatorship! But this dictatorship consists in the *manner of applying democracy*, not in its elimination, in energetic, resolute attacks upon the well-entrenched rights and economic relationships of bourgeois society, without which a socialist transformation cannot be accomplished. But this dictatorship must be the work of the *class* and not of a little leading minority in the name of the class.[76]

Although she unhesitatingly supported the working-class dictatorship directed against the enemies of socialism, she argued that only complete and consistent democracy could ensure the rule of the working class, and could give scope to its tremendous potentialities. She claimed that the Bolsheviks deviated from this conception:

> The tacit assumption underlying the Lenin-Trotsky theory of the dictatorship is this: that the socialist transformation is something in which a ready-made formula lies completed in the pocket of the revolutionary party, which needs only to be carried out energetically in practice. This is, unfortunately—or perhaps fortunately—not the case. Far from being a sum of ready-made prescriptions which have only to be applied, the practical realisation of socialism as an economic, social and juridical system is something which lies completely hidden in the mists of the future. What we possess in our programme is nothing but a few main signposts which indicate the general direction in which to look for the necessary measures, and the indications are mainly negative in character at that. Thus we know more or less what we must eliminate at the outset in order to free the road for a socialist economy. But when it comes to the nature of the thousand concrete, practical measures, large and small, necessary to introduce socialist principles into economy, law and all social relationships, there is no key in any socialist party programme or text book. That is not a shortcoming but rather the very thing that makes scientific socialism superior to the Utopian varieties. The socialist system of society should only be, and can only be, an historical product, born out of the school of its own experiences, born in the course of its realisation, as a result of the developments of living history, which—just like organic nature of which, in the last analysis, it forms a part—has the fine habit of always producing along with any real social need the means

> to its satisfaction, along with the task simultaneously the solution. However, if such is the case, then it is clear that socialism by its very nature cannot be decreed or introduced by *ukase* [edict].[77]

And Rosa Luxemburg predicted that the collective of the Russian workers would not take an active part in economic and social life:

> ...socialism will be decreed from behind a few official desks by a dozen intellectuals...with the repression of political life in the land as a whole, life in the Soviets must also become more and more crippled. Without general elections, without unrestricted freedom of Press and Assembly, without a free struggle of opinion, life dies out in every public institution, becomes a mere semblance of life, in which only the bureaucracy remains as the active element. Public life gradually falls asleep, a few dozen party leaders of inexhaustible energy and boundless experience direct and rule. Among them, in reality, only a dozen outstanding heads do the leading and an elite of the working class is invited from time to time to meetings where they are to applaud the speeches of the leaders, and to approve proposed resolutions unanimously—at bottom then, a clique affair—a dictatorship, to be sure, not the dictatorship of the proletariat, however, but only the dictatorship of a handful of politicians, that is a dictatorship in the bourgeois sense, in the sense of the rule of the Jacobins.[78]

Rosa Luxemburg's criticism of the Russian Revolution, as with all her writing, could give no solace to reformist critics of revolutionary socialism, but could serve as an aid to those who desire to keep the science of working-class action living and untrammelled. Her criticism of the Bolshevik party is in the best traditions of Marxism, of the basic maxim of Karl Marx: 'merciless criticism of all things existing'.

'The Accumulation of Capital'

During the years 1906-13 Rosa Luxemburg lectured on political economy at a German Social Democratic Party school of activists. While doing so she prepared a book on Marxian economics entitled *Introduction to Political Economy*. When about to conclude the basic draft she met with an unexpected difficulty:

> I could not succeed in depicting the total process of capitalist production in all its practical relations and with its objective historical limitations with sufficient clarity. Closer examination of the matter then convinced me that it was a question of rather more than the mere art of representation, and that a problem remained to be solved which is connected with the theoretical matter of Volume II of Marx's Capital and at the same time closely connected with present-day imperialist politics and their economic roots.

In this way Rosa Luxemburg came to write her major theoretical work, *The Accumulation of Capital: A Contribution to an Economic Explanation of Imperialism* (Berlin, 1913). The book is not at all easy to follow, especially for anyone not conversant with Marx's *Capital*. At the same time, without doubt, Rosa

Luxemburg's contribution, whether one agrees with it or not, is one of the most, if not the most, important and original contributions to Marxian economic doctrine since *Capital*.

Marx, in analysing the laws of motion of capitalism, abstracted from it all non-capitalist factors, in the same way as a scientist studying the law of gravity would study it in a vacuum.

The problem with which Rosa Luxemburg deals is as follows: can enlarged reproduction, ie production on an increasing scale, take place under the conditions of abstract, pure capitalism, where non-capitalist countries do not exist, or where any classes besides capitalists and workers do not exist? Marx assumed that it can. Rosa Luxemburg argued that, while in general, for the purposes of the analysis of capitalist economy, abstraction from non-capitalist factors is justified, it is not justified when dealing with the question of enlarged reproduction.

The question is, of course, purely theoretical, as in fact pure capitalism has never existed: enlarged reproduction has always taken place while capitalism has been invading pre-capitalist spheres, either inside the capitalist country itself—invasion into feudalism with the destruction of peasants, artisans, etc—or into wholely agricultural, pre-capitalist countries.

If capitalism has never existed in pure form, one may well ask: what is the importance of the question whether enlarged reproduction is theoretically possible in pure capitalism? After all, neither Marx nor Rosa Luxemburg assumed that capitalism would continue to exist until *all* pre-capitalist formations had been overthrown. However, the answer to this question may throw light on the effect of the non-capitalist sphere on the accentuation or mitigation of the contradictions in capitalism, and on the factors impelling capitalism to imperialist expansion.

Let us begin by explaining how Marx described the process of reproduction as a whole under capitalism.

Marx starts with an analysis of simple reproduction, ie on the assumption—which, of course, could never exist under capitalism—that there is no accumulation of capital, that the whole of the surplus value is spent on the personal consumption of the capitalists, production thus not expanding.

For the capitalist to carry on simple reproduction certain conditions must exist. He must be able to sell the product of his factory, and with the money obtained buy the means of production (machines, raw materials, etc) that he needs for his particular industry; also he must get the labour power he needs from the market, as well as the means of consumption required to feed, clothe, and provide other necessities for the labourers. The product produced by the workers with the help of the means of production must again find a market, and so on.

While from the standpoint of the individual capitalist it makes no difference what his factory produces, whether machinery, stockings, or newspapers, provided he can find buyers for his product so that he can realise his capital plus the surplus value, to the capitalist economy as a whole it is extremely important that the total produce will be made up of certain determined use values, in other words, the total product must provide the means of production necessary to renew the process of production and the means of consumption needed by the workers and capitalists. The quantities of the different products cannot be arbitrarily determined: the means of production produced must be equal in value to the size of the constant capital **c**: the means of consumption produced must be equal in value to the size of the wages bill—the variable capital **v**—plus the surplus value **s**.

To analyse simple reproduction Marx divided industry as a whole into two basic departments: that producing means of production (Department I) and that producing means of consumption (Department II). Between these two departments a certain proportionality must obtain for simple reproduction to take place. It is clear, for instance, that if Department I produced more machines than this department together with Department II needed, machinery would be over-produced, production in Department I consequently paralysed, and a whole sequence of events would follow from this. Similarly, if Department I produced too few machines, reproduction, instead of repeating itself on the same level, would retrogress. The same would apply to Department II if it produced more or less means of consumption than the combined wages bill, or variable capital, and surplus value (**v + s**) in both departments.[79] The proportion between the demand for means of production and that for means of consumption in the economy as a whole depends on the ratio between the portion of capital devoted to the purchase of machinery and raw materials, ie on the constant capital (**c**) of the whole economy on the one hand, and that portion of capital expended on paying wages, **v**, plus the profits of the capitalists in the whole economy.

In other words, the products of Department I (**P1**) must be equal to the constant capital of Department I (**c1**) plus the constant capital of Department II (**c2**):

$$P1 = c1 + c2.$$

Similarly, the products of Department II (**P2**) must be equal to wages and surplus value in both departments together:

$$P2 = v1 + s1 + v2 + s2.$$

These two equations can be combined in one equation:

$$c2 = v1 + s1.$$

In other words, the value of machinery and raw materials, etc, needed by Department II must be equal to the wages plus surplus value of workers and capitalists in Department I.

These equations are for simple reproduction. The formulae for enlarged reproduction are more complicated. Here part of the surplus value is expended on the personal consumption of the capitalists—this we shall denote by the letter **r**—and part is accumulated—this we shall denote by the letter **a**. **a** itself is divided into two portions: part serves to buy added means of production, ie is spent on adding to available constant capital—**ac**—and part goes to pay wages to workers newly employed in production—**av**.

If the social demand for means of production under simple reproduction were expressed by the formula **c1 + c2**, enlarged reproduction would be expressed as **c1 + ac1 + c2 + ac2**.

Similarly the social demand for consumer goods, from

$$v1 + s1 + v2 + s2$$

becomes:

$$v1 + r1 + av1 + v2 + r2 + av2$$

Hence the conditions necessary for enlarged reproduction can be formulated thus:

$$P1 = c1 + ac1 + c2 + ac2$$
$$P2 = v1 + r1 + av1 + v2 + r2 + av2$$

Or:

$$c2 + ac2 = v1 + r1 + av1$$ [80]

Now for Rosa Luxemburg's criticism of Marx's schemas.[81] Rosa Luxemburg showed that a comparison of the formula for simple reproduction with that for enlarged reproduction produced a paradox. In the case of simple reproduction **c2** must be equal to **v1 + s1**. In the case of enlarged reproduction, **c2 + ac2** must be equal to **v1 + rl + av1**. Now **v1 + r1 + av1** are smaller than **v1 + s1** (as **ac1** is deducted from **s1**). So that if equilibrium were achieved under conditions of simple reproduction, the transition to enlarged reproduction would demand not only non-accumulation in Department II but the absurd position of disaccumulation.

And it is no accident, she said, that when Marx used diagrams to illustrate enlarged reproduction, he gave a smaller figure for **c2** than the one he used to illustrate simple reproduction:

Diagram of simple reproduction

I	4000c + 1000v + 1000s	= 6000
II	2000c + 500v + 500s	= 3000
	Total	= 9000

Initial diagram for accumulation on an expanded scale

I	4000c + 1000v + 1000s	= 6000
II	1500c + 750v + 750s	= 3000
	Total	= 9000[82]

Thus the constant capital of Department II is 500 smaller in enlarged than in simple reproduction.

Marx goes on to elaborate the diagram of enlarged reproduction and he shows that, assuming that in Department I as well as in Department II no change in the organic composition of capital (ie, in the ratio of constant capital to variable capital) takes place, that the rate of exploitation remains constant, and that half the surplus value in Department I is capitalised, then the reproduction of capital will result in the following progression:

First year

I	4400c + 1100v + 1100s	= 6600
II	1600c + 800v + 800s	= 3200
	Total	= 9800

Second year

I	4800c + 1210v + 1210s	= 7260
II	1760c + 880v + 880s	= 3520
	Total	= 10780

Third year

I	5324c + 1331v + 1331s	= 7986
II	1936c + 968v + 968s	= 3872
	Total	= 11858

Fourth year

I	5856c + 1464v + 1464s	= 8784
II	2129c + 1065v + 1065s	= 4259
	Total	= 13043

Fifth year

I	6442c + 1610v + 1610s	= 9662
II	2342c + 1172v + 1172s	= 4686
	Total	= 14348[83]

Analysing the above diagram, Rosa Luxemburg correctly points out a peculiarity they show:

While in Department I half the surplus value is capitalised every time, and the other half consumed, so that there is an orderly expansion both of production and of personal consumption by the capitalists, the twofold process in Department II takes the following erratic course:

First year	150 are capitalised,	600 consumed
Second	240	660
Third	254	626
Fourth	290	678
Fifth	320	745

And she adds:

Needless to say, the absolute figures of the diagram are arbitrary in every equation, but that does not detract from their scientific value. It is the quantitative ratios which are relevant, since they are supposed to express strictly determinate relationships. Those precise logical rules that lay down the relations of accumulation in Department I seem to have been gained at the cost of any kind of principle in construing these relations for Department II; and this circumstance calls for a revision of the immanent connections revealed by the analysis.[84]

Here there is no rule in evidence for accumulation and consumption to follow; both are wholly subservient to the requirements of accumulation in Department I.[85]

As regards the progress of the enlarged reproduction, if we assumed that in Department II as well as in Department I there was an orderly expansion of both capital accumulation, and of the personal consumption of the capitalists, there would then have appeared an increasing disequilibrium between the two departments.

Rosa Luxemburg therefore shows clearly that, if any logical rules were laid down for the relations of accumulation in Department I, these rules seem to 'have been gained at the cost of any kind of principle in constructing these relations for Department II'; or otherwise, if the same logical rules were applied to the relations of accumulation in Department II as those applied in Department I, a disequilibrium in the form of overproduction in Department II would appear and grow progressively.

It will now be easy to show, assuming as a point of departure for enlarged reproduction that the constant capital in Department II was not 500 smaller than in simple reproduction, that there would have been disequilibrium between Department I and Department II: the demand of Department I for means of consumption would have been 500 smaller at the beginning of the process than the supply available in Department II of the means of consumption looking for exchange: there would have been overproduction of consumer goods to the value of 500 at the start of the process of enlarged reproduction.

If Rosa Luxemburg did not abstract from a number of other factors, such as the rise in the rate of exploitation and the rise in the organic composition of capital, her argument would have been even stronger. It is easy to prove that if the rate of exploitation rises, so that the ratio of surplus value to wage (**s:v**) is rising, the relative demand for consumer goods as against producer goods will decline, and hence either the rate of accumulation in Department II would be even more erratic than in Marx's diagrams, or increasing surpluses would appear in Department II. Any rise in the portion of the surplus value accumulated would work in the same direction, as well as any growth of the organic composition of capital.

The above-mentioned three tendencies—the rise in the rate of exploitation, rise in the rate of accumulation, and rise in the organic composition of capital—Marx assumed to be absolute and immanent laws of capitalism.

If these were taken into account, Rosa Luxemburg's contention, that under pure capitalism economic disequilibrium would be an absolute, unavoidable, permanent phenomenon, would be greatly strengthened.

However, there is one important factor which cancels out all the above factors and is immanently connected with them: the rise in the relative weight of Department I as compared with Department II. The rise in the organic composition of capital, the improvement of technique, has been historically and logically connected with the rise of Department I compared with Department II. Thus it was calculated that the ratio of net output of capital goods to that of consumer goods was in Britain as follows:

1851, 100:470; 1871, 100:390; 1901, 100:170; 1924, 100: 150.

The figures for the United States were:

1850, 100:240; 1890, 100:150; 1920, 100:80.

The figures for Japan:
1900, 100:480; 1913, 100:270; 1925, 100:240.[86]

To show that the rise in Department I compared with Department II counteracts the factors mentioned by Rosa Luxemburg (as well as those added by the present writer to strengthen Rosa Luxemburg's argument about the tendency of overproduction in Department II), some diagrammatic representation of the effect of the change in the relative weight of Department I to Department II on the exchange relationship between the two departments will be given.

The capital invested in Department I can grow comparatively to Department II in two ways:

(1) by having a higher rate of accumulation in Department I than in Department II;

(2) by the transference of capital from Department II to Department I.
We shall give a diagrammatic example for each of these two processes.

Let us assume that the rate of accumulation in Department I is higher than in Department II, say, half the surplus value in Department I compared with only a third in Department II. We shall assume also that the other factors (the rate of exploitation at 100 percent, the organic composition of capital where constant capital is five times bigger than variable capital) remain unchanged. Then, using Marx's diagram quoted above as a point of departure, the reproduction of capital will result in the following progression (figures are rounded for simplicity):[87]

Point of departure:

I	5000c + 1000v + 1000s	= 7000
II	1500c + 300v + 300s	= 2100

End of first year:

I	5000c + 1000v + 500r + 417ac + 83av	= 7000
II	1500c + 300v + 200r + 80ac + 20av	= 2100

c2 + ac2 = 1580
while v1 + r1 + av1 = 1583.

Thus at the end of the first year, instead of a surplus in Department II as presumed by Rosa Luxemburg, a surplus appears in Department I, amounting to 3.

End of second year:

I	5417c + 1083v + 541r + 450ac + 90av	= 7583
II	1580c + 320v + 213r + 90ac + 18av	= 2220

c2 + ac2 = 1670
while vl + rl + av1 =1714. The surplus in Department I is now 44.

End of third year:

I	5867c + 1173v + 586r + 489ac + 98av	= 8213
II	1670c + 338v + 225r + 94ac + 19av	= 2346

c2 + ac2 = 1764
while vl + rl + av1 =1857. The surplus in Department I is now 93.

From the above diagrams it is clear that if we assume that the rate of exploitation and the organic composition of capital remain unchanged, while the rate of accumulation in Department I is higher than in Department II, then overproduction appears in Department I.[88]

As we have said above, Department I can increase relatively to Department II also by transference of surplus value from Department II to Department I. Let us illustrate this process diagrammatically. We shall assume that the rate of exploitation, the organic composition of capital and the rate of accumulation are the same in both departments and they remain unchanged. At the same time, we shall assume that half the surplus value produced in Department II is being transferred to Department I.

The progress of enlarged production could then be described by the following diagrams:

Point of departure:

I 5000c + 1000v + 1000s = 7000
II 1500c + 300v + 300s = 2100

End of first year:

I **5000c + 1000v + 500r + 417ac + 83av** = 7000
II **1500c + 300v + 150r + 63ac +12av**
(plus surplus value transferred to Department I: **63ac + 12av**) = 2100
c2 + ac2 = 1563
while **v1 + r1 + av1** (plus the **av** transferred from Department II) = **1595**

Thus at the end of the first year, instead of a surplus in Department II as presumed by Rosa Luxemburg, we are faced with overproduction in Department I amounting to 32.

End of second year:

I **5840c + 1095v + 547r + 455ac + 91av** = 7670
II **1563c + 312v + 156r + 65ac +13av**
(plus surplus value transferred to Department I: **65ac + 13av**) = 2187
c2 + ac2 = 1628
while **v1 + r1 + av1** (plus the av transferred from Department II) = **1746**
The surplus in Department I is 118.

End of third year:

I **6000c + 1200v + 600r + 500ac + 100av** = 8400
II **1628c + 325v + 162r + 67ac + 14av**
(plus surplus value transferred to Department I: **67ac + 14av**) = 2278
c2 + ac2 = 1695
while **v1 + r1 + av1** (plus the av transferred from Department II) = **1914**
The surplus in Department I is 219.

Now Rosa Luxemburg argues against this idea that the transfer of surplus value from one department to another can help to bring about an exchange balance between the departments, saying that the 'intended transfer of part of the capitalised surplus value from Department II to Department I is ruled out, first because the material form of this surplus value is obviously useless to Department I, and secondly because of the relations of exchange between the two departments which would in turn necessitate an equivalent transfer of the products of Department I into Department II'.[89] In other words, Rosa Luxemburg argues that Marx's schema is based on the assumption that the realisation of surplus value can take place only through an exchange between departments, and secondly that the presumed surplus in Department II takes a natural form, ie remains as means of consumption, and *cannot* serve directly as means of production. Now the first argument falls through owing to the fact that exchange between enterprises in the same department can serve to realise the surplus value: when an owner of a hat factory sells his hats to workers who produce biscuits, he realises the surplus value produced by his workers. Secondly, quite a large number of consumer goods can serve also as means of production: if a building contractor builds factories instead of flats, this signifies the transference of capital from Department II to Department I; electricity can serve to light flats as well as to move machinery; grain can feed man (consumption) as well as pigs (productive consumption), etc. Thirdly, without the possibility of transference of capital from one department to another, the postulate that the rate of profit throughout the economy tends to equality, which is basic Marxian economics, loses its foundation.

From the diagrams given above it becomes clear that a relative increase of Department I compared with Department II, if all other conditions remain unchanged, brings in its wake surpluses in the exchange relations in Department I.

Can this factor not counteract the one pointed out by Rosa Luxemburg to be the cause of a surplus in Department II? Are the different counteracting factors not in fact two sides of one coin, the progress of capitalist economy? Of course this is so.

Rosa Luxemburg came to the conclusion that a surplus must appear in Department II because she paid attention to only one side of the coin. Considering both sides, it is clear that it is possible in pure capitalism for proportionality between the two departments to exist, while the accumulation in both is regular, not erratic.

However, the theoretical *possibility* of the preservation of correct proportionalities between the two departments, which will prevent overproduction by their mutual exchange while accumulation goes forward on an even keel, does not mean that in actual life the anarchic and atomistic working of capitalism leads to continuous and stable preservation of the proportionalities needed. And here the factor Rosa Luxemburg pointed to—the existence of non-capitalist formations into which capitalism expands—is extremely important. If it is not a prerequisite for enlarged reproduction as Rosa Luxemburg argued, it is, at least, a factor that eases the process of enlarged reproduction, of accumulation, by making the interdependence of the two departments less than absolute. One cannot but agree with Rosa Luxemburg when she says, 'Accumulation is more than an internal relationship between the branches of capitalist economy'; as a result of the relationship between the capitalist and non-capitalist environment:

> ...the two great departments of production sometimes perform the accumulative process on their own, independently of each other, but even then at every step the movements overlap and intersect. From this we get most complicated relations, divergencies in the speed and direction of accumulation for the two departments, different relations with non-capitalist modes of production as regards both material elements and elements of value.[90]

As a matter of fact, the number of factors determining whether certain proportionalities between the departments lead to equilibrium or not are numerous and contradictory (the rate of exploitation, the rate of accumulation in different industries, changes in the organic composition of capital in different industries, and so on) and, once the economy leaves the state of equilibrium, what was proportionality before turns into disproportionality with snowball effect. Hence the exchange between capitalist industry and the non-capitalist sphere, even if it is small in absolute terms, may have a tremendous effect on the elasticity, and hence stability, of capitalism.

In her book Rosa Luxemburg goes backwards and forwards between analyses of the schemas of reproduction—which describe exchange relationships between the two departments of industry—and another set of relations between the two departments: the *potentiality* of means of production to become means of consumption—means of production not only being *exchanged* for means of consumption, but in time being realised in new means of consumption. The proportionalities expressed in Marx's schemas are conditions without which accumulation *cannot* take place; but in order that accumulation *should actually take place* there is need for a progressively enlarged demand for commodities, and the question that arises is: where does this demand come from?

Capitalist prosperity depends upon the increasing output and absorption of capital goods. But this depends in the last analysis upon the capacity of industry to sell an increasing output of consumer goods. However, in trying to sell its products, capitalist industry enters into deepening contradictions, the most fundamental of which is that between production and the limited market: 'The last cause of all real crises always remains the poverty and restricted consumption of the masses as compared to the tendency of capitalist production to develop the productive forces in such a way that only the absolute power of consumption of the entire society would be their limit'.[91]

Rosa Luxemburg argued that the factor making it possible for capitalism to get away from the absolute impediment to accumulation of the limiting market was the penetration of capitalist industry into the non-capitalist territories.[92]

Rosa Luxemburg, more than any Marxist or non-Marxist economist, drew attention to the effect of the non-capitalist frontier on capitalism. Relying on this factor—even if she herself did not develop all the main consequences of it—one can try and sum up the effect of the expansion of capitalism into non-capitalist territories thus:

(1) The markets of the backward colonial countries, by increasing demand for goods from the industrial countries, weaken the tendency for overproduction there, decrease the reserve army of unemployed, and so bring about an improvement in the wages of workers in the industrial countries.
(2) The increase in wages brought about in this way has a cumulative effect. By increasing the internal market in the industrial countries, the tendency for overproduction is weakened, unemployment decreases, wages rise.
(3) The export of capital adds to the prosperity of the industrial countries as it creates a market for their goods—at least temporarily. The export of cotton goods from Britain to India presupposes that India is able to pay for it straight away, by exporting cotton, for instance. On the other hand, the export of capital for the building of a railway presupposes an export of goods—rails, locomotives, etc—beyond the immediate purchasing power or exporting power of India. In other words, *for a time* the export of capital is an important factor in enlarging markets for the industries of the advanced countries. However, in time this factor turns into its opposite: capital once exported puts a brake on the export of goods from the 'mother' country after the colonial countries start to pay profit or interest on it. In order to pay a profit of £10 million to Britain (on British capital invested in India) India has to import less than it exports, and thus save the money needed to the tune of £10 million. In other words, the act of exporting capital from Britain to India expands the market for British goods; the payment of interest and profit on existing British capital in India restricts the markets for British goods. Hence the existence of great British capital investments abroad does not at all exclude overproduction and mass unemployment in Britain. Contrary to Lenin's view, the high profit from capital invested abroad may well be not a concomitant of capitalist prosperity and stabilisation in the imperialist country, but a factor of mass unemployment and depression.
(4) The export of capital to the colonies affects the whole capital market in the imperialist country. Even if the surplus of capital looking vainly for investment were very small, its cumulative influence could be tremendous, as it would create pressure in the capital markets, and strengthen the downward trend of the rate of profit. This in turn would have a cumulative effect of its own on the activity of capital, on the entire economic activity, on employment, and so on the purchasing power of the masses, and so again in a vicious circle on the markets. The export of surplus capital can obviate these difficulties and can thus be of great importance to the whole of capitalist prosperity, and thus to reformism.
(5) By thus relieving pressure in capital markets the export of capital diminishes competition between different enterprises, and so diminishes the need of each to rationalise and modernise its equipment. (This to some extent explains the technical backwardness of British industry, the pioneer of the industrial revolution, as compared with that of Germany today, for example.) This weakens the tendencies to overproduction and

unemployment, wage cuts, and so on. (Of course, in changed circumstances, in which Britain has ceased to hold a virtual monopoly in the industrial world, this factor may well cause the defeat of British industry in the world market, unemployment and cuts in wages.)
(6) Buying cheap raw materials and foodstuffs in the colonies allows real wages in the industrial countries to be increased without cutting into the rate of profit. This increase of wages means widened domestic markets *without* a decrease in the rate and amount of profit, in other words, without weakening the motive of capitalist production.
(7) The period during which the agrarian colonial countries serve to broaden markets for the industrial countries will no longer be in proportion to:
(a) the size of the colonial world compared with the productive power of the advanced industrial countries, and
(b) the extent that the industrialisation of the former is postponed.
(8) All the beneficial effects of imperialism on capitalist prosperity would disappear if there were no national boundaries between the industrial imperialist countries and their colonies. Britain exported goods and capital to India and imported cheap raw materials and foodstuffs, but it did not let the unemployed of India—increased by the invasion of British capitalism—enter Britain's labour market. If not for the barrier (a financial one) to mass Indian immigration into Britain, wages in Britain would not have risen throughout the last century. The crisis of capitalism would have got deeper and deeper. Reformism would not have been able to replace revolutionary Chartism.[93]

One may agree or disagree with Rosa Luxemburg's criticism of Marx's schemas in Volume II of *Capital*, and with all or some of the links in her chain of reasoning leading to the final conclusion that, if the capitalist mode of production was not only the predominant one but the only one, of necessity in a short time capitalism would have collapsed from its internal contradictions. Whatever one thinks, one cannot doubt the tremendous service Rosa Luxemburg did in drawing attention to the effect of non-capitalist spheres on the stability of capitalism. As Professor Joan Robinson states in her introductory essay to the English edition of *The Accumulation of Capital*: '...few would deny that the extension of capitalism into new territories was the mainspring of what an academic economist has called the "vast secular boom" of the last 200 years, and many academic economists account for the uneasy condition of capitalism in the 20th century largely by the "closing of the frontier" all over the world'.[94] Joan Robinson mixes praise of Rosa Luxemburg's analysis with a criticism that Rosa Luxemburg ignored the rise in real wages that occurred throughout the capitalist world—a factor enlarging the market—and thus presented an incomplete picture. However, even if Rosa Luxemburg did not include this factor in her analysis—and it is extraneous to the main line of her argument about the possibility or impossibility of enlarged reproduction in pure capitalism—one cannot explain the rise in real wages itself independently of the main feature Rosa Luxemburg pointed out: the expansion of capitalism into non-capitalist spheres.[95]

Rosa Luxemburg's place in history

Franz Mehring, the biographer of Marx, did not exaggerate when he called Rosa Luxemburg the best brain after Marx. But she did not contribute her brain alone to the working-class movement; she gave everything she had—her heart, her passion, her strong will, her very life.

Above all else, Rosa Luxemburg was a revolutionary socialist. And among the great revolutionary socialist leaders and teachers she has a special historical place of her own.

When reformism degraded the socialist movements by aspiring purely for the 'welfare state', by tinkering with capitalism, it became of first importance to make a revolutionary criticism of this handmaiden of capitalism. It is true that other Marxist teachers besides Rosa Luxemburg—Lenin, Trotsky, Bukharin and others—conducted a revolutionary fight against reformism. But they had a limited front to fight against. In their country, Russia, the roots of this weed were so weak and thin that a mere tug was sufficient to uproot it. Where Siberia or the gallows stared every socialist or democrat in the face, who in principle could oppose the use of violence by the labour movement? Who in Tsarist Russia would have dreamed of a parliamentary road to socialism? Who could advocate a policy of coalition government, for with whom could coalitions be made? Where trade unions scarcely existed, who could think of considering them the panacea of the labour movement? Lenin, Trotsky and the other Russian Bolshevik leaders did not need to counter the arguments of reformism with a painstaking and exact analysis. All they needed was a broom to sweep it away to the dungheap of history.

In Central and Western Europe conservative reformism had much deeper roots, a much more embracing influence on the thoughts and moods of the workers. The arguments of the reformists had to be answered by superior ones, and here Rosa Luxemburg excelled. In these countries her scalpel is a much more useful weapon than Lenin's sledgehammer.

In Tsarist Russia the mass of the workers were not organised in parties or trade unions. There there was not such a threat of powerful empires being built by a bureaucracy rising from the working class as in the well-organised workers' movement of Germany; and it was natural that Rosa Luxemburg had a much earlier and clearer view of the role of the labour bureaucracy than Lenin or Trotsky. She understood long before they did that the only power that could break through bureaucratic chains is the initiative of the workers. Her writings on this subject can serve as an inspiration to workers in the advanced industrial countries, and are a more valuable contribution to the struggle to liberate the workers from the pernicious ideology of bourgeois reformism than those of any other Marxist.

In Russia, where the Bolsheviks were always a large and important part of the organised socialists, even if they were not always the majority, as their name signifies, the question of the attitude of a small Marxist minority to a mass, conservatively-led organisation never really rose as a problem. It remained for

Rosa Luxemburg largely to develop the right approach to this vital question. Her guiding principle was: stay with the masses throughout their travail and try to help them. She therefore opposed abstention from the main stream of the labour movement, no matter what the level of its development. Her fight against sectarianism is extremely important for the labour movement of the West, especially at present, when welfare-stateism is such an all-pervading sentiment. The British labour movement, in particular, having suffered from the sectarianism of Hyndman and the SDF, later the BSP and SLP, then the Communist Party (especially in its 'third period') and now further sects, can gain inspiration from Rosa Luxemburg for a principled fight against reformism which does not degenerate into flight from it. She taught that a revolutionary should not swim with the stream of reformism, nor sit outside it and look in the opposite direction, but swim against it.

Rosa Luxemburg's conception of the structure of the revolutionary organisations—that they should be built, from below up, on a consistently democratic basis—fits the needs of the workers' movement in the advanced countries much more closely than Lenin's conception of 1902-04 which was copied and given an added bureaucratic twist by the Stalinists the world over.

She understood more clearly than anyone that the structure of the revolutionary party, and the mutual relation between the party and the class, would have a big influence, not only on the struggle against capitalism and for workers' power, but also on the fate of this power itself. She stated prophetically that without the widest workers' democracy 'officials behind their desks' would replace the workers' hold on political power. 'Socialism', she said, 'cannot be decreed or introduced by edict.'

Rosa Luxemburg's blend of revolutionary spirit and clear understanding of the nature of the labour movement in Western and Central Europe is in some way connected with her particular background of birth in the Tsarist Empire, long residence in Germany, and full activity in both the Polish and German labour movements. Anyone of smaller stature would have been assimilated into one of the two environments, but not Rosa Luxemburg. To Germany she brought the 'Russian' spirit, the spirit of revolutionary action. To Poland and Russia she brought the 'Western' spirit of workers' self-reliance, democracy and self-emancipation.

Her *The Accumulation of Capital* is an invaluable contribution to Marxism. In dealing with the mutual relations between the industrially advanced countries and the backward agrarian ones she brought out the most important idea that imperialism, while stabilising capitalism over a long period, at the same time threatens to bury humanity under its ruins.

Being vital, energetic and non-fatalistic in her approach to history, which she conceived of as the fruit of human activity, and at the same time laying bare the deep contradictions of capitalism, Rosa Luxemburg did not consider that the victory of socialism was inevitable. Capitalism, she thought, could be either the ante-chamber to socialism or the brink of barbarism. We who live in the shadow of the H-bomb must comprehend this warning and use it as a spur to action.

In the late 19th and early 20th centuries the German labour movement, with decades of peace behind it, sank under the illusion that this situation was everlasting. We who are in the throes of discussion about controlled disarmament, United Nations, Summit Meetings, could do no better than learn from Rosa Luxemburg's clear analysis of the unbreakable tie between war and capitalism, and her insistence that the fight for peace is inseparable from the fight for socialism.

A passion for truth made Rosa Luxemburg recoil from any dogmatic thought. In a period when Stalinism has largely turned Marxism into a dogma, spreading desolation in the field of ideas, Rosa Luxemburg's writings are invigorating and life-giving. Nothing was more intolerable to her than bowing down to 'infallible authorities'. As a real disciple of Marx she was able to think and act independently of her master. Though grasping the spirit of his teaching, she did not lose her critical faculties in a simple repetition of his words, whether these fitted the changed situation or not, whether they were right or wrong. Rosa Luxemburg's independence of thought is the greatest inspiration to socialists everywhere and always. In consequence, no one would have denounced more forcefully than she herself any effort to canonise her, to turn her into an 'infallible authority', a leader of a school of thought or action. She loved the conflict of ideas as a means of coming nearer to the truth.

During a period when so many who consider themselves Marxists sap Marxism of its deep humanistic content, no one can do more to release us from the chains of lifeless mechanistic materialism than Rosa Luxemburg. For Marx communism (or socialism) was 'real humanism', 'a society in which the full and free development of every individual is the ruling principle'.[96] Rosa Luxemburg was the embodiment of these humanistic passions. Sympathy with the lowly and oppressed was a central motive of her life. Her deep emotion and feeling for the suffering of people and all living things expressed themselves in everything she did or wrote, whether in her letters from prison or in the deepest writings of her theoretical research.

Rosa Luxemburg, however, well knew that where human tragedy is on an epic scale tears won't help. Her motto, like that of Spinoza, might have been, 'Do not cry, do not laugh, but understand', even though she herself had her full share of tears and laughter. Her method was to reveal the trends of development in social life in order to help the working class to use its potentialities in the best possible way in conjunction with objective development. She appealed to man's reason rather than to emotion.

Deep human sympathy and an earnest desire for truth, unbounded courage and a magnificent brain united in Rosa Luxemburg to make her a great revolutionary socialist. As her closest friend, Clara Zetkin, wrote in her obituary:

> In Rosa Luxemburg the socialist idea was a dominating and powerful passion of both heart and brain, a truly creative passion which burned ceaselessly. The great task and the overpowering ambition of this astonishing woman was to prepare the way for social revolution, to clear the path of history for Socialism. To experience the revolution, to fight its battles—that was the highest happiness for her. With a will, determination, selflessness and devotion for which words are too

> weak, she consecrated her whole life and her whole being to Socialism. She gave herself completely to the cause of Socialism, not only in her tragic death, but throughout her whole life, daily and hourly, through the struggles of many years... She was the sharp sword, the living flame of revolution.

Editor's note on the text

Rosa Luxemburg was first published in 1959. When it was reissued in 1969, Cliff made two small but significant changes. These reflected the way he had revised his position on Leninism and the revolutionary party in the light of the French events of 1968 and the debate on democratic centralism in the International Socialists in the same year. These changes occur on pp45-46 of the 1980 edition and pp85-86 of this edition.

1959:

Rosa Luxemburg's reluctance to form an independent revolutionary party is quite often cited by Stalinists as a grave error and an important cause for the defeat of the German Revolution in 1918. They argue that Lenin was opposed to the revolutionary Left's adherence to the SPD and continuing association with Kautsky.

There is no truth at all in this legend. Actually, Rosa Luxemburg made a clearer assessment of Kautsky and Co, and broke with them long before Lenin did.

1969/1980:

Rosa Luxemburg's reluctance to form an independent revolutionary party followed her slowness to react to changed circumstances. It was a central factor in the belatedness of building a revolutionary party in Germany. In this, however, she was not alone. Lenin was no quicker to break with Kautsky than Rosa. There is no ground to the Stalinist story according to which Lenin was opposed to the revolutionary Left's adherence to the SPD and continuing association with Kautsky. Actually, Rosa Luxemburg made a clearer assessment of Kautsky and Co, and broke with them long before Lenin did.

1959:

For Marxists, in advanced industrial countries, Lenin's original position can serve much less as a guide than Rosa Luxemburg's, notwithstanding her overstatements on the question of spontaneity.

1969/1980:

However, whatever the historical circumstances moulding Rosa's thought regarding organisation, these thoughts showed a great weakness in the German Revolution of 1918-19.

Notes

1 See J V Stalin, *Works*, vol XIII, pp86-104.
2 R Luxemburg, *Reform or Revolution* (Bombay, 1951), pp14-15.
3 R Luxemburg, *Reform*, p15.
4 R Luxemburg, *Reform*, p16.
5 R Luxemburg, *Reform*, p7.
6 *Vorwaerts*, 26 March 1899.
7 R Luxemburg, *Reform*, p52.
8 The mythological king of Corinth who in the lower world was condemned to roll to the top of a hill a huge stone, which constantly rolled back again, making his task never ending.
9 R Luxemburg, *Reform*, pp50-5l.
10 R Luxemburg, *Reform*, p22.
11 R Luxemburg, *Reform*, pp29-30.
12 P Frölich, *Rosa Luxemburg: Her Life and Work* (London, 1940), p84.
13 R Luxemburg, *Ausgewählhte Reden und Schriften* (Berlin, 1955), vol II, p61.
14 R Luxemburg, *Ausgewählhte*, vol II, p64.
15 P Frölich, *Rosa Luxemburg*, p84.
16 R Luxemburg, *Gesammelte Werke* (Berlin), vol III, pp361-362.
17 R Luxemburg, *Gesammelte*, vol III, p366.
18 R Luxemburg, *Gesammelte*, vol III, p366.
19 *Rote Fahne*, 18 November 1918.
20 R Luxemburg, *Ausgewählhte*, vol I, pp211-212.
21 R Luxemburg, *Reform*, pp58-59.
22 *Die Neue Zeit*, 26 April 1902.
23 *Die Neue Zeit*, 14 May 1902.
24 R Luxemburg, *Ausgewählhte*, vol I, pp227-228.
25 R Luxemburg, *Ausgewählhte*, vol I, pp201-202.
26 R Luxemburg, *Ausgewählhte*, vol I, p274.
27 R Luxemburg, *Ausgewählhte*, vol I, p187.
28 R Luxemburg, *Gesammelte*, vol III, p457.
29 R Luxemburg, *Gesammelte*, vol III, p481.
30 *Dokumente und Materialien zur Geschichte der Deutschen Arbeiterbewegung* (Berlin, 1957), vol I, pp280-281.
31 R Luxemburg, *Ausgewählhte*, vol I, pp391-394.
32 R Luxemburg, *Ausgewählhte*, vol I, p270.
33 R Luxemburg, *Ausgewählhte*, vol I, p269.
34 F Engels, 1895 introduction, K Marx, *The Class Struggle in France*.
35 R Luxemburg, *Ausgewählhte*, vol II, p606.
36 *Dokumente*, vol II, pp704-705.
37 R Luxemburg, *Ausgewählhte*, vol I, p104.
38 *Leipziger Volkszeitung*, June 1913, pp26-28.
39 *Die Neue Zeit*, 1904, p491.
40 Rosa Luxemburg's speech to the Foundation Congress of the German Communist Party.
41 *Die Neue Zeit*, 1904, p535.
42 R Luxemburg, *Ausgewählhte*, vol I, pp235-236.
43 V I Lenin, *Works* (Russia), vol VII, pp365-366.
44 V I Lenin, *Works*, vol VI, p21.
45 V I Lenin, *Works*, vol VIII, p37, quoted in R Dunayevskaya, *Marxism and Freedom* (New York, 1958), p182.
46 V I Lenin, *Works*, vol XIII, p85.
47 Actually this pamphlet was translated into many languages without the commentary Lenin considered necessary.

48 It was no accident that the Russian Social Revolutionaries, future enemies of Bolshevism, warmly approved Lenin's conception of party organisation (I Deutscher, *The Prophet Armed*, (London, 1954), p94n).
49 *Dokumente*, vol II, p135.
50 *Dokumente*, vol II, p525.
51 *Dokumente*, vol II, p528.
52 See, for instance, J V Stalin, 'Some Questions Concerning the History of Bolshevism', *Works*, vol XIII, pp86-104; *Dokumente*, vol II, especially the preface; F Oelssner, *Rosa Luxemburg* (Berlin, 1956).
53 V I Lenin, *Works*, vol XI, p330.
54 V I Lenin, *Works*, vol XI, pp173-176.
55 V I Lenin, Letter to Shliapnikov, 27 October 1914.
56 K Marx, *The Communist Manifesto*.
57 Letter to Sorge, 27 September, 1877, *Marx-Engels Correspondence* (London, 1941), pp348-349.
58 *Correspondence*, p399.
59 *Correspondence*, p399.
60 *Przeglad Socialdemokratyczny*, 1908, No 6.
61 *Die Neue Zeit*, 1895-96, p466.
62 V I Lenin, *Selected Works*, vol V, pp307-308.
63 R Luxemburg, *The Russian Revolution* (New York, 1940), p16.
64 R Luxemburg, *The Russian Revolution*, p56.
65 R Luxemburg, *The Russian Revolution*, p5.
66 R Luxemburg, *The Russian Revolution*, pp54-55.
67 R Luxemburg, *The Russian Revolution*, p55.
68 R Luxemburg, *The Russian Revolution*, p18.
69 R Luxemburg, *The Russian Revolution*, P19.
70 R Luxemburg, *The Russian Revolution*, pp20-21.
71 L Trotsky, *Itogy i Perspektivy* (Moscow, 1919), p80.
72 R Luxemburg, *The Russian Revolution*, p23.
73 R Luxemburg, *The Russian Revolution*, p29.
74 Rosa Luxemburg's criticism of the nationalities policy of the Bolsheviks in power was a continuation of her differences with them on this issue over nearly two decades (see the section 'Rosa Luxemburg on the national question').
75 R Luxemburg, *Ausgewählte*, vol II, p606.
76 R Luxemburg, *The Russian Revolution*, p54.
77 R Luxemburg, *The Russian Revolution*, pp45-46.
78 R Luxemburg, *The Russian Revolution*, pp47-48.
79 Actually, what is needed for smooth reproduction is not only that a certain proportionality be kept between the production of Department I and that of Department II in the whole economy, but that the proportionality between the departments be kept also in every branch of the economy. Thus, for instance, the production of clothing machinery (Department I) will need to fit the demand for this kind of machinery in the clothing industry (Department II).
80 These equations, which are algebraic formulations of Marx's analysis in Volume II of *Capital* were formulated by N Bukharin in his *Der Imperialismus und die Akkumulation Des Kapitals* (Berlin, 1925) and we find them very useful for summing up Marx's many arithmetical examples.
81 Before describing Rosa Luxemburg's analysis of reproduction, it must be clear that she did not develop a theory explaining the cyclical movement of boom, crisis and slump. She took it that the periodical cycles are phases of reproduction in capitalist economy, but not the whole of the process. Therefore, she abstracted her analysis from the cycles in order to study the process of reproduction in purity and as a whole. As she writes: '...in spite of the sharp rises and falls in the course of a cycle, in spite of crises, the needs of society are always satisfied more or less, reproduction continues on its complicated course, and productive capacities develop progressively. How can this take place, leaving cycles and crises out of

consideration? Here the real question begins... When we speak of capitalist reproduction in the following exposition, we shall always understand by this term a mean volume of productivity which is an average taken over the various phases of a cycle.' R Luxemburg, *The Accumulation of Capital* (London, 1951), pp36-37.

82 K Marx, *Capital*, vol II, p596.

83 K Marx, *Capital*, vol II, pp598-600.

84 R Luxemburg, *Accumulation*, p122.

85 R Luxemburg, *Accumulation*, p122.

86 W S and E S Woytinsky, *World Population and Production* (New York, 1953), pp415-416.

87 Editor's note: in these examples Cliff ignores decimals when assigning numbers to individual portions of value, so the totals are correct even if the portions do not appear to add up.

88 Rosa Luxemburg's argument against exactly this idea of a higher rate of accumulation in Department I than in Department II (R Luxemburg, *Accumulation*, pp338-339) is absolutely wrong. We have not the space to deal with it here. The reader should consult the source.

89 R Luxemburg, *Accumulation*, pp340-341.

90 R Luxemburg, *Accumulation*, p417.

91 K Marx, *Capital*, vol III, p568.

92 A different 'Marxist' answer to the capitalist dilemma was given by Otto Bauer in his criticism of Rosa Luxemburg's book. Using much more complicated schemes of reproduction than Marx or Rosa Luxemburg, he tried to prove that 'the accumulation of capital adapts itself to the increase of population...the periodic cycle of prosperity, crisis and slump is an empirical expression of the fact that the capitalist apparatus of production automatically overcomes too large or too small accumulation by adapting anew the accumulation of capital to the increase of population' (*Die Neue Zeit*, 1913, p871). And this is said not by a disciple of Malthus, but of Marx, for whom the primary factor should not be population increase but capital accumulation!

93 By the way, the 'third' buyer—not worker nor capitalist consumer—need not necessarily be the non-capitalist producer, but the non-producing state; hence the permanent war economy can, at least for a time, have a similar effect on capitalist prosperity as the non-capitalist economic sphere. (See T Cliff, 'Perspectives of the Permanent War Economy', *Socialist Review*, May 1957.)

94 R Luxemburg, *Accumulation*, p28.

95 In her argument Rosa Luxemburg made a number of side errors which were discovered subsequently by N Bukharin in his *Der Imperialismus und die Akkumulation des Kapitals*, although he did not disprove her central thesis (even though he thought he did). Thus, for instance, Rosa Luxemburg devoted a good deal of attention to purely monetary problems of capital accumulation—whether, for instance, one should include the production of money commodity (gold, silver, etc) in Department I, as Marx did, or, as she herself proposed, should add a third department. It seems that in a number of places in her book Rosa Luxemburg confuses the question: where does the demand come from? with the question: where does the money come from? But as this is of only secondary importance to her main thesis, we shall not deal with it here. Again, while, if we carefully followed Rosa Luxemburg's own reasoning about the schemes of reproduction, we should say that the weight of her argument is that *a portion* of the surplus value in Department II could not be realised under pure capitalism, Rosa Luxemburg herself sums up the argument as if she proved that no realisation of any portion of the surplus value could take place under pure capitalism. This was pointed out by F Sternberg, in *Der Imperialismus* (Berlin, 1926), p102.

96 K Marx, *Capital*, vol I, p649.

Trotsky on substitutionism

International Socialism (first series) 2, Autumn 1960

Twenty years ago Trotsky was assassinated. The best tribute one can pay to this great revolutionary, who so despised all cant, would be a critical study of some of his ideas. We offer the following study of one problem he so brilliantly posed as a very young man, a problem that plagued him for the rest of his life, and that is still with us: the problem of the relation between party and class, and the danger of the former substituting for the latter.

Quite early in his political activity, when only 24 years old, Trotsky prophesied that Lenin's conception of party organisation must lead to a situation in which the party would '*substitute* itself for the working classes', act as proxy in their name and on their behalf, regardless of what the workers thought or wanted.

Lenin's conception would lead to a state of affairs in which 'the organisation of the party substitutes itself for the party as a whole; then the Central Committee substitutes itself for the organisation; and finally the "dictator" substitutes himself for the Central Committe'.[1]

To Lenin's type of centralised party made up of professional revolutionaries, Trotsky counterposed a 'broadly-based party' on the model of the Western European Social Democratic parties. He saw the only guarantee against 'substitutionism'—the term he coined—in the mass party, democratically run and under the control of the proletarian masses.

He wound up his argument with the following plea against uniformity:

> The tasks of the new regime will be so complex that they cannot be solved otherwise than by way of competition between various methods of economic and political construction, by way of long 'disputes', by way of a systematic struggle not only between the socialist and capitalist worlds, but also many trends inside socialism, trends which will inevitably emerge as soon as the proletarian dictatorship poses tens and hundreds of new...problems. No strong 'domineering' organisation...will be able to suppress these trends and controversies... A proletariat capable of exercising its dictatorship over society will not tolerate any dictatorship over itself... The working class...will undoubtedly have in its ranks

> quite a few political invalids...and much ballast of obsolescent ideas, which it will have to jettison. In the epoch of its dictatorship, as now, it will have to cleanse its mind of false theories and bourgeois experience, and to purge its ranks from political phrasemongers and backward-looking revolutionaries... But this intricate task cannot be solved by placing above the proletariat a few well-picked people...or one person invested with the power to liquidate and degrade.[2]

In Trotsky's words about the danger of 'substitutionism' inherent in Lenin's conception of party organisation, and his plea against uniformity, one can see his prophetic genius, his capacity to look ahead, to bring into a unified system every facet of life.

The history of Bolshevism since 1917 seems to have completely vindicated Trotsky's warning of 1904. But Trotsky never returned to it again. In the present article we shall try to find out why he did not, to reveal the roots of 'substitutionism' in particular, and to look at the problem of the relation between the party and the class in general.

The problem of substitutionism

'Substitutionism' is in the tradition of the Russian revolutionary movement. In the 60s and 70s of the 19th century small groups, mere handfuls, of intellectuals pitted themselves against the mighty autocracy, while the mass of peasants in whose name and interests these heroic Narodniks (Populists) acted remained indifferent or even hostile to them.

In the morass of general apathy, before a mass movement of any kind appeared, these mere handfuls of rebellious intellectuals played an important, progressive role. Marx was not the least to accord them the greatest praise and admiration. Thus, for instance, he wrote to his eldest daughter, in the very year in which the People's Will was crushed:

> These are admirable men, without any melodramatic pose, full of simplicity, real heroes. Making an outcry and taking action are two things completely opposite which cannot be reconciled.

'Substitutionism', however, becomes a reactionary, dangerous element when a rising mass movement already exists and the party tries to substitute itself for this. Trotsky was too scientific a thinker to believe that in the conception, right or wrong, of the party about its role and its relations with the class, one can find sufficient guarantee against 'substitutionism' and for real democracy in the workers' political movement.

The objective conditions necessary to avoid it were clearly formulated by Trotsky a few months before he wrote the above quoted work, when he said at the Second Congress of the Russian Social Democratic Workers' Party (London, 1903):

> The rule of the working class was inconceivable until the great mass of them were united in desiring it. Then they would be an overwhelming majority. This would not be the dictatorship of a little band of conspirators or a minority party, but of

> the immense majority in the interests of the immense majority, to prevent counter-revolution. In short, it would represent the victory of true democracy.

This paraphrase of *The Communist Manifesto* is absolutely in harmony with Trotsky's struggle against 'substitutionism'. If the majority rules, there is no place for a minority to act as its proxy.

During the same period Lenin was not less emphatic in saying that any dictatorship of the proletariat when this was a small minority in society must lead to anti-democratic and, in his words, 'reactionary conclusions'.

When Trotsky, putting aside his own words, called for a workers' government as an immediate aim of the revolutionary movement in Russia, Lenin answered sharply:

> That cannot be! It cannot be because a revolutionary dictatorship can endure for a time only if it rests on the enormous majority of the people... The proletariat constitutes a minority... Anyone who attempts to achieve socialism by any other route without passing through the stage of political democracy, will inevitably arrive at the most absurd and reactionary conclusions, both economic and political.[3]

Trotsky's warning against 'substitutionism' and his emphasis on the rule of 'the immense majority in the interests of the immense majority' as the only guarantee against it is indeed a crying contradiction to his call for a workers' government in 1905 and 1917, when the workers were a tiny minority. Trotsky is torn in the contradiction between his consistent, socialist, democratic conception of opposition to any form of 'substitutionism' and his theory of the Permanent Revolution in which the proletarian minority acts as a proxy for all the toilers and as the ruler of society. Alas, this contradiction is not the result of any failure in Trotsky's thinking, of any inconsistency, but is a reflection of actual contradictions in the objective conditions.

The nature of the revolution, including its actual timing, is not dependent on the size of the working class alone, and not even on its level of class consciousness and organisation, but on many mixed and contradictory factors. The factors leading to revolution—economic stresses, wars or other political and social upheavals—are not synchronised with the enlightenment of the proletariat. A whole number of objective circumstances impel the workers to revolution, while the unevenness in consciousness of different sections and groups in the working class can be quite marked. In a backward country, as Tsarist Russia was, where the workers' general cultural level was low, and traditions of organisation and mass self-activity weak, this unevenness was particularly marked. And there the working class as a whole was such a small minority that its rule, the dictatorship of the proletariat, had to be the dictatorship not of the majority but of a tiny minority.

To overcome the actual dilemma facing the revolution in Russia—to avoid minority rule on the one hand, and to avoid the passive abstentionist attitude of the Mensheviks ('the proletariat should not take power so long as it is a minority in society')—Trotsky looked to two main factors: the revolutionary impulse and activity of the Russian workers, and the spread of the revolution to more advanced countries where the proletariat made up the majority of society.

However, what was the fate of 'substitutionism' with the decline of the revolutionary impulse in Russia itself and, not less decisive, with the breaking of the revolutionary struggles in the West on the rocks of capitalism?

Subsititutionism in Russia

While the relation between the party and the class was affected by the level of culture and revolutionary consciousness of the working class, it was also influenced by the specific weight of the working class in society: by the size of the class and its relations with other classes, above all—in Russia—with the peasantry.

Now, if the Russian Revolution was a simon-pure bourgeois revolution—as the Mensheviks argued—or if it was a simon-pure socialist one—as the anarchists and Social Revolutionaries who did not distinguish between workers and peasants argued—the question would have been simple. A relative social homogeneity of the revolutionary classes would have constituted a large enough anvil on which to batter out of existence any trend toward the Marxist Party substituting for the proletariat.

However, the October Revolution was the fusion of two revolutions: that of the socialist working class, the product of mature capitalism, and that of the peasants, the product of the conflict between rising capitalism and the old feudal institutions. As at all times, the peasants were ready enough to expropriate the private property of the large estate owners, but they wanted their own small *private* properties. Whilst they were prepared to revolt against feudalism they were not for that reason in favour of socialism.

Hence it is not surprising that the victorious alliance of workers and peasants in the October Revolution was immediately followed by very strained relations. Once the White armies, and with them the danger of the restoration of landlordism, had been overcome, very little remained of the peasants' loyalty toward the workers. It had been one thing for the peasant to support a government which distributed land, but it was quite another matter when the same government began to requisition his produce to feed the hungry populations in the cities.

The conflict between the working class and the peasantry was expressed from the beginning of the October Revolution in the fact that already in 1918 Lenin was compelled to take refuge in the anti-democratic measure of counting one worker's vote as equal to five peasants' in the elections to the Soviets.

Now the revolution itself changed the relative weight of the proletariat *vis-à-vis* that of the peasantry, to the detriment of the former.

First, the civil war led to a terrible decline in the specific weight of the working class. The working class victory in the revolution led paradoxically to a decline in the size and quality of the working class.

As many of the urban workers had close connections with the villages, considerable numbers of them hurried back to the countryside as soon as the revolution was over, in order to share in the land distribution. This tendency was further encouraged by the food shortage from which, naturally, the towns suffered the most. Moreover, in sharp contrast to the old Tsarist Army, the new Red Army included relatively more industrial workers than peasants. For all these reasons the town population, and particularly the numbers of industrial workers, declined very sharply between 1917 and 1920. The population of Petrograd fell by 57.5 percent, of Moscow by 44.5 percent, of 40 provincial capitals by 33 percent, and of another 50 large towns by 16 percent. The larger the city, the greater was the relative loss in population. How sharp the decline was is further illustrated by the fact that the number of workers in industry fell from 3,000,000 in 1917 to 1,240,000 in 1921-22, a decrease of 58.7 percent. The number of industrial workers thus declined by three fifths. And the productivity of these workers declined even more than their number. (In 1920 the industrial production of Russia was only some 13 percent of that of 1913!)

Of those remaining, the big majority were the most backward workers who were not needed for the different military fronts or for the administration of the State, trade unions and party. The State administration and army naturally drew most of their recruits from that section of the workers with the oldest social tradition, the greatest political experience and highest culture.

The fragmentation of the working class had an even worse effect. The remainder of the working class was forced by the scarcity of food to behave as small, individualist traders rather than as a collective, as a united class. It has been calculated that in 1919-20 the State supplied only 42 percent of the grain consumed by the towns, and an even smaller percentage of other foodstuffs, all the rest being bought on the black market.[4] The sale by workers of furniture and clothing, and also belts and tools from factories where they worked, was quite common.[5] What an atomisation and demoralisation of the industrial working class!

In their mode of living—relying on individual illicit trade—the individual workers were hardly distinguishable from the peasants. As Rudzutak put it to the Second Congress of Trade Unions in January 1919, 'We observe in a large number of industrial centres that the workers, thanks to the contraction of production in the factories, are being absorbed in the peasant mass, and instead of a population of workers we are getting a half-peasant or sometimes a purely peasant population'.[6]

Under such conditions the class base of the Bolshevik Party disintegrated—not because of some mistakes in the policies of Bolshevism, not because of one or another conception of Bolshevism regarding the role of the party and its relation to the class—but because of mightier historical factors. The working class had become declassed.

It is true that in despair, or in desperation, Lenin could say in May 1921, 'Even when the proletariat has to live through a period of being declassed, it can still carry out its task of conquering and retaining power'.[7] But what an extremely 'substitutionist' formulation this is! Declassed working class rule—the Cheshire Cat's smile after the Cat has disappeared!

In the case of the Narodniks, the 'substitutionist' conception was not a primary cause, but a result of the general apathy and stupor of the people which in turn was rooted in objective social conditions. Now again, in the case of Bolshevik 'substitutionism', it did not jump out of Lenin's head, as Minerva out of Zeus's, but was born of the objective conditions of civil war in a peasant country, where a small working class declined in weight, became fragmented and dissolved into the peasant masses.

An analogy might help to clarify the rise of 'substitutionism' after the October Revolution. One must only imagine a mass strike in which after a prolonged period the majority of the workers become tired and demoralised, and only a minority continue to man the picket line, attacked by the boss, and derided and resented by the majority of workers. This tragic situation is repeated again and again on the battleground of the class struggle. In the face of the White Guard, with the knowledge that a terrible bloodbath threatened the people if the Bolsheviks gave up the struggle, and with the knowledge of their own isolation, the Bolsheviks did not find a way out. 'Substitutionism', like all fetishisms, was a reflection of social impasse.

Substitutionism in the party

From here it is a short step to the abolition of inner-party democracy, and the establishment of the rule of officialdom within it.

Contrary to Stalinist mythology—as well as that of the Mensheviks and other opponents of the Bolsheviks—the Bolshevik Party had never been a monolithic or totalitarian party. Far from it. Internal democracy had always been of the utmost importance in party life, but for one reason or another this has been glossed over in most of the literature dealing with the subject. It is therefore worthwhile to digress somewhat, and devote a little space to setting out a number of cases which illustrate the degree of inner-party democracy and the lack of monolithism in the history of Bolshevism.

In 1907, after the final defeat of the revolution, the party suffered a crisis over the question of what attitude to take to the elections to the Tsarist Duma. At the Third Conference of the Russian Social Democratic Workers' Party (held in July 1907), in which Bolsheviks as well as Mensheviks were represented, a curious situation arose: all the Bolshevik delegates, with the sole exception of Lenin, voted in favour of boycotting the elections to the Duma; Lenin voted with the Mensheviks.[8] Three years later a plenum of the Central Committee of the Bolsheviks passed a resolution calling for unity with the Mensheviks; again the only dissentient voice was Lenin's.[9]

When the 1914-18 war broke out, not one of the party's branches adopted the revolutionary defeatist position which Lenin advocated,[10] and at a trial of some Bolshevik leaders in 1915, Kamenev and two Bolshevik Duma deputies publicly repudiated Lenin's revolutionary defeatist position in court.[11]

After the February Revolution the large majority of the party leaders were not for a revolutionary Soviet government, but for support of the Coalition Provisional government. The Bolshevik faction had 40 members in the Petrograd Soviet on 2 March 1917, but when the resolution to transfer power to the bourgeois coalition government was put to the vote, only 19 voted against.[12] At a meeting of the Petrograd Committee of the Party (5 March 1917) a resolution for a revolutionary Soviet government received only one vote.[13] *Pravda*, edited by Stalin at that time, had a position which can in no way be called revolutionary. It decisively declared its support for the Provisional Government 'insofar as it struggles against reaction or counter-revolution'.[14]

Again, when Lenin came to Russia on 3 April 1917 and issued his famous *April Theses*—a light guiding the party to the October Revolution—he was for a time in a small minority in his own party. *Pravda*'s comment on the *April Theses* was that it was 'Lenin's personal opinion', and quite 'unacceptable'.[15] At a meeting of the Petrograd Committee of the Party, held on 8 April 1917, the *Theses* received only two votes, while 13 voted against and one abstained.[16] However, at the Conference of the Party held on 14-22 April, the *Theses* gained a majority: 71 for, 39 against and eight abstentions.[17] The same conference defeated Lenin on another important question, *viz*, whether the party should participate in the proposed Stockholm Conference of the Socialist Parties. Against his views, it decided in favour of full participation.[18]

Again on 14 September Kerensky convened a 'Democratic Conference' and Lenin spoke strongly in favour of boycotting it. The Central Committee supported him by nine votes to eight, but as the vote was so nearly equal the final decision was left to the party conference, which was to be constituted out of the Bolshevik faction in the 'Democratic Conference'. This meeting decided by 77 votes to 50 not to boycott it.[19]

When the most important question of all, the question of the October insurrection, was the order of the day, the leadership again was found to be sharply divided: a strong faction, led by Zinoviev, Kamenev, Rykov, Piatakov, Miliutin and Nogin, opposed the uprising. Nevertheless, when the Political Bureau was elected by the Central Committee, neither Zinoviev nor Kamenev were excluded.

After taking power, the differences in the party leadership continued to be as sharp as before. A few days after the revolution a number of party leaders came out with a demand for a coalition with other socialist parties. Those insisting on this included Rykov, the People's Commissar of the Interior; Miliutin, the People's Commissar of Industry and Trade; Lunacharsky, the Commissar of Labour; Kamenev, the President of the Republic; and Zinoviev. They went as far as resigning from the government, thus compelling Lenin and his supporters to open negotiations with the other parties. (The negotiations broke down because the Mensheviks insisted on the exclusion of Lenin and Trotsky from the coalition government.)

Again, on the question of holding or postponing the elections to the Constituent Assembly (in December 1917), Lenin found himself in a minority in the Central Committee, and the elections were held against his advice.[20] A little later he was again defeated on the question of the peace negotiations with Germany at Brest-Litovsk. He was for an immediate peace. But at a meeting of the Central Committee and active workers, held on 21 January 1918, his motion received only 15 votes against Bukharin's motion for 'revolutionary war', which received 32 votes, and Trotsky's, for 'neither peace nor war', which received 16.[21] At a session of the Central Committee next day Lenin was again defeated. But at last he succeeded, under the pressure of events, in convincing the majority of members of the Central Committee of his point of view, and at its session on 24 February his motion for peace gained seven votes, while four voted against and another four abstained.[22]

However, inner-party democracy dwindled under the pressure of the objective circumstances referred to above. Isolated, the party became frightened to think aloud, to voice disagreements. It was as if they were in a small rickety boat in the midst of rapids. The atmosphere of free discussion necessarily died.

The breaches of inner-party democracy became worse and worse. Thus, K K Yurenev, for example, spoke at the Ninth Congress (April 1920) of the methods used by the Central Committee to suppress criticism, including the virtual exile of the critics: 'One goes to Christiana, another sent to the Urals, a third to Siberia'.[23] He said that in its attitude toward the Party the Central Committee had become 'not accountable Ministry, but unaccountable government'. At the same Congress V N Maximovsky counterposed 'democratic centralism' to the 'bureaucratic centralism' for which the Centre was responsible. 'It is said', he commented, 'that fish begin to rot from the head. The party begins to suffer at the top from the influence of bureaucratic centralism'.[24] And Sapronov declared, 'However much you talk about electoral rights, about the dictatorship of the proletariat, or the yearning of the Central Committee for the party dictatorship, in fact this leads to the dictatorship of the party bureaucracy'.[25]

At the Eleventh Congress, Riazanov said:

> Our Central Committee is altogether a special institution. It is said that the English parliament is omnipotent: it is only unable to change a man into a woman. Our Central Committee is more powerful: it has already changed more than one very revolutionary man into an old lady, and the number of these old ladies has increased incredibly.[26]

He further accused it of intervening in all aspects of party life. V Kosior gave many examples of local leaders both of the party and of the trade unions being removed by decisions of the Political Bureau or the Orgbureau:

> Many workers are leaving the party. How to explain this? This, dear comrades, is to be explained by the strong hand regime, which has nothing in common with real party discipline and which is cultivated among us. Our party carries wood, sweeps the streets and even votes, but decides no questions. But the not very healthy proletariat finds itself in these surroundings, and cannot stand it.[27]

At the Twelfth Congress Preobrazhensky complained that 30 percent of the secretaries of the gubernia party committees were 'recommended' for the positions by the Central Committee of the party, thus violating the principle of election of all party officials.[28] From here it was but a step to the supreme rule of the General Secretary.

One can say without hesitation that the substitution of a ruling working class for a capitalist class—where capitalism was in its infancy and where the majority of the people were small capitalists (peasants)—was the cause of the substitution of the Marxist party for the working class, and that this led to the substitution of the officialdom for the party, and finally to the individual dictatorship of the General Secretary.

Marx and Engels dealt more than once with the question of what would happen if the working class took power before the historical prerequisites for the substitution of capitalist relations of production by socialist ones were present. They concluded that in such an event the working class would blaze a path for developing capitalism. Engels wrote:

> The worst thing that can befall a leader of an extreme party is to be compelled to take over a government in an epoch when the movement is not yet ripe for the domination of the class which he represents and for the realisation of the measures which that domination would imply…he necessarily finds himself in a dilemma. What he *can* do is in contrast to all his actions as hitherto practised, to all his principles and to the present interests of his party, what he *ought* to do cannot be achieved. In a word he is compelled to represent not his party nor his class, but the class for whom conditions are ripe for domination. In the interests of the movement itself, he is compelled to defend the interests of an alien class, and to feed his own class with phrases and promises, with the assertion that the interests of that alien class are their own interests. Whoever puts himself in this awkward position is irrevocably lost.[29]

Only the expansion of the revolution could have spared Bolshevism from this tragic fate. And on this probability Bolshevism hinged its fate. Only abstentionists and cowards could advise the Bolsheviks not to go to the limit of the revolutionary potentialities of the Russian proletariat for fear of finding themselves at the end of the cul-de-sac. Revolutionary dynamism and international perspectives beat in the heart of Bolshevism.

The inherent danger of substitutionism

However, if the State built by the Bolshevik Party reflected not only the will of the party but of the total social reality in which the Bolsheviks in power found themselves, one should not draw the conclusion that there was no causal connection at all between Bolshevik centralism based on hierarchy of professional revolutionaries and the Stalinism of the future. Let us look at this question somewhat more closely.

The fact that a revolutionary party is at all needed for the socialist revolution shows that there is an unevenness in the level of culture and consciousness of different sections and groups of workers. If the working class were ideologically a homogeneous class there would not have been any need for leadership. Alas, the revolution would not wait until all the masses had reached a certain intellectual level, or level of class consciousness. Oppressed by capitalism, materially as well as spiritually, different sections of the workers show different levels of class independence. If not for this difference in consciousness among different sections of the working class, the capitalist class in the advanced countries would hardly find any social basis for itself. Under such conditions the class struggle would be the smoothest act of gradual progress. There would indeed scarcely be any class struggle to speak of: instead of which workers face the antagonism of other workers—the threat of strike-breakers (workers), and policemen and soldiers (workers in uniform). If the working class were homogeneous there would not be the need for a workers' state either: after the revolution the power of coercion would be unnecessary. Alas, the revolution has nothing in common with such anarchist-liberal daydreaming. Working-class discipline presumes, under capitalism and immediately after the proletarian revolution, not only the existence of more advanced and less advanced workers, ie the existence of leadership, but also the combination of conviction and coercion—the working class cannot free itself by a stroke from the birthmarks of capitalist barbarism.

Under capitalism discipline confronts the worker as an external coercive power, as the power which capital has over him. Under socialism discipline will be the result of consciousness. It will become the habit of a free people. In the transition period it will be the outcome of the unity of the two elements—consciousness and coercion. Collective ownership of the means of production by the workers, ie the ownership by the workers' state of the means of production, will be the basis for the conscious element in labour discipline. At the same time the working class as a collective, through its institutions—soviets, trade unions, etc—will appear as a coercive power as regards the disciplining of the individual workers in production.

This conflict between the individual and the collective, the necessity of uniting conviction with its ugly opposite, coercion, the compulsion on the working class to use barbaric methods remaining from capitalism to fight capitalist barbarism, is but another affirmation that the workers are not liberated spiritually under capitalism and would take a whole historical period to grow to full human stature. Agreeing with the anarchists that the state, even the workers' state, is an ugly offspring of class society, and that real human history will start only by having a really consistent workers' state, it is nonetheless only on this basis that the state will ultimately wither away.

The fact that the working class needs a party or parties is in itself a proof of the cleavages in the working class. The more backward culturally, the weaker the organisation and self-administration of the workers generally, the greater will be the intellectual cleavage between the class and its Marxist party. From this unevenness in the working class flows the great danger of an autonomous development of the party and its machine till it becomes, instead of the servant of the class, its master. This unevenness is a main source of the danger of 'substitutionism'.

The history of Bolshevism prior to the revolution is eloquent with Lenin's struggle against this danger. How often he appealed to the mass of the workers—especially in the stormy months of 1917—against the vacillating, compromising party leadership and its machine. As Trotsky so correctly summed up the inter-relation between Lenin, the masses and the party machine:

> Lenin was strong not only because he understood the laws of the class struggle but also because his ear was faultlessly attuned to the stirrings of the masses in motion. He represented not so much the party machine as the vanguard of the proletariat. He was definitely convinced that thousands from amongst those workers who had borne the brunt of supporting the underground party would now support him. The masses at the moment were more revolutionary than the party, and the party more revolutionary than its machine. As early as March the actual attitude of the workers and soldiers had in many cases become stormily apparent, and it was widely at variance with the instructions issued by all the parties, including the Bolshevik… On the other hand, the authority of the party machine, like its conservatism, was only in the making at that time. Lenin exerted influence not so much as an individual but because he embodied the influence of the class on the party and of the party on its machine.[30]

Men make history, and if these men organised in a party have a greater impact on history than their relative number warrants, nevertheless they alone do not make history and, for better or worse, they alone are not the cause of their greater specific weight, neither of the general history of the class nor even of themselves in this class. In the final analysis, the only weapons to fight the 'substitutionism' of the revolutionary party for the class, and hence the transformation of the former into a conservative force, is the activity of the class itself, and its pressure not only against its social enemy, but also against its own agent, its party.

This is not the place to point out how far Trotsky in practice went in turning a necessity into a virtue, to what extremes of generalisation he turned to justify anti-democratic, anti-working-class, 'substitutionist' practices.

It is enough to mention his arguments in 1921 for the 'militarisation of labour'—compulsory labour imposed by the state. The trade unions, he said, should be statified. We need 'a new type of trade unionist, the energetic and imaginative economic organiser who will approach economic issues not from the angle of distribution and consumption but from that of expanding production, who will view them not with the eyes of somebody accustomed to confront the Soviet government with demands and to bargain, but with the eyes of the true economic organiser'.[31] What about the defence of workers from the state, even from the workers' state? Can the trade unions neglect this? Trotsky did not answer the question, did not even pose it. 'Militarisation', he said at the Ninth Congress:

> …is unthinkable without the militarisation of the trade unions as such, without the establishment of a regime in which every worker feels himself a soldier of labour, who cannot dispose of himself freely; if the order is given to transfer him, he must carry it out; if he does not carry it out, he will be a deserter who is punished. Who looks after this? The trade union. It creates the new regime. This is the militarisation of the working class.[32]

To cap his 'substitutionist' attitude, Trotsky went as far as to say in 1924:

> None of us desires or is able to dispute the will of the party. The party in the last analysis is always right, because the party is the single historical instrument given

to the proletariat for the solution of its basic problems. I have already said that in front of one's own party nothing could be easier than to acknowledge a mistake, nothing easier than to say: 'All my criticisms, my statements, my warnings, my protests—the whole thing was simply a mistake.' I cannot say that, however, comrades, because I do not think it. I know that one must not be right *against* the party. One call be right only with the party, and through the party, for history has no other road for being in the right. The English have a saying: 'My country—right or wrong.' With far more historical justification we may say: my party—in certain concrete cases—right or wrong... And if the party adopts a decision which one or another of us thinks unjust, he will say: just or unjust it is my party, and I shall support the consequences of the decision to the end.[33]

Substitutionism today

As a point of departure for an evaluation of the role of the revolutionary party in its relation to the working class, we cannot but return to *The Communist Manifesto's* statement:

> All previous historical movements were movements of minorities or in the interests of minorities. The proletarian movement is the self-conscious independent movement of the immense majority, in the interests of the immense majority.

From the much higher cultural level of the workers in the industrial countries than in Russia, their greater self-reliance and organisational habits, and the relatively greater social homogeneity of the mass of the toilers in these countries (not engulfed by hordes of peasants) one may deduce that prior to the revolution, during it and after its victory, the unevenness in consciousness of the masses will be much smaller than it was in Russia, although it will not have disappeared completely.

From this a number of conclusions may be drawn.

First, about the size of the revolutionary party as compared with that of the working class as a whole. In October 1906 the Russian Social Democratic Workers' Party (including both Bolshevik and Menshevik factions) numbered 70,000. At the same time the Jewish Bund numbered 33,000, the Polish Social Democrats 28,000 and the Lettish Social Democrats 13,000. Altogether then, the *illegal* Socialist parties numbered 144,000.[34] In August 1917 the Bolshevik Party had 200,000 members. On the average, in 25 towns 5.4 percent of the industrial workers were members of the Bolshevik Party.[35] If the proportion of party members among the working class were the same in the advanced countries as it was in 1917, or 1905, in Russia, the party would have to have millions of members.

Because the unevenness in consciousness and culture is smaller in the advanced countries than it was in Russia, the relative size of the party should be even larger than it was in Russia. (The legality of the workers' parties also contributes to this.) Anyone who draws the opposite conclusion from the *actual* size of the reformist parties does not understand the real role of the masses in the revolutionary struggle. The reformist party is in the main an apparatus for attracting votes in parliamentary and other elections. Hence it does not need a really active mass membership. On the whole the supporters of such a party do not find it necessary to join it actively or to read its press. Active support of masses for a revolutionary party must lead to a comparatively much greater number of workers joining it.

From this it is clear that little groups cannot in any way substitute for the mass revolutionary party, not to say for the mass of the working class.[36]

Now, what about the relation between the revolutionary party and the class?

Every party, whether reformist or revolutionary, whether conservative or liberal, aims to get support in order to lead towards one aim or another. The revolutionary workers' party also aims to lead. But here the similarity stops. The methods by which this leadership is established and the nature of the leadership are totally different.

One can visualise three kinds of leadership that for lack of better names we shall call those of the teacher, the foreman and the companion in struggle. The first kind of leadership shown by small sects is 'blackboard socialism' (in Britain an extreme example of this sort is the SPGB) in which didactic methods take the place of participation in struggle. The second kind, with foreman-worker or officer-soldier relations, characterises all bureaucratic reformist and Stalinist parties: the leadership sits in a caucus and decides what they will tell the workers to do, without the workers actively participating. What characterises both these kinds of leadership is the fact that directives go only one way: the leaders conduct a monologue with the masses.

The third kind of leadership is analogous to that between a strike committee and the workers on strike, or a shop steward and his mates. The revolutionary party must conduct a dialogue with the workers outside it.[37] The party, in consequence, should not invent tactics out of thin air, but put as its first duty to *learn* from the experience of the mass movement and then generalise from it. The great events of working-class history have shown the correctness of this emphasis beyond all measure of doubt. The workers of Paris in 1871 established a new form of state—a state without a standing army and bureaucracy, where all officials received the average worker's salary, with the right of recall of all officials, etc, *before* Marx began to generalise about the nature and structure of a workers' state. Again the workers of Petrograd in 1905 established a Soviet independently of the Bolshevik Party, actually in opposition to the local Bolshevik leadership, and in the face of at least suspicion, if not animosity, on the part of Lenin himself. Therefore one cannot but agree with Rosa Luxemburg when she wrote in 1904:

> The main characteristics of the tactics of struggle of Social Democracy are not 'invented', but are the result of a continuous series of great creative acts of elementary class struggle. Here also the unconscious precedes the conscious, the logic of the objective historical process comes before the subjective logic of its bearer.[38]

The role of Marxists is to generalise the living, evolving experience of the class struggle, to give a conscious expression to the instinctive drive of the working class to reorganise society on a socialist basis.

Because the working class is far from being monolithic, and because the path to socialism is uncharted, wide differences of strategy and tactics can and should exist in the revolutionary party. The alternative is the bureaucratised party or the sect with its 'leader'. Here one cannot but regret Trotsky's sweeping statement that 'any serious factional fight in a party is always in the final analysis a reflection of the class struggle'.[39] This verges on a vulgar materialist interpretation of human thought as growing directly out of material conditions! What class pressures separated Lenin from Luxemburg, or Trotsky from Lenin (1903-17), or what change in class pressures can one see in Plekhanov's zigzags: with Lenin in 1903, against him in 1903, against him in 1905, with him again (and at last breaking, it is true, with Lenin and with the revolutionary movement and joining the class enemy)? Can the differences in the theory of imperialism between Lenin and Luxemburg be derived from an analysis of their position in class society? Scientific socialism must live and thrive on controversy. And scientists who start off with the same basic assumptions, and then use the same method of analysis, do differ in all fields of research.

In order that the party should be able to conduct a dialogue with the masses, it is necessary not only that the party have confidence in the tremendous abilities of the working class in action, but also that the party understand correctly the situation in the country and the conditions of the working class, materially and morally. Any self-deceit on its part must cut short the dialogue and turn it into a boring monologue.

The party has to be subordinated to the whole. And so the internal regime in the revolutionary party must be subordinated to the relation between the party and the class. The managers of factories can discuss their business in secret and then put before the workers a *fait accompli*. The revolutionary party that seeks to overthrow capitalism cannot accept the notion of a discussion on policies inside the party without the participation of the mass of the workers—policies which are then brought 'unanimously' ready-made to the class. Since the revolutionary party cannot have interests apart from the class, all the party's issues of policy are those of the class, and they should therefore be thrashed out in the open, in its presence. The freedom of discussion which exists in the factory meeting, which aims at unity of action after decisions are taken, should apply to the revolutionary party. This means that all discussions on basic issues of policy should be discussed in the light of day: in the open press. Let the mass of the workers take part in the discussion, put pressure on the party, its apparatus and leadership.[40]

Above all, the revolutionary party should follow the guide of the *Communist Manifesto* when it says:

> In what relation do the Communists stand to the proletarians as a whole? The Communists do not form a separate party opposed to other working class parties. They have no interests separate and apart from the proletariat as a whole. They do not set up any sectarian principles of their own, by which to shape and mould the

> proletarian movement. The Communists are distinguished from other working-class parties by this only:
> (1) In the national struggles of the proletarians of the different countries, they point out and bring to the front the common interests of the entire proletariat, independently of all nationality.
> (2) In the various stages of development which the struggle of the working class against the bourgeoisie has to pass through, they always and everywhere represent the interests of the movement as a whole.
>
> The Communists, therefore, are on the one hand, practically, the most advanced and resolute section of the working-class parties of every country, that section which pushes forward all others: on the other hand, theoretically, they have over the great mass of the proletariat the advantage of clearly understanding the line of march, the conditions, and the ultimate general results of the proletarian movement.

The *whole* of the working class will have to mix its level of consciousness and organisation through a prolonged struggle, including a struggle of ideas. As Marx said to revolutionaries who flattered the German workers in his time, 'While we say to the workers: you have 15 or 20 years of bourgeois and national wars to go through, not merely to alter conditions but to alter yourselves and make yourselves fit to take political power, you tell them on the contrary that they must take over political power at once or abandon all hope.'

Notes

1 N Trotsky, *Nashi Politicheskye Zadachi* (Geneva, 1904), p54.
2 N Trotsky, *Nashi Politicheskye*, p105, quoted in I Deutscher, *The Prophet Armed* (London, 1954), pp92-93.
3 V I Lenin, *Sochinenya*, ix, p14.
4 L Kritsman, *Geroicheskii Period Velikoi Russkoi Revolutsii*, (Moscow, 1924), pp133-136.
5 *Chetvertye Vserossiikii Sezd Professionalnykh Soyuzov*, vol 1 (1921), pp66, 119.
6 *Vtoroi Vserossiikii Sezd Professionalnykh Soyuzou* (1921), p138.
7 V I Lenin, *Sochinenya*, xxvi, p394.
8 *VKP, (b) v Rezoliutsiakh*, 4th edn, vol 1, p126.
9 *VKP, (b) v Rezoliutsiakh*, 6th edn, vol 1, pp154-160.
10 L Trotsky, *History of the Russian Revolution* (London, 1932), vol 1, p59.
11 L Trotsky, *History*; V I Lenin, *Sochinenya*, xxi, p432.
12 A Shliapnikov, *The Year Seventeen* (Moscow, 1924), vol 1, p197.
13 A S Bubnov and others, *VPK (b)*, (Moscow-Leningrad, 1931), p113.
14 *Pravda*, 15 March 1917, quoted in L Trotsky, *History*, p305.
15 *Pravda*, 8 April 1917.
16 A S Bubnov and others, *VPK (b)*, p114.
17 *VKP (b) v Rezoliutsiakh*, 4th edn, vol 1, p258.
18 V I Lenin, *Sochinenya*, 3rd edn, xx, p652.
19 V I Lenin, *Sochinenya*, 3rd edn, xx, p526.
20 L Trotsky, *Stalin* (London, 1947), pp341-342.
21 A S Bubnov and others, *VPK (b)*, p511.
22 A S Bubnov and others, *VPK (b)*, p512.
23 9 *Sezd* RKP *(b)*, p52.
24 9 *Sezd* RKP *(b)*, pp62-63.
25 9 *Sezd* RKP *(b)*, pp56-57.

26 *11 Sezd* RKP *(b)*, p83.
27 *11 Sezd* RKP *(b)*, p134.
28 *12 Sezd* RKP *(b)*, p133.
29 F Engels, *The Peasant War in Germany* (London, 1927), pp135-136.
30 L Trotsky, *Stalin*, p204. It is sad to point out that when Trotsky dealt with the question of the dangers of bureaucratic conservatism in the Trotskyist organisations he pooh-poohed the idea, taking flight in a simplicist materialist interpretation of bureaucratism When J P Cannon, the American Trotskyist leader, was accused of bureaucratic conservatism, Trotsky said that the accusation was 'a bare psychological abstraction in so far as no specific social interests are shown underlying this "conservatism".' (L Trotsky, *In Defense of Marxism* (New York, 1942), p81.) What 'special social interests' were underlying the 'committee men' of pre-1917, of which Stalin was the archetype? This Trotsky did not try to show—quite rightly—in his last work, *Stalin*, whose central theme is the conservative, anti-democratic nature of the 'committee men'.
31 L Trotsky quoted in I Deutscher, *Soviet Trade Unions* (London, 1950), p42.
32 *9 Sezd* RKP *(b)*, p101.
33 *13 Sezd* RKP *(b)*, ppl65-166. Trotsky's and Lenin's attitude to the Kronstadt rebellion is often quoted by Mensheviks, anarchists and also some other left critics of Trotsky and Lenin as an example of bureaucratic oppression. Actually the main aspect of Kronstadt was a peasant and semi-peasant rebellion against the towns. Hence all the inner-party oppositions—including the Workers' Opposition of Shliapnikov and Kollontai—took an active part in its suppression, and in its footsteps came the policy of concessions to petty capitalism, to the peasantry—the NEP. However, the question of Kronstadt as well as the different opposition groups which existed prior to Trotsky's going into opposition and which in 1923 joined him under his leadership is a fascinating study which deserves a separate study.
34 V I Lenin, *Sochinenya*, x, p483.
35 *6 Sezd* RKP (b), (Moscow, 1958), p390.
36 Nobody in Russia doubted that Trotsky's group alone—the Mezhrayonka—which in August 1917 had some 4,000 members was much too small to be able seriously to affect the march of events. Similarly one can understand Trotsky when in 1921 be referred to the Communist Workers' Party of Germany (KAPD) as being slight: 'no more than 30,000-40,000' members (L Trotsky, *The First Five Years of the Communist International* (London, 1953), vol 2, p26).
37 Rosa Luxemburg put it thus: 'Of course through the theoretical analysis of the social conditions of struggle, Social Democracy has introduced the element of consciousness into the proletarian class struggle to an unprecedented degree; it gave the class struggle its clarity of aim it created, for the first time a permanent mass workers' organisation, and thus built a firm backbone for the class struggle. However, it would he catastrophically wrong for us to assume that from now on all the historical initiative of the people has passed to the hands of the Social Democratic organisation alone, and that the unorganised mass of the proletariat has turned into a formless filing, into the deadweight of history. On the contrary, the popular masses continue to be the living matter of world history, even in the presence of Social Democracy; and only if there is blood circulation between the organised nucleus and the popular masses, only if one heartbeat vitalises the two, can Social Democracy prove that is it capable of great historical deeds.' (*Leipziger Volkszeitung*, June 1913, pp26-28.)
38 *Die Neue Zeit*, 1904, p491.
39 L Trotsky, *In Defense of Marxism* (New York, 1942), p60.
40 Some cases of secrecy are justified and every worker will understand this. Just as factory meetings can he closed to the capitalists and their newspapermen and other agents, so there are moments in the life of a revolutionary party which have to be kept secret. But in all cases the party should be able to justify this to the workers and convince them that no basic decisions of policy are being hidden from them.

Engels

Talk given at Marxism 1996 conference

I'll start by saying that Engels said about himself that he was the second fiddle to Marx. To be honest with you, to be second fiddle to Marx is quite an achievement. Even to be fiddle 150 to Marx is an achievement! But I'll argue that in fact Frederick Engels underestimated his contribution. In a way, he was very modest about himself. He was more than a second fiddle to Marx, and I will argue that he made a massive contribution, which added greatly to Marxism, and that he did this often *independently* of Marx and *before* Marx.

There is a simple way to test this out. Go through the collected works of Marx and Engels, and find out when the concept of the centrality of the working class first appeared in their writings. Was it Marx or someone else who first made this point? It was Engels, in a book he wrote in Paris in 1844 with the title *The Condition of the Working Class* [*in England in 1844*]. This book is a fantastic introduction to the role of the working class, not only in history, but in the future of society.

What is important for us to understand is that ideas such as are expressed in this book do not develop in libraries. You must be dreaming if you think that great ideas are created there. The truth of the matter is that, as Marx wrote in *The Communist Manifesto*, Communists generalise the historical and international experience of the working class. That means you have to develop ideas from this experience of the class.

Here is an example of how the process works. In *The Communist Manifesto* of 1848, ideas about what will happen after the socialist revolution are very vague. It talks about the dictatorship of the proletariat, but it does not tell you what the dictatorship of the proletariat will look like. Then, in 1871, Marx writes another little book in which he says that under the dictatorship of the proletariat there will be no bureaucracy, no standing army, that all officials will be elected and will all be subject to the right of recall, that they will earn the wage of the average worker, etc. You might say to yourself, 'This shows that Marx has been working very hard in the British Museum. In 1848 he said nothing like this, but in 1871 he does!' Not at all. His views in 1871 were shaped by the Paris Commune of that year, which was a fact of life. The workers of Paris created their Commune without bureaucracy, without a standing army, and so on.

Returning to Engels' discovery of the centrality of the working class—in this, Engels had an advantage over Marx. The advantage was that he lived in Britain before Marx came here, and it was here that the first working class mass movement in the world—the Chartist movement—appeared. You do not study this at school, of course. What you are taught is that revolution is foreign to Britain. It is the Russians that kill Tsars. It is the French that guillotine kings. Don't mention Charles I! Revolution is supposed to be a foreign phenomenon, and therefore the Chartist experience is not mentioned.

But it was in Britain, in 1842, that the first general strike in history happened and, being able to witness it first hand, Engels was tremendously impressed. For example, one of the exciting things about the strike of 1842 was the idea of the flying picket. You may think that we invented it recently, or our generation invented it in the 1970s perhaps. Not at all. It was invented in 1842. They went from one factory to another. They called it turning the factory over, and they turned over industry across the land. It was a fantastic achievement at the time. So Engels' book, *The Condition of the Working Class*, cannot be explained unless you remember that Engels knew the Chartists in Manchester, which was the centre of the 1842 general strike. But there is more to it than his simply being a witness to events.

When you look at the book he wrote you see some fantastic new ideas, things which today we take for granted. It is much easier to draw conclusions long after the events. You have to imagine that you were living in the 1830s or 1840s. Would you have had the same insights as Engels? Bearing this in mind, it becomes clear just what a magnificent book *The Condition of the Working Class* is.

First of all, you should remember that Engels was only 23 years old when he wrote it. And the important thing about it is not so much the descriptions of working class life, though these are very, very interesting. When he writes about working class life he does not adopt the same style as Charles Dickens, along the lines of, 'Oh, the poor devils! Workers are suffering. Please, sir, can I have some more?' No—Engels' style is exactly the opposite. There is fantastic optimism in it, and the workers appear, not as the victims of history, but as the subject of history, as the people who make history. I will give you a quote from *The Condition of the Working Class* to illustrate this:

> The war of the poor against the rich, now carried on in detail and indirectly, will become direct and universal. It is too late for the peaceful solution. Soon a slight impulse will suffice to set the avalanche in motion. Then indeed will the war cry resound throughout the land: 'War on the palaces, peace to the cottages.' But then it will be too late for the rich to beware.

Engels also recognised the importance of trade unions. Many people think today that the trade unions are simply workers' organisations which try to improve conditions. Now, under Blair's influence, it may seem even worse—that unions are workers' organisations that sell out the workers to the employers. The union leaders might not talk openly like that, but in their hands unions are for compromise, compromise, compromise. Engels saw it very differently, because even though it was only at the beginning of trade unionism he could see their potential. In 1844 he already spoke in these terms: 'As schools of war the unions are unexcelled.' For him the unions were schools of war, not schools for compromise. The aim was not to achieve some little gain and stop there, because in a war there is a very simple rule—one side or another wins. The unions, in Engels' view, are a weapon of war. Lenin, many years afterwards, used the phrase, 'Unions are schools of communism.'

Remember that Engels was writing in these terms before he met Marx. To say that Engels recognised the centrality of the working class before Marx is not a criticism of Marx at all. After all, where was Marx living at the time? Has anyone had the good luck to visit his home town of Trier recently? The largest workplace there is probably Marx's house! In contrast to Marx, Engels was in Britain, which at that time was the workshop of the world, and Manchester was the centre of the industrial revolution. So it is absolutely natural that this idea came first from Engels.

Another point about ideas is that you cannot patent them. You cannot say who was the first one, the originator of a great idea, because ideas are like a river and a river is formed from lots of streams. Engels is one of the streams contributing to Marxism. Therefore I don't like the idea of speaking of him as secondary to Marx, because then he is not seen as an independent stream contributing to the overall Marxist movement. But I am happy, by the way, to call ourselves Marxists, because it is much easier to pronounce than Engelsists!

There is sometimes a difference between the work of Marx and Engels, though. If you compare the two men's writings you will find that, while Engels was often the pioneer, Marx went much deeper. I am not trying to put it that Marx simply plagiarised from Engels. That is not true at all. Engels was the pioneer because of his experiences in England, but Marx went beyond—he developed things further.

Take, for example, the definition of communism. How did Engels define it? He wrote the following, using a style that is tremendously compressed and extremely simple (much simpler than Marx's):

> Communism: (1) to ensure that the interests of the proletariat prevail as opposed to those of the bourgeoisie. (These are clear class terms.) (2) to do so by the abolition of private property and replacing the same with community of goods. (3) to recognise no means of obtaining these aims other than democratic revolution by force.

Everything you need for a definition of communism is there. It is achieved by revolutionary force, and is democratic by force, not simply some bloody coup by 50 people who take power from another 50 people.

This definition is very important. And when he explains why we need a revolution, he says that we need a revolution for two reasons. First of all, 'not only because the ruling class cannot be overthrown in any other way, but also because the class overthrowing it can only in a revolution succeed in ridding itself of all the muck of ages and become fit to found society anew.' We come from a class society, and we have a fantastic amount of filth in our heads. The prevailing ideas in society are the ideas of the ruling class, and the ideas of the ruling class dominate everything.

It is not only the obvious and open ideas that influence us. It is not difficult to notice that racism is a bad idea, that it is reactionary. Ruling class ideas affect elementary things. I remember an occasion years back when my daughter was aged seven or eight. She would argue with me. I don't remember what the issue was about. Then she said, 'You must be right.' 'Why must I be?' I asked. 'Because you are older than me, therefore you are cleverer than me.' So I said, 'Alright, so I am cleverer than you. You will be cleverer than your child. So people will become more and more stupid!' Now this idea that the old are better than the young and must be obeyed—that is a hierarchy. It comes from the structure of our society. People don't notice it.

Take the idea that there must be rich and poor. It is said, 'Of course there are rich and poor; there have always been rich and poor.' How many working class mothers say to their children, 'Your father is a worker, your grandfather was a worker, you will be a worker, your children will be workers. There are always rich and poor'? And the conclusion is nothing can be done about it. Somehow the rich must be more talented.

I remember my father used to say to me, 'I can sign my name in nine languages.' That was true. 'But the cheques always bounce.' And then someone who has no abilities can come along and sign a cheque with a cross, but it will pass.

The fact that the prevailing ideas in our society are the ideas of the ruling class means that we cannot get rid of them except through a creative act, the act of revolution. If you think about the revolution as a coup, a tiny minority replacing a tiny minority, with 50 generals being kicked out by another 50 generals at the top, then the masses can remain with the same ideas and the revolution will still happen. But if you speak about the emancipation of the working class being the act of the working class, then we are not fit to bring in the new society until the masses change their ideas. Moses had to take the Israelites for 40 years into the desert to cleanse themselves from the old ideas of the past. Lenin would go on to say that 'in one day of revolution workers learn more than in a century.'

So Engels' idea was that workers need the revolution to get rid of the rubbish in their heads. Only when they fight in the revolution, when they are active in the revolution, do they find the power of the collective and gain the feeling that they do not need anybody to look up to. When someone asks me to sum up this concept, I mention a little story in John Reed's book *Ten Days that Shook the World*. This shows the impact of the Russian Revolution beautifully. Trotsky, the Chair of the Soviet of Petrograd, came to the building of the Soviet and there were two workers checking entry permits. (At this time there was a danger of counter-revolutionaries throwing hand grenades, and so on.) So Trotsky came there, and he looked in his jacket and said, 'I am very sorry, but I don't have the permit, but I am Trotsky.' And the chap said, 'I don't care who you are.' That is workers' power. You need a revolution for someone to dare to say to John Major at the gates of 10 Downing Street, 'I don't give a damn who you are.' This would mean real workers' power. Therefore the idea of Engels, that the revolution is needed for the workers to change themselves, is a fantastic idea.

A few other things about Engels himself. You should know that although on the title page of *The Communist Manifesto* it says that it is written by Karl Marx and Frederick Engels in reality it was written by Marx. But there was a first draft of the *Manifesto*, and Engels wrote this. It is called *Principles of Communism*. Now it is extremely exciting to compare the two drafts. This is because there are a number of questions that are to be found in *Principles of Communism* that are not in *The Communist Manifesto*.

For example, there is one question dealt with exclusively in *Principles of Communism*: can we reach socialism in one country? This is a question that 80 or 90 years later practically led to a bloodbath between Stalin and Trotsky. Engels asks the question, and he answers that, of course, socialism in one country is not possible, because the world is an international economy, and so on. When you look at *Principles of Communism* it gives you a notion of Engels' contribution. All the ideas in *The Communist Manifesto* are already there, put very clearly, very simply, and in not as grand a style. When you look at Marx, you have a sense that he paints for us a fantastic mural, a fantastic big picture. When you look at Engels, you see a smaller picture. But the same basic ideas are there.

A few other points—the question of permanent revolution. All of us talk about Trotsky the teacher, the founder of the theory of permanent revolution. And this is absolutely true, except that long before Trotsky, in 1848, Engels wrote about the permanent revolution. He wrote first of all that the bourgeoisie is cowardly, and the more you go to the East, the more cowardly it is. The English bourgeoisie dared to cut off the head of the king. The French bourgeoisie was also confident enough to cut off the head of a king.

Why was the bourgeoisie more cowardly the further you went to the East? Because they arrived on the scene later (as industry developed there later). Capitalist production was now organised in the form of big productive units with a powerful working class. The bourgeoisie in the 19th century could now see the shadow of this new class. The bourgeoisie in 17th century Britain did not ask itself, 'If we dare to make a revolution will the proletariat rise against us also?' There was no danger of the proletariat rising. The same was true in the French Revolution. Workers did not go on strike. There were riots about food, riots about prices, but there was no concentration of workers in factories.

Engels writes the following about the bourgeoisie: 'Your reward shall be a brief time of rule. You shall dictate laws, you shall bask in the sun of your own majesty, you shall banquet in the royal halls, and woo the king's daughter, but remember, the hangman's boot is on the threshold.' This is a fantastic way of describing what the permanent revolution is all about. The bourgeoisie in the 19th century has become too cowardly to carry its own revolution against feudalism, because it sees behind its shoulders the threat of the working class.

Another point: what is the full name of Marx's *Capital*? If you haven't read it all, you may have read the front page. Its subtitle is *A Critique of Political Economy*. Now that is very interesting. In 1846 Engels wrote a small pamphlet on 'A Critique of Political Economy'. It is true it is not nearly as grand as *Capital*. Marx spent 26 years writing this work and he did a massive amount of research. Engels' pamphlet is nothing like that. But still many of the basic ideas are there—for example the difference between constant and variable capital, exploitation, surplus value, the theory of rent, and so on.

I hate the notion that people think Engels was simply a nobody who followed Marx. The sad thing about Engels was that he was always so modest when it came to Marx. He was so devoted to Marx. You cannot imagine his devotion. It is proved by the fact that, despite all his instincts, he worked as a factory manager for most of his life. It was not that he liked that role at all. He did not believe in class harmony on the lines of 'leave us together, workers with managers', but personally he was a factory manager. His family owned a factory in Manchester and they told him to run it. He hated it every day, every week, every month. He bloody hated it, and you know why he did it? Only for one reason. He did it for Marx, because Marx never earned anything in his life. His mother was absolutely right when she asked him, 'Why the hell do you write a book about capital—why don't you make some capital?' Marx never made any capital. Engels simply supplied the money for his family, for his children, for years and years. When Marx died, it was not that Engels was happy, but he probably gave a sigh of relief because now he could give up managing the factory. He did not want to work in this bloody horrible job.

Not only was his sacrifice absolutely astonishing, the situation also brought out his modesty. Don't tell it outside this room, but when Marx had an illegitimate child, Engels pretended to be the father in order not to hurt Marx's wife. Today we might see such an action as bloody stupid, as an example of 19th-century backwardness. But that is beside the point.

Now I want to make another thing clear. We always talk about historical materialism as the unique contribution of Marx, and so on. But you find this formulation in Engels:

> History does nothing. It possesses no immense wealth. It wages no battles. It is man, real, living, man, who does all that, who possesses and fights. History is not, as it were, a person apart, using man as a means to achieve its own aims. History is nothing but the activity of man pursuing his aims.

Yet quite often people accuse Engels of being a determinist!

To be honest with you, if I know something is predetermined I would do nothing, because if socialism is inevitable I would sit with folded arms and smile: 'Socialism is coming!' So you don't have to do anything about it. You do not have to open the door to history. It will make its own way. Conversely, if I think that the victory of fascism is inevitable, I tell you straight, I will not sit with folded arms, but I would lie on the bed and hide myself underneath the blanket and cry. In both cases I would do nothing. But Engels formulates it absolutely correctly. History is what human beings are doing. It is not French history that stormed the Bastille, it was men and women who stormed the Bastille on 14 July 1789. It is not history that made the Russian Revolution, it was Russian workers and Russian soldiers who made the Russian Revolution.

This is the meaning of historical materialism: that the subject of history is human beings, but they are acting in conditions independent of themselves. There is no question about it—I speak English. Perhaps you don't believe it, but I did not invent the English language. I distort it perhaps a little bit, but English is independent from me. It is not English speaking to you, it is not the language, some mystical thing that speaks to you. No. It is I speaking to you, in broken English, but it is me, part of the active subject of history. That is very important in Engels' formulation.

Today there are some people who have tried to present a picture of Marx being in opposition to Engels. They do this because they want to separate theory from practice. This has happened at other times. During the battle between Stalin and Trotsky, so long as Stalin was alive, the Communist movement by and large supported Stalin. Every time Stalin had a cold and sneezed, the international movement took out the handkerchief. But once Stalin was exposed after his death the same people decided, 'We cannot identify with Trotsky (even though Trotsky did fight against Stalin). We must find somebody who is not a Stalinist but also not a Trotskyist.' They looked carefully around, and they were lucky. There was a man in an Italian prison and, of course, because he was in prison he could not be very active in the daily battle. This man was Gramsci. So they put up Gramsci as the example to follow, as if to say, 'We are not Stalinists, we are not Trotskyists, we are Gramsciites!'

They have tried to do the same with Marx and Engels. It is very difficult to attack Marx, so instead they look for differences between him and Engels. They notice that Engels was the man of practice and so they say that Marx was not—he was a theorist. They say they agree with Marxism, but in their world Marxism is only abstract. It is Volume Three of *Capital*, about the analysis of the transformation of surplus value into the average rate of profit. They are much more interested in the arithmetic, in the maths, than they are interested in the struggle. This is how they distinguish between Marx and Engels. Yet Marx and Engels were like two peas in a pod. You cannot split them in terms of ideas. Engels fed Marx intellectually, and Marx fed Engels.

Even so, in some areas Engels did make a contribution that stands quite independently from Marx. Take, for example, his *The Origin of the Family, Private Property and the State*, written in 1884 (in other words one year after Marx's death). This is a fantastic contribution, because he tackles a new subject. He uses anthropology—what was known at the time from Morgan and others. He goes to the new area and asks a simple question: what about personal relations? What about the family? What about relations between men and women? Are they eternal?

People often think, 'Yes, things change. For example, slavery existed—now there is no slavery but wage labour instead.' They may see that many other things change. But human interpersonal relations are somehow independent and above change. Human nature is something fixed. Engels made it absolutely plain that human nature is part of the historical condition. To put it in a very simple way—look at the question of greed. I come from Palestine. In Palestine nobody would have left milk outside the house after the milkman came. It is not because the weather is so hot that the milk will turn sour, but because people will steal it. Now in Britain, if someone comes and knocks on the door to deliver a TV and finds there is no one there, he will not leave the TV. Yet the milkman leaves the milk. So you say that it is human nature to steal TVs, but it is not human nature to steal milk. It is nothing to do with human nature—it is the circumstances. Milk is cheap—there is a lot of milk, relatively. There are not a lot of TVs. When Engels came to look at the family, at the relations of the family, he explained, basically, that it is rooted in class society. The condition of what we call the family is private property, and all the transformations in the family are affected by this. He showed this brilliantly in his little book, *The Origin of the Family, Private Property and the State.*

The last couple of points are these. What I have talked about up to now is mainly about Engels' ideas, but you cannot speak about Engels without remembering that Engels was a man of action. You know what he was called in Marx's family? He was called 'The General'. Why was he called that? The answer is that while Marx was writing many marvellous articles (during 1848), and so on, it was Engels who was there on the barricades. It was Engels who was fighting in the army. It was Engels, the man of action. And for the rest of his life he was a man of action.

Quite often, because he was a man of action, he lacked the clear picture that Marx gained through having been a little bit distant from events. I am not saying that theory develops just in direct relation to action. If you have a too direct relationship to the action, you do not have the distance. Marx had that distance; Engels sometimes missed it. For example, during the American Civil War, the fight between the North and the South, Engels thought that the South was going to win. Why did he think this? He put forward a whole number of reasons: the South was better organised (that is true); all the army colleges, like Sandhurst in Britain, were in the South; the best generals were in the South; the best officers were in the South; and there is no question that the South, to begin with, was doing better than the North. Yet Marx said, no question about it, the North is going to win. Why? Because wage labour is more productive than slave labour. Full stop! That is the first thing that you can notice. Therefore New York is more advanced than Texas, and therefore the North is going to win. Not only this. Look at the most oppressed section of society—the black slaves. Where did they run to and where were they running from? Did they head from the North to the South, or from the South to the North? From the South to the North. They preferred the North. So despite all Engels' technical military expertise Marx was right about the war, while Engels was wrong.

What is the point of this discussion? The worst thing in the world is hagiography. To come and say Engels knew everything, that he was always right—

that makes me absolutely sick. It is just as bad to say Marx was absolutely right always. Think about what was written about Lenin in Russian history books under Stalin. Not only was Lenin always right, his father was such a militant, such a progressive! The truth was that his father was knighted by the Tsar. And when Alexander II was assassinated in 1881, what do you think Lenin's father did? He went to church to pray for the soul of the Tsar. But people who go along with hagiography cannot admit to this because saints must be born from saints. If you read the New Testament, what does it tell you? This one begat that one and the last one begat Jesus. Everyone's begatting. Therefore I don't want people to come away from this meeting thinking that Tony Cliff said Engels was marvellous, and that he never made a mistake. That would be rubbish.

One good thing about Engels is that he was very active. This was when Marx was alive and, even more important, after Marx died. Between 1883 and 1895, the 12 years when he was on his own, you read again and again that revolutionaries and trade unionists from all over the world were contacting Engels to ask for advice. And Engels was absolutely generous in giving that advice. He was involved in the French socialist movement, in the German, in the Russian and, of course, in the British—in every mass movement.

He was not only an internationalist in word. He was an internationalist in practice, and you can see it from what he was reading. I have the list of what he read every day. He looked at seven daily papers, three in German, two in English, one Austrian, one Italian, and 19 weeklies in a variety of languages. Now Engels himself knew 29 languages. To read a language is much easier than to speak it. I do not say that Engels knew how to speak 29 languages, but he could read them, because he wanted to know what was happening. He wanted to know what the Russians were doing. There were only a few Russian socialists at the time, and you could not follow the movement unless you read Russian. So he studied Russian specially for that. Now that is an achievement.

His contribution and his devotion to the cause were absolutely astonishing. These can be summed up in Engels' own words. This was his speech at Marx's grave:

> For Marx was above all else a revolutionary. His real mission in life was to contribute in one way or another to the overthrow of capitalist society and of the state institutions which it had brought into being. Fighting was his element.

Now these words are exactly the words that fit Frederick Engels. Engels was a fighter. He was not an abstract scientist. His science was simply a weapon in the fight for socialism. The idea of unity of theory and practice is not, as it is sometimes presented, that someone writes a book—that is theory; and you read the book—that is practice. No. The unity of theory and practice is the unity of theory with the class struggle.

I can never understand the idea that is put forward that the party teaches the class. What the hell is the party? Who teaches the teacher? The dialectic means there is a two-way street. Theory by itself is absolutely useless. Practice by itself is blind. Of course in reality practice precedes theory. Before Newton found the law of gravitation apples used to fall. Afterwards he found the theory to explain how apples fell. Practice always precedes the theory, but theory always fructifies the practice.

Therefore we are not simply practical people. We are not simply theoretical people. We are theoretical-practical. But we believe that the most important thing is the practice. Judge our activity in terms of its practical results, both immediately and in the long term. Practice is the judgement of us. Don't support us because you like us. Put us to the test. Put yourself to the test, because the emancipation of the working class is the act of the working class. In practice you have to provide effective practice in the Unison strike in Sheffield libraries, or in other struggles in Britain and elsewhere. Theories are no use at all except in relation to the class struggle.

I will end with a very good story from Heinrich Heine. Heine was a poet and he wrote a little piece called 'The Dream of Professor Marx'. By the way, you should know that it is not Karl Marx that he is referring to, because when Heine wrote it he did not know that there was someone called Karl Marx, and anyway, the latter was still in his shorts. The story is that Professor Marx dreamed about a garden, and in the garden he sees beds. And in these beds it is not flowers that are growing but quotations. And you take the quotations from one bed and put them into another. This was the dream of Professor Marx.

Now that was not the dream of Frederick Engels or Karl Marx. Their dream was not that theory led to theory, theory led to theory, theory encouraged praxis (by the way, that is a very good word because you can impress somebody with it). No, that is a lot of rubbish. The issue is how theory can be related to the struggle in the unions at present; how it relates to the struggle against fascism at present; how it relates to the struggle against unemployment at present; how it relates to war in Chechnya at present. In other words, Marxism is always a guide to action, and above all Engels was a practical man.

Revolutions and the international

Belgium: strike to revolution?

International Socialism (first series) 4, Spring 1961

Since 1886 the Belgian working class has been involved in eight general strikes. We should be hard put to find a better laboratory to study the place of the general strike in the proletarian class struggle, its potentialities and limitations, and the effect of other social and political factors on its development and outcome. The present article tries to help this study.

It will deal, even if sketchily, with three problems:

(1) The economic background to the recent general strike.

(2) The historic roots of Belgium's tradition of general strikes.

(3) The relation between the general strike and the socialist revolution.

The economic background of the recent general strike

The Liège Socialist Party paper, *Le Monde du Travail*,[1] published an article called 'Belgium, the "Sick Member" of the Common Market'. It referred to the fact that the rate of economic growth in Belgium was lagging far behind that of other members of the Common Market: industrial production rose at an average of 2.94 percent per year between 1953 and 1959 as against 5.64 percent in the Netherlands, 7.23 percent in France, 7.92 percent in Italy, and 8.37 percent in Germany. (In 1953 Belgium was producing only 11 percent more than in 1929, 24 years earlier, while the average figure for the other OEEC countries in Europe was some 70 percent.)

Belgian industry is facing severe competition. Approximately 40 percent of its output is exported, mainly in the form of steel products and textiles.[2] And it is precisely these products that have suffered from the change in the structure of world demand over recent decades: from commodities needing relatively unskilled labour towards capital equipment and a wide range of new industries, based on highly-skilled labour.

In Belgium adjustment has proceeded much more slowly than in the other countries of the Common Market. There are a number of reasons for this. First, Belgian industries suffered much less destruction during the war than those of some other countries, notably Germany, which were compelled to re-equip with the most modern machinery. Secondly, the acute demand for basic products immediately after the war and during the Korean boom hid the necessity for developing new types of production. And lastly, Belgian capital found it more profitable to invest abroad than at home.

To add to its troubles, Belgium's main raw material, coal, is produced under extremely bad conditions, so that the effect of the general coal crisis in the industrial countries is felt more acutely than elsewhere. The result: closure of pits on a mass scale over the past few years. The number of underground workers declined by 33 percent between 1 January 1958 and 4 September 1960, and the reduction will no doubt reach 50 percent by the end of 1961.[3]

In an effort to soften the blow, the sacked Belgian miners were given a subsidy by the European Coal and Steel Community. This was to have terminated in October 1959, but was extended to 30 September 1960, when it ceased.

One result of the stagnation of the Belgian economy and the decline of its traditional industries is the large pool of permanent unemployment. Since 1949 the rate of unemployment has kept between 8 and 12 percent of all wage earners.[4]

The Congo debacle

On top of all this came the Congo debacle.

One should not overstate the Congo's importance to the Belgian economy. In 1959 exports to the Congo were only 2.7 percent of total exports, and imports 5.8 percent of total imports. The National Bank calculated that a complete rupture of all economic and financial arrangements with Congo might cause a reduction of, initially, 6 percent in the gross national product and 5 percent in the tax revenue. Nevertheless Congo was quite important in Belgium's balance of payments. She ran an export surplus—$1,660 million between 1953 and 1959, or nearly 3 percent of the gross national product of Belgium—which went largely to helping the 'mother country'. She also helped to cover up the actual deficit in the Belgian budgets.

Had the Belgian economy been growing at the same rate as the French, Italian or West German—7 to 8 percent a year—the loss of the Congo could have been absorbed, but with a rate of growth of only 2 percent.

Above all, 'the Congo debacle…served, it was thought, to put the country in the right mood to accept drastic action'.[5]

Actually, when Eyskens came to power in June 1958, he had already in his pocket a plan similar to that of the *loi unique*, but 'nothing substantial was done' about it.[6]

To drag Belgian capitalism out of the rut two complementary measures were proposed by the government: (1) plums for the capitalists; (2) a cut in workers' standards.

Plums for the capitalists

These are given to Belgian and foreign—mainly American—capitalists to persuade them to invest in industry:

> The Belgian technique of attracting them is to offer a number of temporary fiscal exemptions, including what amounts to 130 percent depreciation allowances for new machinery and plant installed during the development period. In addition to this there are capital subsidies in certain cases. and finance is made available on very advantageous terms by loans which may be as much as 4 percent below market rates.[7]

The result is that:

> ...the American industrialist who builds a factory in Belgium will, in fact, be bringing to the country only a comparatively small contribution to her foreign exchange reserves. He will be borrowing a large part of the money locally, and using the cheap interest rates provided by Belgian government subsidy which have been offered to him as part of the inducement. This, of course, presupposes that Belgium will be able, at all times, to provide the capital funds required'... The effect of this is that the Belgian system will have to find a great deal of the new capital funds, financing the new American and other investments on her territory.[8]

To get these larger capital funds, or at least part of them, a cut in the workers' standards was necessary.

Attack on workers' standards

Belgian workers enjoy wages second only to those of the French in the Common Market area. They earn considerably more than workers in West Germany, some 40 percent more than the Dutch, and some 50 percent more than the Italians.[9]

The aim of the *loi unique* is to cut these standards. The law provides for the introduction of a harsh means test which deprives the unemployed of benefit after a certain number of months. Certain pension rights affecting public employees—railwaymen, postmen, teachers, local government workers—are to be abolished; the pensionable age is to be raised. Indirect taxation is to be raised sharply, the brunt of this falling on the broad masses. The Belgian Socialists estimate that these measures will rob the workers of some 300 to 400 Belgian francs (£21 to £28) a year in cash and, through the reduction of various benefits in kind, amount to a cut of some 10 percent in their standards. The workers answered with a mass strike.

This short economic background makes it clear that the situation in which the strike took place was far from a mature revolutionary one. Capitalism, including Belgian capitalism, is still expanding, even if in an uneven way. Society as a whole was not in an impasse, hence neither of the contending classes felt it necessary to change the balance of forces fundamentally. The working class did not have a strong enough feeling of rebellion to make for a bitter final struggle. Otherwise the strike would not have remained limited mainly to the Walloon workers, the other half of the workers standing aside. Further evidence is the unpopularity of the 'threat' to withdraw the maintenance men and thus flood the mines and cool the steel ovens during the strike. If this had been a life-and-death struggle the workers would not have rejected such desperate means. Yet, although the situation was far from a revolutionary one, it gave us a glimpse of the revolutionary potentialities of the working class. In spite of reformists and revisionists the class struggle goes on. Years of full employment and 'affluence' may put a gloss of conformism on the working class, but they also strengthen its self-confidence and readiness to fight. 'Apathy' is transitory at worst. If workers show such militancy and revolutionary fervour when faced with such a minor deterioration in their conditions, what heights of heroism and initiative will they scale when the contradictions in world capitalism reach really tremendous dimensions, as they are sure to do in the future?

Belgian traditions of general strikes

Belgium has a long tradition of mass industrial strikes. In 1886 a great series of strikes broke out, first in the neighbourhood of Charleroi, then in Liège and over a large part of the Walloon provinces. The main demand was universal suffrage, but there were economic demands as well in some places. Then in May 1891 a mass strike of some 125,000 workers put forward a demand for changes in the electoral system. In April 1893 another strike, embracing about a quarter of a million workers, broke out around a similar demand. The outcome was a universal but unequal franchise, the votes of the rich and 'cultured' counting for two or three times those of workers. Dissatisfied, the workers called another mass strike nine years later, demanding a complete revision of the Constitution.

An even bigger strike—in which 450,000 workers took part—was called by the Socialist Party and trade unions to achieve electoral reform in 1902, and again in 1913.

Another general strike, which wrested a 40-hour week and paid holidays from the capitalists, took place in 1936. In 1950 a general strike led to the abdication of King Leopold.

In 1958-59 the coal miners of the Borinage spontaneously began a general strike not merely for wage demands but for the nationalisation of the mining industry.

Belgian tradition of 'socialist'-conservative coalition governments

There is, alas, another tradition in the Belgian labour movement, that of coalitions with conservative parties.

As early as 1902 the Socialist Party flirted with the conservative party, called Liberals in Belgium, in the midst of the general strike. Between 1919 and 1940 there were 19 Belgian cabinets in all, in 11 of which the Socialist Party partnered a coalition.

To give a theoretical justification to this mania for compromise with capitalism, the theoretician of the Belgian Socialist Party right wing, Henri de Man, put forward views similar to those of Anthony Crosland some two decades later. In his *Plan du Travail*, adopted by the Party and trade unions, he put forward the idea of a mixed economy, with emphasis on control and not on ownership. He tried without success to attract the middle classes and the left wing of the Catholic Party. Finally, in 1940, when the Germans overran Belgium, de Man dissolved the Socialist Party and remained in Belgium as the King's 'adviser'.

After the Second World War the policy of coalition with the conservatives was continued.

Uncommon social democratic party

Despite its right-wing leadership, the Belgian Socialist Party is unique among the parties of the Socialist International. Where else would one find Social Democratic parties repeatedly launching general strikes? What would our Gaitskell or our Carron say to the use of industrial action for political aims—for electoral reforms (as in 1886, 1891, 1893, 1902, 1913), or against the King (1950), or against a government's hunger law (1961)?

Where else would one come across two such typical news items? Early in the strike the Minister of the Interior ordered all mayors to report local government employees who had absented themselves from work without leave. On 26 December the 45 Socialist mayors in the Charleroi district met and unanimously decided 'to refuse to obey the injunctions of the Minister of the Interior'.[10] Socialist mayors in other districts followed suit.

A few days later the papers announced that Socialist MPs, mayors, etc in the Liège district had decided to donate their salaries to strike funds for the duration.[11]

Above all, who in this country would dream that Labour Party and Young Socialist rooms would serve as local headquarters for strike committees all over the country, as happened in Belgium?

Trade unions split on religious-national lines

A deepgoing factor affecting the structure of the Belgian labour movement is the national-religious-political cleavage in the country.

Traditionally Belgium has been divided into two halves, the Flemish-speaking, conservative, Catholic, agricultural North and the French-speaking, anti-Catholic, Socialist, industrial South or Walloon area. (Actually the Flemish make up a little over half the population.) Although the North has ceased to be purely agricultural over the last few decades and contains centres of new industries, the industrial workers in the Flemish areas are not entirely free of Catholic influence. So in many cases the difference between Walloons and Flemish are differences between sections of the working class with different traditions and different levels of development. However, it is also a difference between militant industrial workers and conservative agricultural workers and farmers.

The Belgian Socialist Party is unlike the Social Democratic Party of Germany or the Socialist Party of France, in that it is made up not only of individual members but also of affiliated trade unions, co-operatives and mutual aid societies. In this respect it is similar to the British Labour Party. But there are also basic differences. The British trade unions include all eligible wage and salary earners whatever their politics. In Belgium workers who oppose the Socialist Party from the right belong to unions affiliated to another party—the Catholic party, called Christian Social Party—or to unions independent of both. Their membership can be seen in the following table.[12]

	Number of members of socialist trade unions	Number of members of Catholic trade unions
1890	36,000	-
1900	31,311	-
1905	34,184	(1904) 10,000
1914	127,000	110,000
1951	638,400	533,814
1960	692,000	742,000

Similarly there are Socialist co-operatives and mutual aid societies, and Catholic ones. Indeed the entire pattern of working class organisation in Belgium arose largely from the struggle between Socialists, mainly Walloons, and conservatives, mainly Flemish, aided and guided by the Catholic Church.

The roots of the religious-political cleavage are deep and reach far back. As one British observer remarked half a century ago:

> There is extraordinarily little social intercourse between Catholics and Liberals, and practically none between Catholics and Socialists. Politics enter into almost every phase of social activity and philanthropic effort and it is the exception rather than the rule for persons holding different political opinions to cooperate in any other matter. Thus in one town there will be a Catholic, a Liberal and a Socialist trade union, a Catholic, a Liberal and a Socialist thrift society, each catering for similar people, but each confining its attentions to members of its own political party. The separation extends to cafes, gymnasia, choral, temperance, and literary societies; indeed it cuts through life.[13]

This separation into distinct political groups makes for more intimate relations between the Socialist Party, the trade unions and other workers' organisations. On the other hand, the split in the trade union movement did untold harm to the bargaining power of the unions. Their longstanding weakness—their inability to satisfy the daily requirements of their members—is clear from the repeated defeat of workers on routine economic strikes. In the years 1896 to 1900, 63 percent of all strikes ended in defeat; in 1901-05, 68 percent, and in 1906-10, 60 percent.[14]

As against this, in Britain only 29 percent of strikes ended in defeat in 1911-14 and 26 percent in 1915-18.[15]

Role of co-operatives

The split in the trade union movement has made for greater dependence of all Socialist organisations—not only the Party but also the trade unions—on the co-operatives. The reasons are complex.

The division of workers into different camps under different flags does great harm in the trade union field for obvious reasons. But it cannot harm the co-operative movement to the same extent. A Socialist co-operative store with a few thousand members can flourish even where there is a Catholic one in the same street. So it is that the split in the labour movement between Socialist and Catholic (plus Liberal) wings vested the co-operative movement with relatively great importance compared to the trade unions.

In Belgium the Socialist Party was not formed as the political arm of the trade unions as was the case in Britain. On the contrary, the trade unions were the industrial arm of the Party, and not a very strong arm at that. In the whole pre-1914 period the trade unions 'remained a secondary factor in the Belgian labour movement'.[16]

For many decades the co-operatives formed the backbone of the Party. In 1911 de Man—at that time a Marxist—could write:

> The co-operatives, especially the consumer co-operatives, constitute the material base of the Belgian Labour Party...the co-operatives, with their people's houses, are the organisational and financial backbone of the Party... The political organisations proper, and even the trade unions, are decisively in the minority, in the labour movement.[17]

This situation persisted right up to the First World War: 'Whenever a strike was about to break out the leaders counted much more on solidarity contributions and on the bread deliveries from the co-operatives than on cash from the union strike fund'.[18]

Backwardness of social legislation

The all-embracing nature of the Socialist organisations and the intimate relations between their different wings was a conservative Catholic control of the state and the inability of social legislation in Belgium, in spite of its being such a highly industrialised country [text as in original]. This was due largely to the conservative Catholic control of the state and the inability of the Socialist movement to bridge the gap between the Walloon and Flemish people.

Thus the truck system was abolished as late as 1887. Children below the age of 12 were entitled to work in factories until two years later: 'An official inquiry in 1895 showed that 35 percent of the industrial workers were employed seven days per week; but it was not till 1905 that a law enjoined a six-day limit save where special exemptions were granted (as they since have too freely been)'.[19]

As regards education Belgium lagged far behind—21.4 percent of the working people (above the age of ten) could not read or write as late as 1910, the percentage being lower in the four great towns of Brussels, Antwerp, Liège and Ghent—11.75 percent—and in the Walloon communes 17.34 percent.[20] Compulsory education was not introduced till 1914!

Trade union weakness and conservative social legislation conspired to keep Belgian wages very low. As de Man put it in 1911, 'Today Belgium is the country with the longest working time and the lowest wages amongst the industrial countries of the world'.[21]

Workers' conditions were not only extremely harsh but also unstable, as was to be expected in a small, densely populated country highly dependent on exports and particularly exposed to competition from larger neighbouring industrial countries (Britain, Germany).

Paucity of social legislation coupled with low wages within an advanced industry led the workers to seek help not from the State, but from their movement, which appeared to be an all-embracing and integrated defence against excessive exploitation.

Autonomous trends

Dispersal amongst the small towns so characteristic of Belgium strengthened decentralisation in the trade union structure. Henri de Man wrote:

> This parochialism is the worst characteristic of Belgian trade unionism. Our trade unions are still committed to the principle of federalism, ie of the autonomous branch. There is no industrial country in which the trade unions are more backward than in Belgium.[22]

It was strengthened by the intimate relations between the trade unions and other wings of the labour movement: where the trade union depends largely on the local co-operative centralisation is not encouraged.

Unlike the British movement, the Party and the unions are much more federative. The Belgian equivalent of the TUC—the Fédération Générale de Travailleurs Belges (FGTB)—is made up of over a score of semi-autonomous regional organisations, each comprising the representatives of various trades and occupations in its area. Each regional federation has its centre in a co-operative society building or Maison du Peuple, which serves as a general meeting place for the co-operatives, trade unions and Socialist Party, and also for cultural and recreational activities. Each Federation enjoys substantial autonomy in its own industrial affairs and allows a large measure of independence to the Socialist Party's regional organisation. Thus Liège can pride itself on having a daily Socialist paper, *Le Monde du Travail*, with quite a militant line, very different to the national daily, *Le Peuple*, issued in Brussels by the central leadership. Liège also publishes a trade union daily, *La Wallonie*, edited by André Renard, joint Secretary General of the Belgian trade unions. And Liège has a smaller population than Nottingham!

This all-inclusiveness, together with its deep local roots, made for another specific feature of the labour movement: its composition is almost completely proletarian. As de Man put it, 'Nowhere is a Socialist Party as exclusively composed of proletarian elements as in Belgium'.[23]

Stalemate of parliamentarism and syndicalism

Another reason for the Socialist Party's greater responsiveness to workers' wishes, and for its officials', especially the local and lower echelons, greater tractability, was the early and prolonged check to parliamentary reformism.

The strength of Catholicism in the Flemish half of the country confronted the Socialist Party with a situation in which the winning of a majority in parliamentary elections looked most unlikely. Catholic governments ruled the country uninterruptedly between 1884 and 1914. The Socialist Party could thus not become a complete slave to parliamentarism: although one Walloon worker has equal power with one conservative Flemish farmer in elections, the former is incomparably stronger than the latter in the economic arena.

The national and religious split probably also aided the federalist or autonomic tendencies in the trade unions and the Socialist Party, and so strengthened the non-parliamentary forces in the labour movement.

The result of all this was a militant, non-doctrinaire and purely empirical syndicalism, a mixture of anarchism (without its individualism and with a much greater emphasis on organisation) and trade unionism. It thrived on industrial backwardness and lack of concentration. It gained strength from every betrayal by the right-wing Socialist parliamentarians, which developed among workers a natural suspicion of all political activities. And syndicalism identified the general strike with the socialist revolution rather than looking upon it as only one important element of modern revolution.

However, as much as the syndicalists or syndicalist-inclined people try to overlook politics, it catches up with them, especially during mass strikes. The political arm of the capitalist class—the state with its police and army—is most obvious during such struggles. It is then that syndicalism's lack of political theory, or perspective, leads to empirical, ad hoc measures, indeed to reformist measures.

An extreme example of the syndicalist-nationalist mixture is shown by André Renard, the dynamic and militant leader of the metal workers, joint General Secretary of the FGTB, and the most prominent leader of the Socialist Left, who advocated a federal structure for Belgium in the recent strike.

Disgusted with Van Acker and Co's right-wing reformism, Renard looked for a different solution to that proposed by Van Acker (coalition), but nevertheless confined his perspective within the framework of capitalism. He wanted to transform Belgium into a federal state. 'I am a Walloon', he declared, 'and I am a federalist, and I shall remain one. We do not want to submit to Flemish clericalism any longer.' And in a leaflet distributed at one of his meetings in the Walloon colours of yellow and red his point was expressed succinctly: 'For a Walloon Wallonia; against the *loi unique*; against the misery in the Borinage; against the oppression of unitary government; against the Flemish government; against the murderers of the Walloon people.[24]

Whether this slogan of federalism squares with the general trend towards increasing economic and political integration, and above all whether it squares with the spirit dominating the fighting, marching workers who again and again sang the Internationale, is not for us to deal with here. The basic criticism of Renard's federalism is that it is reformist: it calls for changes in the structure of the state on national lines instead of the social revolutionary overthrow of the capitalist state and the establishment of workers' power which of course might or might not entail a change in the national form.

In sum, it was the comprehensiveness of the labour movement, its federative structure, its extra-parliamentary slant that formed fertile ground for using the general strike as a recurrent weapon of class struggle. It well-suited the requirements of a working class in a highly industrialised country suffering from extremely harsh and unstable conditions, and prevented from using purely trade union or parliamentary methods of struggle.

True, all these mass strikes were not general strikes. On the whole they embraced only the Walloon workers; in the 1902 general strike, for instance, the Walloons made up 90 percent of the strikers, and in 1913, 75 percent.[25] But in a country like Belgium where industry is highly concentrated in a few sectors and dependence on foreign trade great, a limited mass strike—a stoppage in coal mining and steel production—is much more effective than would be a similar strike in a few big industries in a large and economically more diversified country.

'Properly speaking,' wrote the great bourgeois historian Pirenne, 'this party is more than an ordinary party. It makes the observer think of a state and a church in which the class spirit takes the place of the national or the religious spirit'.[26]

In conclusion

The combination of factors behind the numerous general strikes in Belgium shows both the weaknesses and strengths of the labour movement in that country.

The fact that the trade unions exclude half the organised workers is a weakness. But it is partially also a source of strength: those organised in socialist trade unions are more militant.

The movement's heavy dependence on the co-operatives is a weakness, but the help the co-operatives give can be a source of strength.

Backward social legislation can be a sign, a result and a source of weakness, but it can push the workers to greater self-reliance, to greater efforts and self-mobilisation.

Tendencies towards decentralisation and local autonomy can reflect a lack of unity and a narrow-minded parochialism, but it can also mean that the central bureaucracy is relatively weaker and less of an impediment to rank and file activities.

The almost purely proletarian composition of the Socialist Party results in a narrow empiricism and a lack of the theoretical horizons which are indispensable for changing the working class into a revolutionary class, but it can also inhibit right-wing middle-class Party leaders from poisoning the movement.

Above all, the factor that made the general strikes endemic to Belgium, as distinct from other labour movements, namely the split into more or less equal halves of the organised workers, also impeded the development of general strikes beyond themselves into workers' power.

The general strike and the socialist revolution

Being the country that experienced many more general strikes than any other, Belgium is well placed to show the role of the mass strike in the class struggle, its potentialities as well as its limitations.

On the basis of the 1902 general strike in Belgium, Rosa Luxemburg came to the conclusion that the mass strike was a specifically proletarian weapon, the central factor in the revolutionary struggle for workers' power.[27] She developed the idea in the light of the 1905 Revolution in Russia, when she wrote:

> In former bourgeois revolutions where, on the one hand, the political education and leadership of the revolutionary masses was undertaken by the bourgeois parties, and, on the other hand, the revolutionary task was limited to the overthrow of the government, the short battle on the barricades was the appropriate form of the revolutionary struggle. Today, at a time that the working class must educate, organise and lead itself, in the course of the revolutionary struggle, when the revolution itself is directed not only against the established state power but also against capitalist exploitation, mass strikes appear as the natural method to mobilise the broadest proletarian layers into action, to revolutionise and organise them. Simultaneously it is a method by means of which to undermine and overthrow the established state power as well as to curb capitalist exploitation. In order that the working class may participate *en masse* in any direct political action it must first organise itself, which above all means that it must obliterate the boundaries between factories and workshops, mines and foundries: it must overcome the split between workshops which the daily yoke of capitalism condemns it to. Therefore the mass strike is the first natural, spontaneous form of every great revolutionary proletarian action. The more industry becomes the prevalent form of the economy, the more prominent the role of the working class, and the more developed the conflict between labour and capital, the more powerful and decisive become mass strikes. The earlier main form of bourgeois revolutions, the battle of the barricades, the open encounter with the armed State power, is a peripheral aspect of the revolution today, only one moment in the whole process of the mass struggle of the proletariat.[28]

A general strike has a dual effect: it organises the working class and disorganises the authority of the capitalist state. The greater and the more general the anarchy produced, the greater the disarray of the state machine and the better consolidated, organised and enthused the proletariat, the nearer is the victory of revolution.

Nevertheless, by itself the mass strike cannot defeat the capitalist class. They have much greater resources than workers and can hold out much longer. If it is to end in complete, final victory over capitalism, the logical and necessary climax of the mass strike is armed insurrection. And this is what tends to happen in the surge of general strikes—they tend to transcend themselves. In the Russian Revolution of 1917, for example, the most revolutionary sectors of the class, educated and forged in previous mass strikes, started rejecting this method of struggle as ineffective after a time. Trotsky tells us that in the last few months before October the more advanced workers did not on the whole take part in any more mass strikes:

> The strikes were especially stormy among the more backward and exploited groups of workers. Laundry workers, dyers, coopers, trade and industrial clerks, structural workers, sausage makers, furniture workers, were striking, layer after layer, throughout the month of June. The metal-workers were beginning, on the contrary, to play a restraining role. To the advanced workers it was becoming more and more clear that individual economic strikes in the conditions of war, breakdown and inflation could not bring a serious improvement, that there must be some change in the very foundations.[29]

> ...the workers were striking, layer after layer... Only those layers of the working class did not enter the strike conflict which were already consciously moving towards a revolution.[30]

It is clear that at a certain stage in its own development the revolution—of which the mass strike is a central organising and educating element—transcends the mass strike. Under revolutionary conditions the mass strike poses the question of power—which class is to dominate?—but in itself it does not solve it. A general strike may well grow into armed uprising, but it does not necessarily do so. Many a cocoon has died before becoming a butterfly.

How and why is shown quite clearly in this 'laboratory' of general strikes—Belgium.

The general strike and parliamentarism

In the eyes of the anarchists and anarcho-syndicalists the general strike is a complete negation of day-to-day parliamentary political work. And indeed, as an act of direct and complete involvement of the masses outside the parliamentary perimeter, it is such a negation. But it is not a complete negation. After all, the 1886, 1891, 1893, 1902 and 1913 mass strikes in Belgium aimed at achieving universal suffrage.

As Rosa Luxemburg put it:

> The attempt to find a contradiction between the day-to-day public activity and especially between parliamentarism on the one hand, and the general strike on the other, has no foundation in reality, as the general political strike does not aim to *substitute* for parliamentary activity or other small activities, but joins as a link in the chain of propaganda and struggle. Moreover, in itself it serves as a servant of parliamentarism. It is worth pointing out that all general strikes hitherto came out to defend parliamentary rights or to conquer them.[31]

To the extent that the struggle for broadening or defending workers' electoral rights under capitalism is a progressive one, the general strike may well play a progressive role without overthrowing the capitalist state, but only shaking concessions out of it. In this way the mass strike, a revolutionary weapon *par excellence*, may well serve limited, reformist, aims.

The general strike: economics and politics

For reformists there is a Chinese wall between political struggle for economic aims and political struggle for revolution. The mass strike shows it up for what it is—pure chimera. The police and army—the political weapons of the ruling class—are there for all to see as decisive factors in the struggle. As a demonstration for Lenin's saying that politics is nothing but concentrated economics, there is nothing better than the mass strike.

If politics is concentrated economics, not every economic struggle, however wide, will necessarily lead to concentration in a political movement for the overthrow of the capitalist order. Whether or not it does so depends on both objective factors—whether the immediate interests of the workers can be satisfied only by a complete overthrow of the system—and subjective ones—whether there is a mass revolutionary party which represents, as against national and local group interests, the interests of the proletariat as a whole, and throughout the different stages of the class struggle, whether it represents the final aim of working class freedom.

By their very nature, and even if one overlooks the bureaucracy's hold over them, the trade unions represent the workers' current, day-to-day, partial interests, ie local and national interests. A revolutionary party, in the words of *The Communist Manifesto*, would be the unifying element of the present with the future and as such is a necessary element for revolutionary trade unionism.

One can agree that in 'every strike one can see the hydra-head of revolution'—and that this is certainly true of general strikes—without drawing the conclusion, as many a vulgar Marxist does, that every strike *leads* to revolution. After all, Belgium has witnessed mass political strikes, combined with economic struggles, trade unionism with parliamentarism, for over 80 years. And still no revolution. There is no talisman, no one weapon, for the liberation of the working class from capitalism.

The 'disciplined' mass strike

The mass strike would seem to be the epitome of direct involvement and therefore of mass spontaneity. But not always are things so clear cut. In Belgium there have been general strikes practically fully organised and disciplined by a bureaucratic leadership, such as, to take an extreme case, the strike of 1913. It is worth studying it for a moment, since in every general strike the bureaucracy has acted as straitjacket, even if somewhat less effectively than in 1913.

The 1913 one was prepared and organised for months in advance by the leadership of the Socialist Party and the trade unions. If they were pushed into the strike by the masses, they never lost their control, which was practically complete, over all the levers of the strike. They insisted on 'the centralisation of the means of propaganda'. One bourgeois student of this strike showed the reason:

> A moment's thought will show the wisdom of this principle under the conditions of high emotional pressure among the masses. But for the strong central control of propaganda the militant wing, and especially the 'young guard' of the Socialists might easily have run away with the movement and have ended in anything but a non-violent general strike.[32]

After the strike started, all speakers at strike meetings were definitely appointed by the federation whose members were holding the meeting, 'lest tumult should arise from uncertified orators':

> In spite of all these precautions and propaganda, even to the end of the strike, the majority of the leaders secretly feared that the general strike might become violent. Hence it was rather natural that such bitter terms as '*agents provocateurs*', 'traitors', 'criminals', were applied to any who sought to incite to violence.[33]

Special labour 'strike police' were organised. These 'police' were present at all trade union meetings, all fetes, games or conferences. The surroundings of factories and workshops were guarded by them. Each member of this force carried his identity card, to be shown wherever intervention became necessary. Any 'incident' had to be promptly reported to the local committee, and in the meantime, to secure discipline, 'no parades or processions were permitted save with the official sanction of the regular trade union committee'.[34]

In this way the mass strike, the 'natural form of every great revolutionary proletarian action', to use Rosa Luxemburg's words, was tamed. In different forms, and in different degrees, this was repeated in later mass strikes in the country.

The mass strike and the revolutionary party

The mass strike is part of the general working class struggle. It accentuates all the strength of the class and all its weaknesses—the influence of bureaucracy, ideological immaturity.

To use Rosa Luxemburg's words, the workers of Europe and the world should learn to 'speak Belgian'. But they will also have to break with its dialect, its empiricism, narrow trade unionism, bureaucratic conservatism and nationalism.

Notes

1 *Le Monde du Travail*, 22 December 1960.
2 OEEC, *Belgium-Luxemburg Economic Union* (Paris, 1960), p32.
3 *La Gauche*, 26 November 1960, quoting the High Authority of the European Coal and Steel Community.
4 *Le Monde du Travail*, 22 December 1960. This compares with 1.9 percent in Britain at present.
5 *Economist*, 31 December 1960.
6 *Economist*, 31 December 1960.
7 *Statist*, International Banking Supplement, 17 December 1960.
8 *Statist*, International Banking Supplement, 17 December 1960.
9 Economist Intelligence Unit, *Britain and Europe* (London, 1957), p31.
10 *La Wallonie*, 27 December 1960.
11 *La Wallonie*, 31 December 1960.
12 D S Chlepner, *Cent Ans d'Histoire Sociale en Belgique* (1956), pp115-116, 118, 272-273.
13 R S Rowntree, *Land and Labour: Lessons from Belgium* (London, 1911), p24.
14 D S Chlepner, *Cent Ans*, p122.
15 K G J C Knowles, *Strikes: A Study in Industrial Conflict* (Oxford, 1954), p243.
16 E Vandervelde, *Le Parti Ouvrier Belge* (1925), p279.
17 H de Man, 'Die Eigenart der Belgischen Arbeiterbewegung', Supplement to *Die Neue Zeit*, 10 March 1911, p18.
18 E Vandervelde, *Le Parti*, p279.
19 H Pirenne, *Historie de Belgique* (1932), vol VII, p343.
20 R C K Ensor, *Belgium*, 1915.
21 R S Rowntree, *Land and Labour: Lessons from Belgium* (London, 1911), p264.
22 H de Man, 'Die Eigenart', p6.
23 H de Man, 'Die Eigenart', p26.
24 H de Man, 'Die Eigenart', p3.
25 *Times*, 10 January 1961.
26 W H Crook, *The General Strike* (Chapel Hill, 1931), p101.
27 R Luxemburg, 'The Belgian Experiment', *Die Neue Zeit*, 26 April 1902; R Luxemburg, 'Yet A Third Time On The Belgian Experiment', *Die Neue Zeit*, 14 May 1902.
28 *Ausgewählte Reden und Schriften* (Berlin, 1955), vol I, pp227-228.
29 L Trotsky, *History of the Russian Revolution* (London, 1934), p431.
30 L Trotsky, *History*, p847.
31 R Luxemburg, 'Yet A Third Time', *Die Neue Zeit*, 14 May 1902.
32 W H Crook, *The General Strike*, p74.
33 W H Crook, *The General Strike*, p80.
34 W H Crook, *The General Strike*, p95.

France—the struggle goes on

With Ian Birchall, 1968*

> A Frenchman travelling abroad feels himself treated a bit like a convalescent from a pernicious fever. And how did the rash of barricades break out? What was the temperature at five o'clock in the evening on 29 May? Is the Gaullist medicine really getting to the roots of the disease? Are there dangers of a relapse? Even if these questions are not put directly, one can read them on the headlines displayed in all the news-stands and bookstalls.
>
> But there is one question that is hardly ever asked, perhaps because they are afraid to hear the answer. But at heart everyone would like to know, hopefully or fearfully, whether the sickness is infectious.
>
> Robert Escarpit, *Le Monde*, 23 July 1968

Introduction

Suddenly, as if out of the blue, the revolt of the French working class burst upon a shocked capitalist world. It changed the political and social climate. As Premier Pompidou prophetically told the National Assembly on May 22, 'Nothing will ever be exactly the same.'

Sparked off by militant action on the part of revolutionary students—Trotskyists, Maoists, Anarchists—and fanned by police brutality, the flames of revolution spread to the working class. All the pent-up frustrations of the exploited and oppressed burst out.

The giant working class brought the country to a standstill. It seized all industry from the hands of the helpless capitalist class. Everywhere it raised the red banner of socialism. The state looked on, paralysed and powerless.

Chorus girls and taxi drivers, soccer players and bank clerks, participated in the general strike and occupation of their place of work. Journalists and TV men refused to lie to order, and printers censored their employers' press. Schoolchildren, joined by their teachers, took over the schools.

The strike involved a 'cultural revolution' in the best sense of the term. This centred on the students in the Sorbonne but spread everywhere. The vast creative potential of unalienated men was glimpsed once again, as it had been at other revolutionary moments of history.

Unhappily, the working class did not manage, in one fell swoop, to get rid of the burden of the past, of the shackles of the traditional reformist organisations—above all the French Communist Party (PCF). For this failure the working class had to pay dearly.

The social crisis that gripped France shows vividly that none of the capitalist powers of our era is stable enough to be immune from proletarian revolution. The fact that social equilibrium could be endangered by clashes between the authorities and students shows how precarious is the stability of world capitalism in our era of 'prosperity'.

The theory spread by many, among whom C Wright Mills and Herbert Marcuse are notable, that the working class has lost its revolutionary potential, that it has been seduced by the TV and the motor car, and is inseparably integrated into capitalism, was put to a crucial test; and the refutation of Marcuse's statement that 'in the advanced industrial countries where the transition to socialism was to take place, and precisely in those countries, the labouring classes are in no sense a revolutionary potential,' could not have been more vivid and thoroughgoing.

France has shown, more clearly even than Hungary or the Belgian general strike, that the working class of the advanced countries has not been bribed or integrated into complacency, but retains enormous revolutionary potential—even though France has the most sophisticated form of planned Western capitalism. The exceptional militancy of workers in the most modern sectors of industry, including motors and electronics, has shown that such militancy is no hangover from the past, but a crucial portent for the future.

The crisis has clearly indicated the role of such social groups as students. The French students played a central role, acting, as it were, as 'detonator' for the social explosion. They were not able themselves to act as the agents of social change, but merely as stage-setters for the working class. Nor were they able to hold out on their own after the workers returned to work.

For the ten long years of the Gaullist regime the workers witnessed the impotence of the traditional reformist forms of struggle: parliamentary skirmishes, 'demonstrative' strikes, uninspired marches, and so on. The social crisis submitted all methods and all doctrines to a searching and merciless examination. However short and transitory revolutionary crises are, they nevertheless throw a penetrating light on the deepest social processes.

All the ideas that the students and workers brought with them to the struggle, that had been the subject of theoretical discussion alone among a small number of political elements—the strength of the revolutionary potential and its limits, the role of revolutionary organisations, including the revolutionary party, the role of workers' councils and the trade unions, etc—were put to the test in the struggle itself.

The French revolutionary struggle of May and June 1968 was part of the international struggle against capitalism. The fight against the Algerian war, and later against the Vietnam war, were central elements in forging the revolutionary students' movement. The Japanese Zengakuren and the German SDS contributed their share. The accumulation of grievances and frustrations in the French working class were the outcome of the increasing contradictions in world capitalism, refracted through the prism of the authoritarian Gaullist regime.

The French revolutionary struggle is internationalist above all because a victory of the French proletariat cannot but transform the whole world scene by raising to unprecedented heights the confidence and militancy of workers everywhere, and casting fear and despair in the camp of exploiters. Paris and Berlin, Prague and Moscow, Tokyo and London are intimately united.

It is therefore imperative for socialists everywhere to study the May and June days.

The student revolt

The storm breaks out

On 20 November 1967 Nanterre witnessed the largest student strike in France to date. Ten thousand students took part. On 13 December university students all over France held a one-day strike and six secondary schools joined in.

On 21 February 1968 a mass demonstration of university and secondary school students took place in Paris. One of its acts was to rename the Latin Quarter 'The Heroic Vietnam Quarter'. On 22 March a mass demonstration took place in Nanterre protesting against the arrest of a number of militants in the previous demonstration. On this occasion the March 22 movement was formed. The students occupied the university.

On 29 March the students of Nanterre decided to hold a day of political discussion at the university. The rector closed the university for two days, during which large-scale clashes took place between members of March 22 movement and the fascists of the Occident group.

May 2 and 3 were to be days of demonstration against imperialism. On 2 May the rector again closed the university. Disciplinary procedures were initiated against Daniel Cohn-Bendit and six other members of the March 22 movement. On 3 May a meeting of 500 students took place in the Sorbonne. Several revolutionary organisations participated: JCR, FER, the March 22 movement and others. The rector of the University, Roche, called the police in at 4pm. The Sorbonne was invaded by the police and all the students arrested. Immediately after, spontaneous demonstrations began in the Latin Quarter and they fought the police until 11pm. The Sorbonne was then closed and no one allowed in. A general strike of the university was called to protest against the arrests and the presence of the police in the Sorbonne.

On 6 May the students of Paris organised a new, even more massive demonstration. On 7 May another demonstration of students started off from Denfert-Rochereau. The trade unions refused to participate. When it started at 6.30pm there were several thousands in the streets. As they had no definite destination they made a sort of 'long march' through Paris. People listening to the radio in the evening when they came home from work learnt from it where the demonstration was, and many joined it in the evening. In the end there were 50,000 in the Champs-Elysées with red banners and singing the Internationale.

On 8 May 20,000 took part in a peaceful demonstration around the Latin Quarter.

On 9 May, notwithstanding the promise of the Minister of Education, Peyrefitte, that the Sorbonne would be opened, it remained closed. A number of spontaneous meetings were held all over the Latin Quarter.

On 10 May more than 50,000 students of the University and secondary schools joined many young workers gathered at Place Denfert-Rochereau. The demonstration tried to go toward boulevard Saint-Michel where it was met by a massive police force. Sixty barricades were built. The Battle of the Barricades, starting at 17 minutes past 2 at night, went on until 7 o'clock in the morning. The local population actively sympathised with the students and young workers on the barricades. They gave them oranges, cakes and other food, took care of the injured and took them into their homes, where they gave what medicines they could. They threw water on the pavement, as the demonstrators had asked, to neutralise the effects of gas.

On 11 May representatives of UNEF (Union Nationale des Etudiants de France—National Union of French Students), CGT (Confédération Générale du Travail—General Confederation of Labour) and CFDT (Confédération Française et Démocratique du Travail—French Democratic Confederation of Labour) met and decided to declare Monday 13 May a day of general strike and demonstrations against police brutality towards the students.

On 13 May 10,000,000 workers went on strike, and the whole country was brought to a standstill. A million took part in a demonstration, mainly made up of workers, but including tens of thousands of students. On the evening of the same day the students reopened the Sorbonne and occupied it.

On 13 May the main centre of gravity of the struggle moved to the working class.

Role of the CP in these fateful days

On 3 May Georges Marchais wrote an article in *L'Humanité* entitled 'Unmask The Pseudo-Revolutionaries!'

> The activities of the 22 March group at Nanterre run counter to the interests of the majority of students and can only lead to provocations by the fascists... [These grouplets] are also trying to give lessons to the working class. More and more they are to be found at factory gates or in areas inhabited by immigrant workers distributing leaflets and other propaganda...
>
> In spite of their contradictions these grouplets—a few hundred students—have united into what they call the 'Mouvement du 22 Mars Nanterre', led by the German anarchist Cohn-Bendit... These false revolutionaries must be energetically unmasked;

> for, objectively, they serve the interests of the Gaullist government and the big capitalist monopolies...
>
> The views and activity of these 'revolutionists' are laughable; in as much as they are generally the children of big bourgeois, contemptuous of students from working-class origins, who will soon dampen their 'revolutionary flame' to go and run papa's business and exploit the workers in the best traditions of capitalism.

The closing of Nanterre did not merit much comment by the CP. *L'Humanité* of 3 May relegated these developments to the bottom of three columns on the sixth page, quoting very long excerpts from an article by the dean, Grappin, accompanied by the following commentary:

> Thus the activities of pseudo-revolutionary groups—which we have ceaselessly condemned—have led to a measure which, on the eve of examinations, badly harms the bulk of the students. The great majority of the students in Nanterre want to work in the best conditions. And, a few weeks before exams, their preoccupations have nothing in common with those of the trouble-makers. They proved it yesterday when a hundred 'leftists,' ensconced in a lecture hall, tried again to stop the class for the 450 other students who were waiting.

L'Humanité of 4 May carried out its policy of isolating the mini-groups by appealing to the self-interest of students awaiting exams (this was the day after the closing of the Sorbonne):

> Three weeks from the exams thousands of students are being prevented from normal preparation which for some, the poorest, means the end of their studies. The authorities, whose openly proclaimed objective is to place the maximum limitation on entry into the university, have every reason to rejoice at the deterioration in the situation.

There was no doubt about who was responsible for this deterioration. After the police invasion of the Sorbonne on 5 May, where a *peaceful* meeting had been called to protest against the closure of the faculté de lettres at Nanterre and against the summoning of seven student leaders, including Cohn-Bendit, to appear before a university disciplinary committee, the Union des Etudiants Communistes (UEC) issued a statement saying:

> The leftist leaders are taking advantage of government neglect and speculating on the discontent of the students in an attempt to prevent the running of the faculties, and stop the mass of students studying and passing their exams. Thus these pseudo-revolutionaries objectively act as allies of the Gaullist regime and its policies which harm the majority of students, especially those from the humblest backgrounds.

L'Humanité-Dimanche of 5 May described in detail an oral question which Louis Baillot, a Communist deputy from Paris, put to Peyrefitte (the minister of education). Its audacity shows the extent to which the Communist leaders had grasped the stakes in the battle. He asked the minister what measures he intended to take to:

(1) enable the students to study normally and prepare for their examinations under good conditions;
(2) offer real answers to the legitimate demands of the students (housing, cafeterias, scholarships);
(3) put into operation an emergency plan for building universities and IUTs (instituts universitaires de technologie—technical universities) in the Paris region.

None of the measures proposed by Baillot were to capture the students' attention in subsequent days. It was not that they were opposed to them but they were not fighting to patch up the existing system: they wanted to destroy the old university system to create a new one.

On 8 May, after more riots, *L'Humanité* at last came round and announced, 'The Government Bears The Responsibility'.

Changing role of students

For more than a century the student community had identified itself with bourgeois society. The students were the more extreme exponents of middle-class values. During the rise of the bourgeoisie, when it headed the democratic forces, it was the students who waved the banner of liberty and progress most enthusiastically—as happened in Vienna in 1848. However, when the same bourgeoisie turned its guns on the revolution, as happened in Paris in June of the same year, the students were on the same side of the barricades as the bourgeoisie, facing the workers on the other side. With the ageing of the bourgeoisie, the students became conservative and reactionary. In Britain student attitudes led them to strikebreak practically as a body.

It was natural in those days for Marxists to consider the bourgeois intelligentsia as collectively hostile to socialism, although individuals could be won to the socialist movement. To quote a typical statement of Trotsky in 1910:

> It is not only Europe's intelligentsia as a whole but its offspring, too, the students, who decidedly don't show any attraction towards socialism...the intensification of the struggle between labour and capital hinders the intelligentsia from crossing over to the party of labour. The bridges between the classes are broken down, and to cross over, one would have to leap across an abyss which gets deeper with every passing day...this finally means that it is harder to win the intelligentsia today than it was yesterday, and that it will be harder tomorrow than it is today.[1]

During the last decade or so the student scene has changed radically, from the Zengakuren in Japan—who in June 1960 led millions in massive demonstrations, successfully overthrowing the Kishi government and preventing Eisenhower from visiting the country—to students in Birmingham, Alabama, and Berkeley, California, to the London School of Economics, to the SDS in Germany...to the Sorbonne and Nanterre!

Why?

First of all, there is the university explosion.

Just before the Second World War the percentage of the student age group in Britain that attended university, or a similar institution of higher education, was 2.7; today it is above 11. Similarly throughout Europe the number of students per 1,000 of population rose from two in 1950 to six in 1965, tripling in only 15 years. There are at present 6 million university students in the United States, 3 million in Western Europe, 1.5 million in Russia and over 1 million in Japan. As a result of changes in capitalism and in the employment of intellectuals, the majority of students are not being trained any more as future members of the ruling class, or even as agents of the bosses with supervisory functions, but as white-collar employees of state and industry, and thus are destined to be part and parcel of the proletariat.

A central aspect of the 'third industrial revolution' is the integration of manual with mental labour, of intellectual with productive work: the intellectual element becomes crucial to the development of the economy and society. But this productive force comes into sharpening conflict with the irrational nature of capitalism. The conflict expresses itself in university life as a contradiction between the demand for the streaming of education dictated by the immediate needs of industry and the need to allow a certain amount of intellectual freedom. This applies especially to the social scientists, who have to 'solve' capitalism's social problems—according to the theory of the ruling class—and at the same time have to understand, at least to a certain extent, what generates the revolt against capitalism.

The central contradiction of capitalism is that between the production of what Marx called use-values, and the production of value. The first are natural. The second are specific to the capitalist order of society. In the university this is reflected as a contradiction between the ideal of unlimited intellectual development, free from social, political and ideological restraint, and the tight intellectual reins imposed by capitalism. The liberal mystique of education clashes with its social content.[2]

Because students, or, even more, graduates who have left the university, are progressively more pivotal to the development and salvation of all advanced industrial countries, it is more and more essential for these countries to ensure that students and technologists fulfil their assigned role. And this means that any attempt by these groups to put forward demands on their own behalf which conflict with the needs of capitalism will inevitably be resisted by ruling interests. With increasing international competition and the narrowing of profit margins on the one hand, and the need to produce more graduates on the other, the pressure is fierce to cut expenses per student, which involves greater streamlining of courses, regimentation of standards and increasing resistance to students' claims.[3]

Another factor fanning the revolt among students is the feeling of insecurity as to what the morrow of graduation will bring in their personal lives. The student of a previous generation knew in advance the slot into which he would fit—in the higher brackets of society. Not so the student of today. At the university he has not found the kind of education he was looking for, and when he graduates he finds it more and more difficult to get the kind of job he was led to expect. The feeling of instability, of uncertainty, creates unease, which easily combines with other factors to create a revolutionary combustion.

Another important element encouraging student rebellion is that students are more and more concentrated in the same areas. This was particularly the case in Nanterre, where 12,000 students were gathered in the same buildings, many living on the university campus all the year round.

The special medium in which the student is trained—theorising and generalising—facilitates the synthesis of the different elements of unease and rebellion. Students at present rebel more readily than workers because they are less shackled mentally by the traditional, ie bureaucratic, organisations, like the Socialist parties and the Communist parties. The rootlessness of the student acts as oil to the wheels of revolt.

In speaking of student rebellion one should avoid the extremes.

The first is that put forward by the Stalinist bureaucrats both east and west and followed by a number of so-called 'orthodox' Marxists who deny the progressive revolutionary capacity of students. The other is that of C Wright Mills and Herbert Marcuse, who deny the revolutionary potentiality of the working class and hence describe students and intellectuals as the main vehicle for revolutionary action now and in the future.

Actually the rebelling students have at one and the same time great strength and great weakness.

They are a small minority of the population. They are outside production. They are not the big battalions that can overthrow the social order.

Being outside production is a source of weakness, but it is also a cause for quick advance, as it is so much easier for the students to move into action. If a small minority of the university community wants to act on an issue, it can go ahead and do so. Thus at the beginning only a tiny minority of London School of Economics students identified themselves as left-wing militants: they demonstrated on one issue after another. Every demonstration was an act of propaganda, of educating themselves and others. The situation of a militant minority in the factory is radically different. It cannot act—by strike action or occupation of the factory—unless the overwhelming majority of all the workers employed are carried along. In the factory the level of consciousness and the morale of the majority may act as a dead weight on the militant minority. This situation may prevent individuals in this minority from identifying one another, hence individual militants find it difficult to make explicit even to themselves their own potentialities. Only as a mass collective can factory workers act, and thus assert themselves.

Hence the temperature bringing students into combustion is incomparably lower than the one necessary to inflame the workers. But unfortunately the lifespan of their fire is also shorter. They lack the stamina that workers as a collective have. Because separate social forces do not come to the arena of open combat with capitalism at one and the same time, it is in the interests of the ruling class and its hangers-on to separate the students from the workers, to engage the students, if need be, in a fight to the finish, before the great battalions arrive. It is at the same time in the interests of the rebellious students to call on the heavy battalions of the working class for supporting action—action, of course, on their own account. The synchronisation of student rebellion and working-class revolution is one of the most important things confronting the revolutionary movement in the advanced industrial societies.

The student cannot act as the vanguard, as the leadership, of the working class. A number of features in the student make-up impede him from carrying out meaningful propaganda and agitation among workers. Workers' thinking is basically concrete. It grows from bread and butter issues that are with him all his life, from trade union consciousness. Socialist consciousness transcends trade union consciousness. The student thinks in abstracts; trade union consciousness hardly plays any role in his life. The knowledge that being a student is a transitory situation for him of a few years' duration, and that at the university the most irksome exploitation is not the openly economic, but the intellectual, explains this. Behind the complaint about the tangible reality of low grants, bad food, strict rules and overcrowded amenities, the student feels the intangible manipulation of his mind. Because of the different nature of student exploitation, his response does not fit the traditional trade union pattern. That is why practically all student revolts were started by political elements. Conversely, the overwhelming majority of workers' strikes since the beginning of capitalism were initiated and led by workers who did not have revolutionary political convictions.

Only by being in a revolutionary organisation that includes workers, by rubbing shoulder to shoulder with workers, can the socialist student learn the 'language' necessary to communicate with workers in normal times, ie not revolutionary periods.

To lead the workers in a factory one must be in daily touch with them. During 'normal' periods the role of revolutionaries is necessarily limited to propaganda and agitational activities for the dissemination of their ideas, connecting these with the concrete struggle of the workers. A small revolutionary organisation or, even better, a revolutionary party, can do it, as it is composed of workers and intellectuals together. Students alone cannot.

The student as a detonator

If students as such cannot organise and lead the working class, they can, and in May and June did, act as the detonator of the revolution.

In 1936 it was the electoral victory of the Popular Front that acted as a detonator for the general strike and occupation of the factories. In 1944-45 it was the military victory over Nazism. This time it was the students' struggle, culminating in the Night of the Barricades.

The feeling, perhaps confused, but nevertheless very real, of being exploited, of injustice being meted out to him daily, is in the mind of every worker. However, the mere knowledge does not lead to rebellion; it may indeed lead to resignation. In order to rebel, the worker must entertain the hope of change—change for the better. It is this hope, or the lack of it, that has made the history of the labour movement, with its ups and downs. And it was the new hope, the dream of a better world, that the students gave first to young workers, and then to the working class as a whole.

The workers enter the arena

The spark inflames the young workers

The student rebellion first caught the imagination of young workers. They, more than anyone else, are hurt by the economic crisis of French society. It is very difficult for them to find a job and, if they do, it is often dead-end. From childhood they are roughed up by the police as 'delinquents' or rebels. They are hurt by the ideological and moral crisis of society.

When the students proved on 6 May that not only were they ready to fight the police, but were also able to stand their ground against them, thousands of young workers joined. The number increased even more on 10 May, the Night of the Barricades. Since then thousands of workers started visiting the Sorbonne. The revolutionary élan there caught their imagination. As one middle-aged Renault worker said:

> In the first few days of May every evening I took five or six workers—quite often members of the Communist Party—in my car to the Sorbonne. When they returned to work next day they were completely changed people. Through the students and the 'groupuscules' they got the political education they did not get from the CP. There was a completely libertarian atmosphere at the university, so different from the totalitarian atmosphere at the factory. The student demonstration created an environment in which people were free to coin their own slogans. In the official trade union demonstrations only certain, centrally determined, slogans were permitted. When Renault was occupied, the workers experienced a change from control by the management, which uses modern manipulative techniques, to control by the CP bureaucracy, which is completely totalitarian. In Renault their freedom was alienated. In the Sorbonne they felt free. When a worker went to the Sorbonne he was recognised as a hero. Within Renault he was only a thing. In the university he became a man. This atmosphere of freedom in the sense of being considered human gave great combativity to the young workers. Returning from the Sorbonne the young workers in Renault organised self-defence with Molotov cocktails. The CP officials forbade the use of Molotov cocktails against the police. When the students came to Billancourt the CP officials distributed truncheons to the workers to fight the 'Trotskyists'; at the same time we were told by the officials that if the CRS were to come we should avoid violence—we should come out of the factory holding our heads high. In the student demonstrations we were free to throw paving stones at the police. On the official trade union demonstration the main slogan was 'Beware of provocateurs'. On the student demonstration, anyone ready to pick up a paving stone was considered a comrade.

The same Renault worker also pointed out the following:

> The students communicate to the workers an image of a combative working class, an image very different to the one seen on the surface. Many young workers rediscovered there in the Sorbonne the historic idea of the revolutionary traditions of the working class, and started to talk the language of revolution.

However, not all the workers reacted like these young ones. Only a minority came into close contact with the revolutionary students and with the revolutionary groups. The overwhelming majority of the workers remained under the influence of the traditional organisations—above all the CP and its trade-union federation, the CGT.

The trade unions step in

The first edition of *L'Humanité* on Saturday 11 May, the day after the Night of the Barricades, called for a demonstration on Tuesday evening, 14 May, to march from Place Saint-Michel to Gare de l'Est. However, on the same Saturday representatives of UNEF, the CGT and CFDT met; as a result a call was issued for a general strike on Monday 13 May. *L'Humanité* issued a special edition entitled 'Stop The Repression'.

The trade union leaders wanted a one-day token strike—one more in the long chain of token strikes. But the response on 13 May was nothing like token. Ten million workers came out, four times more than the number organised in trade unions. The whole country was paralysed. In Paris a demonstration of 1 million people took place. Notwithstanding the efforts of the CGT and CP leadership, practically no tricolores were to be seen on the demonstration—one observer counted three—while thousands of red flags fluttered. The CGT leaders raised the slogan 'Des sous, Charlot' (Money, Charles) and 'Défense du pouvoir d'achat' (Defend purchasing power). The students shouted 'Le pouvoir aux ouvriers' (All power to the workers), 'Le pouvoir est dans la rue' (Power lies in the street), 'Libérez nos camarades' (Free our comrades), 'De Gaulle—assassin', 'CRS=SS'. The main slogans taken up by the mass of the workers were neither those of the CGT (and CP leadership) nor of the revolutionary students. Their main slogans were 'Dix ans, c'est assez' (Ten years is enough), 'A bas l'État policier' (Down with the police state), 'Bon anniversaire, mon Général' (Happy anniversary, General). Whole groups mournfully intoned a well-known refrain: 'Adieu de Gaulle'. They waved their handkerchiefs to the great merriment of all.

Serious political differences lie behind the difference in the choice of slogans.

The CGT and the CP leaders hoped that the one-day strike and demonstrations would serve as an effective safety valve—that this would be the end of the struggle. But they did not reckon with the rank and file, who entered the arena off their own bat.

On 14 May the workers of Sud Aviation in Nantes declared an unlimited strike. They occupied the factory and imprisoned the manager in his office.

(*L'Humanité* next day tried to overlook the event. It gave it only seven lines on page nine).

Next day, 15 May, Renault-Cléon was occupied.

On 16 May the strike and occupation movement spread to all Renault factories. At Billancourt the strikers declared their demands: for a minimum of 1,000 francs a month, immediate return without loss of pay to 40 hours a week, retirement at 60, full pay for the days of the strike, trade union freedom in the factory. These demands were taken up *in toto* by all the large enterprises in the country.

In the footsteps of Renault all the engineering factories, the car and aeroplane plants, went on strike and were occupied by the workers. On 19 May the trams stopped along with mail and telegraph services. The subway and bus services in Paris followed suit. The strike hit the mines, shipping, Air France, etc, etc.

On 20 May the strike became general. Some 9 million workers were now on strike. People who had never struck before were involved—Folies Bergères dancers, soccer players, journalists, saleswomen, technicians. Red flags fluttered from all places of work. Not a tricolore was to be seen, notwithstanding the statement of the CGT and CP leaders that 'Our banner is both the tricolore and the Red Flag'.

The leadership of the PCF and CGT made it abundantly clear, however, that they wanted to limit the movement to struggle for economic reforms, to avoid raising it to the overthrow of the capitalist system.

On 17 May at a press conference, Séguy stated, 'This general strike is developing without our having called for it, and it is developing under the responsibility of the workers themselves.' He was quite right about this, for the strike wave was growing far faster than the CGT was able to anticipate or cope with.

Perhaps the most revealing official PCF statements of the crisis came in an interview with Séguy broadcast on the Europe No 1 station on 19 May, the text of which was given by *L'Humanité* on 2 October:

> Question: Nearly everywhere the workers on strike are saying that they will go all the way. What do you understand by that? What are your objectives?
> Séguy: The strike is so powerful that the workers obviously mean to obtain full satisfaction at the end of such a movement. 'All the way' for us trade unionists means the satisfaction of the demands for which we have always fought but which the government and bosses have always refused to take into consideration... 'All the way' means a general increase in wages—no wage less than 600F a month [Frank Cousins' 'minimum' is £15 a week!]—guaranteed employment, earlier retirement age, reduced working hours without loss of pay, and the defence and extension of union rights...
> Q: I wanted to ask you why you did not call a general strike today.
> A: That is a very interesting question. It has been put to us numerous times in the past 24 hours. Well! Quite simply, because the general strike is under way without our having had to give any order and is under the control of the workers themselves without any necessity for a decision from the central national leadership. We much

prefer that it should be under the control of the workers themselves…
Q: Unless I am mistaken, it is written in the statutes of the CGT that its aim is the overthrow of capitalism and its replacement by socialism. In the present circumstances which several times this evening you have said were exceptional and important, why has the CGT not seized this unique opportunity of issuing a call to this effect?
A: It is true that the CGT offers the workers a conception of trade unionism which we consider the most revolutionary in as much as its final objectives are the elimination of the bosses and wage labour. It is true that this objective appears in the first article of out statutes. And this objective remains fundamentally that of the CGT… If they [the other left-wing parties] decide to consult us, the trade unions representing the workers, to decide on such a programme, the CGT will willingly pledge itself to such a project and play its full part in the action of the left-wing parties to secure the victory of a democratic alternative in our country, for this, it seems to me, is in the interests of the workers and their families.

Under the pressure of events the CP and the CGT leadership, frightened of being outflanked by a big chunk of the working class, even if a minority, decided to support the strike movement, in order to contain it, discipline it and manipulate it.

There was hardly a journalist in France at the time who did not see this quite clearly. Thus, for instance, the Paris correspondent of the *Observer* described the situation:

All over France a calm, obedient, irresistible wave of working-class power is engulfing factories, dockyards, mines, railway depots, bus garages, postal sorting offices.

Trains, mails, air flights are virtually at a standstill. Production lines in chemicals, steel, metalworking, textiles, shipbuilding and a score of industries have ground to a halt.

Nearly a million men and women in key industries are seizing their places of work and closing the gates. Many a baffled and impotent manager is being held prisoner in his own carpeted office.

The paralysis, creeping hour by hour across the country, has been ordered by the French Communist Party and its trade union arm, the CGT, and followed by other unions. It is an imposing demonstration of the Communists' organised strength. They are the arbiters of the situation. If the Government wants a settlement, it must deal with them.

But the paradox which underlines this controlled chaos is that the Communist unions and the Gaullist Government they appear to be challenging are really on the same side of the barricades. They are defending French society as we know it.

The turning point of this crisis came late on Thursday night. In near desperation, the establishment—not only the Government but also the bureaucrats of the great Communist unions—rallied to its defence.

This is the real significance of the vast Communist-ordered strike movement. Like a gendarme astride the French economy, the CP has held up and stopped the traffic. 'We are in charge here', the Party is saying.

Only by this dramatic mobilisation of its troops can the orthodox Communist Party outbid the student agitators and isolate their revolutionary virus.[4]

The gathering storm

To say that the student movement acted as the detonator, the spark, inflaming the working class, is true. But by itself it goes only a short way to explaining the explosion. There must have existed a lot of dry tinder for the spark to catch on to. As a matter of fact the last couple of years saw a rapid heightening of the struggle in the factories. Again and again there were outbreaks of violent industrial disputes, including the occupation of factories, the imprisonment of managers by the workers, bloody fights with the CRS. These conflicts were the dress rehearsals for May 1968. The same years saw the CGT time and again organising demonstrative strikes including one-day general strikes. The leadership in these struggles mixed political-electoral issues with straightforward bread and butter demands. These again were dress rehearsals for the bureaucracy's action in May and June 1968.

On 17 May 1966 an all-trades strike was called. This was probably one of the most important strikes of the Fifth Republic. It was directed against the National Employers' Federation as well as against the government, and was very widespread.[5] For 23 November the Paris unions of the CGT and CFDT planned a demonstration to leave Gare de L'Est and march toward Place de la République. However, on 19 November the police forbade the demonstration. The trade unions then called it off. However, about 4,000 people did march to Boulevard Magenta and occupied it, at which point they came into conflict with the police.[6]

On 1 February 1967 a new mass strike was called, principally involving state industry, and some civil servants, while private sector workers were left out of the movement, except in the provinces: 75 percent of electricity workers came out for 24 hours; the railways went on a 48-hour strike; the post office brought out 40 percent of the Paris and 24 percent of the provincial postmen in a 24-hour strike; a substantial proportion of the Paris transport workers took part in a 24-hour strike; practically 100 percent of the teachers in primary schools and a quite large percentage of secondary school teachers came out for a day. In private industry the support for the strike was very uneven; it was also difficult to gauge its extent as many plants closed down due to a power cut.[7]

The employers retaliated in a number of cases to the 1 February strike with lock-outs aimed at breaking down the workers' strength. The most important cases were a lock-out at the Dassault factories in Bordeaux and at the Sidelor-Micheville steelworks in Villerupt.

After the Dassault lock-out a spontaneous rank-and-file strike broke out and continued for three weeks. This particular strike is remarkable for its militancy. It had been preceded by stoppages and other actions in the previous December. In some shops the men stopped work and just manufactured banners. When the president of the board of directors visited the factory, he was surrounded by the men, who would not release him until he promised to do something about their wages. The question of taking over the factory was discussed, but not acted upon. The workers went on demonstration after demonstration in the streets.

They captured and then put to flight the local mayor. Generally they saw to it that their demonstrations and actions received all the publicity that the streets could afford them. Their struggle sparked off *solidarity movements*; an inter-trades march through Bordeaux, a two-hour solidarity strike by the three steel workers' federations, etc. The workers won.[8]

This strike strongly influenced those that followed straight after in the Lyons region.

The Dassault strike had only just finished when the Rhodiaceta strike started. Rhodiaceta is an artificial fibre-textile factory at Besançon, which employs 3,000 workers. The workers had a massive picket, occupied the factory and refused entry to the director. The pickets and occupation were denounced by the CGT as an infringement of the owners' legal right and were ambiguously supported by CFDT. The strikers held meetings on political economy, folk-song recitals and an auction of paintings by local artists. Not as much rank-and-file control was evinced as at Dassault, but still the workers were not fooled into relaxing by the management and union initiatives. The strike spread to Vaise, Saint-Fons Belle Etoile, Vénissieux (near Lyons) and Péage-de-Roussillon (Isère). Altogether 14,000 Rhodiaceta workers were on strike.

Then the strike spread to the Berliet factory—truck producers—which employs 12,000 workers. The CGT and CFDT called only a two-hour strike, but the workers went on unlimited strike and occupied the factory. Berliet declared a lock-out and called on the CRS to evacuate the factory. However, only slight gains were achieved as there was lack of coordination between the unions.

This strike was followed by a strike on 1 March of 3,000 metal workers at St Nazaire. The course of this strike was like that at Dassault in that morale throughout was high. The strike was not led from above, but was conducted through meetings of the strikers.

On 18 March there was a lock-out of 8,000 shipyard workers at Chantiers de l'Atlantique on the pretext of indiscipline.

On 30 March there was an inter-trades demonstration in Nantes. Collections for this were organised in a number of different towns (Vannes, Lorient, Marseilles, Le Havre, St Etienne, Decazeville).

On 11 April there was a general strike in St Nazaire in both private and public sectors. There followed almost daily demonstrations of strikers. After seven weeks of strike a vote taken at a mass meeting of strikers showed 87 percent in favour of continuing the strike. However, when it ended after two months, the workers won only a small rise in wages.

On 27 April a 24-hour general strike was called in the whole of Loire-Atlantique.

A general one-day strike was called for 17 May by the three trade union confederations, CGT, CFDT and FO (Force Ouvrière, the right-wing socialist federation), as well as by FEN, the teachers' union. The aim of the strike was to protest against government schemes to mutilate Social Security. In the public sector the strike was almost 100 percent solid; in the private sector it was massive but far from all-embracing. In a demonstration in Paris in support of the strike 150,000 participated. There were also demonstrations in the provinces, notably Lyons, Marseilles, St Etienne and Bordeaux.

Although the central slogans in these demonstrations were opposition to the mutilation of Social Security, the slogan which actually drew the greatest response was 'All power to the workers'. In all the demonstrations the Internationale replaced the Marseillaise.[9]

On the eve of the introduction of the new Social Security measures (31 October) a new wave of official one-day mass strikes and demonstrations took place. Strikers at Le Mans, among whom were Renault workers who had already been demonstrating for a week, not content with demonstrating at the five points on the perimeter of the town that the police authorised, marched on the police prefecture and fought the CRS. Stones were used against teargas grenades, bare fists against helmets and matraques, the civilian crowd against armoured cars.

21 October saw a big demonstration of some tens of thousands in Paris from the Bastille to Place de la République. In Marseilles on the same day a march of 3,000 took place, which passed without incident, the police escorting it all the way.

At Renault-Flins there were two-hour stoppages on 12 and 13 October, which most of the workers supported. Nearly 5,000 gathered in front of the factory, many of the usually hesitant joining in. In the evening the CGT and CFDT decided to repeat this action the next Monday. But on that day a squabble took place between the CGT and CFDT and the demonstration was then sold out by the unions. As a result, on the Tuesday the CFDT managed to call out only 300 workers in a depressing demonstration.[10]

Another national action day was called for 13 December. Workers were beginning to show clear signs of weariness with these gesture strikes. In private industry the strike was very limited—three hours at Renault, small-scale strikes in the building industry, in food, banks and commerce. It was a great comedown compared with the 17 May strike.[11]

The advent of 1968 saw an important strike in Cannes, where 4,800 workers at Saviem Blainville came out. It started on 22 January. At the end of the first week the police charged a demonstration of strikers, sympathisers from other factories and students in a particularly ferocious manner. Barricades were built and a heroic resistance put up to the CRS; 205 were wounded (of whom 16 were kept in hospital), 85 arrested and 13 convicted to between 15 days and three months in prison; one Portuguese was deported after serving his time. The management then tried to split the workers by promising no victimisation and the unions tried to quell them by agreeing to withdraw the pickets. The strike ended finally on 6 February. The strike did not end in victory, but it was not defeated either, as sanctions against the workers were withdrawn. Of great importance, however, was the fact that it injected a spirit of real struggle into the scene.

This potted history of strikes in the two years before May 1968 shows that there were many rehearsals for the great event, both on the part of the workers and on that of the union bureaucracy. The wave of strikes was rising quickly, their militancy meeting with greater violence from the CRS; and the expertise of the union bureaucracy in diverting semi-insurrectionary struggles into 'demonstrative', 'warning', 'rotating' strikes was put to the test again and again.[12]

The role of the trade union bureaucracy as a brake on the real struggle of the workers was summed up by the theoretical organ *Voix Ouvrière*:

> Since World War Two French trade unions have practically never organised or led strike movements to victory in any area. But for a few rare exceptions, the only strikes of long duration which have taken place, (the Civil Servants' strike in 1953, the strike of the West coast shipyards in 1955, the strike of the coal miners in 1963), were either launched without the trade unions, or pursued in spite of their opposition. In all cases the trade unions have endeavoured to send people back to work and have finally succeeded in doing so without having obtained any satisfaction for the strikers.

However, the trade union bureaucracy could not preserve its influence over the workers and its control over the movement if it was openly antagonistic to all workers' resistance to exploitation. Hence its indulgence in 'struggles':

> If not real economic struggles, the CGT must at least organize parodies of them; whence the so-called 'demonstrative' strikes, 'warning' strikes, 'rotating' strikes, 'partial' strikes, general strikes...of 24 hours, etc...which the bourgeoisie tolerates, given what they are, that is, a necessary evil but not a threat. This is ineffective, but the workers generally impute this inefficacy to the political situation (a 'reactionary' government, etc...). And even if the workers are convinced of this inefficacy and of the duplicity of the national leadership of the unions, the bureaucratic apparatuses have become masters in the art of unpriming social conflicts. As soon as the workers are ready to start a fight in any area they are engaged in strikes limited to one or two hours a day, which are sterile, ineffective, and demoralising. It is the best means that the bureaucrats have found to prevent the most combative workers from bringing along those that are less combative: they are made to fight alone. Sometimes even a 24-hour strike is organised for a whole branch or even for the whole country... After such a day the militants declare to the workers that the general strike is a symbolic act with no follow-up and that harassing actions are therefore better. After 20 years the end of such actions is not yet in sight, and the French workers are still caught in the strait jacket which the union bureaucracies have tailored for them.[13]

The strike

The May 1968 strike was a reaction against the years of frustration, and the futile policies of the traditional organisations. Hence its violence, its semi-insurrectionary temper. Unfortunately, the workers could not throw overboard the traditional organisations in one fell swoop as they lacked a credible alternative. The strike, therefore, was very confused and ended neither in total victory nor complete defeat, but in stalemate.

It is virtually impossible to get a clear overall picture of the development of the strike, the forms of action and level of involvement, and to see precisely how the return to work was brought about. All that can be done is to put together some of the recorded incidents in specific situations, and try to discover some common patterns.

The first point to note is that in only very few instances were strike committees democratically elected. In practically every plant the trade union nominated the delegates to the strike committee. In Renault there were a few attempts to get elections by the rank and file, but they were squashed by the CGT and the CP except in one department. In the central Citroën factory the officially-appointed strike committee was not challenged, but in one of its subsidiary factories—in Nanterre—it was, but the attempt failed. As against this, in the Chemical factory Rhône-Poulenc-Vitry, the demand for a rank-and-file strike committee was so strong that the official one was overthrown and a new one elected by union and non-union workers alike.[14]

It is interesting that even in Citroën, where for 16 years there had not been a strike, and where only 7 percent of the workers were organised in trade unions, the union bureaucrats still managed to prevent the election of a democratic rank-and-file strike committee, and imposed a nominated one. They hastened to do this even before the strike began, as they were afraid that, because of the weakness of the union, things might get out of hand. This is also the reason why it was the CGT full-time officials who took the initiative in calling the strike.

The general policy of the union was to minimise the involvement of workers in the strike and the occupation of the factories. The overwhelming majority of the workers, probably as many as 80 or 90 percent, were sent home. Those remaining in the factories were mainly members of the CP and the CGT. These were prevented from meeting the revolutionary students, which was the real reason for locking the factory gates.

Another factor affecting the involvement of workers, and also the morale, was the *voluntary withdrawal* of young workers from the factories during the strike.

The young workers, who played a key role in encouraging militancy and developing new ideas preferred—because of the bureaucratic atmosphere prevailing in many factories—to leave them and participate in the student struggles in the streets—thus leaving the factories to the bureaucrats.

Also, once the strike had passed its peak, the sense of involvement waned. At Rhône-Poulenc, which had had a vigorous rank-and-file committee in the early days, the failure to make the struggle active led to apathy. Towards the beginning of June a certain intellectual tiredness crept in, so many of the subjects for discussion having been exhausted.

On the return from the Whit holiday the occupation was just as strong, but the spirit was not at all the same: the long discussions were replaced by games of cards, bowls and volleyball.[15]

Another factor militating against involvement in the strike was the relative isolation of the immigrant workers, who constitute quite a sizeable proportion of the working class of France.

Foreign workers are often less integrated into the existing organisations and are more particularly vulnerable. At Citroën, for example, after the return to work, the management threatened to confiscate foreigners' residence permits (an illegal action) if they did not cooperate in overtime working.[16]

Some places presented a very different scene. Thus at Nantes and St Nazaire the strike committee took over the administration of the town. The strikers controlled prices. Their wives distributed vegetables direct to the consumers. Strikers manned the petrol pumps and distributed petrol:

> Furthermore, care of strikers' children was taken charge of by unionised teachers and supervisors of children's holiday camps... Families of strikers in the worst financial situations had food coupons issued to them by the unions. The coupons were equivalent to a certain quantity of food. For each child under three there was a coupon for 1 franc [1 shilling 9 pence] of milk, and for each person over three a coupon for 500 grams [just over 1 lb] of bread and a 1 franc coupon for general foodstuffs.[17]

The most obvious lack in the strike was a network connecting the different strike committees. It did not exist even for factories belonging to the same firm.

If the CGT could not stop the strike, it was able to sabotage it by fragmenting the movement—taking what had been a mass movement of the class as a whole and reducing it to a series of disconnected struggles in different industries. Thus on 27 May the Administrative Commission of the CGT declared: 'What the Government and employers have not agreed on a national, inter-trades level, we must obtain from them on other levels by means of negotiations which we must demand immediately in each separate branch of industry and trade, such as are being carried on in the nationalised and public sectors.'

Thus negotiations with different employers transformed the strike from being general into a collection of separate strikes.

Not only was there no network of strike committees, but in practice the trade union bureaucracies did their best to isolate one strike committee from another. Thus, for instance, the Renault Billancourt CGT refused on 23 May to receive a delegation from Renault Flins.[18]

Unfortunately there was no national organisation strong enough to agitate for strike committees democratically elected by all workers, union or non-union, and to show the need for linking them up. If these had existed, they would have been basically the same as the soviets of 1917 or the Workers' Councils of Hungary in 1956.

The return to work

On 27 May the Grenelle 'Agreements' were reached between the representatives of the trade unions and the employers under the arbitration of the Ministry of Labour. The agreements can be summed up as follows:

— The Minimum Guaranteed Wage for all industries is increased from 2.22 to 3 francs per hour. For a 40-hour week this makes 519 francs per month. The unions were demanding 'no wages below 600 francs'.
— A general increase in wages, fixed for the private sector at 7 percent on 1 June 1968, plus 3 percent on 1 October. But from these percentages must be deducted increases already granted during the year.

In the public and nationalised sectors, separate negotiations are to be carried on sector by sector.
— Payment for the period of strike—an ambiguous formulation: 50 percent will be paid, but must be made up by overtime working. In fact, it is simply an advance on wages.
— The exercise of union rights in the factory. There was no agreement on this question, merely the listing of a certain number of points which are to be the subject of further discussions.
— Social Security. A patient's contribution to medical expenses is to be reduced from 30 percent to 25 percent. The increase from 20 percent to 30 percent introduced in 1967 has not been withdrawn.

On other points—working hours, retirement, a sliding scale of wages—there was no agreement.

Even then it took the Trade-Union leadership a long time—nearly three weeks—to bring the strikes to an end, and they had to cow the workers in one factory after another.

Benoît Frachon, President of the CGT and a leader of the CP, declared that the agreements 'will bring to millions of workers a well-being that they had never hoped to attain'—on 600 francs a month, mind you (£10 a week—less than the minimum of £15 a week demanded by Frank Cousins). Stating this to the assembled workers in Renault Billancourt he was astonished, it seems, to be booed.[19]

As a matter of fact, the strike movement reached its peak after the Grenelle 'Agreements'.

But the pressure of the trade union and party bureaucracies did eventually yield results, and what *L'Humanité* (6 June) called 'The Victorious Return To Work' started. In some places resistance to this was sharp.

On 1 June an attempt was made to run trains by force at the Gare de L'Est, Paris. This was prevented by the railway workers lying down on the tracks.[20] On 3 June workers at Sud Aviation (Nantes), where the first occupation had begun, issued a statement urging all workers to maintain the general strike to 'total victory'.[21] Elsewhere the response was more ambiguous. At CSF (Levallois) there was a referendum in which two thirds of the workers voted dissatisfaction with the management offer, but only one third voted to continue the strike.[22] In the big Paris stores there was a demoralising drift back to work, with some workers recommencing before others.[23]

The failure to end the strike in some sectors was, according to the CGT, due to the:

> ...particularly retrograde and stubborn attitude of the bosses who were refusing to make the concessions granted everywhere else. The CGT strongly insists that

> the settlement of claims in the metal, rubber and other industries in the same spirit which has prevailed in the other large sectors of the economy, is a national affair requiring the attention of the government and the CNPF...
>
> The CGT calls upon the whole of the public which has had the opportunity of appreciating the responsibility of the CGT, and the calmness of millions of strikers, to give powerful support to the victims of an unjust and scandalous act of discrimination.[24]

The sheer duplicity of the CGT in calling for solidarity with those still out on strike, after it had itself destroyed the best form of solidarity by persuading workers elsewhere to go back to work, is disgusting.

On 7 June there was a return to the charge of collusion between the 'groupuscules' and the government after the abortive attempt to re-occupy the Renault factory at Flins. 'It is difficult to believe that the high-handedness of the engineering industry employers, the support they get from the government, and the police brutalities and these attempts at provocation are not concerted,' said the local CGT official.

In most cases the return to work was decided by a 'democratic' vote. In the most militant factories the vote was often very close. Thus at Renault, after the CRS attack, the vote went as follows: at Billancourt, where the union delegates voted openly for the return, 78 percent of the workers followed them. But at Flins, where supporters of the strike prevented the CGT delegate from speaking, the percentage fell to 58 percent (4,811 votes for, 3,890 against, 25 spoilt ballot papers).[25]

At Peugeot, on 9 June, the vote was closer. Out of 25,800 workers, only 5,279 participated; 2,664 voted for return, 2,615 against. Work was restarted on 10 June, but a new strike began the next day, and continued to 20 June, when 84.7 percent of the 15,000 who voted supported a return.[26]

At Citroën, Paris, following the intervention of leading CP bureaucrats, out of 24,738 workers, 18,519 voted, of whom 13,184 (71.18 percent) supported a return.[27]

The role of the CGT in these votes was at best confusing and at worst criminal. At Citroën, on the occasion of the first vote, organised by the management by secret ballot outside the factory, the CGT took no action but simply declared, 'People are free to vote'.[28] At the second vote different coloured ballot papers were used, and CGT observers carefully scrutinised how workers voted.[29] At Polymécanique (Pantin) the CGT confused the issue by announcing that the vote was not for or against a return, but for or against the management proposals.[30] At Crédit Lyonnais Paris, there was no supervision of the ballot so one could vote several times.[31] At Thomson-Gennevilliers, before the ballot took place, the CGT distributed a leaflet and sold *L'Humanité*, both declaring that Thomson had returned to work having gained great advantages. To make sure their declarations would be proved correct, they allowed non-strikers to vote.[32] At Sev-Marchal, Issy-les-Moulineaux, not only non-strikers but also foremen, supervisors and even management were allowed to participate in the vote on the return.[33]

In this situation of fragmented return, the role of information was crucial, for obviously the decision whether or not to return was dependent on decisions elsewhere. The bourgeois state and press combined their efforts with the CGT. Teachers first learned that they were to return to work by a radio announcement.[34] A standard technique of the CGT was to announce in one factory that other factories had decided to return.[35]

In Paris transport—underground and buses—the trade union representatives were the only ones who went from one depot to another. To the workers of each depot they said, 'You are against the return to work, but you are on your own. Everybody else wants to return to work.' Thus, while the Depot Rue Lebrun had voted to carry on the strike, other depots had been told that it had voted 85 percent for a return. After talking to the union officials, the elected strike committee at Lebrun, hearing that all the other depots were back at work, ordered a return, ignoring the vote already taken. At last, as a result of this method, after four weeks of strike, the transport workers were demoralised enough to vote for a return to work.[36]

The various local Action Committees distributed leaflets trying to put the real facts before the workers, but there was no organisation to coordinate the vital information in time. What a difference would have been made by a revolutionary party with a daily newspaper and possibly even a radio transmitter!

On the surface the role of the formerly Catholic trade unions, CFDT, was a bit more militant than the CP-controlled CGT. As is well known, they opposed the CGT at Billancourt and welcomed the student deputation. Where they were in a minority they were able to act a demagogic role and in some cases prevented CGT sell-outs. Thus at Thomson-Gennevilliers the CGT was impeded in its desire for a return to work by the strength of the CFDT. But the CFDT were only able to work within a bureaucratic framework—thus at Thomson-Gennevilliers it accepted a vote on the return to work carried out by secret ballot, and factory by factory rather than over the whole company.[37] Likewise at Citroën Paris the CFDT called for continuation of the strike—but made no attempt to organise a boycott of the vote.[38]

Elsewhere the role of the CFDT was openly anti-strike. Thus at Rhône-Poulenc (Vitry) the CFDT decided to return to work on 12 June despite a vote of 580 to 470 by occupying workers against a return.

Analyses et Documents[39] sums up the role of the CFDT as follows:

> There were also cases where the CFDT, because it was in the majority, fully exercised the function entrusted by the bourgeoisie to the union organisations, the return to order. This happened notably at Berliet, Peugeot, Rhodiaceta. We saw that at Peugeot it was the CGT which opposed the return. The same happened at Berliet-Vénisseux. There the CFDT signed an agreement, ratified by the FO and the CGC [Confédération Générale des Cadres—Union of Supervisors and Technicians]. The CGT opposed it, which allowed the CFDT delegate to play the role played elsewhere by the CGT, in denouncing 'the behaviour of a sectarian and anti-democratic minority'. The return to work was to be decided on 19 June, by only 56 percent of these voting.

> There were also, more frequently, attempts by the CFDT to outflank the CGT, at Citroën, Sud-Aviation, Renault-Flins. At the last, the decision for indefinite strike on 19 June, cancelled the next day, shows clearly that it was in no way an attempt to mobilise the workers, but just a tactical manoeuvre directed against the CGT.

Relations between the CGT and CFDT, good before May, have much worsened; some recent elections of factory committees show that at SAVIEM (Caen), where the CFDT was formerly in the majority, the CGT have gained votes, but at Berliet, where the CGT was in the majority, it is the CFDT that has gained.[40]

In Renault Billancourt members of the CGT left and joined CFDT: in the shop commonly known as The Kremlin, where there was only one member of CFDT before the strike, now the number of CFDT members is equal to that of the CGT.

The Social-Democratic Trade Union Federation, FO, despite its slender resources, also fulfilled its norms of strikebreaking. At the Ministry of Supply representatives of the FO, the strongest union in the establishment, had no advice to offer other than that the strike was illegal.[41]

All the Trade Union Federations thus came up to the expectations of the regime, as formulated clearly by *Le Monde*: 'The employers, like the state, have...a vested interest in the existence of a strong union organisation, that is a union organisation that will do as it's told!'[42]

Even in the purely economic terms to which the CGT tried to reduce the struggle, there were advantages for those sectors which continued the struggle. At Citroën, where the CGT controlled the situation, the gains were minimal—from the 10 percent wage increase an increase already given in January was deducted. In return for services rendered, the unions gained the right to circulate papers in the factory.[43] At Renault some significant gains were made over and above the Grenelle 'Agreements'—further wage increases of 2 to 4 percent, and reduction of working hours by one hour a week without loss of pay.[44] It was in the public sector, Electricity, Gas, Railways, Paris Transport, Post Office, that the biggest additional gains were made.[45]

But the general return to work far from marked an end to the struggle. On the contrary, the experience led to a new level of militancy, and the return to work will allow the development of new forms of organisation.

Although the full maturation of an unofficial strike movement can be expected only in the autumn, there is already a high level of struggle. At CSF Issy-les-Moulineaux the workers reacted quickly to attempts to discriminate between strikers and non-strikers. There were immediately several short strikes, called at a few minutes notice, and involving 700 or 800 workers.[46] At Renault, on 19 June, there were stoppages to defend foreign workers (who had been very active in the strike) against the threat of non-renewal of contracts. The CFDT initially supported this action, but withdrew using the excuse of non-participation by the CGT.[47]

At Renault (Flins) after an attempt to restart work on 10 June, the workers reoccupied on 11 June, despite opposition from both CGT and CFDT.[48]

One of the main issues now facing workers is recuperation—that is, overtime working to make up pay lost during the strike period. Many workers are anxious to make up earnings before the holiday period. This is an immediate cause of friction. Thus at Roussel-UCLAF, Romainville, the workers were allowed to vote on the principle of recuperation, but not on the form, and many are being asked to work an hour later, so that they come out at a time when transport is virtually impossible.[49] At Renault, where a computer is used to calculate the pay slips, the main aim seems to be to prevent workers discovering how much is due to them or how it is calculated.[50]

Added to this is the question of sackings. At Citroën 925 monthly paid workers have already been given notice.[51] At Citroën, where before May there had not been a single strike for over ten years, there have already been about 50 short stoppages. The unofficial strike, hitherto almost unknown in France, is becoming more widespread, and there may be a wave of them in the autumn.

In such struggles the unions are continuing to play their obstructive role. At the Assurances Générales, Paris, where there is compulsory recuperation of half an hour per day—even for non-strikers—the unions have opposed this in principle, but refused to call a strike of half an hour a day.[52]

At Citroën the CGT, trying to settle accounts for a dispute during the strike when they tried to prevent workers defending the factory from the CRS, went so far as to issue a leaflet fingering a militant:

> ...they tried to pass to another stage of their activity and tried to proceed to sabotage. X [the original leaflet names a worker, but our source refuses to perpetuate the fingering] has himself confessed this to the CGT commission.
>
> We denounce such attempts as foreign to the orientation of the CGT and harmful to the working-class movement. We call on the CGT leadership to react firmly against such attempts if they know about them, for they are to the advantage of the Citroën management and to the Gaullist regime itself. People like X and others of his group have no place, not only in the CGT, but in the factory.[53]

The picture, then, is a very confused one—not least because we have detailed information only from those factories where there happen to be revolutionary militants who communicate their experience to journals outside. But the main lines—of union betrayal and continuing militancy—are clear.

The Action Committees

A vacuum existed on the left. There were not even the embryos of Soviets—workers' councils linking up democratically elected strike committees. Neither was there a revolutionary party so desperately demanded by the situation.

As a substitute Soviet that did not exist and a substitute revolutionary party that did not exist, arose the Action Committees!

What a magnificent improvisation !

The Action Committees reflected the great unevenness in the level of consciousness of the fighting people—above all the big difference between the students and the bulk of the industrial workers.

The initiative to establish the Action Committees was in the main taken by students, including members of all the 'groupuscules' (Trotskyists, Maoists, Anarchists and members of no group). At the end of June there were in Paris some 450 Action Committees. Many hundreds existed up and down the country.

The Action Committees and the 'Comités de Base' (Rank-and-File Committees) took widely differing forms in different places, and one can merely quote some.

Rhône-Poulenc (Vitry): There were 39 Rank-and-File Committees. They each delegated four representatives to the Central Committee; this therefore had 156 members of whom 78 sat permanently. These representatives were elected and could be recalled at any time. The meetings of the Central Committee took place daily and were public.54

Ministry of Supply: Every morning a general assembly of the staff was called; this was the leading body of the strike, and every day it elected a different chairman, whose role was limited to allowing free discussion (thus up to 8 June there were 18 successive chairmen).

Outside the factories the main need was to organise food supplies. The March 22 movement assisted in the creation of organisations to distribute chickens and potatoes in the factories of Courbevoie. At Rennes contacts were made with the peasantry who offered poultry and rabbits as gifts in solidarity.[55]

These structures, while being highly democratic in nature, were essentially geared to the strike situation, and in particular to the context of an active strike, where the workers begin to control the means of production. With the end of the strike the same forms could not survive. But some continuity was possible. Thus at CSF, Issy-les-Moulineaux, a more permanent Comité de Base has been established.

The duration of the mandate of members of a rank-and-file committee is six months. The committee is composed of delegates elected by all the staff of the unit corresponding to the committee, the number of these delegates being around 10 percent of the total workforce. Half of them are replaced every three months; no delegate can be re-elected twice running. The objective to be attained by these measures is to allow a rotation of all workers in positions of responsibility. Delegates can be recalled at any time.[56]

But the role of these rank-and-file committees was necessarily an ambiguous one. There was wide discontent among unionised workers with the part played by the leadership of the trade unions in the strike, and out of this discontent grew the recognition of the need to create alternative forms of organisation. In many cases these new organisations were able to put pressure on the unions in the negotiations and to limit the extent to which the unions were able to sell out. But in the short and hectic period available the new forms of organisation were not able to take over from the unions, but only to exist alongside them in uneasy compromise.

One reason for this was the need to very rapidly overcome previously-held attitudes. For example, one of the striking achievements of the Comités de Base was the way they were able to involve workers who had not been unionised hitherto—some of the best militants came from this section—but initially the demand for representation of non-unionised workers in strike committees produced an unfavourable reaction from workers who had already been unionised and for whom trade-union consciousness was an important step forward.[57]

The weakness of the Comités de Base was increased by the attitude of the management, who much preferred to negotiate with the bureaucratic unions. At CSF, Issy-les-Moulineaux, the management refused to meet the elected delegates of the workers.[58]

However, the Rank-and-File Committees quite clearly represent a new development in the factories. Thus at Roussel UCLAF, Romainville, workers elected delegates in their own workshop, without any legal formality and without the intervention of the unions to put up candidates—a practice almost unknown in France previously.

Similarly, reports from Rhône-Poulenc (Vitry) suggest that the Rank-and-File Committee was well on the way to replacing the unions in the first fortnight of the strike: all propositions were listened to, discussed and the best put to the vote (for example, the admission of a non-unionised worker to the Executive Committee). We should also stress that throughout this period union members cooperated within the Rank-and-File Committees without any internal conflicts. In effect, we can say that there were no longer union or non-union members, but only occupiers. The Executive Committee was entirely under the control of the decisions of the Central Committee.[59]

There are at present three main types of Action Committees: (1) of the locality—anyone who lives in a certain locality can join this body; (2) of the place of work (Comités de Base); (3) joint student-worker Action Committees. The last, which played an important role during the strike, is now in decline. The first two types are more active at present.[60]

The greatest weakness of the Action Committees is their fragmentation and lack of perspectives. Members of the Action Committees are frightened, quite rightly, of bureaucracy. Quite often, however, they identify any centralised organisation with bureaucratism, thus throwing out the baby with the bath water. As a result there is hardly any coordination between Action Committees.

It is much too early to estimate whether in the Action Committees—through action and discussion—a political differentiation and regroupment will take place that will lead to the building of a revolutionary party. It is possible also that the Action Committees, and especially the Comités de Base, will serve to ginger up a rank-and-file industrial leadership, something not unlike the shop stewards (that exists in Britain but not in France).

The party of permanent treason

The counter-revolutionary role of the PCF is an old story. In the space available we will quote only a few examples out of this long and ugly history.

The Popular Front period

Following the Franco-Soviet Pact of May 1935 the PCF moved quickly toward class collaboration. Shortly after Foreign Minister Pierre Laval returned from Moscow and announced, 'Stalin fully approves France's policy of national defence in order to maintain its armed forces at a level sufficient to preserve its security,' the CP, in a letter to the Radical Party Congress, declared, 'Private property, the fruit of labour and saving, must be respected'.[61]

When in May and June 1936 a mass sit-in strike spread spontaneously throughout France, involving some 1.5 million workers, the PCF proved itself to be the 'Party of order'.

It took upon itself the role of trying to control the strike wave. The leadership was bewildered by the revolutionary nature of the struggle. Cachin said, 'We are confronted—we and the others—by the fact of the strike'.[62] Communist militant Henri Raynaud and Socialist Jules Moch were not admitted to a factory by the striking workers with whom they went to discuss.[63] On 11 June Thorez addressed a party meeting:

> If it is important to carry out a movement of demands properly, it is also important to know how to bring it to an end. It is not a question of taking power at the moment… If the aim now is to achieve satisfaction for demands of an economic character, while progressively raising the level of consciousness and organisation of the masses, then one must know how to stop a strike as soon as satisfaction has been obtained.[64]

1944-47

In August 1944 the armed resistance movement, consisting mainly of workers, used the fall of German power to take control of Paris. They seized the main factories, and, arms in hand, patrolled the town, disarming the collaborating police. The '200 families'—the financial magnates of France—had no popular support at all, as they had willingly collaborated with Hitler and done good business under Nazi rule. Indeed, one can unquestionably say that the knell of French capitalism had sounded. How, then, did it survive? *The answer is to be found mainly in the conduct of the French Communist (and Socialist) parties.*

After de Gaulle signed the 20-year Franco-Soviet alliance in December 1944, Thorez declared him a 'great friend and ally of the Soviet Union'. The Party acted in the spirit of this 'friendship' and immediately after his return from Moscow agreed to the disarming of the popular militia, a measure which it had opposed earlier in the year. Thorez then raised the slogan 'One State, one army, one police force', and the Stalinist cabinet ministers, Thorez, Tillon and Billoux, voted for the decree dissolving the people's militia.

The 'one police force' which was to remain was the very same as had served the strikebreaking government of Daladier, and later that of Vichy and the Gestapo, the same force which persecuted the Resistance for four years and which had not since been purged. Thorez could shamelessly declare, 'We do not put forward any socialist demands.' And another leader of the party, Duclos, could say on 19 November 1945, 'Since the Liberation we have contributed to the re-establishment of order in the country. We have led a campaign for the disarmament of the armed groups and for production.'

How the CP leaders encouraged productivity and prevented strikes is clear, for instance, from Thorez's speech at Waziers on 21 July, 1945, where he caught a genuine [Lord Alfred] Robens-like accent:

> It is true that only we, the Communists, had enough authority to put a stop to the strikes in June 1936, and that only we, five months ago, had enough authority to say: we must stop playing at civil war and not allow provocations against the working class and our country.
>
> Besides, it isn't true that miners do not love their work. You know I come from a family of miners... Old miners love their work like sailors love the sea.
>
> I want to come back to the question of absenteeism. Many reasons and pretexts are being given for absences. I must say, dear comrades, that I am not fully convinced by the reasons given to justify absences.
>
> I will tell you, dear comrades, that in the Loire basin the same question came up in the winter when there was so much flu and food shortage. The union got together the delegates to the Welfare Fund and told them, 'Examine the medical certificates and discuss with the doctors,' and they were told, 'These doctors, for the most part, are not your friends. They give certificates too easily. They, who have for a long time been the enemies of the working class and of nationalisation, easily give certificates; they are encouraging disorganisation.' There are going to be elections to the Welfare Fund. The union must demand that these questions are raised everywhere and say to the delegates to the Welfare Funds that you are going to elect, 'You must be intransigent; we have finished with such methods, because it is anarchy, an encouragement to idleness.'
>
> I was told the other day that at the Escarpelle pit about 15 lads asked to knock off at six o'clock to go dancing. This is impermissible.

Similarly, in 1945, Thorez denounced as 'agitators' the civil servants who threatened strike action.[65] But despite this there were strikes, for the PCF did not have total control of the workers—Paris printers in January 1946, Post Office workers in July 1946, and the Renault strike of April 1947 which coincided with the CP change of line.[66]

Support to imperialism

On 4 April 1946 the Stalinist Deputies in the French parliament voted for the following message of congratulation to the French troops fighting in Indo-China against the Viet Minh: 'The National Constituent Assembly sends to the troops of the Expeditionary Force in the Far East and to their leaders the expression of the country's gratitude and confidence on the morrow of the day in which their entry into Hanoi sets the seal on the success of the government of the Republic's policy of peaceful liberation of all the peoples of the Union of Indochina.' Again, 'On the occasion of Christmas, the Commission of National Defence sends to the French soldiers in Indochina the expression of its affectionate sympathy and salutes their efforts to maintain in the Far East the civilising and peaceful presence of France' (10 December 1946).

In March 1947, when the PCF was still in the government, the Political Bureau issued a statement instructing Communist deputies to abstain on the vote of credits for the military expedition to Vietnam, but added, 'There is no need for Communist Ministers to break Ministerial solidarity'.[67] Later, although some dockers and other individuals took direct action against the Vietnam war, the Party failed to organise mass demonstrations.[68]

On the Algerian question, which roused the emotions of French people much more strongly, the Party's role was worse.

Before the war the French Party had never seriously considered the problem of Algerian nationalism. In January 1937 the Popular Front government dissolved Messali Hadj's Etoile Nord Africaine.[69]

In May 1945, after a nationalist demonstration in Algeria which led to riots, there was sharp repression by the authorities leading to at least 10,000 Muslim deaths, probably many more. The French government at the time of the reprisals contained two Communist ministers,[70] and *L'Humanité* of 19 May contained the statement, 'It is necessary to mete out the punishment they deserve to the Hitlerite killers who took part in the events of 8 May, and to the pseudo-nationalist leaders.' Thorez's report to the Tenth Congress of the PCF (June 1945) gave some indication of the reasons: 'We are short of food. Algeria could provide us with a million sheep every year, if water supplies were improved.' And Caballero, General Secretary of the Algerian Communist Party, 'concluded by emphasising that the Algerian people had the same enemies as the French people, and do not want to be separated from France. Those who claim independence for Algeria are the conscious or unconscious agents of another imperialism'.[71]

In 1954, when the Algerian war broke out, the PCF had neither the excuse of famine nor governmental responsibility.

The Mollet government in 1956 asked for special powers to deal with the Algerian situation—the PCF deputies voted for them—giving the excuse, 'The essential aim of this vote was to make the scales lean to the left and free the government from the pressures of reaction'.[72]

Demonstrations in protest against the recall of demobilised soldiers to Algeria, called by local CP militants, were disavowed by the Party, while the Socialist government exercised repression against such demonstrations. The PCF leadership forbade direct contact between French and Algerian Communists.[73]

After de Gaulle took power, the Soviet Union obviously was worried about the situation; the USSR only recognised the Provisional Government in October 1960; Khrushchev urged a negotiated settlement, and the USSR was chary about arms or non-military supplies.[74]

When a PCF militant, Albert Liechti, refused to bear arms in Algeria and was imprisoned, the PCF did not wage a campaign on the issue for nearly a year.[75] When the *Manifesto of the 121*, supporting the refusal to bear arms against the Algerians, was published in 1960, the Party replied (though nine members had signed it) that it could not 'approve, in any form, the appeal for insubordination or the organisation of it'.[76]

The resilience of the PCF

After all the damage the French Communist Party has done to the working class, how can one explain the fact that still the overwhelming majority of the French workers remain loyal to it? The two greatest periods of growth of the Party were during the Popular Front period in 1936, and the Liberation of 1945; both were occasions when it held back a working-class thrust towards power, and diverted it into safe parliamentary channels. The great resilience of the Party was shown also at the time of the Hungarian Revolution. Certainly the rank and file did not support the Russian action there, and the leaders of the CGT were unable to get their members to endorse it, which compelled them to leave it as an open question; but the Party lost few members or votes over the question.

An analysis of the sources of the enormous strength and resilience of the French Communist Party is necessary. To do this requires a recognition that Stalinism has a coherent logic. Whatever may be the motives of the leadership, the rank-and-file militants who have beaten up leftists and turned students away from the factories have done so out of sincere acceptance of the Party position.

Certainly one important reason is the fact that the workers cannot see any viable alternative. They cannot leave the Communist Party in spite of all its crimes unless they can replace it with another party.

A second reason is the innate conservatism which characterises all mass organisations. After all, a couple of generations of the working class have gone through the PCF. This has created a strong tradition. Workers feel deep loyalty to those who reared and educated them.

These two factors explaining the stability of the mass support of the PCF apply also to the mass Social Democratic Party. There are, however, some specific features that distinguish the Stalinist PCF from traditional Social Democracy, which add greatly to the resilience of the former.

Like Social Democracy, the PCF has a social base in the labour aristocracy, in the management of town councils and local administrations. Its members who are trade union delegates get subsidies from the state. It has many members in the trade union bureaucracy. It benefits from the privileges accorded by French capitalism to the higher social layers of the labour movement. But, unlike Social Democracy, the PCF is more able to protect its flank from attacks from the left, as its relation to the ruling capitalist class of France is more ambivalent. The Kremlin never offered the PCF for sale to l'Elysée, but only for hire. The fact that again and again the PCF broke out, or was thrown out of official society, helps its leaders to refurbish their tarnished image.

To keep its influence among the workers the PCF leaders time and again organise 'struggles', naturally always contained and controlled, but nevertheless struggles.

The historical background of the PCF explains why it can indulge in such struggles, while Social Democracy can not.

The degeneration of Social Democracy took place during a period of rising capitalism with relative social peace, the period preceding the First World War. It had grown into bourgeois conformism, as it did not need to use methods of 'struggle' to keep its rank and file in tow. When a prolonged period of crises and upheavals came, Social Democracy could not adapt itself to the new methods needed to keep its mass base. The degeneration of the Communist International took place under completely different conditions, during the period of big convulsions following the greatest revolutionary crisis the world had known.

The above factors—dependence on the Soviet bureaucracy (and only in the second place on French capitalism), and preserving its capacity to indulge in 'struggles'—give rise to another factor, quite significant in the stability of the PCF: its totalitarian nature.

Social Democracy as a bourgeois party has much more centralism than democracy in it. The well-clad bureaucrats at the top of the party are quite free from any real control by the rank and file. As with the rest of capitalist society, decisions are made by a small group at the top and handed down to the people below. Freedom to discuss issues (and choose 'representatives') once in so many years is all that remains to the rank and file. If the need arises to settle accounts with the revolutionaries, as in Germany in 1919, it is not the Social Democratic Party members who grew up in bourgeois conformism and legalism who need do the dirty job, but the military and police arms of capitalism.

The Communist Parties were formed in opposition to the bourgeois legalism of Social Democracy, and countered this legalism by proclaiming the necessity for revolutionary violence. Following their bureaucratic degeneration the Communist Parties the world over, while losing the revolutionary content of their action, still kept their attitude of support for violence. Freed from squeamishness on this score, the Communist Parties educated their own militants to hunt down oppositionists. The apparatus was strong enough to isolate the revolutionaries from the rank and file of the Communist Party and its trade unions for decades.

For a whole generation no Trotskyist was allowed by the PCF to sell newspapers at the factories or in their neighbourhood. Again and again the sellers were severely beaten up. Never for a moment did the PCF relax its vigilance in hunting down Trotskyist militants and expelling them from the unions.

One need but think of the 13 May demonstration in Paris when something like 20,000 CP stewards linked arms to separate the workers from the students! No Social Democratic Party has anything like this apparatus of strong-arm men.

Connected with all the above factors is another strengthening the PCF control over the masses. No channel of spontaneous rank-and-file organisation and expression is available not only in the Party but also in the Party-controlled union, the CGT.

The local branches and sections of the CGT have general members' meetings only in exceptional cases, hardly once a year. The only union meetings which take place are those for the union apparatus. Generally these meetings are called 'CE' (Executive Committee) meetings, and are attended only by workers allowed 'special time' (paid as work hours) in order to carry out their mandate as 'délégués du personnel' (elected representatives of the employees) and as members of the 'Comité d'Entreprise' (committee of workers and management representatives dealing with labour conditions).

Whenever the CP can, it tries to penetrate throughout the union structure and keep all posts entailing responsibility in the hands of Party members. 'Unreliable' elements are kept away from meetings. The 'delegates' are elected from union lists. Thus, unlike in England, a worker may be elected as steward by workers who, though he is in the same union,[77] do not know him, or even personally detest him. Each delegate is entitled to 15 paid hours every month:

> The CGT may decide that a rotating strike of half an hour or quarter of an hour every fortnight is the best way to fight the management. This decision is not put to the vote of the workers, but in the workshops or sections some convinced workers are sent to organise broad democratic debates on the problem of organising the rotating strike. Thus the choice of day and time is entrusted to the decision of these rank-and-file assemblies. Anyone who intervenes to say he is not in agreement with the principle will soon find himself told that that is not the subject under discussion.[78]

Lines of communication are by and large open only to the CP and the CGT. The CGT is able to transmit information from one group to another—telling one shift or shop that the others are already in agreement for (or against) the strike, and thereby convincing them to act as required.[79]

The CP's disciplinary powers in industry are strong. To quote just one example cited by a worker at Renault:

> In 1960, the management sacked nearly 3,000 workers. These, helped by some others, demonstrated their hostility violently by breaking the management's windows...the next day...a leaflet from the CGT attacked the smashers as provocateurs and by implication pointed to three of the culprits. As a result two were sacked for this; the only charge against them was the said leaflet. The three named were members of other unions.[80]

On the basis of the totalitarian nature of the PCF a highly developed leader cult arose.

In particular, a cult grew up around the person of Maurice Thorez. Ever since 1946 official lists of the membership of the Central Committee put Thorez at the head of the list and not in his place in alphabetical order.[81] In May 1950 a National Exhibition was held to celebrate Thorez's fiftieth birthday.[82] At this time the Party issued recruiting forms headed 'I join the Party of Maurice Thorez', which only named the Communist Party in small print at the bottom.[83]

On the occasion of Stalin's death the Party sent a message to Thorez including the following:

> It seems to us that in the immense space of the great hall your voice echoes—your voice which created our party... Your presence gives a face to all our hope. And we feel you present within each one of us.[84]

Accepted by millions as the only party of the working class, while at the same time more and more implicated in bourgeois politics—parliamentarism, 'peaceful co-existence', and so on—the PCF bolsters the bourgeois prejudices of its supporters, and is itself fed by them. Many of the Party supporters at present do not regard it so much as the embodiment of the ideas and traditions of October 1917, but as the embodiment of reformist opportunism. Thus a survey carried out in 1952 by IFOP (French public opinion polls) of voters for various parties found the following concerning the PCF: 29 per cent thought the party not intransigent enough (as against 13 percent too intransigent and 42 percent just right); 41 percent favoured reform by means of revolution, 50 percent by means of reform; 40 percent thought the Party should never take power by force; 32 percent voted Communist to support the struggle for peace, and 39 percent for its anti-capitalist programme; 46 percent thought war was the most important problem and 32 percent the cost of living; 74 percent thought France should stay neutral in a general war.[85]

As in the social democratic parties, the supporters of the PCF participate less and less in any party activity, even so far as reading the party press. Thus, for instance, while the CP retained its vote of around 5 million for more than two decades, the circulation of *L'Humanité* fell from around 400,000 in 1947 to around 200,000 today.

The strength of the PCF lies above all in the fact that for many years it has been the only political power of the opposition, the only left-wing force, which crystallises round itself all the hopes of change.

However, the mole of history burrows on...

In May 1968, for the first time, a serious threat from the left rose before the PCF; for the first time since the degeneration of the Communist International the extreme left appeared as a political force in the country that was not negligible. Tens of thousands of youth, including tens of thousands of young workers, turned towards revolutionary politics. For the first time a mass movement independent of the CP arose. It was limited practically only to the youth. It was confused, but it was there.

There are a number of other circumstances that will make it much more difficult this time for the PCF to retain custody of the working class. In 1936 it was the party on the extreme left, as the main working-class party was still the Social Democratic Party (SFIO). At that time the CP attracted to itself the poorest sections of the working class—the unorganised workers. In 1945 the PCF was the party of the Resistance, and attracted many skilled workers and petit bourgeois elements who had hitherto been the social base of Social Democracy. Now the PCF is *the* leadership, hence it is in an exposed position. Above all, the constellation of international political forces is completely different from that of 1936 or 1945: Moscow has lost its magical influence in the world.[86]

Unfortunately the PCF may succeed in carrying through a third, fourth and fifth betrayal of the working class if no credible revolutionary alternative arises, if no revolutionary party comes into being. If the study of history—even the most recent—were enough by itself to solve political questions, Social Democracy would have died a long time ago, and so would Stalinism. Alas, this is not how history works. And there is nothing more foreign to socialism than fatalism.

The non-CP 'left'

Although it is the Communist Party which has the main grip on the French working class, and is therefore primarily responsible for its betrayal, certain representatives of the non-Communist left attempted to play a role in the crisis. In order to understand why the working class treated them with the contempt they deserved, it is useful to look at the history and record of these men and institutions.

The principal section of the non-Communist left in France is the Socialist Party—SFIO—French Section of the Workingmen's International: its name is virtually the only connection it retains with either internationalism or the working class.

The SFIO since the Second World War has never managed to have an effective working-class base. In 1951 it was estimated that 32 percent of Socialist votes came from communes of less than 2,000 inhabitants, and only 31 percent from towns of more than 20,000 inhabitants. It is strongest in the South West and Mediterranean areas.[87] Its membership is declining—in 1945 it had 335,000 members, in 1950 it had 140,000, and in 1962 it had 91,000.[88]

The party made little impact on youth, partly due to witch-hunts; in 1947 the youth sections lost their autonomy for Trotskyist heresies; ten years later youth sections existed in only 48 of 90 departments.[89] The party is openly imperialistic. Jacques Fauvet notes that the party had never been so united right across the spectrum from Mollet and Lacoste to Defferre (who often took a more left line) than on the Suez intervention.

It should be noted that among non-members of the SFIO Mitterrand wholeheartedly supported Suez and Mendès-France gave it qualified approval.[90]

It should be remembered that the SFIO still describes itself as a Marxist and revolutionary party, and uses appropriate language.

Typifying this is Guy Mollet, the General Secretary of the SFIO since 1946, who has shown unparalleled skill at manipulating the party machine.

Mollet was brought to power by the left of the party. At the 1957 Socialist conference he still remembered enough of Marx to produce a quotation to justify the Suez adventure.

Yet what was Mollet's record? Apart from Suez and his policy over Algeria, the following points might be noted:

He played a key role in de Gaulle's return to power in 1958—an issue on which the SFIO was divided. On 30 May Mollet met de Gaulle, and told the press that the meeting 'had been one of the great moments of his life'.[91] During the election that November, Mollet—not opposed by a Gaullist candidate—waved an autographed photo of de Gaulle at election meetings.[92]

Mollet remained in the de Gaulle government till December 1958—he then wrote to de Gaulle saying, 'I do not regret any of my decisions since May, and am happy and proud to have been able to help you found the institutions of the republic on a firmer basis'.[93] The SFIO continued to support de Gaulle's regime throughout the duration of the Algerian war.

Among other worthies of the SFIO we may mention:

Jules Moch: Minister of the Interior, 1947-50—reorganised the police force, appointing, following Vichy precedents, eight super-prefects to control the police effectively; was responsible for the CRS shooting strikers, killing two and wounding many.[94]

Robert Lacoste: Appointed by Mollet as Resident-Minister in Algeria. Among the 'achievements' of his reign there may be noted the torture of Henri Alleg, and the disappearance and murder of Maurice Audin. As the Algerian crisis of 1958 came to a head, Lacoste's role, linked to that of the 'Algérie Française' elements, became clearer.

(In the recent elections Messrs Mollet, Defferre and Lacoste were all supported by the CP in the second ballot.)

In the Fifth Republic the SFIO has, for electoral purposes, merged with various smaller left groups into the FGDS (Fédération de la Gauche Démocrate et Socialiste—Federation of the Democratic and Socialist left).

The Federation, as the coalescing of several bureaucracies, represents the combination of the defects of all the groups it contains. We may note particularly its policy of selecting candidates, which guarantees renomination to sitting deputies of any of the constituent groups—this means little chance for new blood to get into Parliament; it also means that the Federation must endorse and campaign for men like Max Lejeune, personally responsible for the kidnapping of Ben Bella in 1956, leader of the extreme 'Algérie Française' tendency of the SFIO, and for a time de Gaulle's Minister of the Sahara; or even Georges Bonnet, vicious anti-Communist of the 1930s, Foreign Minister at the time of Munich, personal friend of Ribbentrop and debarred from Parliament in 1944-53 as a wartime collaborationist. Bonnet and Lejeune were both re-elected in 1967 with CP support in the second ballot.

The presidential candidate and leader of the Federation is Mitterrand, of the UDSR (Union Démocratique et Socialiste de la Résistance).

In 1953 Mitterrand wrote:

> For me, the maintenance of the French presence in North Africa, from Bizerta to Casablanca, is the first imperative of national policy... I believe in the virtues of firmness and the necessity of prestige.[95]

Travelling in Algeria before the outbreak of the rebellion in 1954, he refused to meet representatives of the nationalist parties.[96] When the rebellion broke out, he immediately dissolved the main nationalist party,[97] and said:

> Algeria is France, and from Flanders to the Congo there is one nation, one Parliament. That is the Constitution, that is our wish.[98]

Although his position on Algeria shifted pragmatically later, Mitterrand nonetheless appeared as a defence witness for Salan at his trial in 1962.[99]

The Federation has also inherited those sections of the Radical Party which were unable to accommodate themselves to Gaullism. The Radical Party, with a petit bourgeois and peasant base, had been the dominant party in the 1930s; it combined Jacobin language with conservative policies (opposition to votes for women, etc). Its weak Resistance record left it a divided and declining party in the Fourth Republic. It sought allies opportunistically, uniting with the Gaullists in the municipal elections of 1947, and the Socialists in the 1951 General Election.

Most of its deputies supported Suez and the special powers in Algeria. Between June 1957 and April 1958 two Radical prime ministers governed France; in this period the army got increasingly out of hand, torture was rife in Algeria, and Sakiet in Tunisia was bombed.

To the Federation, Radicalism offers a touch of middle-class respectability and appeals to nostalgia for the Popular Front; to Radical career politicians, like Félix Gaillard (prime minister at the time of Sakiet), the Federation offers a Parliamentary seat and Communist votes on the second ballot.

A more cautious treatment is required to deal with the PSU (Parti Socialiste Unifié), which took by far the best line of any of the official parties during the May events. The origins of the PSU go back to 1958 when some members of the SFIO, unable to tolerate Mollet's leadership and in particular the Algerian policy and support for de Gaulle, left; this group included former ministers and was not exclusively left. It formed the Parti Socialiste Autonome which by 1960, with some dropouts and new elements from outside the Socialist Party, developed into the PSU. Its real growth was based on its clear opposition to the Algerian war, in opposition to the CP's foot-dragging.

As a result, the PSU's ideology is vague—the *Canard Enchaîné* once maliciously commented that in the coming elections each party would present its policy, except the PSU, which would present two. In 1965 it organised a seminar at Grenoble for the 'couches nouvelles', the technocratic elite, on economic problems, and showed a strong tendency to become the political expression of the technocracy. In particular it has developed the strategy of the 'counterplan', an essentially reformist device.

After saying this, and making it quite clear that the PSU is in no way a revolutionary Marxist party, it must be stated to its credit that it is an open party in which free discussion can take place, and in which revolutionaries can work and propagandise. In the recent events it not only strongly supported the students, but defended the dissolved left groups, and in the elections it invited non-members from the Comités d'Action to stand as PSU candidates on Action Committee programmes.

For foreign observers, there is a danger that the PSU will be confused with Pierre Mendès-France, a politician much more loved outside France than in it: Mendès-France represents the extreme right of the PSU, and unlike other PSU members receives electoral support from the Federation.

The Mendès-France government of 1954-55 showed Mendès-France up for the opportunist and neo-capitalist he was and has remained. He did indeed negotiate the peace in Indochina, but his motive was clear. As he said, "We must choose—We shall not make an army in Europe as long as the haemorrhage in Indochina lasts'.[100]

When the Algerian rebellion broke out, Mendès-France's neo-colonialist liberalism seemed to be on the wane—he said:

> The departments of Algeria are part of the Republic... Never will France, never will any Parliament or any Government yield on this fundamental point.[101]

We have already noted the actions of his Minister of the Interior, Mitterrand. It was, furthermore, Mendès-France who sent Jacques Soustelle to Algeria as Governor-General.

More recently Mendès-France supported Israel, and declined to take sides over Vietnam.[102]

During May and June 1968 he became more and more estranged from the PSU, where the 'Centre', led by Michel Rocard and Marc Heurgon, wanted to support the rebellious students to the end, while Mendès-France wanted to stick to the PSU's former line, which was the development of a 'new left' within a union of the entire left, including both the PCF and the FGDS. (A few days later it was announced that Mendès-France resigned from the PSU.)[103]

Was there a revolutionary situation?

The central theme in the 'theoretical' self-justification of the PCF leaders was that the situation in France was not revolutionary. Thus on 8 June René Andrieu, editor in chief of *L'Humanité*, gave an interview to the *Morning Star*:

> Q: Some of the leftist leaders made their strongest propaganda on the platform that last month there was a revolutionary situation in France in which the chance of revolution was betrayed. These leftist leaders labelled the coming elections as treason to the revolutionary cause. These same arguments have been reflected in the British papers. How would you answer them?
> Andrieu: In reality there was in France an unprecedented movement of people's demands. But for there to be a revolutionary situation two conditions must be fulfilled:
> (1) It is not enough that the main forces of the nation should be moving—which was the case—it is also necessary for them to be won to the idea of socialist revolution. But this was not the case, for all the 10 million workers on strike, let alone for the middle sectors (especially the peasants).
> (2) It is necessary for the State to be disintegrating. But even if the government was crippled the regular army with its tanks and its planes was holding itself ready to seize the pretext of the least adventure to drown the workers' movement in blood and to install a military dictatorship.

The same analysis was given by Séguy on 14 June:

> To tell the truth the question of deciding whether the time for insurrection had arrived or not was never raised either in the Bureau Confédéral or the Administrative Commission composed, as is well known, of serious, responsible militants who are not in the habit of allowing themselves to take their desires for reality. If the workers were momentarily disturbed about this matter, the funeral black flag of anarchy waved hysterically by the members of the so-called 'comités révolutionnaires' soon opened their eyes and brought them over to our side, the side of those who in the struggle combined the red flags of the workers of the world with the tricolore of France, and the revolutionary history of our people. No, the 10 million workers on strike did not demand power for the working class but better conditions of life and work, and the overwhelming majority expressed their attachment to democracy in their opposition to personal rule.
>
> Let us deal with each argument separately.

The armed forces

First the question of the army (and police).

When Andrieu says that 'even if the government was crippled the regular army with its tanks and its planes was holding itself ready' and therefore a revolution was impossible in France at present, he actually excludes revolution altogether. Does he really expect the army generals to order their troops to join the revolutionary workers?

A peaceful conquest of the army to the side of socialism is even less possible than the peaceful conquest of parliament. As Trotsky aptly wrote, 'The army is a copy of society, and suffers from all its diseases, usually at a higher temperature'.[104] The hierarchy of command in capitalist society is reflected in a more extreme form in its armed forces. The officer castes keep in close touch with the capitalists, while the mass of soldiers, to a much weaker extent, reflect the mood of the workers' community from which they came. Soldiers cannot dare to disobey their officers' command before they are convinced that the path of insurrection and victory is open:

> During the revolution, inevitable oscillations will occur in the army, an internal struggle will take place. Even the most advanced section will not go over openly and actively to the side of the proletariat unless they see with their own eyes that the *workers want to fight and are able to win.*[105]

> The first task of every insurrection is to bring the troops over to its side. The chief means of accomplishing this are the general strike, mass processions, street encounters, battles at the barricades.[106]

In fact only a revolutionary policy could have probed the reliability of the French army as a support for capitalism. This did not take place in the recent crisis.

Five years before, when de Gaulle threatened to use military force against workers, his bluff was called.

During the miners' strike of 1963 he issued a requisition order, ordering the miners to return to work unconditionally. The miners disregarded this, and received expressions of solidarity from many quarters, while de Gaulle's standing was considerably weakened.[107]

Throughout the recent mass strike de Gaulle did not dare to pit the army or the police against the workers. The CRS was used only against students, and later on, when the majority of strikers had already returned to work, against individual factories. Ten million workers could not have been intimidated by the army or the police. Thus the occupation of Renault Flins by the CRS, which was accompanied by bitter clashes with workers and students, in which one student was killed, took place on 7 June. The prolonged battle of the CRS with the workers of Peugeot at Sochaux, in which two workers were killed, took place on 11 June. In both cases nearly all other workers had gone back to work and these two factories were isolated.

One must remember that the army is predominantly made up of conscripts. Even without the clear lead of a mass revolutionary party, there were signs of rebellion in the armed forces. Thus the *Canard Enchaîné* of 19 June refers to reports of a mutiny on the aircraft carrier *Clemenceau*, which at the end of May was bound for the French nuclear test in the Pacific, but was brought back to Toulon. Three families were informed that their sons had been 'lost at sea'. *Action*, journal of UNEF, which carried a fuller report in its 14 June issue, was seized. Obviously if such a report had been publicised while the situation was still seething, the effect on other sections of the armed forces could have been dramatic.

Both *La Nouvelle Avant-Garde* and *Partisans*,[108] two Socialist journals, reproduce a statement of the 153° RIMCA (Régiment d'Infanterie Mécanisée), stationed at Muntzig, and dated 22 May. The following are extracts from the statement:

> The military bureaucracy, with its outdated traditions, is recruited in a socially selective manner designed to preserve the owning classes. The extremely rudimentary training in arms given in the army represents the desire that the popular classes should merely be passive herds to be manoeuvred in any forthcoming conflict...
>
> The equal right for all to receive instruction in arms in no way justifies keeping men in barracks for 14 to 16 months. This scandalous concealed unemployment is perhaps justified by economic pseudo-reasons, but it is not our concern because we have no real part in the management of French society. Hundreds of thousands of young people are thus every year legally reduced to a degrading semi-detention...
>
> Military instruction must be an equal right for all. Military instruction and sex education must be administratively, geographically and chronologically integrated into the whole system of National Education from the earliest age, and controlled according to the same principles now demanded in Universities and schools; dialogue and joint management...
>
> Like all conscripts, we are consigned to barracks. We are being prepared to intervene as repressive forces. The workers and youth must know that the soldiers of the contingent WILL NEVER SHOOT ON WORKERS.
>
> We Action Committees are opposed at all costs to the surrounding of factories by soldiers.

Tomorrow or the day after we are expected to surround an armaments factory which 300 workers who work there want to occupy.

WE SHALL FRATERNISE.

Soldiers of the contingent, form your committees!

Our immediate demands are:

— Military service reduced to eight months with effective military training.

— Abolition of obsessional discipline not essential to the content of military instruction.

— Freedom of political and trade union organisation in the contingent.

—Educational reform of military instruction based on dialogue, and joint management of all activities with the instructors.

LONG LIVE SOLIDARITY OF WORKERS, SOLDIERS, STUDENTS AND HIGH SCHOOL PUPILS.

LONG LIVE WORKERS' DEMOCRACY.

LONG LIVE JOY, LOVE AND CREATIVE WORK!

Even police morale suffered a grave crisis. The *Sunday Express* published this report from Paris:

> As 10,000 reinforcements from the provinces were being drafted into Paris to help maintain law and order, a delegation from the police unions called at the Ministry of the Interior with an urgent demand for increased pay.
>
> The demand was backed by a statement from the unions representing 51,000 riot police and gendarmes. This statement warned the Government, 'A climate of extreme tension exists at the present time in all the police bodies of the nation'.[109]

The *Times* reported:

> 'My men are underpaid and tired', said a police officer. 'They are permanently on duty...'
>
> They are seething with discontent over their treatment by the Government, and the branch dealing with intelligence about student activity has been deliberately depriving the Government of information about student leaders in support of an expenses claim...
>
> Nor have the police been impressed by the Government's behaviour since the troubles broke out. 'They are terrified of losing our support', said one man.
>
> Such dissatisfaction is one of the reasons for the apparent inactivity of the Paris police in the past few days. Last week, men at several local stations refused to go on duty at the crossroads and squares of the capital.[110]

In the next issue of the same paper its defence correspondent, Charles Douglas-Home, wrote, 'In an extreme emergency the troops could be brought into operation, but it is appreciated that they could be used only once, and then only for a short while, before the largely conscript army was exposed to a psychological battering in a general campaign of subversion which it would probably not withstand'.[111]

The general strike—actualities and potentialities

The French general strike was by far the largest general strike in world history. Never before have there been anything like 10 million workers on strike. Wrenching industry from the hands of the capitalists, the workers faced a completely paralysed state: the question of state power was posed nakedly. This happens in every general strike. As Trotsky put it, 'The general strike is, by its very essence, a political act'.[112]

> The general strike, as every Marxist knows, is one of the most revolutionary methods of struggle. The general strike is not possible except at a time when the class struggle rises above particular and craft demands, and extends over all occupational and district divisions, and wipes away the lines and the parties, between legality and illegality, and mobilises the majority of the proletariat in an active opposition to the bourgeoisie and the state. Nothing can be on a higher plane than the general strike, except the armed insurrection. The entire history of the working-class movements proves that every general strike, whatever may be the slogans under which it occurs, has an internal tendency to transform itself into an open revolutionary clash, into a direct struggle for power.[113]

> The fundamental importance of the general strike, independent of the partial successes which it may and then again may not provide, lies in the fact that it poses the question of power in a revolutionary manner. By shutting down the factories, transport, generally all the means of communication, power stations, etc, the proletariat by this very act paralyses not only production but also the government. The state power remains suspended in mid-air. It must either subjugate the proletariat by famine and force and constrain it to set the apparatus of the bourgeois state once again in motion, or retreat before the proletariat.
>
> Whatever may be slogans and the motive for which the general strike is initiated, if it includes the genuine masses, and if these masses are quite resolved to struggle, the general strike inevitably poses before all the classes in the nation the question: *Who will be the master of the house?*[114]

However, posing the question is not the same as answering it. The morale, consciousness and organisation of the contending classes determine whether the general strike will be transcended by a proletarian seizure of power.

The outbreak of the general strike, with the semi-insurrectionary temper of the working class accompanying it, shows that the situation was actually pre-revolutionary, potentially revolutionary. Whether the working class as a whole was conscious that the question of state power was at the centre of the struggle or not, the duty of the revolutionary leadership was to make this explicit, to develop the confidence of the workers in themselves and in their organisations. And it was just this that the PCF and the CGT *did not do*.

Economics and politics in the strike

One of the central arguments of the PCF was that the movement in May was essentially a movement for economic reforms: for higher wages, a shorter working week, etc.

However, if there is a time when the absence of a Chinese wall separating the struggle for economic reforms from the political struggle for power is exposed, it is during a general strike.

Long ago Rosa Luxemburg pointed this out:

> The movement does not go only in one direction, from an economic to a political struggle, but also in the opposite direction. Every important political mass action, after reaching its peak, results in a series of economic mass strikes. And this rule applies not only to the individual mass strike, but to the revolution as a whole. With the spread, clarification and intensification of the political struggle, not only does the economic struggle not recede, but on the contrary it spreads and at the same time becomes more organised and intensified. There exists a reciprocal influence between the two struggles. Every fresh attack and victory of the political struggle has a powerful impact on the economic struggle, in that at the same time as it widens the scope for the workers to improve their conditions and strengthens their impulse to do so, it enhances their fighting spirit. After every soaring wave of political action, there remains a fertile sediment from which sprout a thousand economic struggles. And the reverse also applies. The workers' constant economic struggle against capital sustains them at every pause in the political battle. The economic struggle constitutes, so to speak, the permanent reservoir of working-class strength from which political struggles always imbibe new strength. The untiring economic fight of the proletariat leads every moment to sharp isolated conflicts here and there from which explode unforeseen political struggles on an immense scale.
>
> In a word, the economic struggle is the factor that advances the movement from one political focal point to another. The political struggle periodically fertilises the ground for the economic struggle. Cause and effect interchange every second. Thus we find that the two elements, the economic and political, do not incline to separate themselves from one another during the period of the mass strikes in Russia, not to speak of negating one another, as pedantic schemes would suggest.[115]

It is an oversimplification of the situation either to reduce the French general strike entirely to a movement for higher wages and improved conditions, or to condemn as betrayal any raising of political or economic demands as opposed to 'pure' revolutionary demands. In different sectors, different industries, different regions, there was a wide range of demands—some simply for higher wages and longer holidays, some for purely political changes, like the sacking of Pompidou or de Gaulle, many for control or participation in some form.

France has shown the falseness of the purely economistic—bread and butter— trade union perspective. A revolutionary movement does not grow naturally out of a mere accumulation of partial economic struggles. It was only after a direct political confrontation that we saw the unleashing of a vast movement of economic demands.

On the other hand, in a crisis situation concrete economic demands may be more revolutionary than an abstract political line imposed from outside. Many economic shells can hide a political kernel.

If any proof that the movement was far from being purely economic is necessary, one can single out the fact that relatively few workers joined the trade unions during the May-June days and their aftermath. One must remember that in 1936 the membership of the CGT rose from 1 million to 5 million, and of the CFTC from 150,000 to 500,000. In 1945, again, the number of trade unionists rose from nothing to 7 million. This time the CGT claims to have gained 450,000 recruits and the CFDT 280,000.[116]

De Gaulle had no doubt at all of the anti-capitalist revolutionary essence of the general strike when he spoke on the TV on 7 June to announce the snap elections. He went out of the way to declare himself an opponent of capitalism. His emphasis on 'participation' of labour and capital was but evidence of the attraction of socialism: imitation is the homage of hypocrisy to virtue.

Consciousness of the class

When Andrieu said that the 10 million workers on strike were not won to the idea of socialist revolution, whose fault was this if true? It was the CP that had insisted from the outset that there was no revolutionary situation, regardless of the great changes in the temper of the workers that took place from the beginning to the end of May.

Class consciousness is not a 'natural' product of objective conditions à la vulgar mechanical materialists. Nor is it the accidental product of the subjective thought of individuals or parties. The consciousness of the class is the product of the interaction of acting men—including parties—and the objective given world.

Regularly leaders complain that the workers are passive. And quite often this is so. But are the leaders free from blame for this passivity? Is workers' activity like a revolver that can be kept unused for years in the pocket of the leaders and then taken out at will? To overcome the inertia—the product of helplessness and hopelessness—workers have to win confidence in themselves, and in the party that organises and leads them.

One has the feeling that one has been here before. Trotsky's words on the French situation in May-June 1936 fit perfectly the evaluation of the French situation in May-June 1968:

> The situation is revolutionary, as revolutionary as it can be, *granted the non-revolutionary policies of the working-class parties*. More exactly, the situation is pre-revolutionary. In order to bring the situation to its full maturity, there must be an immediate, vigorous, unremitting mobilisation of the masses, under the slogan of the conquest of power in the name of socialism. This is the only way through which the pre-revolutionary situation will be changed into a revolutionary situation. On the other hand, if we continue to mark time, the pre-revolutionary situation will inevitably be changed into one of counter-revolution.[117]

The parliamentary election fraud

And for what did the PCF and the CGT call the strikes off? For the prospect of a parliamentary election.

As long as the strike went on de Gaulle was completely helpless and could not have carried out the elections. When, on 24 May, he called for a referendum, it turned out that not a single printshop in France would print the General's ballot papers, and when in desperation he tried to have the ballot papers printed in Belgium the Belgian workers refused, out of solidarity with their striking brethren.

After de Gaulle's speech of 30 May the PCF threw everything it had into the electoral campaign. Its central theme was that the PCF was 'the Party of order'. Waldeck Rochet, the General Secretary of the PCF, elaborated on this in an interview on Radio Luxembourg on 20 June:

> Q: The outgoing majority accuses you of having desired to seize power during the recent events. You have denied this accusation. Does that mean that your party envisages only the parliamentary road to power?
> A: In claiming that the PC envisaged recourse to force in order to seize power, the Gaullist leaders are indulging in the most gross deceit. Contrary to the slanderous insinuations of M Pompidou the PC carried out all its actions in support of the working class *within the framework of republican legality. This position is not in the least one of expediency but fully conforms to our principles.*

When the means of communication and the machinery of state are in the hands of a hostile ruling class, one cannot expect parliamentary elections to do anything other than play into the hands of this class. Parliamentary elections always distort the real correlation of class forces. The Bolsheviks got only a quarter of all votes cast for the Constituent Assembly (9 million out of 36 million votes). And this after being in power, after the inauguration of many of the most important and popular revolutionary measures: land to the peasants, workers' control in industry, etc. This did not prevent the Bolsheviks from winning the civil war. In the years of the civil war the overwhelming majority of the Russian people fought on the side of the Bolsheviks, thus effectively demonstrating that Lenin had more accurately gauged popular feeling than the results of the Constituent Assembly appeared to indicate. Lenin never identified the indices of parliamentarism with the actual correlation of forces. He always introduced a radical correction in favour of direct action.

In our epoch not a single serious issue can be decided by ballot. In the decisive class battles bullets will decide. The capitalists will be counting the machine-guns, bayonets and grenades at their disposal.

The electoral cretinism of the PCF did not even pay in parliamentary terms. First of all, the youth (below 21), the most dynamic element in the strikes and demonstrations, was barred from voting. Secondly, foreign workers, who are numerous in France, and played quite an important part in the strike, also could not vote. Thirdly, with the retreat from the strike, many workers in disgust abstained from elections, while the forces of the Right organised to take advantage of the situation.

The PCF lost 12 percent of its vote nationally (604,000 votes) compared with the year before. The loss was in direct relation to the amplitude of the struggle in the May-June days, and to the nakedness of the betrayal of the PCF and the CGT. Thus in the constituency of Montbéliard (where the Peugeot-Sochaux factory is) the PCF vote declined by 28 percent; and in the constituency of Meulan-Poissy (where Renault-Flins is) the PCF declined by 25 percent.

In the Paris region and Seine-et-Oise, the PCF lost eight of its previous 13 seats. In the Latin Quarter as many as 35 percent of the electors abstained.

At the same time as the PCF lost 604,000 votes, the Federation of the Left lost 570,000 votes—or 14 percent. The only party of the Left that considerably increased its vote was the PSU, which had been alone in flirting with the revolutionary students. Its vote rose by 379,000 or 90 percent.

De Gaulle made use of the CP to re-establish law and order, but even so did not show it any gratitude (except perhaps for doing it the service of banning the small groups of the extreme left, but that was something de Gaulle did primarily for himself).

De Gaulle campaigned in the name of an anti-Communist crusade. It is not surprising that the campaign attracted the attention of everybody in France who is conservative or hesitant, since EVERYBODY including the CP presented the students' struggle, the continuation of the strike, counter-attacks or even just defence against the anti-strike actions of the police as 'adventurist' acts, or 'provocation' incited by goodness knows what professional troublemakers, even by 'foreign agents'.

Nobody could sort things out...and if 'adventurism' was to be condemned, why not vote for the Gaullists rather than the CP or the Federation of the Left? The Gaullists at least had a clear policy: they had never followed those they condemned, whereas the CP and the Federation 'supported' the strike at the same time as they condemned those who had set it going and wanted to carry it on, and they attacked demonstrations, calling them adventurist, while going on demonstrating themselves. The 'left' had two faces during the strike: it displeased everybody, both the workers and the petite bourgeoisie.[118]

One good result of the electoral exercise of the PCF is that it will be very difficult to repeat it. As *Lutte Ouvrière* put it:

> The government, the bourgeoisie and de Gaulle himself were able to realise that an electoral majority is not everything, anyway. The strike of May broke out less than a year after the election which, like the ones before, had returned a Gaullist majority to the Chamber.
>
> De Gaulle, the bourgeoisie and the Government were able, this time, to end the strike by promising new elections to the workers...it is true, with the complicity of the CGT leaders, who proclaimed that the new assembly would be able to provide what the prematurely-terminated strike could not have provided...but a trick like that will not work twice.
>
> De Gaulle et al well know this, and they also know well that the majority they

have just obtained does not provide them with any additional means for facing up to a new offensive by the workers.[119]

After the swing to the right on the first ballot, the PCF's verdict was that it was entirely the fault of the leftists. *L'Humanité* of 24 June declared, 'Each barricade, each car set on fire, swung hundreds of thousands of votes to the Gaullist party: that is the truth.'

Of course, the CP was right: the left 'provoked' reaction.

Liberalism has always said to the workers that by the class struggle they 'provoke' reaction. The reformists have repeated this accusation against the revolutionaries. These accusations reduce themselves, in the final analysis, to the profound thought that if the oppressed do not stir the oppressors will not be obliged to beat them. If you do not try to make a revolution, there is no danger of a counter-revolution! Keep submissive and inert, and nobody will hurt you!

The contrast between the growth of reaction in parliament and the growth of insurrection in the streets and factories is a further confirmation that the victory of socialism cannot be realised by parliamentary means, but only through revolution.

In conclusion

The main condemnation of the PCF is not that they did not carry out a victorious socialist revolution in May or June. No one could have guaranteed that this could be done. What was necessary was to raise the self-confidence and organisational strength of the workers to enhance the combativity of the working class.

The PCF prevented the election of democratic strike committees. It prevented the link-up between committees. It sent the majority of workers away from the factory. Those who were left were engaged in games instead of serious political discussion. It did its best to insulate the workers from the revolutionary students and young workers.

To attain workers' power a number of steps were necessary: (1) the establishment of rank and file committees in the factories and their generalisation into local, regional and finally national councils of workers' deputies (Soviets); (2) arming the picket lines first and then the mass of the workers, against the CRS and scabs; (3) starting to run the factories under the control of the workers' committees; (4) decisively smashing, disarming and dismantling the armed forces of the capitalists.[120]

The accusation against the PCF is not that it did not win an assault on the citadels of capitalism, but that it prevented anyone from even starting the assault.

The swing back of the pendulum—the 1936 precedent

One of the decisive lessons of history of the last 50 years is that if a pre-revolutionary situation is not taken advantage of by a revolutionary party, the situation can swiftly change into a counter-revolutionary one. Is France now going to have another long wave of reaction, as happened after June 1936? This is the first question every socialist must be asking.

The similarity between May-June 1936 and May-June 1968 is quite uncanny. The 1936 general strike also started spontaneously.

The first factory occupation—nobody knows the individual responsible for the idea of the tactic—was at the Bréginuet factory at Le Havre on 11 May following the sacking of militants who had not worked on May Day. On 13 May there was an occupation at Toulouse, on 14 May at Courbevoie—they were hardly heard of in Paris, except through the bourgeois press which mentioned them briefly—*L'Humanité* did not mention the occupations till 20 May. However, an article in *Humanité* on 24 May discussed the tactic of occupation and its particular advantages, and this undoubtedly contributed to the spread of the strikes. The strikes with occupation now spread rapidly, in two ways: in the localities between neighbouring factories, and between different factories of the same company. By the end of June the strike wave had spread to Belgium, and if it had continued there were signs it might reach Germany.

The strikes were quite clearly spontaneous—both in their instigation and later in the many refusals to accept solutions negotiated by the unions. It was in industries with a very low rate of unionisation that the strikes started first and spread most quickly—metalworkers (4 percent unionisation), textiles (5 percent), food supplies (3 percent), big stores (1 percent). An eyewitness tells how a girl from the Prix Unique store came into the union offices, trembling, to announce that she had got the store workers out on strike and didn't know what to do next. The union sent officials to help her prepare a list of demands.[121]

The extent of the strike was smaller than in 1968. There are no reliable figures of the total number of strikers, but Salengro, Minister of the Interior, estimated one and a half million at the high point. Many areas had virtually no strike. The employers resisted any suggestion of using force to end the factory occupations.[122]

Then the SFIO and CP came and sold the strike for economic gains at the Matignon Agreements. The workers got a number of concessions all the same. The working week was cut to 40 hours, the average wage raised by 11 percent.[123] The trade unions grew by leaps and bounds. The CGT claimed to have grown from 1 million to 5 million members; the CFTC from 150,000 to 500,000.

Of the gains made by strike action, many rapidly disappeared: in February 1937 Blum admitted that '[t]he rise in the cost of living during the last eight months imposes on a wage-earner's family a burden heavier than the advantages gained by measures taken in their favour'. Even between 9 July and 3 September 1936 there were massive price rises—a kilo of bread rose from 1.60 francs to 1.90 francs, a dozen eggs from 7.25 francs to 8.35 francs. Over a somewhat longer period, from 1935 to 1939, average weekly wages for male workers increased, in Paris by 49 percent, in the provinces 42 percent; in the same period the cost of living increased in Paris by 57 percent, in the provinces by 52 percent.[124]

The 40-hour week did not have a long life. In a broadcast of 12 November 1938 Daladier announced the restoration of a working week of 48 hours.

The political results of the 'failed revolution' were even more dismal. Alexandre Lambert-Ribot, vice-president of the Comité des Forges, and a leading representative of the French employers, said on 18 November 1937, 'The Matignon Agreements saved France from singularly terrible events, from grave riots liable to degenerate into civil war.' The acceptance of a compromise gave the ruling class a chance to regroup. An offensive was undertaken against the workers all over France.

The workers fought back. There were further factory occupations in March and April 1938—Citroën, Gnôme-et-Rhône—but the movement was now demoralised; the class as a whole was not prepared to go through the same experience twice. When the Blum government fell in April 1938, it was replaced by a moderate government without Socialists, under Daladier. This government, under a man whom the CP had instructed the working class to support in the 1936 election, signed the Munich agreements, broke the CGT general strike in November 1938, and on 26 September 1939 made the Communist Party illegal. The CP was bitten by the mouth it had so earnestly fed.

The demoralisation in the working class after June 1936 made possible the capitulation to fascism in 1940.

An Italian precedent

Even more dramatic was the attack of reaction after a deep-going and massive sit-in strike in Italy in September 1920. The occupation came after three months of unsuccessful negotiations by the unions on bread-and-butter demands: an increase in wages due to the rise in the cost of living. The negotiations finally broke down, and the unions reacted with a go-slow which was to start on 21 August. The Alfa-Romeo factory in Milan, however, locked out the workers, and on 28 August the factory was occupied. By 1 September all metalworkers and engineers had occupied their factories in Turin, Milan, Genoa and Savona, and in the following days this was extended to all of Italy. In Turin and in some other towns the workers moved into other types of factories as well.

The factory councils took the lead, and from the outset became responsible for the running of the factories. Production was kept up throughout the strike in so far as conditions allowed. Success varied from place to place, and often, in spite of the solidarity of other workers, especially the railwaymen, who brought raw materials and primary products to the factories, the factories were starved of resources. Making the strike operative served a double purpose: it tested and proved the responsibility of the workers, and the products once sold could have constituted a useful means of supporting strikers in the absence of strike funds. The latter scope was not, however, realised, and the workers on strike had to rely on the generous collections of other categories to keep going.

Red armed guards were created for the protection of the factories, but with the exception of a few isolated incidents they were not actually needed since the compactness and militancy of the workers were enough to keep away unwelcome visitors.

Started on economic demands, the strike soon acquired a clear political content and became in fact about the recognition of workers' councils and, indeed, workers' control.

The industrialists varied in their reactions from frantic calls to the government to use force to what amounted to complete resignation. Giolitti refused to intervene in the strike other than as negotiator, well knowing that the movement would be strangled by the PSI and the CGL—the Italian Socialist Party and the TUs.

After one month of occupation the reformists set up a very ambiguous referendum with the utopian promise of workers' control sometime in the future. The strike thus ended, without having ever posed the question of power where it counts. The capitalist state was not overthrown. Power was not seized by the working class.

The bourgeois reaction was not very long in following. The capitalist class was very frightened by the occupation. Thus Agnelli, the owner of Fiat, was so demoralised that he was ready to hand the factory over to the workers. All social classes came out of the crisis convinced that the old order had been shaken for ever.

However, the fact that the strike had not raised the political question of the overthrow of the bourgeois state gave time to the bourgeoisie to regroup and to substitute its own 'new order' on the dying liberal state. The victors were soon shown to be the victims.

Thus the roots of Fascism lie in the defeat of 1920, but for its success a number of other factors needed to be present: first, and most decisively, the economic slump of 1921 which deprived the workers of their bargaining power and dealt shattering blows to their self-confidence.

Immediate prospects

No economic collapse of Western capitalism—in the form of a slump and mass unemployment—is on the agenda for the coming few years. The expansion of French capitalism will continue with ups and downs. If on average the annual rate of growth of total output between 1950 and 1960 was 4.4 percent, and if between 1963 and the first quarter of 1968 it was 2.0 percent, one can expect a continued growth, even if somewhat slowed down.

At the same time, because of speedy technological changes, accompanied by sharpening international competition, and the acceleration of mergers in industry, we can expect creeping unemployment, inflation and pressure on wages.

The financial position of France deteriorated very seriously as a result of the May-June events. In May France lost $306,000,000 out of her reserves, in June $1,088,600,000, and in July $666,800,000. Altogether in three months she lost $2,055 million, which is almost a third of the reserves held at the end of April.[125] Even before the recent events the international financial situation was not too good. In the past two years the French balance of payments has plunged from a healthy surplus to a deficit of $33 million in 1967.

Even before the recent events French industry found international competition tough. According to a report by the production committee of the French parliament, France's share in United States imports of industrial products from the OECD nations is 4.5 percent against 19 percent for Germany and 11.5 percent for Great Britain. Its share in Japan's imports for the same producers is 3.5 against 14 percent for Germany and 11.3 for Britain. France covers its total imports of manufactured goods by its exports at the rate of only 107 percent (figure for 1966) against 100 percent for Japan, 230 for Germany, 220 for Britain.[126]

With the lifting of the last customs barriers between the Common Market countries (1 July 1968), French industry is bound to feel the pressure more than ever. Her strength compared with her main partner/competitor, Germany, is not very great. German production capacity is 70 percent greater than the French in mechanical construction, 90 percent in steel, 200 percent in plastics, 200 percent in organic dyes.[127]

The rise in wages after the May-June events will affect the French situation in the export market. A recent poll of the IFOP market research organisation for the economic fortnightly *Les Informations Industrielles et Commerciales* showed that 60 percent of the industrialists expected their foreign sales to fall.[128] Only 19 percent considered the wage increases 'bearable', while 66 percent regarded them as 'very heavy', and 13 percent as 'catastrophic'.[129]

The area of manoeuvrability open to the French capitalists is not very wide. Even before the May-June wage rises the squeeze on profit margins over the past few years was very severe.[130]

Some of the industries and firms will be able to absorb the wage rise much better than others. Some of the heads of large firms made this clear.

Sommer's (textile) extra costs will not affect their financial return. In fact, plans for a new improvement in productivity should provide the necessary compensation.

The president of Pechiny (chemicals) has clearly posed the alternatives as 'making an effort to keep course *with the most efficient*' or falling into mediocrity.

Baumgartner, president of Rhone-Poulenc, says, 'For the corporations the extra cost will only be apparent.' He thinks that measures must be taken to:

> ...consolidate the situation of the producers on whom the competitive faculties of our country undoubtedly depend... As for us, we shall continue to revise those of our activities which do not satisfy present demands and develop those which meet the needs of the market, etc.[131]

Mergers will take place at an accelerated pace compared with the past.[132]

Unemployment will rise, although it is very difficult to forecast how steep this will be. The poll carried out by the market research organisation referred to above showed that about a quarter of the companies questioned expected to see a fall in employment, while the vast majority said they would not take on any more workers for the time being.[133] Some economists forecast as many as 1 million unemployed in the coming winter.

At the same time inflation is expected to take its toll. Nine out of ten French companies intend to raise their prices by between 5 and 10 percent as a result of the recent wage increases.[134] According to a report laid before the Economic and Social Council, French retail prices may rise between 6 and 7 percent this year as a result of the general strike.[135]

Thus in the immediate period we can expect a sharpening of the industrial struggle in France, increasing in bitterness, sometimes fragmented, but often fused into massive confrontations, not only with the bosses, but also with the State.

The way ahead

The limitations of spontaneity—the need for a revolutionary party

The May-June events raised the two issues of the limitation of the effectiveness of spontaneity and the need for a revolutionary party in the sharpest and most urgent way.

Revolutions do indeed start as spontaneous acts without the leadership of a party. The French Revolution started with the storming of the Bastille. Nobody organised this. Was there a party at the head of the people in rebellion? No. Even the future leaders of the Jacobins, for instance Robespierre, did not yet oppose the monarchy, and were not yet organised into a party. The 14 July 1789 revolution was a spontaneous act of the masses.

The same was true of the Russian Revolution of 1905 and the February 1917 Revolution. The 1905 Revolution started through a bloody clash between the Tsar's army and police on the one hand, and the mass of workers, men, women and children, on the other, led by the priest Gapon (who was actually an agent provocateur of the Tsar). Were the workers organised by a clear decisive leadership with a socialist policy of its own? Certainly not. Carrying icons, they came begging their beloved 'little Father'—the Tsar—to help them against their exploiters. This was the first step in a great revolution. Twelve years later, in February 1917, the masses, this time more experienced, and among whom there were a greater number of socialists than in the previous revolution, again rose spontaneously. No historian has been able to point a finger at the organiser of the February Revolution, for it was simply not organised.

However, after being triggered off by a spontaneous uprising, revolutions move forward in a different manner. In France the transition from the semi-republican government of the Gironde to the revolutionary one, which completely annihilated feudal property relations, was not carried out by unorganised masses without any party leadership, but under the decisive leadership of the Jacobin party. Without such a party at the helm this important step, which demanded an all-out fight against the Girondists, would have been impossible. The people of Paris could spontaneously, leaderlessly, rise up against the king after decades of oppression. But the majority of them were too conservative, too lacking in historical experience and knowledge, to distinguish, after only two or three years of revolution, between those who wanted to drive the revolution to an extremity and those who aimed at some compromise. The historical situation required a struggle to the bitter end against the party of compromise, the allies of yesterday. The conscious leadership of this great undertaking was supplied by the Jacobin party which fixed the date and organised the overthrow of the Gironde on 10 August 1792 down to the last detail. Similarly the October Revolution was not a spontaneous act but was organised in practically all its important particulars, including the date, by the Bolsheviks. During the zigzags of the revolution between February and October—the June demonstration, the July Days and subsequent orderly retreat, the rebuff of the rightist Kornilov putsch, etc—the workers and soldiers came more closely under the influence and guidance of the Bolshevik Party. And such a party was essential to raise the revolution from its initial stages to its final victory.

Spontaneity is inevitably irregular and uneven, and while all revolutions in history have begun spontaneously, none have ended so. The May days in Paris showed clearly that, while a few hundred students or workers can build a barricade, to overthrow the capitalist regime and seize state power a much larger centralised organisation is necessary.

The pivotal role of the party in the socialist revolution was summed up clearly by Trotsky:

> ...events have proved that without a party capable of directing the proletarian revolution, the revolution itself is rendered impossible. The proletariat cannot seize power by a spontaneous uprising. Even in highly industrialised and highly cultured Germany the spontaneous uprising of the toilers—in November 1918—only succeeded in transferring power to the hands of the bourgeoisie. One propertied class is able to seize the power that has been wrested from another propertied class because it is able to base itself upon its riches, its cultural level, and its innumerable connections with the old state apparatus. But there is nothing else that can serve the proletariat as a substitute for its own party.[136]

> The part played in bourgeois revolutions by the economic power of the bourgeoisie, by its education, by its municipalities and universities, is a part which can be filled in a proletarian revolution only by the party of the proletariat. The role of the party has become all the more important in view of the fact that the enemy has also become far more conscious. The bourgeoisie, in the course of centuries of rule, has perfected a political schooling far superior to the schooling of the old bureaucratic monarchy.[137]

If only the workers of Paris in 1968 had remembered the experience of Paris in 1936 or the Italian workers in 1920! The revolutionary party is, so to say, the memory of the class, the store of experience of the class struggle internationally, the university of the class.

Facing the strictly centralised and disciplined power of the capitalists there must be no less centralised and disciplined a combat organisation of the proletariat.

Both centralism and democracy are essential:

> *Centralism*—because it is imperative to assure unity in action of all sections of the proletariat and the simultaneity of demonstrations under a single common slogan: this can be achieved only if there is a genuine concentration of leadership in the hands of responsible central and local bodies, stable in their composition and in their attitude to their political line.
> *Democracy*—because these leading central and local bodies, which under certain conditions may be very small, must be elected by all party members, controlled by them and accountable to them.[138]

Because of the instability built into a capitalism that is on the whole expanding, the class struggle is going to have many sharp turns. Because changes in the objective economic conditions do not find immediate expression in the consciousness and activity of the class, as the latter are impeded by the dead weight of traditional reformist organisations, we must expect many zigzags in the struggle, from economic strikes to political battles and vice versa; from a semi-revolutionary situation to its opposite; from lulls to mass strikes whose scope and temper are insurrectionary. The unevenness between sections of the class, between different factories and industries, is going to continue, with sometimes an upward levelling, sometimes a downward, when equilibrium achieved will be again upset. Workers in advanced factories with long experience of the CGT and PCF will more and more be inclined to move away from them, while in the backward ones many will still join these organisations.

What is necessary under such conditions is a revolutionary organisation that is able not only to distinguish between a revolutionary situation and a counter-revolutionary one—this is quite easy—but between all the nuances in the transitional intermediate stages between them. An organisation like this should be able to show initiative, being stringent in its principles and highly adaptable and elastic in its tactics, always aware of the sharp turns in the situation.

For the revolutionary left in France there are now much better openings to build such a party than have existed for some 40 years.

For the first time a whole section of society—the students and tens of thousands of young workers, indeed youth in general—is free from the influence of the PCF; a base to the left of Stalinism has been established.

Now the central job for revolutionaries is to win the confidence of the majority of the working class. Only then can workers be summoned to an open revolutionary assault on capitalism, for workers' power.

Lacking the lead of a revolutionary party, millions of French workers again and again become disillusioned and passive. For revolutionaries to win their confidence is not an easy task. However, it is necessary by word and deed to conquer the confidence of thousands, and thence of millions of workers.

During the period following May 1968, during the many grey days ahead, the workers will be absorbed in current concerns and cares, in defence of wages and conditions. Revolutionaries must try and unite the workers on the soil of economic resistance to the bosses, as well as on the soil of political resistance to the state. It is necessary to carry on an active agitational campaign for the creation of factory and shop committees embracing all workers in each plant, irrespective of whether they are in the unions or not. The aim of such committees should be to carry on the resistance to capitalist exploitation, and to further it to the introduction of workers' control over the conditions of work and production. Revolutionaries can win mass confidence only on the basis of taking a leading part in the struggle for transitional demands. The long haul ahead will be the work of years, rather than of months.

The fantastic depth, width and power of the spontaneous mass movement showed itself vividly in all its glory in the May days. However, its limitations were no less vividly shown. Even strike committees, not to say Soviets, could not be established spontaneously in the face of the opposition of the counter-revolutionary PCF with its hold over the proletariat. Even with the first skirmishes on the path toward workers' power, spontaneity proved to be inadequate.

Lessons for British revolutionaries

In a number of ways the situation of the British labour movement is different from that of the French. Some should facilitate the work of socialists. Some will make it harder.

First, unlike the mass workers' party, the PCF, which finds itself in opposition to official society, and hence able to engage in 'struggles', however contained, the Labour Party is in power. While Waldeck Rochet may from time to time show his 'left' face, Wilson is compelled to show only his numerous 'right' faces. The task of exposing Wilson is therefore incomparably easier than that of Rochet.

Secondly, the PCF has deep organisational roots in the factories; the Labour Party has none. The PCF has strong-arm men to prevent Trotskyists, Maoists, Anarchists, from selling their literature at the factories; not so the Labour Party. The PCF could mobilise some 20,000 stewards to separate the students from the workers in the 13 May demonstration. The Labour Party has not 20,000 activists.

Thirdly, the British workers, unlike the French, are quite well organised at the grass roots—with shop stewards democratically elected. The British workers are engaged in thousands of unofficial strikes every year, while the French have up to now had relatively very few spasmodic unofficial strikes.

As against the above factors that make the building of a revolutionary organisation easier in Britain than in France, there are big hurdles that make the British situation more difficult.

First of all, the strength of the shop stewards' organisations in individual factories in Britain is paralleled by a lack of link-up between them. Strikes involving a number of factories, not to speak of whole industries, are almost unknown in Britain, while they are quite common in France.

Secondly, in Britain, trade unionism is very much accepted as completely separate from politics, so that strikes for political issues are unknown, while in France they have a long tradition.

Thirdly, as Marx already pointed out, the British labour movement very much lacks a disposition toward generalisation and theory.

France today, Britain tomorrow!

We cannot be sure of the rhythm of events, but there can be no doubt that there will be an acceleration. One thing has been made abundantly clear by the French crisis: a theme that was the kernel of Luxemburg, Lenin and Trotsky's make-up—the immediacy of revolution—immediacy, of course, in the scale of history. We cannot gauge the timing, duration and sweep of the coming revolutionary crisis in British capitalism, but it is not far off.

The rapidity with which the French explosion took place, and the failure of the revolt to supercede the limits of a general strike, show how urgent is the need for revolutionaries in Britain to work towards the establishment of links with the mass of the workers in their daily struggle, and through that struggle to form a combative revolutionary party.

For a long time what was lacking in the West was mainly a spontaneous and massive opposition of the working class. This is being changed, and tomorrow can change very quickly. Then, in the great battles of the future, what will be vitally needed is a dedicated revolutionary organisation which will link the opposition together, and focus not on the maximum concessions obtainable from the present regime, but on revolution, on workers' power.

Notes

* For help in research for this work we wish to thank: Jairus Banaji, Sean Dunne, Colin Gill, Andrew Hornung, Dave Purdy, Nick Richmond and Barbara Williams. Without them the research would have taken much longer and the results would have been poorer. Special thanks are owed to two French Marxists who because of the persecution of revolutionaries in their country must remain anonymous. They read the manuscript carefully and made criticisms and suggestions which have been of great value. —Tony Cliff, Ian Birchall, 10 August 1968.

1 L Trotsky, *The Intelligentsia and Socialism* (London, 1966), p12. (By the way, it is very odd to see the above statement published today without a note to show how inapplicable it is to the student scene today.)

2 How far the PCF was from coming to terms with the rebellion of students against the content of bourgeois education can be gleaned from the article in *L'Humanité* of 15 June, the day after the Gaullist police drove the students out of the Odéon. The article, entitled 'Concerning "Student Power"', says: '...the very notion of "*student power*"...seems particularly pernicious to us from all points of view...

'We are for the new university institutions, those that existed before May 1968. We think that students and teachers must contribute to building these institutions which will assure collaboration between them in the future.

'Without paternalism *vis-à-vis* the students, and without demagogy, we are acting in a responsible way in strongly criticising the very principle of "student power" no matter what its form.

'A student in the first or second cycle [secondary school and first years of university] cannot judge the scientific value of a professor. He can and ought, naturally, possibly to criticise his technique in transmitting knowledge but his criticism must stop there.

'By the third cycle things are no doubt different but even there the idea of challenging basics cannot be accepted without extreme caution.'

3 At the start of the present academic year there were 514,000 university students in France, 156,000 of them in Paris. There are only 500 seats in the university library in Paris. Practical work in science laboratories is often done in batches of 40 or more, and it is not unknown for a small lecture room to be crammed with 500 students trying to take notes from one lecturer. It is estimated that 12 per cent of French students fail to graduate. In Britain it is some 13 percent (*Guardian*, 8 August 1968). In 50 years the number of students has increased five times, but the number who have got degrees has only doubled (Ambassade de France, *The Problems of Higher Education in France* (London, 1967), p9).
4 *Observer*, 19 May 1968.
5 *Analyses et Documents* 124.
6 *Analyses et Documents* 127.
7 *Analyses et Documents* 130.
8 *Analyses et Documents* 133.
9 *Analyses et Documents* 136; *Pouvoir Ouvrier*, May-June 1967.
10 *Voix Ouvrière*, 31 October 1967.
11 *Analyses et Documents* 145.
12 The cold figures of the number of days lost in strikes over the last few years also show the great rise in strikes:
1965: 979,860 days lost.
1966: 2,523,500 days lost.
1967: 4,222,000 days lost.
13 *Class Struggle*, December 1967.
14 *Action* 6.
15 *Cahiers de Mai* 2, p11.
16 *Lutte Ouvrière* 4, p7. *Partisans* 42, p86, published a leaflet issued by the 'Maghreb Action Committee' which declared, 'The mortal blow which the French proletariat will strike to capitalism and imperialism will be a first step towards the destruction of the dictatorships of which we are the victims in our own countries and of which our brothers in the Third World are victims.' It is impossible to say how far such initiatives extended among immigrant workers.
17 *Cahiers de Mai* 1.
18 *Analyses et Documents* 155.
19 *New York Times*, 28 May 1968.
20 *Analyses et Documents* 156, p6.
21 *Partisans* 42, pp162-163.
22 *Lutte Ouvrière* 2, p6.
23 *Partisans* 42, p158.
24 *L'Humanité*, 6 June 1968.
25 *Analyses et Documents* 156, p15.
26 *Analyses et Documents* 156, p16.
27 *Lutte Ouvrière* 2, p5.
28 *Lutte Ouvrière* 2, p5.
29 *Analyses et Documents* 156, p18.
30 *Lutte Ouvrière* 2, p5.
31 *Lutte Ouvrière* 2, p6.
32 *Lutte Ouvrière* 2, p6.
33 *Lutte Ouvrière* 2, p7.
34 *Analyses et Documents* 156, p21.
35 *Nouvelle Avant-Garde* 1, p9.
36 *Action* 5.
37 *Lutte Ouvrière* 2, p6.
38 *Lutte Ouvrière* 2, p5.
39 *Analyses et Documents* 156, p19.
40 *Le Monde*, 21 July 1968.
41 *Cahiers de Mai* 2, p13.

42 *Le Monde*, 31 January 1967.
43 *Lutte Ouvrière* 2, p5.
44 *Analyses et Documents* 156, p15.
45 *Analyses et Documents* 155, p8.
46 *Cahiers de Mai* 2, p7.
47 *Analyses et Documents* 156, p13.
48 *La Grève à Flins* (Cahiers Libres, Maspéro, 1968), pp61-62.
49 *Lutte Ouvrière* 2, p7.
50 *Lutte Ouvrière* 4, p7.
51 *Lutte Ouvrière* 4, p7.
52 *Lutte Ouvrière* 2, p7.
53 *Analyses et Documents* 156, p17.
54 *Cahiers de Mai* 2, p1.
55 *Partisans* 42, pp159,166.
56 *Cahiers de Mai* 2, p6.
57 See for instance, *Lutte Ouvrière* 5, p5.
58 *Lutte Ouvrière* 2, p8.
59 *Cahiers de Mai* 2, p10.
60 We exclude Action Committees that are nothing but front organisations of political parties. Thus the PCF built its own Action Committees for a Popular Government, and so did the PSU.
61 M Thorez, *Fils du Peuple* (Editions Sociales, 1960), p124.
62 Quoted in L Trotsky, *Whither France?* (New York, 1936), p152.
63 G Lefranc, *Juin 36* (Juillard, 1966), p134.
64 Within the CP there was some opposition, notably Ferrat, a member of the Central Committee, who attacked the CP for supporting the Matignon Agreements as a compromise holding back mass action. He was expelled (G Lefranc, *Juin 36*, pp235-237).
65 *Histoire du Parti Communiste Français* (Unir), III, p23.
66 G Lefranc, *Le Syndicalisme en France* (PUF, 1964), p104.
67 *Cahiers du Communisme*, March-April 1947, p340.
68 *Histoire*, III, p65.
69 E O'Ballance, *The Algerian Insurrection* (Faber 1967), p30.
70 E O'Ballance, *Algerian*, p33.
71 *L'Humanité*, 30 June 1945.
72 F Bonte, in *France Nouvelle*, 17 March 1956.
73 *Histoire*, III, pp146-147.
74 E O'Ballance, *Algerian*, pp155-159.
75 *Histoire*, III, p189.
76 J Fauvet, *Histoire du Parti* (Fayard, 1965), p310.
77 D Mothé, *Militant chez Renault* (Seuil, 1965), pp40-41.
78 D Mothé, *Militant*, p50.
79 D Mothé, *Militant*, p54.
80 D Mothé, *Militant*, pp28-29.
81 *Histoire*, p16.
82 *Histoire*, p65.
83 M Duverger, *Political Parties* (Methuen, 1959), p181.
84 J Fauvet, *Histoire du Parti*, II, p260.
85 P M W Williams, *Crisis and Compromise* (London, 1964), pp509-510.
86 By the way, the only bookshop in Paris that does not display books on the May events is the Communist Party bookshop.
87 A Philip, *Les Socialistes* (Seuil, 1967), p173.
88 A Philip, *Les Socialistes*, p174.
89 P M W Williams, *Crisis*.
90 J Fauvet, *La Quatrième République* (Fayard, 1954), pp321-322.
91 A Werth, *De Gaulle Revolution* (London, 1960), p162.

92 A Werth, *De Gaulle*, p375.
93 A Philip, *Les Socialistes*, p169.
94 P M W Williams, *Crisis*, p347; *Histoire*, III p50.
95 *L'Express*, 5 September, 1953.
96 *Histoire*, III, p124.
97 P M W Williams, *Crisis*, p46.
98 *Histoire*, III, p125.
99 In the *Archives Secrètes de la Wilhelmstrasse*, IV, p433 (Plon, 1953), Ribbentrop gives the following account of a meeting with the French Foreign Minister Georges Bonnet: 'He told me that on the one hand they didn't want to receive any more Jews coming from Germany—we should take measures to see that they do not come to France—and on the other hand that France would have to get rid of about 10,000 Jews and send them anywhere—possibly Madagascar.'
100 J Fauvet, *La Quatrième République*, p189.
101 *Histoire*, III, p125.
102 *International Socialist Journal* 22, p608.
103 *Times*, July 30 1968.
104 L Trotsky, *The Revolution Betrayed* (London, 1937), p211.
105 L Trotsky, *Whither France?*, p95.
106 L Trotsky, *History of the Russian Revolution* (London, 1934), p1,031.
107 A Werth, *De Gaulle*, p364.
108 *La Nouvelle Avant-Garde* 1; *Partisans* 42, pp188-190.
109 *Sunday Express*, 19 May 1968.
110 *Times*, 30 May 1968.
111 *Times*, 31 May 1968.
112 L Trotsky, *Whither France?*, p89.
113 L Trotsky, *Whither France?*, p79.
114 L Trotsky, *Whither France?*, p87.
115 R Luxemburg, *Ausgewählte Reden und Schriften* (Berlin, 1955), vol 1, pp201-202.
116 *L'Express*, 24 June 1968.
117 L Trotsky, *Whither France?*, p50.
118 *Lutte Ouvrière* 2. The pretext for the dissolution of the left groups by de Gaulle's regime was that they were armed. It should therefore be noted that the first reference to them in these terms—'the armed bands of Geismar'— was in *L'Humanité* of 5 June, five days before the ban. On 12 June the government banned street meetings, dissolved the 'groupuscules'. This was reported by *L'Humanité* without comment, let alone protest.
119 *Lutte Ouvrière* 2.
120 A revolutionary organisation that catches the ear of only a few workers has to adjust the same programme tactically. As the point of departure for real revolutionary leadership is the experience of the workers themselves—their own views and attitudes—a small revolutionary group would have to be very modest in putting forward the above-mentioned transitional demands. While its agitation should have concentrated on the demand for democratically-elected strike committees, and the need to link them up, its main propaganda demand should be the final demand—for workers' power, for all power to the Soviets (that do not exist yet). There is not a time where the connection between propaganda and agitational slogans is of more importance than at a time of deep social crisis. However, there is no time where the mixing of the two, ie using the one instead of the other, is more pregnant with danger. The temptation for the small revolutionary groups in France to have an auction with the PCF—'You ask for money; we demand workers' power'—is very great. Verbal extremism often accompanies actual impotence. Without the achievement of democratic strike committees the slogan of workers' power must remain empty.
121 G Lefranc, *Juin 36*, p185.
122 G Lefranc, *Juin 36*, p116.
123 It is remarkable too how similar was the persecution of the Trotskyists. On 12 June 1936 the

Blum government, with CP backing, seized a Trotskyist paper, *La Lutte Ouvrière*, which called for workers' power.

124 G Lefranc, *Histoire du Front Populaire* (Payot, 1965), p324.

125 *Times*, 6 August 1968.

126 Paul Moch's report on the French Economic Council, *Times*, 29 November 1967.

127 Paul Moch, report on the French Economic Council.

128 *Financial Times*, 29 June 1968.

129 *Financial Times*, 9 July 1968.

130 This reflects itself clearly in share prices in the capital goods industries over the past few years:

SHARE PRICE INDICES (END 1961=100)

	Motors	Mechanical Engineering	Electrical Engineering	Iron and steel	Chemicals	General index
End 1961	100	100	100	100	100	100
End 1962	141	88	84	74	93	104
End 1963	122	72	59	62	77	88
End 1964	105	63	54	60	77	82
End 1965	109	61	48	52	70	75
End 1966	88	40	48	35	60	70
End 1967	81	33	48	34	63	73

France, Phillips and Drew, *Investment in the Common Market* 5 (London, 1968), p13.

131 *Analyses et Documents* 157, pp3-4.

132 In the first eight months of 1966, 1,600 mergers took place as against 450 in the whole of 1957 (M Kidron, *Western Capitalism since the War* (London, 1968), p15).

133 *Financial Times*, 9 July 1968.

134 *Financial Times*, 29 July 1968.

135 *Financial Times*, 4 July 1968.

136 L Trotsky, *Lessons of October* (New York, 1937), pp23-24.

137 L Trotsky, *Lessons*, pp100-101.

138 L Trotsky, *The First Five Years of the Communist International*, vol II (New York, 1953), p157.

Portugal at the crossroads

International Socialism (first series) 81, 82, September 1975*

Chronology of events

1974:

April

25	MFA overthrows Caetano regime. Spinola appointed President. Promise of free elections within one year.
26	Secret Police, PIDE, disbanded and members hounded through streets. Taken into military custody for protection.

May:

1	100,000 march through streets of Lisbon.
9	1st Provisional Government set up. CP takes Ministry of Labour.
30	CP trade union leaders in the Intersindical attack workers who have been striking for higher wages. CP denounces bakery workers as 'fascists'.

June:

Strike wave continues, including nearly every major group of workers.

18	Postal workers' strike starts in Lisbon. Bitterly attacked by CP.
22	New Press Law passed—allows fines and suspensions of papers. A Maoist editor is imprisoned. PRP paper *Revolução* fined for expressing discontent of rank and file soldiers.

July:

12	Second Provisional Government. Vasco Gonçalves appointed prime minister.
20	Two officers who refuse to break postal workers' strike arrested and imprisoned.
27	Spinola forced to issue statement supporting immediate independence for Portuguese colonies.

August:

During August the Press Law is used against a number of Portuguese papers, including *Republica*, which is suspended. The minister responsible is Raoul Rego.

2 Guinea-Bissau recognised as independent.

29 New strike law passed, outlawing occupations and setting up 30-day cooling-off period. CP remains in the government which passes this law and makes no protest.

September:

11 Lisnave workers' one-day strike. CP supports government ban on march.

23 TAP workers, who have been on strike for a month, stage massive demonstration against the use of the army to break their strike.

27-28 Spinola plots coup. Demonstration of the 'silent majority' called for by Spinola is stopped by workers. Workers build barricades in Lisbon and Oporto. Bridges are blocked. Railway workers strike. Motor transport is stopped and searched by armed workers and rank and file soldiers. MFA leaders forced to back workers' mobilisation. Many right wingers arrested.

30 Spinola forced to resign as President. Replaced by his former chief of staff in the African Wars, General Costa Gomes.

1975:

January:

Discussion of new trade union law. CP and revolutionary left call for a single trade union centre. Socialist Party and right wing call for several trade union federations—designed to split workers along religious and political lines. CP support for single federation not entirely impartial as they have firm bureaucratic control over the existing single centre, the Intersindical.

14 Mass demonstration of 100,000 workers in Lisbon in favour of single trade union federation.

26 COS, a right-wing party led by former fascists, holds rally in Oporto attended by British Tories, including Geoffrey Rippon. The hall is besieged by left-wing demonstrators. Police attack demonstrators. Troops called in side with demonstrators against the police.

February:

7 40,000 workers march in Lisbon organised by the Interempresa. The Interempresa (inter-factory committee) was a body set up on a PRP initiative in the Lisbon area. It grew to include the representatives of 40 of the most militant factories in the area. The demonstration is called over the fight against unemployment and in protest against the manoeuvres of the NATO fleet off Portugal.

9 30,000 farm workers, landless labourers from the Alentejo region in the South, demand the confiscation of the landlords' land. A wave of land seizures begins in the South.

21 Elections postponed to 25 April, a sign of the mounting tension in Lisbon.

March:

7 Police fire on left-wing demonstrators in Setubal, killing one worker.

11 Right wing, led by Spinola, attempt coup. The RAL 1 barracks in Lisbon attacked from the air and ringed by paratroopers. Workers down tools, build barricades, demand arms from soldiers. The police barracks in Lisbon besieged by crowds of workers. Other police barracks are stormed and weapons taken by workers. Paratroopers attacking RAL 1 are surrounded by workers who argue with them. The attempted coup peters out. After the coup Spinola a flees to Brazil and many right-wing officers are purged from the army.

12 Bank workers occupy banks to prevent economic sabotage.

14 Government forced to nationalise banks. Foreign-owned banks and agricultural credit institutions are excepted.

25 Fourth Provisional Government declared. Election campaign begins.

28 MRPP banned from election on grounds that it refuses to change its symbol, which the CP claims is too much like its own. Although this Party, the AOC and the semi-fascist PDC are all subject to legal restrictions during this period, and some members of the MRPP are arrested and held for brief periods, the left-wing parties continue to be able to operate completely openly.

April:

19 The first Congress of the CRTSM (Councils of Revolutionary Workers, Soldiers and Sailors) movement is held in Lisbon. The PRP is the only organisation in Portugal putting forward any perspective of workers' democracy at this stage. All other parties are obsessed with lecturing workers via their free television time, etc.

25 Elections held. The SP wins largest number of seats in the Constituent Assembly, although it, like all the other main parties, has agreed with the MFA that it is to continue to dominate Portuguese politics. The big SP vote finds no reflection in the government, so Soares launches his long campaign to force concessions. CP gets only 12 percent of the votes, and the parties to the left of it about 4 percent.

May:

1 Massive May Day rally in Lisbon. Soares tries to force his way onto the platform. PRP organise smaller demonstration in support of CRTSMs.

29 MRPP members arrested in Lisbon and other towns. Held in same jail as ex-PIDE members.

Throughout May and June the SP backs attempts of one of its leaders, Rego, to prevent workers influencing contents of paper, *Republica*. SP claims this is a 'Communist takeover'.

June:

16-21 Crucial meeting of Armed Forces Movement assembly ends in compromise. Discussion centres around building of revolutionary councils. On Tuesday 17, 40,000 march through Lisbon on a demonstration organised by CRTSMs calling for the dictatorship of the proletariat. The same week the reports begin to come in of the first right-wing rallies in the Azores.

July:

Radio Renascenca becomes focus of struggle between workers and bishops of Catholic Church.

1-7 Contradictory statements by government ministers as to what is going to happen to Renascenca.

1 Army occupies Lisbon Telephone Exchange to break strike.

3 Army announces withdrawal from Telephone Exchange. Morale of troops has broken down. During this week workers picketed the main Lisbon stations, persuading workers not to buy tickets in protest at fare increases. The CP Youth Organisations organise gangs of thugs to beat up pickets. Military Police sent in to break pickets, fraternise.

4 30,000 workers march through Lisbon in support of TLP workers.

8 MFA Assembly approves compromise document on 'Popular Power'.

10 *Republica* produced under control of workers. Policy is well to the left of the CP and critical of it.

10 Soares leaves government, threatening to paralyse country unless SP demands are met.

15 Soares starts to put threats into practice with first rally in Lisbon. It is small and middle class, but shows right-wing politics.

16 Soldiers and workers demonstrate in Lisbon calling for implementation of the MFA plan for 'Popular Power'.

18-20 SP programme of rallies gets under way. CP tries to set up barricades in Lisbon and Oporto to stop Socialist Party. Barricades taken over by Army. From this point on, attacks on CP, trade union and other left offices, and the beating up of militants, become regular throughout the North of Portugal.

21-26 Attempts to set up Fifth Provisional Government. Vasco Gonçalves still Prime Minister.

25 PRP offices in Sao Joao da Madeira attacked by reactionary mob. PRP members open fire and drive off crowd.

26 Second Conference of CRTSMs called in Lisbon.

August:

10-16 Battle of the Documents: rival groups of army officers put forward proposals for reorganising the country. The 'nine' produce right-wing document. Some officers of COPCON produce a left-wing alternative.

20 Mass demonstration in Lisbon by workers and soldiers demanding implementation of COPCON document.

24 United Front formed between CP, centrist groups and PRP.

27 United Front calls mass demonstration in Lisbon against threat of right-wing government. CP break unity and get Costa Gomes to speak. PRP contingent march off the demo in disgust.

28 CP start talks with SP and expelled from the United Front.

September:

29 August-5 September Military officers discuss political situation. Gonçalves removed as Prime Minister, rejected as Army Chief of Staff. Admiral Pinheiro de Azivedo appointed new Prime Minister. Begins discussion of new government. It looks likely that the new government will represent a sharp shift to the right.

Glossary

Organisations of the State, etc

AFM: Armed Forces Movement [MFA]. Originally a small group of career officers, it organised the coup of 25 April 1974. Its Council has become one of the main battlegrounds between left and right in the armed forces, The Assembly is dominated by officers but does contain some sergeants and ordinary soldiers.

COPCON: Continental Operations Command. The command unit of the military operations of the army in Continental Portugal. The term also signifies a small number of units of crack troops regularly used for internal security purposes. These units are among the most radicalised in Portugal. The commander of COPCON is General Otelo de Carvalho.

Supreme Revolutionary Council: Body of officers who exercise considerable power. Probably more important than the actual government.

PIDE/DGS: Former fascist secret police.

Provisional Government: The nominal government of Portugal.

PSP: Portuguese Security Police. Paramilitary fascist police. Still exist as a disciplined armed body.

GNR: National Republican Guard. Another paramilitary police force. They also still exist.

Political parties, etc:

Right-wing groups:

PCS: Christian Social Party. Banned extreme right-wing group.

CDS: Centre Democrats. Another extreme right-wing group. Both the above groups are havens for ex-fascists.

PPD: Popular Democrats. Claim to be 'social democrats' but in fact right-wing anti-working-class party.

ELP: 'Portuguese Liberation Army'. Clandestine terrorist organisation based in Spain. Made up of fascists and PIDES.

Reformist groups:

PS: Socialist Party [SP]. Largest party in terms of votes. Its leadership is extreme right wing of social democracy. At least until recently it commanded support from many workers, some of whom sincerely believed that it was a socialist party. It is undoubtedly the main organising centre for the Portuguese and international ruling class. Left dissidents are regularly expelled by the leadership.

PC: Communist Party [CP]. Large, bureaucratic party with considerable support in state apparatus, trade union bureaucracy and among sections of workers. Traditionally pro-Moscow.

Centrist groupings:

MES: Movement of the Socialist Left. Led by middle-class lefties but commanding some working-class support.

FSP: Popular Socialist Front. Left split from Socialist Party.

LUAR: League for United Revolutionary Action. Loose armed group with history of armed action. Some influence among workers.

There are also a number of small 'Trotskyist' groups, none of which have any significant base.

The centrist groups contain all sorts of politics. Many of them are obsessed with overcoming their isolation by trying to influence the Communist Party. They are quite unable to play any significant role.

Liberation movements:

FRELIMO: Liberation movement in Mozambique.

PAIGC: Liberation movement in Guinea-Bissau.

MPLA: Angolan liberation movement. Moscow-backed.

FNLA: Right-wing Angolan 'liberation' movement, backed by CIA, Zaire and China.

UNITA: Another right-wing 'liberation' movement in Angola. Allegedly also CIA backed.

Portugal at the crossroads

The Portuguese Revolution began in Africa. The Angolan risings of early 1961, partly stimulated by the Belgian withdrawal from the Congo (Zaire) in 1960, temporarily destroyed Portuguese control in much of northern and part of central Angola. The massive military effort required to regain partial control and contain the subsequent guerrilla war imposed a heavy burden on the weak Portuguese economy, which was intensified after FRELIMO began military operations in Mozambique (towards the end of 1964) and PAIGG forces liberated parts of Guinea-Bissau.

By the beginning of 1974 an army of 200,000 men was eating up half the state budget of the poorest country in Western Europe, and was locked into a series of African wars that could be neither won nor ended by the heirs of Salazar's dictatorship.

In 1920 Lenin had argued that revolutionary movements in the colonial world, 'the revolutionary masses of those countries where there is no, or hardly any, proletariat, ie the oppressed masses of colonial Eastern countries', could play a big part in the overthrow of the imperialist states and the capitalist system in the developed capitalist countries, the imperialist homelands.[1]

In the event, the major powers of western capitalism, helped by profound changes in the balance of their economies, managed in the period after 1945 to avoid the costs and consequences of endless colonial wars. They were able to concede formal independence to, generally speaking, conservative 'local' ruling classes in their former colonies whilst retaining, in many cases, a good deal of indirect control, both economic and political. Neo-colonialism was born.

Independence was not, of course, conceded very willingly—and most certainly not bloodlessly. In Vietnam, Indonesia, Malaya, Egypt, Kenya, Algeria, Cyprus and South Arabia the imperialist powers fought savage rearguard actions accompanied by murderous repression equalling or surpassing anything done by the Portuguese in Africa. But these wars were fought—sometimes successfully and sometimes not—within a strategic framework of the withdrawal from direct colonial rule in favour of neo-colonialism. They were the exceptions, profoundly important exceptions, but exceptions nonetheless. Portuguese imperialism was at once too weak and too rigid to adopt the neo-colonialist strategy in time. The 13 years of colonial wars led directly to the overthrow of the dictatorship in Portugal itself.

Fascism would have been overthrown many years earlier if not for the fact that Portuguese capitalism was locked into international capitalism and strongly supported by it. British capitalism had dominated the Portuguese economy throughout the 19th century—hence the mythology of 'our oldest ally'. Indirectly the British ruling class had control over the Portuguese empire and profited from it; that is why the Portuguese colonies survived the 'scramble for empire' by the USA, Germany, France, Britain and Japan in the decades before the First World War. They survived because they were an appendix of the British empire.

Portuguese fascism survived through the 1930s and the Second World War. Salazar, like Franco, survived the downfall of Hitler and Mussolini. As the 'Cold War' got under way, the Portuguese empire became one of the pillars of the free world, a founder member of NATO (1949), and recipient of modern arms and expert advice on techniques of repression. The African wars could not have continued for very long without NATO weaponry and equipment.

NATO gave the dictatorship a new lease of life, but not for good. International capitalism, through its contradictions, went on burrowing beneath the structure of Portuguese society. Foreign capital was flowing into Portugal on a massive scale. The multinationals moved in to exploit an abundant supply of cheap and well-policed labour. The result was comparatively rapid growth of the previously stagnant economy and a very considerable growth in the size of the working class.

When, on 25 April 1974, sections of the army officer corps overthrew Salazar's successor, Caetano, a wave of working-class struggles created a mass working-class movement almost overnight. And that movement, with all its illusions and political weaknesses, is at a higher level than any other in Europe. It has prevented, up to the present, the consolidation of a new conservative regime—whether military, fascist or 'social democratic'—and has put the socialist revolution on the agenda in a European country for the first time for years. The potential consequences are enormous. The history of the last 18 months in Portugal is an excellent illustration of the interdependence and interrelations of apparently diverse events.

The African wars, the growth of the multinational corporations, the development of the EEC; all contributed to the present situation in Portugal. The defeat of the threatened counter-revolution in Portugal and the seizure of power by the Portuguese workers would shake capitalism in the major countries of Western Europe.

The ruling classes are well aware of it. That is why, for example, British TV, press and radio—which ignored for years on end the brutal fascist dictatorship in this 'oldest ally'—now devote unprecedented time and space to presenting the right-wing forces in Portugal as defenders of 'democracy'.

The outcome is still undecided. A revolutionary situation exists in Portugal, a situation of fragmentation of power—leading to powerlessness. It cannot continue for long. Either the crisis will be resolved by the working class or by the forces of reaction. Such situations are the supreme test of parties, programmes, policies. In the last resort, all the political tendencies in the working-class movement are to be judged by their willingness and their ability to lead the working class forward to power in the time of crisis—or by their contribution to its defeat. Today Portugal is the touchstone for organisations claiming to be socialist or communist.

The collapse of the fascist regime[2]

A fundamental objective prerequisite for a revolution is the impasse of the old regime. Among the symptoms of a revolutionary situation, Lenin pointed out the following:

> ...when it is impossible for the ruling classes to maintain their rule without any change; when there is a crisis, in one form or another, among the 'upper classes', a crisis in the policy of the ruling class, leading to a fissure through which the discontent and indignation of the oppressed classes bursts forth. For a revolution to take place, it is usually insufficient for 'the lower classes not to want' to live in the old way; it is also necessary that 'the upper classes should be unable' to live in the old way.[3]

The deeper the general crisis, the more different sections of the ruling class quarrel with each other. The deeper the crisis and the greater the general hostility of the masses of the people towards the regime, the sharper are the fissures and conflicts within the ruling class. This is exactly what has happened in Portugal.

The collapse of the fascist regime in Portugal was just the result of the loss of confidence of the ruling class that things could continue in the old way.

The coup which overthrew the Caetano regime on 25 April 1974 was the work of the Armed Forces Movement (MFA), consisting of 400 middle ranking officers. But its success depended on the feeling within the most powerful sections of business and among the upper ranks in the forces that Caetano's government was too inflexible to deal with the main problems facing Portuguese capitalism. When it came to the crunch, no substantial section of society was willing to side with the old regime.

The colonial revolution

The most important problem was that of the African colonies. Portugal's army was facing defeat in Guinea, and was bogged down in endless wars in Mozambique and Angola. The cost was eating up nearly half the government budget. Yet for the most advanced sections of big business Guinea and Mozambique at least were a declining asset. In the last ten years the proportion of Portugal's exports bought by the colonies had declined from 25 percent to 11.3 percent, while Portuguese sales to Europe had increased from 49 percent to 65 percent. It was hardly surprising that people in high places began to ask themselves whether they could not replace colonial rule by indigenous rule, while keeping in their own hands the main economic wealth of these countries—as Britain had in Zambia, Kenya, Nigeria and so on.

Further tipping the balance against Caetano was the economic condition of Portugal itself.

The economic basis of the ruling class has been undergoing substantial changes in the last 20 years. The economy remains the most backward in Europe, with output per head only two thirds of the Spanish level. But some industrial development has been taking place, gradually changing Portugal from an overwhelmingly agricultural country to one where industry plays an important role. In 1950 half the population lived off the land (in agriculture, fishing or forestry) and only a quarter worked in industry; by the late 1960s the proportion in industry had risen to 35.5 percent and that in agriculture fallen to 33.5 percent.

This change has been based upon a massive flow of foreign capital into Portugal and the Portuguese African colonies. In the years 1943-60 the total foreign investment in Portugal was 2 billion escudos; in the years 1961-67 it rose to 20 billion.

In the year 1971 alone private foreign investment was three or four times larger than between 1943 and 1960.

In the years 1961-71 foreign capital made up 66.9 percent of all new investment in Portugal.[4]

American and German capital flowed into Portugal at a much faster rate than British capital. But the total British investment is still greater than that of any other country.

Portugal became a semi-colony of the advanced western imperialist countries. There are 200 companies in Portugal associated with British capital, with total investments of £300 million. They include Plesseys, GEC, Babcock and Wilcox, British Leyland, BICC, British Steel Corporation, Rootes-Chrysler, and Metal Box. Other international companies, notably ITT, are also there.

The aim of the multinationals was to exploit the low-paid labour of the Portuguese working class. In Lisbon the average wage for a 45-hour week was between £7 and £10; elsewhere wages were even lower. In some districts infant mortality was as high as 10 percent, and the Portuguese have the lowest life expectancy in Europe.

The most backward capitalism in Europe was likely to be hardest hit by the developing world crisis. Inflation was already greater than anywhere else apart from Greece; estimates suggest it had reached 30 percent a year by March 1974. The inevitable by-product was continual unrest in industry which the crudest repression could not stop.

At the same time, the massive scale of arms spending on the colonial wars made impossible any attempt to deal with the grave social problems that face the majority of the Portuguese. More importantly for the ruling class, it has hampered the expansion of Portuguese industry keeping up in any way with that in the rest of Europe.

As the *Economist* pointed out three years ago, 'Many of the bright young men rising to prominence in the banks and the economic ministries are ready to argue very strongly that the price of holding on to Africa has been the diversion of investment funds from vital development projects in the home country'.[5]

Spinola's programme

The coup finally took place when some of Portugal's biggest monopolies decided that the time had come to change course. One of these, Champalimaud, which controls banks and the steel industry, had for some time followed a 'liberal' line, reflecting the fact that it was more closely linked with a group of foreign-trained technocrats who had had some influence in the early years of the Caetano regime. They were closely associated with the journal *Expresso*, which advocated a policy of reforms and liberalisation. Also associated with them was the former Education Minister Veiga Simao (a graduate of Manchester and Cambridge Universities), who had begun the reform of Portugal's archaic education system by developing technical and vocational education.

Shortly before the coup another of the big monopolies, CUF, which owned 10 percent of Portuguese industrial capacity, moved to a position of opposition to the regime. CUF has many interests in Africa and traditionally has been much more reluctant to consider decolonisation, but recently has been increasingly anxious about the outcome of the colonial wars. It was a firm owned by CUF that published Spinola's book which advocated a political solution to the African wars.

This recognition of the need for a change of line by the monopolies coincided with the growth of discontent among the army, and in particular the middle-ranking army officers. This discontent had at first been economic in origin; soldiers were badly paid and had to do four years military service. There was a serious shortage of officers, so that many career officers had done several tours of duty in the colonies, and reservists up to the age of 36 were being recalled for service. Many workers of military age emigrated rather than serve; it is estimated that there were over 100,000 draft dodgers throughout Europe.

The discontent in the army was growing even though the Caetano government had recently increased pay; there had been demonstrations in the Military Academy. More and more the demand for economic improvements was spilling over into the demand for an end to the colonial wars.

At home too there was considerable pressure for an end to the wars; demonstrations had taken place, and there was a significant anti-war movement among Catholic priests.

General Spinola was the person best suited to bring together the big monopolies on the one hand, and the captains' movement in the army on the other.

Spinola's past—as a supporter of Franco and Hitler—gave him credentials as a reliable conservative. As governor and commander in chief in Guinea-Bissau, Spinola followed a policy described by Dr Manuel Boal, one of the leaders of the liberation movement PAIGC, as 'systematic terrorism': 'He bombed defenceless villages in the liberated zone, destroyed our crops and always burned hayfields at the end of the dry season to prevent us constructing huts for the rain season… He is a man with blood on his hands and a smile on his face.' One of his feats was to help in organising the murder of the PAIGC leader Amilcar Cabral.

When Spinola came to the conclusion that the African wars were unwinnable, he dissociated himself from the Caetano regime. His book, *Portugal and the Future*, published in February 1974, was a bombshell; it was the first time anyone in such a position had admitted that a purely military solution to the African wars was impossible.

Spinola's actual proposals combined ambiguity with Utopianism. He stopped far short of urging complete independence for the colonial territories, preferring such phrases as a 'scheme of the pluri-national state type' and a 'federal solution cemented by solidarity'. His hopes that political agreement could be established with the liberation forces were a belated neo-colonialism. Yet in the total dead end that Portuguese imperialism had reached his proposals seemed the best available.

Though he played no part in the organisation of the April coup, indeed had no connection with the MFA, Spinola was its natural beneficiary. He became President with the agreement of both the MFA leaders and Caetano—the latter being only too glad to hand over office to such a conservative figure and make his own escape.

The coup and the popular movement

Spinola's problem was that he could not implement his programme for satisfying the new needs of Portuguese big business without getting rid of the old regime. And the armed forces could not do that without paralysing the repressive forces that had kept the mass of the population in check previously.

The destruction of the old regime required more than the replacement of one or two men at the top. Throughout the bureaucracy of the state, the armed forces and the police were individuals who owed their advancement to the methods of Caetano and his predecessor, Salazar. The officers of the Armed Forces Movement feared that unless these were purged they would regroup and reverse the coup.

The officers might then find themselves on the receiving end of the torture of which the secret police were notorious practitioners.

Three years ago a senior government official told the *Economist*, 'Portugal is like a pressure cooker, the lid has been kept on for a very long time and if some fool lets all the steam out at once, the thing will blow up'.[6] That is exactly what Spinola was forced to do. He had to prevent the exercise of power by the secret police in order to protect his own pro-capitalist supporters. But when he did that, he inadvertently permitted the mass of the population to give expression to all the discontents that had been accumulating for half a century.

In the explosion that followed, a process of radicalisation took place far greater than Spinola intended. He did not aim to dismantle the hated secret police, the PIDE, but that is what has happened as a result of spontaneous mass pressure.

The moment the purge began, it took on a life of its own. The bonds that had tied down the rest of Portuguese society for nearly 50 years snapped. In the factories, in the media, on the streets, workers began to turn against those who had inflicted so many injuries on them in the past. The army was forced to take secret policemen into protective custody before they were lynched. Army officers were called to the factories to negotiate an end to strikes for the dismissal of fascist managers. In virtually every industry there were struggles for massive wage increases.

The bourgeoisie found that a movement aimed initially to rationalise its rule had got out of hand. From singing about 'freedom' and 'unity' in May it began to scream about anarchy, until a significant sector of it backed the abortive right-wing coups in September 1974 and March 1975. The failure of the coups and the fall of Spinola, however, aggravated its problems, and ensured that the months ahead in Portugal will be very stormy indeed.

Reading accounts of events in Lisbon after 25 April 1974, one is vividly reminded of Marx's account of the revolution of February 1848 in Paris, when one section of the bourgeoisie was overthrown by another aided by the middle classes and the workers:

> The provisional government which emerged from the February barricades necessarily mirrored in its composition the different parties which shared in the victory. It could not be anything but a composite between the different classes . . . this was the February revolution itself, the common uprising with its illusions, its poetry, its visionary content and phrases...
>
> In the minds of the proletariat, who confused the finance aristocracy with the bourgeoisie in general...the rule of the bourgeoisie was abolished with the introduction of the republic. At that time all the royalists were transformed into republicans and all the millionaires of Paris into workers. The phrase which corresponded to this imaginary abolition of class relations was fraternity, universal fraternisation and brotherhood. This pleasant abstraction from class antagonism, this sentimental reconciliation of contradictory class interests, this visionary elevation above the class struggle, this *fraternity* was the real catchword of the February revolution... The Paris proletariat revelled in this magnanimous intoxication of fraternity.[7]

But the euphoria of February 1848 was shattered four months later when the fundamental class divisions in modern society showed themselves to be more important than temporary divisions of interest within the ruling class. The bourgeois republicans consolidated their rule by turning the guns of their armed forces on the working class.

> Fraternity, the fraternity of the antagonistic classes, of which one exploits the other, this fraternity, proclaimed in February, written in capital letters on the brow of Paris, on every person, on every barracks—its true, unadulterated, its prosaic expression is civil war, civil war in its most frightful form, the war of labour and capital. This fraternity flamed in front of all the windows of Paris on the evening of 25 June [1848] when the Paris of the bourgeoisie was illuminated, while the Paris of the proletariat burnt, bled, moaned unto death. Fraternity endured just as long as the interests of the bourgeoisie were in fraternity with the interests of the proletariat.[8]

The lesson of 1848 has been repeated dozens of times since. Whenever one section of the ruling class turns against an established authoritarian government for its own reasons there is always talk of 'national unity', 'popular unity' or 'anti-fascist unity'. This leaves the ruling class free to disrupt the 'unity' when conditions are most suited to its own victory.

The masses enter the arena

The mass of the workers did not wait for the Government or for the labour leaders to tell them what to do, but immediately and effectively entered upon the historical arena. The collapse of fascism raised their expectations. Revolutions are impatient, and the revolutionary masses are impatient. The downtrodden were looking for radical changes in their lives, for enlarged horizons.

Revolutions break the wall between the partial economic struggles and the general political struggle. Each kind of struggle reciprocally encourages the other.

The weeks and months following 25 April 1974 proved to the hilt how wrong were those who see a Chinese wall between partial struggle for economic reforms and the political struggle for revolution, and how correct Rosa Luxemburg was when she pointed out that in a revolutionary period the economic struggle grows into a political one and vice versa:

> The movement does not go only in one direction, from an economic to a political struggle, but also in the opposite direction. Every important political mass action, after reaching its peak, results in a series of economic mass strikes. And this rule applies not only to the individual mass strike, but to the revolution as a whole. With the spread, clarification and intensification of the political struggle not only does the economic struggle not recede, but on the contrary it spreads and at the same time becomes more organised and intensified. There exists a reciprocal influence between the two struggles. Every fresh attack and victory of the political struggle has a powerful impact on the economic struggle, in that at the same time as it widens the scope for the workers to improve their conditions and strengthens their impulse to do so, it enhances their fighting spirit. After every soaring wave of political action, there remains a fertile sediment from which sprout a thousand economic struggles. And the reverse also applies. The workers' constant economic struggle against capital sustains them at every pause in the political battle. The economic struggle constitutes, so to speak, the permanent reservoir of working-class strength from which political struggles always imbibe new strength. The untiring economic fight of the proletariat leads every moment to sharp isolated conflicts here and there from which explode unforeseen political struggles on an immense scale.
>
> In a word, the economic struggle is the factor that advances the movement from one political focal point to another. The political struggle periodically fertilises the ground for the economic struggle. Cause and effect interchange every second. Thus we find that the two elements, the economic and political, do not incline to separate themselves from one another during the period of the mass strikes in Russia, not to speak of negating one another, as pedantic schemes would suggest.[9]

After 25 April 1974 the immediate task was to recover from the years of fascist repression and unite the workers split up by the multitude of unions in a particular plant, and a multitude of plants and small production units throughout industry.

The Portuguese working class took the task of unification into their own hands. In factories all over Portugal workers' committees were elected to lead rank and file struggles, not only on a local basis but also for whole industries and throughout monopolies.

In the electronics industry a combine has been formed which has workers' delegates from all the electronics firms—Plesseys, STC, ITT, etc. Many factories and sections of workers are regularly producing newspapers and bulletins for the rank and file. In some cases, such as the wool and textile industries, the docks, and the steel industries, these papers are produced for the workers of entire industries.

These are not alternative trade unions, but are made up of delegates elected by the rank and file of the trade unions in the plants, and are designed to give a responsive, democratic leadership to the factory. The factory committees co-ordinate the struggles on a day-to-day basis and all policy decisions are taken by mass meetings. Negotiations with the management are reported to the rank and file.

From the start, political and economic demands have been closely linked in the workers' committees. *Saneamento* (purging) meant much more than simply locking up the secret policemen. Effectively and thoroughly carried out, it means to virtually destroy the structure of the bourgeois state. Because the corporate state meant control over every level of social life, banks, churches, schools, universities, offices and factory managements, a complete *saneamento* would mean the destruction of the entire social hierarchy from board of directors right down to foremen.

In the big companies, multinationals especially, economic demands went alongside struggles for the purging of all members of the management or administration that were in any way connected with the fascist regime: 'In some places this means the sacking of them all'.[10]

During May 1974 alone over 200,000 workers in the key sectors of textiles, shipbuilding, transport, hotel and catering, electronics, the post office, and banking, were on strike for better wages and conditions as well as for *saneamento*.

In Lisnave 8,400 workers went on strike, occupying the shipyards of Margueira and Rocha do Conde de Orbidos. Main demands were £130 minimum wage per month and a 40-hour week.

In textiles, about 6,000 workers of the Lanificios of Corvitha, Tordozendo and Unhais de Serra decided to begin a strike on 12 May in order to back their demand for a £13 monthly increase. The strike spread to several factories in Porto, Castanheira de Pera, Castelo Branco, Cebolais de Lima, Lisbon, Portalegre, Mira d'Aire and Arelar.

About 1,600 miners in Panasqueira began a strike on 13 May. Demands were a £100 minimum monthly wage, an annual bonus of a monthly wage, free medical care, the purge of all people linked with the fascist regime and one month's holiday. The strike ended on 20 May and all the workers' demands were met.

Firestone workers in Lisbon, Alcochete, Porto and Coimbra began a strike on 13 May and occupied the plants. They demanded the purge of elements of the administration connected with the fascist regime and went back to work on 20 May.[11]

By the end of June significant advances had been made. *Saneamento*, although by no means complete, had resulted in the most compromised and prominent right wingers being cleared out of offices, newspapers, radio and television stations, local government structures, churches and factories throughout Portugal, the most sustained and far-reaching purging being conducted in the factories where the repression which followed the wave of strikes preceding the coup was still fresh in the memory of the class.

For the multinationals the legislation of a national minimum wage by the government in June, and the militancy with which the working class fought to enforce it and with which shop floor organisation developed, meant the end of the era of super-exploitation of cheap and repressed labour. Companies such as Plesseys, Timex and ITT started repatriating capital, and attempted to close down parts of their operations and move out. Many of the small and medium enterprises have gone bankrupt and closed down or simply been abandoned by their owners.

The struggle against redundancies began in June 1974. By September 1975 there were 300,000 out of work in the industrial sector alone. The harsh facts of Portugal's capitalism continue to drive the working class to defend itself.

Many factories have been taken over by the workers, and the workers' committees, which were elected soon after 25 April 1974, have started to run them. But the bosses didn't give up without a fight. They tried to bring in the Strike Law against the workers. In Charminha, a small garment factory outside Lisbon, they tried to pay salaries with bounced cheques. The Austrian manager fled the country, and the workers, mainly women, set up a cooperative to sell their work to the people. In Eurofil, which makes plastics, fibres, rope and sacking, etc, and was run on 40 percent casual labour, the management tried to make the company go bankrupt. The workers occupied the factory and continued production. They have kept out the bosses and are demanding nationalisation without compensation under workers' control.

In Tintura Portugalia, the biggest network of dyers in Portugal, the bosses answered the list of workers' demands with a list of redundancies and a lockout. The workers occupied the factory and started a work-in. The bosses, who claimed the company faced a critical financial situation, nevertheless started to run a highly expensive campaign of smear and slander against the workers in the national press and radio. Their plans were foiled by workers in the radio station who blacked the campaign and broadcast the workers' version of the struggle instead.

A new wave of very bitter redundancy struggles has been sweeping Portugal since January. In the first six weeks of this year there have been more than 250 struggles around this issue.

Strikes are no longer the main tactic being used in these struggles. Instead, an ever growing number of factories have been occupied. Some, like the Nutripol supermarket chain, are being run under workers' control, and in a number of cases workers have demanded nationalisation—in the CUF, a sprawling conglomerate that has now been nationalised, and the Nefil Furniture factory where a spokesman for the workers' committee explained the tactic as follows:

> We do not have any illusions in workers' management under capitalism. We are using it as a weapon, as an emergency solution. We started to run the factory because we had to in order to survive after the management had abandoned the factory on 27 December... We are thinking about demanding that the government nationalise the firm—under workers' control. We do not want a phoney nationalisation which only helps the bosses.

In the ITT-owned factory of Standard Electrica at Tascais 150 redundancies were announced out of a total workforce of 1,800, with the rest to go on short-time working. There was an immediate mass meeting, which was attended by delegates from other electronics factories, and which adopted the following demands: that the government take action to stop redundancies and that all sacked workers be reinstated; the immediate withdrawal of all troops from the overseas territories; government legislation to control profits made by multinationals; the creation of new jobs; and that steps be taken towards freeing Portugal from imperialist domination.

In the first week of May 1975, 150,000 workers went on strike for better pay and conditions. They were mainly from the chemical industry and from the hotel and catering industry who, as in Britain, are amongst the lowest paid sections of the working class.

Again, 280,000 wool weavers and garment workers throughout Portugal have recently been involved in a go-slow. They are demanding a 40-hour week, rest day on Saturdays for wool weavers and on bank holidays for garment workers, and a minimum wage of £20 a week.

A great many of these workers are employed by multinational companies (both Courtaulds and ICI have interests in Portugal). They work with imported raw materials and a high proportion of the goods manufactured with their cheap labour is then exported to Europe. The workers have held demonstrations of several thousands in Oporto and the textile town of Covilha.[12]

On 25 June over 3,000 workers of TAP, the Portuguese airline, surrounded the main administrative offices and trapped the company managers in their offices, demanding the settlement of their 15 month old wage claim.[13]

To gauge how far the workers' struggle went, one must mention that it is estimated that some 300 undertakings have been taken over by the workers![14]

Struggle for control of the media

One of the foremost working-class battles—important economically, politically and ideologically—was over control of the media.

First the battle over *Jornal do Comercio*.

It started in April 1974, straight after the coup, and went on for five long months. The workers presented the administration with demands over wages, working conditions and, above all, the expulsion from the firm of the fascist supporters of the previous regime. Journalists, printers and office workers were unanimous on one point—all the demands were negotiable except for the expulsion of the director, Carlos Machado. He was accused by the workers of being reactionar and incompetent, and of exploiting the workers.

The refusal of the administration to sack Carlos Machado led the workers to strike and occupy the *Jornal do Comercio*.

During the occupation the workers published a 'strike paper' in spite of being told by the army not to do so. Following the issue of this strike paper the army sealed *Jornal do Comercio* off. Pickets were organised and the workers devised ways of communicating with the people and raising funds, through public meetings, shows and the publication of a booklet on the strike. Their unity and class consciousness prompted solidarity action from many sectors of the working class, including a 24-hour solidarity strike of all Lisbon and Oporto dailies except *O Seculo*. Workers from many firms contributed one day's pay to the strike fund, and the mass media workers gave space and time to publicise their fight.[15]

On 29 August the army occupied *Jornal do Comercio*.

The strike ended when, on 28 September, during the abortive right-wing coup, the owner of the paper, who was deeply involved, fled the country. The workers of the paper took it over.

A second battle for the media was fought out in *Republica*.

The *Republica* affair started in early 1975 when the print workers became concerned at the paper's declining sales. They feared redundancy and asked for discussions about safeguarding their jobs. They asked for information on the overall situation including the political line of the paper.

The editor, Paul Rego, refused any such discussion. Instead he started sacking workers. Some 17 journalists, who in one way or another opposed what was going on, were forced out.

Paul Rego is an interesting man. He is one of the top leaders of the Socialist Party. He was Minister of Information in the Spinola government, in which office he suspended publication of four newspapers; one of them was *Republica* itself. He also fined the paper. So he was not very popular, to say the least, among its workers.

Under Rego's editorship the paper moved away from being an independent, nonparty 'paper of information', as it is registered, to a journal more and more closely allied with the Socialist Party. It went as far as to exclude statements from any other political organisation, or gave them very small space during the general election campaigns. Rego's arrogance drove the workers to strike action on 2 May.

After long negotiations, on 7 May an agreement was struck between the management and the workers. It contained, at the request of the printers, the following paragraph: 'The newspaper will not be a party newspaper, in the sense that it will not reflect the predominance of a particular party in its column. All progressive parties should have identical treatment, coverage depending only on the importance of the events connected with each party.'

Rego broke the agreement. When the workers threatened to take it over

Rego asked the MFA to shut it down.

When COPCON came to give him the keys to reopen *Republica*, Rego demanded that they come down with him and help him sack some 15 workers, a number which suggested that he was out to sack the entire 15-strong workers' committee.

The COPCON major concerned would not go along with this. He went down to *Republica*, sought out a Socialist Party member of the workers' committee and gave him the keys to reopen.

The whole international campaign of the capitalist press describing the battle round *Republica* as a battle between the Communist Party and the Socialist Party is a lot of rubbish. As a matter of fact Communist Party members are in a minority on the *Republica* workers' committee—two out of 15. *Republica* on the whole reflects very much the views of the extreme left and very often is highly critical of the Communist Party.

Another very important battle for control of the media was waged by Radio Renascenca.

This radio station had always been in the hands of the Catholic Church. Even after the collapse of fascism it still held to its strong right-wing bias. For instance, on the arrival of Soares and Cunhal at the airport after the fall of the fascist regime, Radio Renascenca refused to broadcast their statements. In the following few months a number of clashes took place between workers and management, largely caused by the sacking of workers.

On 19 February 1975 an all-out strike started throughout Radio Renascenca. But on 11 March, when the right-wing coup broke out, the workers decided to go back to work, and they put the station at the disposal of the working class.

The workers expected that, since their boss was one of the most reactionary in Portugal, they would now win their case. But that was not to be. On 14 March the government appointed a mixed committee to run the station, with a delegate from the Ministry of Labour, the government, the technicians, and so on.

The workers were so dissatisfied that on 27 May they occupied the Lisbon station. The Oporto station remained in the hands of the Church hierarchy.

On 17 July the government told the workers that the station would be returned to the Church. The workers refused to hand over the station. During the next three days a number of mass demonstrations took place in support of the Radio Renascenca workers.

Then the Supreme Revolutionary Council of the MFA countermanded the decision of the government.

The workers took over complete control of the station. Their leadership was largely that of the revolutionary left. The programming of the station is done by a general assembly. Reports of struggles all over the world are regularly broadcast. The struggles going on in the factories, tenants' committees and so on are given a wide hearing.

The ideological/political importance of *Jornal do Comercio*, *Republica* and Radio Renascenca is that both contending forces—the revolutionary left and the reactionary bourgeoisie—see them as symbols of their power.

Community action

As one factory after another was occupied by its workforce, and workers' committees were elected to run them, there was a growing number of examples of workers mobilising on a neighbourhood basis in order to take control of other areas which affect their lives such as health, transport, education and housing.

Soon after the coup of 25 April, the families living in the shanty town of Bairro da Boavista in the outskirts of Lisbon took over a housing estate that had stood empty for three years. This housing estate, like many other new estates in the outskirts of Lisbon, was part of a speculator's plan to rehouse families living in the centre of the town in properties of high speculative value which would then be demolished and give place to high rise blocks that would house the posh headquarters of some bank or a first class hotel.

An army company, fresh from the events of 25 April, was deployed to force the families back to the corrugated iron lean-tos of the shanty town. The officer in charge, a member of the young Armed Forces Movement, faced with determined opposition from the whole community, followed the routine practice of any operation in the colonial wars of Africa and went straight to what he thought was the weakest link, an old widow who had just moved with her six sons to a two-bedroom flat with electricity, water and toilet. She replied, 'You better shoot me right here. All my life I have had the earth for a floor. At least I will die on a proper floor.' The officer stood there for a moment. Outside the men, women and children who had assembled to resist any eviction were speaking with the soldiers: 'This could be your shanty town! Remember that you too are the people! Turn the guns on the speculators, and not on your brothers and sisters!' The officer understood and, taking the company with him, left the estate. The occupation had been 'legalised' by the AFM.

In a country where over 2 million people live in slums and shanty-towns, houses are no longer being allowed to stand empty. They are being occupied. Left-wing parties, trade unions and broad-based neighbourhood assemblies are all behind a movement through which hundreds of houses and buildings either unused or misused have been occupied and transformed into nurseries, social centres, clinics, old people's centres and a multitude of other purposes tailored to the needs of the community.

On 9 March a general assembly of local residents in Oporto decided to occupy a four-house complex of 24 flats owned by the Ministry of Justice, which had stood empty for 15 years.

In Cascais, a suburb of Lisbon, local workers occupied an exclusive sports club and formed a local residents' committee to run it as a day nursery.

In Areiras de Cima a mansion belonging to an absentee landowner was taken over on 27 March by local people. They formed a committee to transform it into a clinic, nursery, cinema and cultural centre.

In Lisbon workers in the Portuguese Institute of Rheumatology converged on a building in the city centre, empty for nine years, and in it are setting up a proper therapy centre for a disease which up until now has had inadequate treatment in Portugal.

Another empty building in Lisbon, the dilapidated Frankfort Hotel, empty for two years, was the target of Lisbon shop workers who occupied it on 7 April. They organised groups of workers to clean it, repair it and to guard it by night. They issued a communiqué stating the aims of the occupation. They intend to create 'a nursery, library, canteen and common rooms where workers can discuss, read and in different ways create a better class consciousness, a better political consciousness and a better spirit of cooperation'.

In Corroios, another luxury hotel was occupied on 7 March by local people. A member of the occupation committee commented:

> The working people will devote their time to transforming this luxurious hotel complex of the rich into a place for workers to enjoy themselves—into a people's canteen, a child care centre and an old people's centre. The workers want to show their exploiters and prove to themselves that they are capable of solving their own problems.

Not only empty buildings, but local services, especially clinics and hospitals, have been requisitioned by neighbourhood committees, who through them are running a people's health service suited to the needs of the local community.[16]

A group of workers in Mafra decided to occupy a large building because they felt the need to have a place where they could leave their children during working hours. The workers distributed leaflets to the population, explaining the purpose of the occupation, and urging the people to participate in the occupation itself and in organising the creche.

A neighbourhood committee in Ajuda occupied a mansion which belongs to the Azevedo e Silva family, owners of an electrical material firm. For the last five years part of the mansion has been used as a warehouse for the firm and the other half has not been used at all. The mansion is going to be used as a creche for the children of the workers who live in the area. The workers are demanding the immediate removal of all the materials still in the mansion and immediate expropriation without compensation.

The residents of Alhandra have occupied a local squire's mansion and surrounding grounds to establish a much-needed nursery and junior school for local children. A voluntary committee has been set up to run the nursery, which already caters for 57 children.[17]

The workers' parties

The Communist Party supports Spinola's government

Straight after 25 April the Communist Party joined Spinola's government. The government was set up under the premiership of Palma Carlos, a conservative law professor who sat on the board of directors of some of Portugal's big companies. It was made up of a coalition of forces as diverse as the Popular Democratic Party (PPD), a party of big business, with two Communists and four Socialists. The Minister of Labour was a member of the Communist Party.

To pay their passage, the leaders of the Communist Party argued that nothing should be done that might upset Portuguese capitalism.

First of all, Portugal in the immediate future could not, and should not, go beyond the limits of capitalism, argued Alvaro Cunhal, the General Secretary of the Communist Party, in a speech in June 1974:

> It is necessary, for good and all, to get rid of the idea that there exists in Portugal a popular government in a position to carry out thorough social reform. Also illusions should not be nurtured that in the present circumstances the workers can force these through. The Provisional Government is formed of a broad coalition of social and political forces, whose programme—the Movement of the Armed Forces programme—does not envisage profound reforms of the socio-economic structure. This is one point. Another point to stress is that this same programme of an anti-monopolist strategy will make use of emergency measures. These can easily be implemented without altering the present structures of Portuguese society. There has been a small advance in this direction. We must advance.[18]

He further remarked:

> In the present political conditions, the demands put forward by the workers must be realistic, must not be at a level which cannot be borne by the enterprises or by the national economy...there are some bosses who demagogically say they are prepared to give all that the workers ask for (and even much they do not ask for). They incite workers to strike, and try to quickly unload these burdens onto the back of the State and the consumers, leading the country back into the old vicious circle of inflation that we saw in the days of fascism... The workers will not back strikes encouraged or supported by bosses who are suspiciously generous. They will not pull the chestnuts out of the fire for their own exploiters to consume.
>
> To do this would make the workers the dupes of fascism and the reaction. The workers will not do this.
>
> Because they are not ready to be duped, the workers have to show that they understand that, in present circumstances, *the strike* (a legitimate weapon necessary and indispensable in a struggle to win demands) must be used only as a last resort after other means of struggle have been tried.[19]

Excessive wage claims are 'counter-revolutionary', he stated:

> A typical example of counter-revolutionary activity is the recent incitement to strike on the part of administrators in large companies and the old government delegates in public enterprises. These people, who have always lived by the exploitation of workers, are suddenly leaping to the 'defence' of the workers, giving wage rises much higher than those demanded by the unions, wage rises that cannot be met in the present economic situation. They are pushing workers into striking and struggling against the Provisional Government.
>
> We see here what amounts to an orchestrated attack aiming to create a climate of insecurity in society, in such a way as to paralyse transport, prevent the distribution of essential commodities (bread and milk), disrupt the economy, destroy

> small and middle-sized businesses, spread popular discontent and encourage a conflict between the popular masses and the armed forces.[20]
>
> 'The vast majority of employers are perfectly capable of satisfying, certainly not all the unrealistic demands that some demagogues are foisting on the workers, but the major rises in wages demanded and other important and just demands.[21]

The small and medium businesses are less able to pay, hence workers should show restraint when putting wage claims to them: '...those who can should pay more and those with fewer resources should pay less'.[22]

And with some justification Cunhal goes on to say:

> Our enemies proclaim that communists threaten small businesses... The truth is that communists defend, not only the interests of the working class and peasantry, but all classes and middle layers. Small farmers, small industrialists, small businessmen—all these can look to us communists as the true defenders of their legitimate interests.[23]

The same line of opposition to workers' 'excessive' demands was put by the Intersindical (the Portuguese TUC), which the Communist Party very much influences. Antero Martins, as the delegate of the Bank Workers' Union, expressed the majority view of the Intersindical: 'In most cases the Intersindical takes action with the aim of avoiding big groups going on strike, while with groups that are already on strike it discusses the problem and, taking any opportunity, encourages a return to work.'

Such views were not confined to words. They were repeatedly translated into action. When the first big strikes took place after 25 April, the Communist Party exerted all its efforts to get them called off.

In the weeks which followed every major industry was hit by strikes and occupations. The Communist Party did not only order its own militants to argue against strike action: it went further and spread various slanders, arguing that strikes of bakers and transport workers in Lisbon were fomented by 'fascists'. When 35,000 postal workers (97 percent of the workforce) struck, the Communist Party claimed that the right was once again behind the strike and that the committee running the strike was unrepresentative. It supported the use of troops to break the strike, and organised meetings on street corners and demonstrations outside the post offices against the strikers.

Cunhal stated:

> *The strike of the CIT* [Postal Workers] *is an example of a strike that should neither be called nor implemented.* It is an example of a strike that is not only useless but damaging to the workers. Firstly, some of the demands, such as the 35-hour week, are unrealistic, demagogic and economically insupportable. Talks were proceeding. The strike was in no way justifiable. Clearly its promoters did not hope for an improvement in the workers' standard of living... The aim of these people was not the improvement of living standards. The aim was to paralyse a service essential to the life of the country, disturb economic and social life, and turn the workers against the Provisional Government.[24]

The demand for a 35-hour week unrealistic! When massive unemployment grips Portugal!

Excessive wage demands threaten the national interest, and in Portugal according to Cunhal:

> These events show that, in the struggle for the complete destruction of fascism and the defence of liberty, a new battlefront emerges in which all the people are involved: *the battle to prevent the disruption of economic life and a deep economic crisis*.
>
> It is time to say that this is a great danger, if not the greatest danger that is threatening the Portuguese road to democracy.
>
> A serious economic crisis that will hit broad layers of the population and will mean a general sharpening of social conflict will not only bring in its wake a wave of unemployment and new serious economic problems for the workers but will be the most favourable breeding ground for opening the way to counter-revolution.
>
> For the defence of the workers' interests, the defence of the national interest, liberty and democracy, it is in the vital interests of the Portuguese people that they avoid such a crisis and do all they can to this end.[25]

Harold Wilson could hardly improve on Cunhal!

The lesson was driven hard into the postal workers, and in September, when the government, still loyally supported by the Communist Party, issued a call for a 'Voluntary Day of Labour' in order to save the national (and capitalist) economy, the union leadership issued the following statement:

> The CPS [Union Organising Committee] believes that the struggles of the toiling masses, led by the proletariat, must be continued. And it is for this purpose that we call on all postal workers to go to their places of work on that day. The CPS points out that taking part in this day of labour is voluntary and the workers must decide what to do according to their revolutionary consciousness. We must use this day to raise our consciousness, to improve our organisation, and to step up the struggle that we have been waging to purge the administrators connected to the old regime, to win a higher standard of living and to build the union... The CPS suggests that the workers demand that the pay rate this Sunday be the same as other days of the week, since this work is voluntary.
>
> The CPS proposes that the money we get for this extra day be turned over to the union funds for workers who have been laid off and for comrades on strike. We advise all concerned that such a contribution would also be voluntary.
>
> As we all know we are not used to working Sundays, so it would be natural for less work to be done. Therefore, the CPS calls for using our breaks and refreshment periods to discuss the present crisis, to sharpen our vigilance in the struggle against fascism and capitalist exploitation. Let us turn this working Sunday into a day of struggle for purging the administrators connected to the old regime, for building the union, and against fascism and capitalist exploitation.'[26]

The idea that the day of labour should be used for union organising, that it should be paid at the normal rate, and that it was unlikely that so much work would be done as on a normal day was presumably not what the government had in mind.[27]

The labour law

The Communist Party leadership supported the Spinola government's Labour Law. Despite the claim that it legalised strikes for the first time for 40 years, it actually put restrictions on them which were much more severe than those in the Industrial Relations Act of the British Tory government.

The first two articles in the text of the Strike Law guaranteed to the workers of Portugal the Right to Strike in principle, describing it as 'the collective recourse of workers to defend and promote their collective professional interests'.

Having so established the workers' rights, the law continued with a further 29 articles of conditions, restrictions and exceptions which chipped away at these rights, leaving a law which attempted to block and suppress the struggles of the working class at every turn.

Firstly there were the exceptions. The army, the police, judges, prison officers and firemen were forbidden to strike, and a special law was to deal with the rights of civil servants and employees in public institutions.

Secondly the types of strikes permitted under the law were severely limited. It was illegal to strike for 'political motives'. It was illegal also to strike in solidarity with workers in a different trade. Isolated strikes by small sections of a company's workforce were illegal, as were occupations of factories or places of work by strikers. The only form of picketing that was allowed was outside work premises to prevent companies from employing blackleg labour. Strikes were also illegal if they occurred whilst a negotiated agreement was in operation. This meant that if workers signed, say, a two-year wage agreement with management, they were powerless against the effects of inflation until the agreement had run its course.

There remained, though, a residue of situations where strike action was legal, and so the bulk of the law went into creating complicated procedures and restrictions upon the actions of strikers that forced them to walk a delicate tightrope between what was permitted by law and what was not. No strike could take place until 30 days of negotiations had elapsed, counted from the moment the workers presented their demands in writing. Then a further seven days notice had to be given to both management and the Ministry of Labour. Strike action became illegal if the workers' demands were met either in whole or even 'to a significant degree' by management, and the Ministry of Labour was to be the arbiter of that last vague situation.

A strong feature of the law was its attempt to bureaucratise the actions of the workers themselves. A strike was only legal when conducted through an official trade union or unions representing the majority of the workers in a factory. In addition a strike committee had to be elected, and the identity of its members communicated to the management and the Minister of Labour.

Once elected, moreover, it could not be changed for six months. A decision to strike must have the support of a majority of the workforce in a factory, and all those absent at a strike vote were to be counted as anti-strike voters.

Lock-outs by management also became illegal under the terms of this law, but to this there were many loopholes. Lock-outs were justified if the workers tried to occupy the factory, if they damaged or destroyed goods or equipment, if they infringed any clause of the strike law, or if for any technical reasons it was impractical to keep the factory open—all vague clauses leaving much room for management manoeuvre. But the trump card was held by the government, which reserved the right to intervene to break a strike if in their view it was 'against the national interest'.

The law carried penalties of stiff fines for failure to abide by its procedures, and imprisonment of up to six months for violence in the course of a strike.[28]

In practice the strength of the working class was such that the law remained a dead letter.

In August 1974 the workers of TAP, the Portuguese National Airline, one of the most militant sections of the working class, were involved in a struggle against management which led to an attempt by the government to curb the strike wave. Troops were sent in to try to enforce the law, arresting and sacking strike leaders.

The TAP workers quickly drew the lessons of their struggle. In a leaflet published on 25 August 1974, they asked:

> What kind of government makes laws against us the workers and does not revoke the fascist laws?
>
> What kind of government represses workers who are fighting for their just demands and allows PIDE agents and the most notorious reactionaries to remain at large? What kind of government plants in TAP a lackey of Champalimaud [a huge Portuguese monopoly] who had been purged from the Siderugia [National Steel Works] when we are fighting for *Saneamento*?
>
> This government is not on our side. It is a government which sides with the bosses. For us, the workers, there are redundancies, a rise in the cost of living, repression. For the bosses, a free hand to exploit us better.[29]

Similarly 4,000 workers of Lisnave shipyard staged an afternoon strike and marched on the Ministry of Labour. The workers wore their blue overalls and coloured helmets in the demonstration, which was particularly impressive for its discipline, organisation and unity. They were joined by a large delegation of Post Office workers and hundreds of supporters, and were all the way applauded by the population. The march opened with a huge banner ('Down with Capitalism'), and the other dominant slogan ('Right to strike, yes. Lockout, no') made the recently published anti-strike law the main target of the demonstrators.

The workers completely ignored the ban on the demonstration declared by the government and the Armed Forces the day before, as well as the show of strength of the Army, which brought hundreds of soldiers and armoured vehicles to the streets, and sealed off the whole area around the Ministry. The head of the demonstration was stopped for half an hour by a line of COPCON troops across the street. The workers appealed directly to the soldiers over the heads of the officers. They explained the anti-working-class nature of the strike law, and appealed to the soldiers as 'sons of workers, brothers of workers, future workers'. Some of the soldiers broke down weeping. When the officers saw they were losing control of the soldiers, they were forced to let the march pass.[30]

The minimum wage law

During the last few months of the fascist regime a large number of strikes took place—at Plesseys, Standard, Grundig, General Instruments, Lusitania, British Leyland, Signetics, ITT, Fabrica de Leinas Uniao, Fabrica Leao and many others.

The focus of the Communist-Party-controlled trade union centre—the Intersindical—was the campaign for a national minimum of £100 a month, which provided the basic demand for many of the struggles that took place.

The Provisional Government declared a national minimum wage of £55 a month. This law did not cover agricultural workers, domestic servants and employees in establishments with less than five workers.

The Communist Party leaders declared their support for this law, denounced the demand for £100 as unrealistic and refused to support the many strikes based on the demand. And this notwithstanding the fact that since 1973, when the Intersindical first raised the demand for £100 minimum, the cost of living rose by at least 50 percent.

Communist Party bureaucratic control of the trade unions

In order to control the workers, Salazar had established a union structure that divided the workers into tiny groups. Corporate unions were horizontal structures, organised on the basis of profession/trade; a machine operator therefore would belong to the metalworkers' union, whether he worked in a brewery, car factory or airport. These bodies were also divided on the basis of sex—tailors and 'seamstresses' belonged to different unions. There were over 400 unions in Portugal when the coup took place—in some factories there were 30 to 40. In CUF there were as many as 100. In the Lisnave shipyards there were 24 separate craft unions of which most of the 7,000 shipbuilders were members.

Approximately 2 million workers were divided among these bodies. In 1969, 80 percent of the unions had average memberships under 1,616 and only eight unions had more than 20,000 members. Some of them were federated on a regional basis, as for example the Union of Electrical Workers of the South.

The Communist Party, which controlled the Intersindical after 25 April, did not smash the existing structure but took hold of it.

The trade unions are still suffering from the fragmentation imposed by the fascist regime. A very large number of unions still exist which are divided both according to trades and according to district. Metal workers, for instance, who form a large proportion of industrial workers in Portugal, have separate unions in each of the major cities. The same is true of the bank employees' unions.

Other forms inherited from fascism and the lack of historical tradition in independent trade union organisations have recently led to some serious problems in several trade unions. The rules imposed upon the unions by the fascist regime ensured that the final decision-making body of each union is not a delegate conference but a General Assembly which all members of a union are entitled to attend. Under fascism these decisions could not be freely implemented due to state control. The rule was uncritically accepted as democratic after 25 April.

In practice, this method of establishing policy can become highly undemocratic. The geographical location of the General Assembly and its timing can determine which particular group of workers is more likely to attend. Anomalies thus created are considerable.

To look at a few examples: the Executive of the Bank Employees Union of Oporto organised a series of local meetings and a delegate conference to discuss their proposed demands, a reduction of the working hours. In practically all these meetings, which were all well attended, the proposal was overwhelmingly agreed. However, when the General Assembly was called, its attendance barely surpassed that of some of the local meetings and the executive proposal was defeated. This decision, according to the rules of the union, had to stand as official union policy, even though the majority of the membership was clearly opposed to it.

The rule has allowed certain union executives to maintain bureaucratic control over the union. In some cases, it has reduced trade union activity to political parties mobilising their supporters to attend General Assemblies and thus outvote the supporters of rival political lines.

In the Metalworkers' Union of Lisbon, for example, the executive, which is sympathetic to the Intersindical line, has sacked a number of full time officials who had supported strikes which the executive opposed.[31]

Oppressive press law

The Communist Party leaders also supported all the repressive measures taken by the Spinola government against the press.

By the end of July 1974 the radio and TV networks had been put under military control and left-wing newsreaders sacked. Fines have been imposed on three newspapers, and Saldanha Sanches, editor of *Luta Popular* and a member of the Maoist group MRPP, had been imprisoned.

On 1 August *Diario de Lisboa* was suspended for two days, and *A Capital* and *Republica* for one day, for publishing reports on a demonstration two days earlier against the colonial wars. The Ad-Hoc Committee administering the law also took exception to an 'alarmist' article in *Diario de Lisboa* describing the uneasy situation in Angola.

The press responded the following day with a protest strike at the suspension, and *Diario Popular* was the only evening daily paper to appear on the streets. The pickets, organised to prevent the distribution of the strike-breaking paper, were the victims of the most overt police repression since the coup.

Five days later the police made another appearance, this time joined by 11 tanks, numerous military police vehicles and several hundred soldiers, to suppress a demonstration in protest against the imprisonment of Sanches and the indefinite suspension of *Luta Popular*. The demonstration was peaceful, and its break-up showed a determination to control the media and suppress critical groups. The colonial problem and the workers' struggles were the most sensitive areas.

The offences are described in such vague terms as 'incitement to strike' and 'ideological aggression'.[32]

In July a provisional press law was introduced pending a fully-fledged Press Law. It aimed at imposing 'self-control' upon the press, and an Ad-Hoc Committee was set up along with it as a watchdog with the power to impose fines and/or suspension orders on the offending papers. This was the first measure to censor the Portuguese press. No court of law was required to operate the sanctions. A victim could appeal, but meanwhile the sanctions would already have been applied and have served their purpose.

The main victims were the small local papers and party organs which could least afford to pay fines and suffer losses through suspensions.

Bureaucratic manipulation: the Communist Party's role

After 25 April the Portuguese Communist Party was the only political party organised on a national scale. It had a significant base in the working class, an estimated membership of 5,000, and the credibility and respect earned by consistent opposition and action throughout the years of fascist rule. The Communist Party weekly *Avante* was the only clandestine newspaper to come out regularly during those 48 years, and many Party militants were imprisoned and killed for their part in working-class opposition to fascism. After the coup the Portuguese Communist Party alone was in a position to give leadership and unite the struggles that developed. Instead it set about establishing bureaucratic control over the trade union structures in their existing fragmented form—Communist Party members were elected, or replaced fascists, in the leaderships of most of the trade unions. Communist Party control over the Intersindical was firmly consolidated.

In some 200 municipalities the local government structure was taken over by Communist Party members. This, of course, in no way raised the consciousness and morale of the masses. On the contrary, as events in recent weeks in North Portugal show, Communist Party control of local government structures played into the hands of fascist provocateurs who could entice people against the local mayor who refused to help, or who was involved in corrupt practices.

Side by side with bureaucratic takeovers of trade unions, local government, and government and army offices, the Communist Party carried out a massive recruitment campaign. Soon the Communist Party claimed a membership of 100,000—a massive influx.

In the provisional government the Communist Party initially shared power with the Socialist Party and the PPD (Popular Democratic Party), the parliamentary expression of Portuguese capitalism, and eventually with the Movement of the Armed Forces. To maintain and justify this position it faced an enormous contradiction—on the one hand, to retain its influence it had to retain its base within the working class; on the other hand, it considered that a powerful offensive from the masses would threaten its position in the government and therefore its ability to carry through the 'democratic' as opposed to the socialist stage of the Portuguese Revolution. The Communist Party therefore performed a balancing act—between supporting some but not all the major struggles that took place.

What characterised the Communist Party's behaviour, above all, was manoeuvring and manipulation.

The Socialist Party

The Socialist Party did not exist before 1973. Soares and the other leaders of the Socialist Party were a handful of individuals without a party in the period of Salazar and Caetano.

They were the sort of lawyers who would defend political prisoners or take up workers' compensation claims in the courts.

After 25 April 1974 the Socialist Party entered the government. At first it had next to no local organisation but with the PPD still participated in the electoral front run by the Communist Party under Caetano (the CDE—later the MDP-CDE). They only withdrew from this in the late summer.

There is little doubt that, in the early post-25-April period the Communist Party effectively *built up* the Socialist Party and Soares, eg in a mass demonstration in Lisbon in July 1974 the audience was supplied by the Communist Party but Soares was one of the star speakers. At that time the Socialist Party did its best to cultivate a left image. Indeed, the Socialist Party statement of aims sounds almost revolutionary, as a few extracts show:

> The Socialist Party fights the capitalist system and bourgeois domination... The Socialist Party is implementing a new conception of life that can only be brought about through the construction of workers' power...
>
> The struggle against fascism and colonialism will only be achieved by the destruction of capitalist society and the construction of socialism... The Socialist Party refutes those who say they are social democrats but continue to preserve the status quo, the structures of capitalism and the interests of imperialism.[33]

Soares spoke of a 'multi-tendency party' including revolutionary leftists. He even threatened to resign from the government over certain right-wing measures that the Communist Party supported (the press law of summer 1974 and the slow pace of decolonisation allowed by Spinola).

At that time the Socialist Party put forward a double image. Big meetings for international speakers featured Altimirano, the left-wing Chilean Socialist Party leader, but also Mitterrand, the right-wing leader of the French Socialist

Party who is currently aligned with Harold Wilson, Schmidt, Palme and company in defence of 'democracy' (meaning capitalism) in Portugal.

The workers the Socialist Party recruited at the time could be to the *left* of the Communist Party cadres in the factories. The Socialist Party never carried the attacks on strikers under the first two provisional governments (until 28 September 1974) as far as the Communist Party (which held the Ministry of Labour). There were cases of Socialist Party members standing on joint electoral lists with the revolutionary left (eg Oporto bank workers).

But the Socialist Party never became a workers' party in the way in which the Communist Party is: although much of its support has come from workers its cadres, its activists, have been mainly petty bourgeois. This possibly explains its ability to make some leftist noises in summer 1974—its cadres did not have to carry the policies of the first two provisional governments in the factories. The onus was on the Communist Party to do this, because the Communist Party was seen as the party controlling the factories. But because its activists are not in the factories, the Socialist Party could swing very quickly to the right once it had built up a national organisation. This happened last autumn, under pressure from Western social democracy. Last autumn the Socialist Party and the PPD withdrew from the MDP-CDE. Then they began agitation for the right of unions to exist independently of the Intersindical (the agitation over the union law—not to be confused with the strike law).

At first the argument over this issue was quite confusing—the military wanted to impose a single union federation (with Communist Party support); the Socialist Party and PPD were clearly leaving the ground open for a split in the union (as with the Force Ouvrière in France in 1948).

In reality two things were at stake: the clash between the supporters of NATO and the Warsaw Pact over who was to control bits of the state apparatus in a strategically important country, and the desire of the 'West' (via the Socialist Party) to divide and weaken the workers' movement.

Shortly prior to 11 March the Socialist Party opposition to the Communist Party hardened (one of the things that prompted the attempted coup of 11 March). But the Socialist Party did not support the extreme right on either 28 September or 11 March. Why not? Because, firstly, on the African question the Socialist Party represented that section of the bourgeoisie (and petty bourgeoisie) that had decided it could no longer afford the African wars. Secondly, if the coups of 28 September or 11 March had succeeded, the right would probably have decided they could govern without politicians like Soares.

Since 11 March the Socialist Party has sought to win back, for pro-western bourgeois elements, those sections of the state machine in the hands of the Communist Party and areas of society under control of the workers. Hence the party's repeated threats to withdraw from the provisional government and its eventual departure.

But the Socialist Party still fears to completely lose its working-class support. So its speakers can still make very left-wing speeches in the South (eg before its last big demonstration in Lisbon it played records over a loudspeaker system from its party headquarters—the Internationale, the Bandera Roja, the Workers United Front song of Brecht, etc)—even while well-heeled middle-class youths were driving expensive cars to put out propaganda for the demonstration. It also fears that it will unleash right-wing forces that will dispense with its services. Its slogans are 'For a government of national salvation' but also 'No to Spinola, No to Communist Dictatorship'.

At present the Socialist Party, as a petty bourgeois party par excellence, represents everything that is immature and confused in the masses' consciousness. Everybody who had not inherited from the period of fascism a clear political consciousness, ie belonged neither to the fascist right nor to the Communist Party nor the 'ultra-left' groups, now found himself ready to support the Socialist Party. This meant supporting the 25 April revolution without any further commitment: its banner is the simple one of 'pure democracy'—commitment to the revolution in general.

What characterises the petty bourgeoisie, however, is their fear and mistrust of the masses, and their cringing before the rich and mighty. A long time ago Engels explained the role of petty bourgeois democracy in a letter to Bebel (11 December 1884) on 'pure democracy':

> ...pure democracy...when the moment of revolution comes, acquires a temporary importance...as the final sheet-anchor of the whole bourgeois and even feudal economy... Thus between March and September 1848 the whole feudal-bureaucratic mass strengthened the liberals in order to hold down the revolutionary masses... In any case our sole adversary on the day of the crisis and on the day after the crisis will be the whole of the reaction which will group around pure democracy, and this, I think, should not be lost sight of.

And Marx elaborated: '...from the first moment of the victory, and after it, the distrust of the workers must not be directed any more against the conquered reactionary party, but against the previous ally, the petty bourgeois democrats, who desire to exploit the common victory only for themselves'.[34]

The floodtide of revolution brought hundreds and thousands without experience into political life, and the first leaders they support are those who were not capitalist, but also not very strongly or clearly defined. They assemble behind the banner of the Socialist Party.

The petty-bourgeoisie are a massive transmission belt of influence between the capitalists and the mass of the people, including sections of the proletariat. The big capitalists are an insignificant minority of society. But the ruling class does not live in isolation. Through a network of institutions it enmeshes sections of the lower middle classes. And these shade into sections of the proletariat, especially the less organised and backward ones. While the upper layers of the petty bourgeoisie are directly linked to the big bourgeoisie, its lower layers merge into the proletariat and the lumpen proletariat.

The Socialist Party is the party with whose aid capitalism preserves the hopes of the petty bourgeoisie and the backward workers in a progressive improvement of their situation. The deepening crisis of Portuguese capitalism will inevitably undermine the power of this party, and it will deliver its supporters either to the revolutionary proletariat or to the extreme right—to the fascist forces. So long as the masses hesitate between revolution and reaction, they continue to support the Socialist Party. But this situation of hesitation cannot last long.

The deepening crisis pushed masses of aroused petty bourgeoisie to support the Socialist Party with its demagogy against the present impasse and the Gonçalves government that is identified with rising prices, high taxation, etc. But this is only a transitory stage for the petty bourgeoisie. All historical experience shows that fascism finds its mass support mainly in the enraged petty bourgeoisie. Ruined by capitalism, losing the belief in peaceful reformist social democracy, masses of petty bourgeoisie can quite quickly veer to fascism. This is bound to happen to the Portuguese Socialist Party in the present general crisis of society unless its mass following is attracted by the revolutionary left, which in practice will show its ability to smash all blocks on the road to a better future for the masses, including the lower petty bourgeoisie.

The Communist Party is now frightened it is going to be kicked out of the government and lose control over the unions. So it has been attempting to resist Socialist Party and PPD pressures. But at the same time it is still refusing to mobilise the rank and file of the workers' movement for an all-out struggle.

The speeches the Communist Party leaders made at the 1975 May Day rallies simply urged workers to 'work harder', and 'wait patiently' in the hope that one day unemployment would disappear. Instead of developing a massive rank and file movement, the Communist Party has placed its main hope in a continuing alliance with a section of officers in the armed forces. That is why the trade union law it supported provides for unity at the top of the unions but opposes attempts to form united rank and file organisation between workers in different factories in any town. That is why the row over the union law has not led it to campaign against the labour law.

The zigzagging policy of the Communist Party, the appointment of leaders from the top, whether in the trade unions or the municipalities—the lies and deception of the masses—played into the hands of the Socialist Party leaders. Instead of encouraging the formation of rank and file workers' and soldiers' committees, the Communist Party has been trying to maintain its hold over the trade unions by bureaucratic manipulation and by deals with the leaders of the Armed Forces Movement. This could only drive more workers to fall for the Socialist Party's talk of 'democracy'.

The Maoists

Until 25 April the Maoist groups were almost entirely confined to the universities (and via them to sections of conscript officers).

Their leaders had been in the Communist Party (in one or two cases part of its leadership) until the early 1960s. They broke at the time of the Sino-Soviet dispute and then later when the Communist Party was under internal pressure because of its failure to turn the mass agitation of the early 60s into armed insurrection (despite its verbal pledges to armed action). All the Maoist groups accept the Chinese designation of Russia as 'social imperialist' and see the Communist Party as an agent of 'social imperialism'.

They all accept, to some degree or other, a Stalinist stages theory, by which the first task in Portugal is 'national democratic' revolution. (Hence the name of the Popular Democratic Union (LTDP) and the stress on the slogan 'National independence'.)

All the Maoist groups accept a variant on the Stalinist notion of the party, claiming that their aim is to 'reconstruct' or 'reconstitute' the Communist Party as it existed before Cunhal. (Eg a communiqué put out by UDP and FEC organisations speaks of 'a different period that began 11 years ago when the first Marxist-Leninists decided to abandon the Communist Party, after it had been completely taken over by the renegade Cunhal... Since then the Marxist-Leninists have fought for the reconstruction of the destroyed Communist Party'.)

Such a conception of the Party allows them, in practice, to justify all the manoeuvring, the duplicity and the bureaucratic tricks that characterised Stalinism in its heyday. (They all carry portraits of Stalin, sell his books, etc.)

But their Stalinism inevitably means *splits* between them because it cannot fit the needs of the revolutionary Portuguese situation, and because of disputes over who is Stalin/Mao in Portugal today.

These points apply to all the organisations. But they draw different conclusions from their basic assumptions.

[Editor's note: Cliff described both the Maoist and centrist organisations in more detail elsewhere in the original article. These boxes of information have been reproduced on pp255-258 in this version of the text.]

PRP-BR (Proletarian Revolutionary Party-Revolutionary Brigades)

The Revolutionary Brigades were formed in 1969 by a group of activists who split from the Communist Party, accusing it of being reformist. For a number of years they carried out armed actions against the fascists and the colonial apparatus, including the blowing up of a NATO base, blowing up trucks destined for the colonial wars, trying to blow up power lines on May Day 1973 (the theory being that this would allow workers to leave factories to hold meetings and demonstrations) and releasing pigs dressed in naval uniforms during the choosing of a naval officer as president in 1972.

The Revolutionary Brigades always made it clear that for them 'the practice of armed actions was never separate from the need to create a revolutionary organisation of the proletariat which would link the armed struggle with the mass struggles'.

The key theme underlying the BR analysis was that the fight against imperialism could not be separated from the struggle for socialism. Thus the BR completely opposed the Menshevik-Stalinist-Maoist theory of stages—first should come the democratic revolution, and then, only after a passage of time, the socialist revolution, a theory at the service of class collaboration.

In September 1973 the BR joined with a number of revolutionary communists and other groups to constitute the PRP-BR. The manifesto issued by the conference made it clear that the task of the Portuguese Revolution was the establishment of the dictatorship of the proletariat:

> The crisis of Portuguese capitalism, in the context of the general crisis of the imperialist world system, is especially aggravated by the colonial war: this creates a situation of instability at the level of power. This situation throws open to the revolutionary forces, to the proletariat, the perspective in the short term of the conquest of power and the triumph of the Socialist Revolution.

The manifesto sharply attacked the reformist concept of the peaceful road to socialism accepted by social democrats and Stalinists:

> Faced with this crisis situation the revisionists and social democrats have attempted to make reformist alternatives seem credible. Even in countries with a bourgeois democracy, eg with Popular Fronts, this alternative has failed time and time again in different ways. The recent tragic events in Chile, which led to the butchery of left-wing militants and the working-class movement of the country, by the united forces of reaction and imperialism, are yet another example of what the pacifist legal road can lead to—this is the real adventurism.

The manifesto made it clear that the armed revolution is absolutely necessary in order to overthrow the power of the capitalist class:

> Only the socialist revolution with the taking of power by the proletariat can be the solution. But this is only possible by its own organisation for revolutionary violence. Only the revolutionary violence of workers can counter the economic, social and political violence of the bourgeoisie. Only through violence can power be wrested from the bourgeoisie.

Finally the manifesto makes it clear that the Portuguese Revolution is part and parcel of the international revolution of the proletariat and the colonial peoples:

> The struggle for the socialist revolution in Portugal is not an isolated struggle; it is an integral part of the internationalist struggle of the proletariat against imperialism. Its internationalist character is further reinforced at this moment by the historic coincidence between the interests of the Portuguese proletariat and the interests of the peoples of the colonies, which is expressed in a common front against colonialism and imperialism.[35]

In all its propaganda the PRP-BR put the stress on the need for autonomous organisations of the working class, and the necessity for the party to be made up mainly of proletarians and not of a few intellectuals adopting the mantle of leadership.

Because of the emphasis on the autonomous organisations of the working class the PRP was able to give a certain necessary direction to the revolutionary left as a whole. It was influential in pushing for the formation of the Interempresas Committee which held very successful demonstrations on 28 September 1974 and 7 February 1975. Party militants were very involved in solidarity campaigns in other factories, with TAP workers, etc. The PRP played a central role in propagandising the ideas of CRTSMs—Revolutionary Councils of Workers, Soldiers and Sailors.

The PRP's stress on the autonomy of the class was a definite advantage to it in the period after 11 March 1975. During the general elections to the Constituent Assembly, there is no doubt that many militants got fed up with the different and numerous political organisations competing for working-class votes. Militants felt that their unity in struggle prior to 11 March was being disrupted for votes. *Apartidarism* (non-partyism) corresponded to the feelings of much of the advanced section of the class. When the PRP raised the question of workers' and soldiers' councils it got a response from the advanced section of the class, and also from revolutionaries within the armed forces. Hence the successful CRTSM demonstration of mid-June 1975 involving some 40,000 people.

But the PRP did not have the implantation in the working class to establish real councils (soviets) as opposed to making propaganda for them.

The CRTs popularised the notion of workers' power among a section of the class, but could not directly contend for power. [For more on this problem see pp277-280, 'Revolution deflected from soviets'.]

The PRP is an authentic revolutionary Marxist organisation which argues for the need for armed revolution, stands squarely for the dictatorship of the proletariat, and believes in the need for autonomous organisations of the proletariat—councils (soviets).

The PRP is very clear in grasping the nature of the Communist Party. It refuses to speak of 'social fascism', hence its superiority over the Maoists. At the same time it recognises that although the Communist Party has a base in the class (unlike the Socialist Party) it is a reformist party that cannot be pressurised into revolutionary actions (hence its superiority over the centrists like those of the MES and FSP).

It understands the need for a united front in defence of workers' organisations.

The healthy emphasis on self-activity by the proletariat, however, is accompanied by a certain lack of clarity about the relations between the revolutionary party and the proletariat.[36]

'Centrist' organisations

In any revolutionary situation all sorts of centrist political tendencies grow up that vacillate between the reformists and the revolutionary left. Usually such vacillation is an ingrained political characteristic for the leaders of these tendencies. But the rank and file is often made up of serious, committed, militant workers who are breaking politically with reformism but are not yet convinced of the full revolutionary organisation. The leaders try to maintain their control of the rank and file by verbal revolutionism while in practice giving ground to the reformists.

In Portugal there are a number of such groups.

MES (Left Socialist Movement)

Originated from fusion of three groups: (a) Radical Catholics, intellectuals involved in the anti-war movement. The leadership and cadre of the organisation are predominately from this background. (b) Rank and file workers won in the opposition to the Communist Party strategy of infiltration of the official unions. Working-class base mainly in textile industry. President and vice-president of textile union MES members. Played part in 1973 TAP strike, and as a result held for a while the presidency and vice-presidency of the Metalworkers Union. (c) Group of Marxist intellectuals, who have now left and form the 'Ex-MES' group, some of whose members have been the 'extreme left' in some of the provisional governments. At rank-and-file level MES militants line up with the revolutionary left. But at the national level, they have tended to act as a pressure group on the Communist Party, not as a revolutionary organisation out to replace it. The Communist Party has often welcomed the MES's presence as enabling itself to have a slight 'left' coloration.

FSP

Created around Manual Serra, a radical Catholic worker leader from way back (in and out of jail, etc). He had a group around him, the MSP (Popular Socialist Movement), which soon after 25 April joined the Socialist Party. After the Socialist Party Congress in December 1974, in which they put up an alternative slate which was lost, Serra accused Soares of rigging the election and of moving to the right. He then left with the bulk of the original MSP and formed the FSP. The FSP has always refused to go into government, but has been very close to the Communist Party, and has been used by the Communist Party to voice attacks on the Socialist Party which the Communist Party would not want to make officially itself. Little organisation and little base.

LUAR

Secretary General the charismatic Herminio Paima Inacio—a Dick Turpin figure in Portugal. A bank robber, he made three dramatic escapes from prison. LUAR was started in the late 1960s with the Figueira de Foz bank robbery. They organised the world's first hijack, hijacking a plane over Morocco, and using it to distribute leaflets all over Lisbon. Base amongst workers, and in the Alentejo and Algarve. Led in the formation of neighbourhood committees and in the occupations of houses.

LUAR often works as part of the revolutionary left. But it talks in Populist terms, without posing the need for revolutionary party. Can play an important part in revolutionary action at the local level, but could never take initiative in raising the question of class power nationally.

Maoist organisations

PCP-ML, front name AOC, leader Vilar

The organisation enjoys Chinese support. It argues that the main danger in Portugal today is social fascism.

It points out that Dimitrov said you should unite with the bourgeois liberals and social democrats against fascists. It therefore supports Socialist Party and 'liberal' bourgeoisies against Communist Party, goes on Socialist Party demonstrations and has helped make attacks on 'social fascists' in the North. It took over the Chemical Workers Union of the South after 25 April in the same bureaucratic manner that the Communist Party took over most other ex-fascist unions.

It did not have a good record of struggle in the interests of workers, and was even said to give arguments about the need for 'restraint' in the 'national interest'—similar to those of the Communist Party. Eventually it lost control to the Communist Party, and tried to cling to power in the union through Communist-Party-type thuggery.

It supported the pre-11-March mixed-economy economics plan of Melo Antunes, as a 'defence of national independence'.

MRPP

The biggest 'revolutionary' organisation in the University, it seems to recruit sons of upper class CDS supporters. Its membership is characterised by a religious fervour. It was quite heroic under fascism, but even then spent much of its time denouncing the rest of the revolutionary left. Typically, today it runs slogans like 'Long live the glorious MRPP—Arnaldo Matos (Secretary of MRPP), glorious leader of the proletariat', etc.

It gained some influence in a few firms when the Communist Party was involved in strike-breaking—eg it has some influence in TAP and the TLP (telephone workers).

But its influence is restricted in Lisbon to at most five workers' committees.

It is extremely unpopular with COPCON rank and file because of its references to them as the 'new PIDE'.

Its position *used* to be distinct from that of the PCP ML/AOC, in that it did not openly back the Socialist Party. But the Socialist Party saw an advantage in claiming to defend the MRPP against the Communist Party. And recently the MRPP has provided a convenient weapon for the Socialist Party to use to break the hold of the Communist Party on certain unions in Lisbon (journalists, bank workers, clerks).

The MRPP sees the events in the North as a ' peasant uprising against social fascism'. When the Communist Party defended its headquarters in Leiria, the MRPP spoke of it 'shooting down peasants'.

There seems to be some sort of convergence here between the sons of the bourgeoisie and their parents.

FEC-ML (Communist Electoral Federation)

Refers to 'social fascism'. But does not draw conclusion about need to defend social democracy against social fascism.

Its headquarters in the North have been attacked by the right. It is stronger in the Oporto region than in Lisbon (while the UDP is strong in Lisbon, weak in Oporto).

Its central plank has been need to reconstruct Communist Party, eg in an interview in magazine *Flama* three months back, it said that it was utopian to raise question of revolution until Party had been reconstructed. It claimed that all talk of workers' councils, of workers' control or dual power was a utopian attempt to build islands of socialism within capitalism. In practice, this must mean abstention from raising question of class power. Instead allows policy of trying to take over unions by diplomacy, manoeuvre, etc.

UDP (Popular Democratic Union)

A front for two-three Maoist groups

By far the largest of the Maoist groups within the working class.

But its politics (its Stalinist politics) put great impediments in front of its following anything like a correct revolutionary policy.

It is still half-stuck on a stages theory which calls for a bourgeois democratic revolution in Portugal, so it cannot raise the question of workers' power as the central question.

The UDP tries to distinguish itself by stressing 'national independence from the imperialisms' (stress on the plural) as if Russian imperialism were the same sort of immediate threat as US imperialism in Portugal.

One of its main criticisms of the United Revolutionary Front was for not demanding, 'No to the superpowers, unity with the Third World', and, 'No to the imperialisms, national independence'.

On the revolutionary demonstration of 20 August 1975, the UDP people seemed to be stressing only such 'national democratic' slogans, and they objected very strongly to a banner which said 'Out with the scum, power to those who work'.

They cannot talk in terms of a united front with the Communist Party even of a limited, defensive character, while they refer to it, even if only occasionally, as 'social fascist'.

The situation has demanded going beyond 'national democratic' slogans. Insofar as the PRP has been able to agitate in this sense it has been able to force the UDP to follow its strategic lead.

But, because the UDP is quite big, there must be many workers who cannot decide whether to join the UDP or the PRP and so join neither. The UDP can certainly restrict the success of PRP initiatives like the CRTSM.

Two failed right-wing coups

The rise in the mass action of the working class, its temper and breadth, were very much affected by a lashing from the right. A long time ago Marx said that the revolution from time to time needs the whip of counter-revolution.

Two attempted coups by the Right—on 28 September 1974 and 11 March 1975—gave a fantastic fillip to the revolution.

28 September 1974 coup

It is one of the characteristics of a revolutionary situation that the balance of class forces changes very swiftly, and in no preconceived fashion. Hence uncertainty is in the air. And the only way to find out the real strength of the contending forces is by testing them in action. Hence again and again the bourgeoisie is tempted to a trial of force.

In the months after the fall of fascism, despite the support of the Communist and Socialist Party leaders, and the willingness of the MFA to use limited repression, the Portuguese bourgeoisie failed in its attempts to hold back the workers' movement. After a lull in late July and early August, a new wave of strikes and occupations developed, with strikes in textiles, among agricultural workers, in the shipyards, at TAP, and on the daily paper *Jornal do Comercio*. In the Lisbon area at least these strikes were much more political than previously. The Lisnave workers demonstrated for the purging of fascists from their management. Their slogans included 'opposition to the labour law, support for the struggles at TAP, *Jornal do Comercio*, Siderurgia and Texmales, and support for the Armed Forces so long as they support the struggle of the oppressed and exploited classes against the oppressing and exploiting classes.'

Such a development itself was enough to worry the bourgeoisie. But there were other factors at work as well, which turned this worry into complete panic among sections of big business and certain generals.

One was the complete failure of the 'centre' to develop as a political force capable of resisting the growing strength of the workers' organisations. The Communist Party could not prevent the development of independent working-class activity to the left of it. But it did predominate in large parts of the country compared with the political parties to the right of it. Big business began to feel that the only possible counterweight lay with those political forces it had itself dismissed only five months before—the former members of Caetano's political apparatus.

Finally there was the unresolved problem of Africa.

The handing over of power to FRELIMO made the ruling class fear that the government would allow a potentially very rich Angola to slip out of Portugal's grasp.

Those industrialists like the Champalimaud family, who had welcomed the coup in April, now began to denounce the provisional government in the bitterest terms. It was not a far cry from denunciation to organised opposition.

Spinola gave expression to this change of mood within the ruling class. He had invited Communists into his government in May in order to control the popular movement. Now he venomously criticised the representatives of the left parties in the privacy of the council of state and denounced unnamed 'political forces' in public. He hinted that he opposed the handing over of Mozambique to FRELIMO and called for the 'silent majority' who opposed 'anarchy' to take action.

The organisation leading to the abortive putsch was primitive. Leading industrialists, such as representatives of Champalimaud, the Banco Spirito Santo and Mabor met together with a few of the generals, including at least three who were in the Junta, and leading former supporters of Caetano. Spinola made a speech calling on the 'silent majority' to demonstrate, and the industrialists and right-wing politicians tried to mobilise behind it on the streets. Groups of fascists were supplied with arms.

The aim was to give the impression of mass popular opposition to the left. This was to culminate in a pro-Spinola march which was intended to be 300,000-strong. The arms were not meant to enable the fascists themselves to take power, but to create such disorder as to give the generals an excuse to intervene, attacking the left and re-establishing 'order'.

Yet despite the crudeness of the scheme the right nearly won.

The demonstration was called for Saturday 28 September. All that morning the leaders of the MFA begged Spinola to call it off. He ignored them and kept them in a state of virtual arrest in the presidential palace. From there they could not move their units of troops against the right. For several crucial hours COPCON was paralysed. Meanwhile troops commanded by Spinola supporters were operating. The two ministries directly under the control of pro-Spinola officers, the Defence Ministry and the Ministry of Communications, prevented the appearance of all newspapers and put an armed guard on the radio stations.

However, the one thing missing from the calculations of the generals was the reaction of the mass of workers. No doubt they were lulled into a sense of false security by the willingness of the main workers' parties to sacrifice themselves. But this time the future of the left parties themselves was at stake, and they knew from Spinola's previous outbursts at the Council of State what he had in mind.

The evening before the rally was due to take place, a number of unions came out calling for opposition to it. The Communist-controlled Intersindical called upon the people to be 'vigilant'. The railway union went further, and instructed its members to refuse to man special trains carrying rightists to Lisbon and to search other trains for them. It called upon the coach drivers' union to do the same, with the result that only two coachloads of demonstrators ever left for Lisbon.

The Left began to set up roadblocks throughout the country. At the same time representatives of a number of groups of the revolutionary left met. They decided to assist in the organisation of roadblocks and barricades, and to call for a demonstration in the centre of Lisbon to clash with the rightist demonstration. Representatives of workers from the most militant plants in Lisbon—TAP, Lisnave, CTT (postal workers), Standard Electric, *Jornal do Comercio*—had decided on the same approach, and the two demonstrations were merged. What began as a demonstration 10,000-strong soon grew until it was at least 40,000-strong.

By the way—and this is an important pointer—the first workers to demonstrate on the streets were those whose struggle had been criticised by the Communist Party and attacked by the army in recent weeks: the Usnave shipyard workers, the TAP maintenance staff, the *Jornal do Comercio* workers and the same postal workers who were alleged by the Communist Party a few weeks ago to be led by 'reactionaries'.

Such a movement of workers did not fail to penetrate the barrack walls. Those officers backing the rightist line began to find themselves isolated. Soldiers began to join civilians on the barricades, despite broadcasts from Spinola's supporters ordering removal of the roadblocks.

The mass mobilisation on the streets shifted the balance within the army command from Spinola to the MFA. Spinola made one last desperate bid for the Council of State to grant him dictatorial power, and then called off the rally. The MFA forces moved into action at long last, taking control of the radio stations from the right and searching the city for anyone who might have been associated with the coup plans.[37]

On 30 September General Spinola, together with two Ministers and three members of the Council of State and the military Junta, resigned. Two hundred people involved in the plot were arrested.

Neo-colonial solution

One of the central issues that led General Spinola to hatch the coup was that of Portuguese colonial policy. He was afraid the Portuguese Revolution would undermine completely his neo-colonial 'solution' to the African wars.

Spinola's book *Portugal and the Future* was clear in projecting a Lusitanian federation in which the colonies would enjoy self-government under Portuguese auspices. On taking power, Spinola was careful to distinguish between 'self-determination' (which he supported for the colonies) and 'independence' (which he didn't, since there had been 'insufficient preparation' for the peoples of the overseas territories 'to be able at present to decide for themselves about their future').[38]

At the beginning of May 1974 General Costa Gomes was sent to Angola and Mozambique. While in Luanda, he put an ultimatum to the liberation movements. They were to enter negotiations for a ceasefire immediately, or else the colonial war would be relentlessly pursued. He declared:

> The armed struggle will continue against the partisan fighters as long as they refuse a political solution. We intend to carry on fighting... I am convinced that Angola will decide to remain Portuguese. She must strengthen her relations with South Africa and Rhodesia.[39]

Above all Spinola and his friends were very anxious to hold on to Angola.

This was Portugal's richest colony. It is the biggest producer of oil in Africa after Nigeria. Being rich in natural resources Angola attracted the attention of the multinationals, which concentrated in key areas of the economy. Besides Gulf Oil at Cabinda, Portuguese, Belgian and South African capital is involved in the diamond industry, Portuguese and Belgian capital in iron mining, and Portuguese, Belgian, South African, French and American capital in the petroleum industry. South Africa is also heavily involved in the Cunene River dam project in Southern Angola, as well as in numerous other joint projects with the Portuguese.

Angola far surpassed the other two Portuguese colonies, Mozambique and Guinea-Bissau. Guinea-Bissau was of little economic importance to Portugal, and Mozambique had become increasingly economically integrated with South Africa, providing harbour facilities at Lourenço Marques (now Cam Phumo) and a huge amount of cheap labour for the gold mines of the Rand. Angola's natural resources and her industrial development make her, by contrast, potentially one of the richest countries in Africa.

There is another difference between Angola on the one hand, and Mozambique and Guinea-Bissau on the other. In Mozambique and Guinea-Bissau there was one dominant liberation movement. In Mozambique FRELIMO, in Guinea-Bissau PAIGC. In Angola there were three rival movements, none dominant, none weak enough to be ignored—MPLA, FNLA and UNITA.

The MPLA from its foundation in December 1956 orientated itself on the black working class of Luanda and other centres, developing roots among the urban masses that were to survive until now.

The FNLA is a tribalist movement led by Holden Roberto, the brother-in-law of President Mobutu of Zaire. Traditionally the Mobutu regime has been one of the US's best friends in Africa. American corporations are heavily involved in Zaire, and there are 5,000 US government personnel, both civil and military, in the country. Involvement by the US governmerit in Zaire dates back to 1960, when the country became independent of Belgium. The CIA intervened in strength to stabilise the situation for foreign capital, organising the overthrow and assassination of the radical nationalist premier, Patrice Lumumba.[40] It was rumoured that an agreement of several years standing existed between Zaire, FNLA and Gulf Oil under which Roberto's troops would steer clear of Cabinda. It is certainly true that the only attacks on Cabinda came from the MPLA based to the north east in Congo-Brazzaville, rather than from the FNLA from Zaire in the south.[41]

The third force, UNITA, is a split from the FNLA, and is also largely tribalist—supported by the Ovimbundu of the south. When the 25 April coup took place, UNITA was clearly the weakest of the three.

The anti-imperialist struggle was weakened by the deep divisions in the national movement in Angola and the existence of a very large white settler community 400,000-strong.

However, the policies of Spinola and company aiming at a neo-colonial 'solution' were constantly undermined by the continuing struggles and victories of the national liberation movements—the victories above all in Guinea-Bissau and Mozambique. On 24 June the railway line from Beira to Tete, an important supply line for the Cabora Bassa dam, was simultaneously disrupted at 28 points. In the southern provinces (Monica and Sofola) a number of military outposts and arsenals were attacked. On 15 July the strategically important town of Morrumbula was finally captured by FRELIMO units.

But Spinola was fighting hard to preserve his neo-colonial policies. On 13 July 1974, at a time when the failure of the federalist approach had already become apparent in the fruitless talks with FRELIMO, MPLA and PAIGC, Spinola defended his 'decolonisation strategy' at a press conference in Lisbon. It had basically four immediate goals:

(1) Agreement to a ceasefire with the liberation movements.

(2) Development of industry and administration in the colonies.

(3) Creation of democratic institutions.

(4) A referendum in the colonies where those entitled to vote would choose between three solutions:

(a) a close federation of mother country and colonies

(b) a loose federation of all the territories

(c) complete independence

He allowed no doubt that he considered solution (c) 'unrealistic and premature' and that his African strategy was closely linked with the idea of the referendum, which would allow the longest possible presence of the Portuguese colonial administration and troops. The hopes of the Portuguese bourgeoisie that the people in Africa would understand this clearly proved to be illusory.[42]

But Spinola was more and more isolated from the MFA on colonial policy. On 10 July the Portuguese Constitution was changed through a law recognising the right of the colonies to independence. On 4 August the Provisional Government declared that it officially recognised the Republic of Guinea-Bissau and supported its entry into UNO as an independent state.

Spinola still hoped to reverse the trend. In his speech of 10 September appealing to the 'silent majority' of Portuguese, Spinola warned of 'abandoning the African population (of the colonies) to the domination of new dictatorships'.[43]

However, the neo-colonial policies of Spinola collapsed. They were smashed by a combination of a mass working-class movement in Portugal and a deep and widespread colonial revolution in Africa.

The March coup

The capitalists would not accept the defeat of the coup of 28 September as final. Having been defeated on this occasion, the reactionary forces were more determined than ever to regroup themselves for a violent attack on the working class.

Throughout January and February 1975 it was becoming clear that the government was losing control of the situation. Neither the Communist Party nor the MFA appeared able to curb the level of struggle. And the wave of action had spilled over from the factories, involving massive sections of the population. School students throughout the country were on strike. Buildings were being taken over by people living in the sprawling slum areas around the big towns. Workers were taking over the land. Added to this, the most powerful right-wing organisations, the CDS and PPD were having their meetings broken up. In the forefront of this mass movement was the fight against redundancies, and against the closure of workplaces, closely linked to the demand for *saneamento*. This struggle was generalising into a major working-class offensive. Every new confrontation could become a direct political challenge to the ruling class, whose 'April dream' was rapidly taking on the proportions of a nightmare.

On 11 March 1975, barely a month before the scheduled election, a new plan to restore the right wing to power was put into action. It was organised by a group of right-wing officers around Spinola, who was living in the countryside outside Lisbon since the failed coup of 28 September lost him the Presidency of Portugal. Centred on the Tancos Air Force base, 100 miles north east of Lisbon, it should have involved a simultaneous uprising of military units in and around Lisbon.

The plan was a disaster, miscalculated and mistimed and virtually unsupported—two Fiat T-6 fighters and two helicopters bombarded the RAL 1 (1st Light Artillery) barracks by Lisbon, backed up by a ground force of paratroopers. Two hours later the second attempt since 25 April last year had fizzled out. While the bewildered paratroopers fraternised with the RAL 1 soldiers, explaining, 'We are no fascists—we are your comrades,' Spinola was fleeing to Spain and the rest of the conspirators were being rounded up.

The coup was not unexpected. It had been rumoured for at least a week beforehand. Otelo Carvalho, Commander of COPCON and military commander of Lisbon, had already stopped all fuel supplies to the military region around Tancos. But just as on 18 September, it was workers and people in Lisbon and throughout the country who took decisive and immediate action against the right wing, in advance of the military. Barely two hours after the attack on RAL 1, barricades had been set up around Lisbon sealing off all main roads, manned by workers from adjacent factories. Many were armed and they used everything they could lay hands on as reinforcements. Bulldozers, lorries and cement were expropriated from factory yards. Agricultural workers armed themselves with spades and hoes. The banks were occupied, closed down and encircled by pickets—so were factories and schools. Offices and shops were similarly closed down. Workers in the press and radio issued continuous news bulletins. Newspapers printed special editions and used lorries to distribute them to those manning the barricades.

Trade unions and workers' committees throughout the country issued leaflets. From the Union of Office Workers in the Oporto District:

> Comrades, in defence of democracy—stop all work immediately, and set up pickets around workplaces, seize control of all communication between sites (telephones, telexes, etc)...those workers not needed to guard buildings should go to the streets to demonstrate.[44]

In Barreiro, a centre of industry south of Lisbon, factory and fire engine sirens shrieked continuously, and workers formed pickets and barricades which stopped and searched all vehicles.

In Sacavem, near the bombarded barracks, workers formed a dense barricade across the main road, backed up with four bulldozers and tons of cement.

A representative from the workers' committee at a local construction firm went to the barracks and asked that the workers be armed, so they could join in the fight.

At Cartaxo the barricade was built from lorries from the occupied brewery works of SCC, and was quickly joined by hundreds of workers from other factories, armed with clubs, spades or anything else that was at hand. Revolutionary organisations joined in the struggle. They put up barricades in Algueirao-Martins, after attacking a post of the National Guards (a force that identifies with the extreme right) and forcing them to join the barricades.

In Baixa de Banheira they seized the weapons of the National Guards and, in Moita, those of the police. They took control of the bridge and the ferries which connect Lisbon to the industrial areas to its south, and searched cars suspected of bringing weapons into the city.

In the Lisnave shipyards the workers stopped work, joined the barricades and sent pickets to protect the children in the local school.

The frontier roads to Spain were blocked off, and all over the country groups of people were guarding the roads. In Coirribra, the third biggest city, cars were driven onto the airport runway after a plane had been seen flying low over the city.

Huge demonstrations were jamming the streets of Lisbon, Oporto and the other towns. All papers were sold out. Many printed second editions or special broadsheets, as did the workers' committee of the big Lisbon daily *O Seculo*. Thousands of leaflets were handed out by the trade unions and workers' committees denouncing the attempted coup.[45]

The role of the revolutionary left was far greater than during the September events. Revolutionaries joined the barricades alongside the workers and Communist Party militants. They seized control of the 25 April (previously Salazar) bridge, which spans the river Tagus, and the ferries that ply across the Tagus between Lisbon and Cacilhas. Although the Communist Party and the Intersindical were also involved, their role and influence appeared considerably less than in September.

Two weeks before the coup the results of elections to the air force, army and navy councils of the Assembly of the MFA showed a decisive swing to the right among the officer corps at grass roots level. Key members of the Coordinating Committee such as the commander of COPCON, Otelo Carvalho, lost their positions. These men are no 'extremists'. Carvalho himself was courting the centre within the officers' corps. The results of these elections probably led the ruling class and the right-wing generals grouped around Spinola to judge that the time was ripe to strike. They must have believed that a current of reaction within the lower hierarchy of the military was strong enough to carry the right wing back to power. The right-wing tendency within the officers was not consolidated. These men did not have the confidence to change the leadership of the MFA on the one hand, or the confidence in their own control over the rank and file of the army on the other. For some of them, to order their soldiers against the workers would have been tantamount to suicide, and instead of leading the army against the working class, the coup resulted in radicalising the rank and file.

In many units soldiers simply refused to carry out the orders of officers known to be right wing, and in those units whose officers were loyal to the leadership of the MFA, the orders were superseded by the rank and file. Soldiers openly fraternised with workers manning the barricades. Some handed over the arms demanded by the workers. And for the first time ever, mass meetings of officers and soldiers were held. In the bullet-ridden barracks of RAL 1 the following resolution was passed unanimously by such a meeting:

The second communiqué of the soldiers and officers of RAL 1:
To all the soldiers and sailors, workers and peasants, to all anti-fascists and democratic officers.

Comrades, while the PIDE agents continue to be treated with gentleness, while the fascist parties continue to exist legally while the people are fired on in Setubal, while the soldiers and all the officers in struggle against fascist oppression in the barracks are imprisoned, the people will continue to be oppressed with more ferocious exploitation and oppression.

> Comrades, the soldiers and all the offers of RAL 1, who up until now have struggled against fascism and its accomplices, will continue and intensify this struggle against the exploiters and the oppressors.
>
> We demand the immediate execution of fascists and their accomplices, whether or not they are officers, whether or not they are generals.
>
> **Death to Fascism, Popular Justice**
> **Imperialists out of Portugal**
> **Immediate Execution of the Fascists**
> **The Soldiers are the Sons of the People.**[46]

The right-wing coup collapsed, as the paratroops embraced the light artillery men they were supposed to be attacking.

Right-wing generals who sought refuge in the headquarters of the GNR (National Guards) were arrested. Among other conspirators picked up were the directors of one of the biggest banks and of the biggest monopolies, CUF and Champalimaud.

By 5pm the MFA was in control of all radio stations and calling on the people to leave the barricades so the military could take them over, but to remain vigilant and united.

But that was by no means the end of the popular movement.

That evening left-wing demonstrators ransacked the headquarters of the GNR, Spinola's house and the headquarters of the extreme right-wing CDS and Popular Democrat parties.

Workers' pickets remained on the post offices, the telephone exchanges, the government buildings, cutting off the means of communication to the right wing. The roads in the centre and south of the country continued to be blocked by barricades, with workers belonging to the Communist Party and the revolutionary left wearing red armbands and armed with shotguns, waving down and searching all vehicles.[47]

Workers learn the lesson

Immediately after the coup hundreds of thousands of Portuguese workers held mass meetings to demand further action to press home the revolution. Here are some examples of the resolutions they passed.

The Draughtsmen's Union said that reaction was able to act 'to a great extent because of the lack of revolutionary action from the Provisional Government'.

A mass meeting of workers at the Portuguese airline, TAP: 'We support the Armed Forces Movement so long as they are on the side of the workers.'

The leadership of the Electrical Workers' Union of the south: 'There is one lesson to be learnt: it was the hesitation of the organs of power that gave the fascists an opportunity to reorganise.'

From the postal workers' union:

> The move by the reactionaries was only possible because the process of purging was not completed, so that many PIDES (members of the former secret police), legionaries and other reactionaries remained not only in our industry but also in

many others. And all this with the benevolence of various government bodies, despite the many workers' strikes and demonstrations aimed at expelling from the workplaces individuals linked with fascism.

The most significant resolutions came from within the army. For the first time mass meetings of rank and file soldiers were held. The regiment under attack, RAL 1, issued a communiqué from 'all soldiers, seargeants and officers':

> Why the attack on RAL 1? Because the soldiers of RAL 1 know that our enemies are the capitalists and fascists that have oppressed us and that we have a role to play whether the generals like it or not: to defend the workers and to fight all reactionaries.
>
> For those who started to cause bloodshed between us it only remains to demand their immediate shooting. Comrades, an armed people will never be defeated. Death to fascism. Death to capitalism.[48]

The defeat of the coups of 28 September and 11 March show the power of the working class. But this should in no way lead to the conclusion that the counter-revolution is finished. It is worth recalling that in Chile the right wing tried to overturn the Allende government three times before it finally achieved success. In Portugal the splits in the armed forces and the freshness of the memory of fascism in the consciousness of the population will make its task more difficult. But it can succeed in Portugal too, eventually, unless the working class develops its own, independent forms of class-wide organisation, led by a coherent revolutionary leadership.

The Armed Forces Movemement

Revolution and the army

The Armed Forces Movement (MFA) is a unique phenomenon. No revolution other than the Portuguese has seen anything like it.

Let us start with the historical experience of armies in periods of revolution.

One result of all past revolutions was the disintegration of the existing army.

'Surely, the fact is evident', wrote Engels to Marx on 26 September 1851, 'that a disorganised army and a complete breakdown of discipline has been the condition as well as the result of every victorious revolution.'

Look at the experience of Russia in 1917. Already in the months preceding the February 1917 Revolution, discipline in the Tsarist army was falling to pieces. The February Revolution accelerated the process. After all, the revolution took place not only without the officers, but against them. Many of the officers, a couple of days after the revolution, rushed to pin on red ribbons, But could the soldiers trust them?

V B Stankevich, an officer who joined the revolution 'five minutes after it started', and became a prominent leader in the army between the February and October revolutions, recorded quite clearly what the actual feelings between officers and soldiers were in the early days after the February Revolution:

> It was the fact that the soldiers, breaking discipline, left the barracks not merely without their officers but even despite their officers, and in many cases against their officers, even killing some of them who tried to fulfil their duty. And now by universal, popular, official acclaim obligatory for the officers themselves, the soldiers were supposed to have realised by this a great deed of emancipation. If this was indeed a heroic exploit, and if the officers themselves now proclaimed it, then why had they not themselves led the soldiers out onto the streets—for you see that would have been easier and less dangerous for them than for the soldiers. Now after the victory is won, they adhere to the heroic feat. But is that sincere and for how long? You see, during the first moments they were upset, they hid themselves, they changed into civilian clothes... Even though next day all the officers returned. Even though some of the officers came running back and joined in five minutes after the going out of the soldiers, all the time it was the soldiers who led the officers in this, and not the officers the soldiers. And those five minutes opened an impassable abyss cutting off the troops from all the profoundest and most fundamental presuppositions of the old army.[49]
>
> Officially they [the officers—TC] celebrated, eulogised the revolution, cried 'Hurray!' to the fighters for freedom, adorned themselves with red ribbons, and marched under red banners... Everyone said, We, our revolution, our victory, and our freedom. But in their hearts, in their tête-à-têtes, they were horrified, trembled, felt themselves prisoners of a hostile elemental force that was travelling an unknown road.[50]

The open antagonism between the soldiers and the officers meant that even the right-wing labour leaders—the Mensheviks and Socialist Revolutionaries—had to accept the need for soldiers' committees to control the officers. The revolutionary mood among the troops was such that the compromisers thought it impossible to simply preserve the old disciplinary set-up. The result was a compromise, Order number 1, issued by the Petrograd Soviet on 1 March:

> 'In all companies, battalions, regiments, parks, batteries, squadrons, in the special services of the various military administrations, and on the vessels of the navy, committees from the elected representatives of the lower ranks of the above-mentioned military units shall be chosen immediately.
>
> 'In all its political actions, the military branch is subordinated to the Soviet of Workers' and Soldiers' Deputies and to its own committees.
>
> 'The orders of the Military Commission of the [government] shall be executed only in such cases as do not conflict with the orders and resolutions of the Soviet of Workers' and Soldiers' Deputies.
>
> 'All kinds of arms, such as rifles, machine-guns, armoured automobiles and others, must be kept at the disposal and under the control of the company and battalion committees, and in no case should they be turned over to officers, even at their demand.
>
> 'In the ranks and during their performance of the duties of the service, soldiers must observe the strictest military discipline, but outside the service and the ranks, in their political, general civic and private life, soldiers cannot in any way be deprived of those rights that all citizens enjoy. In particular, standing at attention

> and compulsory saluting, when not on duty, is abolished.
>
> 'Also, the addressing of officers with the titles "Your Excellency," "Your Honour", etc, is abolished, and these titles are replaced by the address of "Mister General", "Mister Colonel", etc. Rudeness towards soldiers of any rank, and, especially, addressing them as "thou" [ty] is prohibited, and soldiers are required to bring to the attention of the company committees every infraction of this rule, as well as all misunderstandings occurring between officers and privates.
>
> 'The present Order is to be read to all companies, battalions, regiments, ships' crews, batteries, and other combatant and noncombatant commands.'
>
> Within a matter of days officers were faced with committees which presented demands, requested explanations, countermanded orders, and instituted controls over arms and ammunition. Not infrequently officers were requested to recognise the committee structure by issuing special orders. All attempts by officers to explain that the Order was unofficial, and in any case applied only to Petrograd, were in vain.[51]

A clear dual power situation appeared in the army: in every unit of it. On the one side the officers, with hardly any *real* power, on the other side—the soldiers' committees.

With the army so clearly divided vertically between officers and men, no wonder the latter found it natural to combine together and send delegates to the Soviets (or Councils) which were formed as Soviets or Workers' and Soldiers' Deputies.

The Bolsheviks, who detested equivocation, came out clearly for the abolition of dual power in the army, by getting rid of the appointed officers.

Thus Lenin posed the question, 'Should officers be elected by the soldiers?' And he answered, 'Not only must they be elected, but every step of every officer and general must be supervised by persons especially elected for the purpose by the soldiers… Is it desirable for the soldiers, on their own decision, to displace their superiors?' And he answers, 'It is desirable and essential in every way. The soldiers will obey and respect only elected authority'.[52]

The MFA

In the Portuguese army up to now there has been no clear vertical division between officers and men. Nor has there been a horizontal one, between a clearly defined body of revolutionary officers and men on the one side, and a reactionary body of officers and men on the other.

In the coup of 25 April 1974 two very different military bodies collaborated. On the other hand the Junta, on the other the MFA.

The senior officers who ran the Junta had, by and large, risen to their present positions by currying favour with the Salazar and Caetano regimes. Spinola himself had identified sufficiently with Salazar's fascist goals to fight for Franco in the Spanish civil war and for Hitler on the Russian front.

But the Junta had not made the coup d'état. It had only benefited from its outcome. The main force in carrying through the coup had been the middle rank officers of the Armed Forces Movement, some 400 in number. Their attitudes and goals were by no means identical with those of the generals.

Among the junior officers a large number were conscripts. In the Portuguese armed forces anyone who is conscripted after being a student is enrolled as an officer (unless he has committed some political or criminal offence).

Since 1962 Portuguese university students had been involved in effective and organised anti-regime activity. Since 1968 Portuguese universities have been in continuous turmoil. Practically no student could have avoided participating at one time or another in these activities. Thus these conscript officers, ex university students, brought into the army a degree of political experience which was shared by only very few of the career officers. Most of the ex-students resented being dragged off to fight in a futile war in Africa and many continued to retain some of the left-wing ideas picked up in their student days.

More significant, however, was the development to dislike tour after tour of duty in remote parts of the colonies, fighting an unwinnable war, on behalf of privileged groups of white settlers who had much higher living standards than themselves. Their resentment led to organisation against the regime when it became clear that the war was threatening their own career prospects. The turning point for many was a proposal in 1973 to change the training programme for officers which they saw as threatening the established career structure through 'dilution'.

The middle-rank officers on the Coordinating Committee of the Armed Forces Movement found that their goal of breaking the hold of the old political elite and ending the African wars could not be guaranteed merely by relying on the generals of the Junta. They maintained their own organisation, the Coordinating Committee of the MFA, to act as a watchdog on the Junta.

The overall result was that Portugal emerged from the coup with at least three centres of power: the Junta, the Provisional Government and the Coordinating Committee of the MFA.

Spinola tried to reconcile these different forces by the establishment of a new organ, the Council of State, made up of equal numbers of representatives of the Junta, the MFA and civilians appointed by Spinola. This was given the power of vetting all governmental decrees and new laws.

But the new arrangement never worked perfectly. From the first days after the coup of 25 April the mass pressure of workers affected the MFA. Portuguese workers immediately demanded and got, with the support of sections of the MFA, the immediate abolition of the hated secret police, the PIDE/DGS. The attempts by the generals to restrict the scope of the purge of the old regime led to clashes with the MFA. In one incident, for instance, the generals arrested an officer who refused to stop examining secret files on the connection between the PIDE and the CIA. Representatives of the MFA went to the barracks and released him.

With the repressive apparatus of the PIDE/DGS broken, the working class continued their offensive through strikes, occupations and demonstrations. They demanded an immediate improvement of their desperately low standard of living and the widening of their democratic rights. This led to increasing resistance from the capitalists, gathered round General Spinola. The sharpening class struggle was reflected immediately in the armed forces and within the MFA itself, some sectors being drawn towards the bosses and some towards the workers. The Coordinating Committee of the MFA was only able to maintain a semblance of unity by alternately supporting and repressing the working class.

In July 1974 the leaders of the MFA joined the government, and the chairman of the movement, General Vasco Gonçalves, became the Prime Minister. Other key posts taken by the MFA were Labour (replacing the Communist Party Minister of Labour in the first Provisional Government), Defence, and Economics—seven in all out of a total cabinet of 16. By entering the government, the MFA hoped to be able to control the situation more effectively and avert increasing class conflict. But they failed to achieve this. For the same reasons on 8 July the MFA created COPCON—Continental Operation Command. COPCON is a separate military establishment whose task was to 'intervene directly in support of the civilian authorities and at their command', under General Otelo Saraiva de Carvalho, the mastermind of 25 April.

Over many months the military have been balancing between left and right, trying to avoid coming down decisively on one side or the other.

Troops were used last summer to break the strike of the postal workers, to attack strikes at TAP, the Portuguese airways, and *Journal do Comercio*, and to attack demonstrations of shipyard workers from the huge Lisnave yards.

COPCON supported the strike law passed in September, which virtually eliminated the legal basis of the right to strike, and was a determined attempt to break the strength of the growing independent rank-and-file working-class movement.

The coup of 28 September was a turning point in the role of the MFA and COPCON. Since then—until August this year, by and large—the MFA in general, and COPCON in particular, sided with the left against the right.

Take the case of the Corane strike. The 300 workers of this factory, which makes metal equipment for heavy industry, decided to occupy the plant. They had voted unanimously at a mass meeting to do this because they had evidence of consistent sabotage by their boss, ex-air-force commander Dos Santos Nogueira.

Simoa, a member of the workers' committee, explained how they organised the takeover:

> After the decision in the mass meeting, we telephoned the workers' committee in the bank and explained why we wanted them to freeze the accounts of the firm. They agreed to do this.
>
> We then telephoned COPCON, and told them we had taken over the factory and that we were going to occupy the parent company SAPREL. COPCON said: 'OK, it's your problem—this is revolutionary legality.'
>
> The laws here mean nothing, because in a revolution the only laws are those made by the revolutionary process.[53]

Then again, both at the 28 September coup and the 11 March coup, as we have seen, the MFA sided with the workers.

Everything to paper over the cracks...

Since 25 April the main political parties have tried to outdo each other with declarations of support for the MFA. As a matter of fact, the talk of Communist Party leaders, as well as of Socialist Party leaders, about the need for 'national unity', 'sacrifice and austerity', were echoes of what the MFA leaders said, and vice versa.

One need but compare the words of the Communist Party leader, Alvaro Cunhal, quoted earlier, with the words of Vasco Gonçalves.

On taking office as Prime Minister of the Second Provisional Government on 18 July 1974, Gonçalves said:

> This must be the motto for us all: without arduous work by the Portuguese, without a gigantic effort at all levels (the State, management and working class) in national reconstruction and modernisation we will never end the underdevelopment of the country. At the same time, we must all, during this period, live in an atmosphere of real austerity, wasting less on unessential goods and saving as much as possible in a universal effort of investment. This, I repeat, must be the concern of everyone.[54]

A few weeks later, on 30 September, Gonçalves made it clear that in the national unity *all* classes had to be included: 'It should be understood that, as we understand it, an anti-monopolist strategy does not mean an attack on private property'.[55]

And again: 'The people, and by that I mean the population of the whole country, workers, peasants, intellectuals, students, small businessmen, small and middle-sized industralists—all, all of us must be on the alert against demagogues and reactionaries'.[56]

Under the slogan of 'Unity of the People and the Movement of the Armed Forces', he went on to say, 'You must be patient, because being impatient today means being a fascist',[57] a position which is indistinguishable from that which the Communist Party has taken up since 25 April.

Split in the Supreme Revolutionary Council

At the beginning of August Major Melo Antunes, former Foreign Minister and a leading supporter of the Socialist Party, together with another eight members of the Supreme Revolutionary Council of the MFA (out of 28) issued a document called 'It is a Time of Great Decisions, a Time to End Ambiguity'.

This has become a war statement of the right wing of the MFA

Antunes' document argued that nationalisation had gone too far—at an impossible speed'.

> From day to day an open rift is appearing between a very small minority social group (part of the proletarian zone of Lisbon and the south), who support a certain revolutionary project, and practically the whole of the rest of the country, who are reacting violently to the changes that a certain revolutionary vanguard is trying

> to impose without thought for the complex reality of the Portuguese people's historical social and cultural life.
>
> We see a progressive decomposition of state structures. Everywhere wildcat and anarchistic forms of the exercise of power have taken over little by little, reaching as far as the Armed Forces.

The Antunes document called for a 'social bloc encompassing the urban and rural proletariat, petty bourgeoisie and broad strata of the medium bourgeoisie'.

And as regards foreign policy, the document called for the 'maintenance of links with Europe, reinforcing and deepening relations with certain economic bodies (EEC, EFTA)'.[58]

Antunes' document became the rallying call for a massive campaign against the left wing of the MFA leadership identified by Antunes as being front runners of the Communist Party.

In reply to the nine who signed the Antunes document, a group of officers in COPCON published a counter-document arguing that the crisis in Portuguese society was a result of the country not going far enough in the direction of overthrowing capitalism and fighting imperialism:

> The degeneration of the economic situation and its effects on the political and social life of the broad masses of the people is due above all to a failure to define an objective political line and a consequent governmental programme. It is futile to believe there is a combination of economic measures that can solve this degeneration within the existing capitalist structure while at the same time maintaining total dependence on imperialism and all its consequences, such as the closing of factories, the flight of foreign exchange, unemployment, scandalous political pressure on our sovereignty.
>
> The solution for the present situation, for which the MFA is heavily responsible, cannot be found in right-wing palliatives as the aforementioned document proposes. The maintenance of the coalition government will certainly not lead to the construction of socialism.
>
> The proposal put forward led to the Right advancing, opening the way to the destruction of the revolution.
>
> The proposed economic perspective of links with the EEC and EFTA will reinforce the country's subjection to degrading economic and political dependence.
>
> How can a project calling itself left wing miss out the role of the masses and reject the action of its vanguard? How can it criticise the rate of nationalisation? If the bourgeoisie keeps possession of the means of production what will be left for the people?

The signatories of Antunes' document did not know or hide the fact that is 'the central point of the current political situation—the growing activity of fascism.'

The COPCON document suggests a number of reforms: financial and technical aid to the peasantry, public works to help the unemployed, cutting down and limiting house rents, socialisation of the health service, nationalisation of the drug industry.

Unfortunately the COPCON document is far from adequate to deal with the crisis. For instance, there is no reference in it to the need to expropriate foreign capital that dominates the key positions in the economy. Above all, the COPCON document is defective in its kernel—the organisational suggestions regarding the armed forces themselves. It states:

> (a) Organised form for ranks:
>
> The military people must be organised in accordance with existing different ranks, freely debating problems in their rank and democratically electing their representative to the ADU[59] who will transmit the decisions taken. Decisions taken by the AGU[60] with bearing on the collective life of the unit must be debated in the ADU to form a general consensus—this is the indispensable basis for cohesion and discipline.
>
> (b) Social privileges:
>
> Immediate measures must be taken to cause a visible rise in the private's standard of living, in particular by the modernisation of facilities, substantial pay rises, general distribution of the family subsidy and family bonus, etc.
>
> (c) Reinforcement of discipline:
>
> Expanding the internal dynamisation of the units, debating and collectively analysing without restriction, consolidating cohesion through a voluntary discipline leading to a clarification of ideas—only this will make the military man dedicated to his patriotic mission of unyielding defence of the interests of the Portuguese people.[61]

No dealing with over-representation of the officers in the army assemblies, no election of officers by the rank and file, no equality of pay between officers and men, no abolition of the separate messes.

Middle-class revolutionaries

The leaders of the MFA are middle class through and through. One of the characteristic features of the petty bourgeoisie is its lack of clear political-social physiognomy, as it is suspended between the capitalist class and the proletariat.

Practically all the officers of the MFA come from sections of the middle class. Their fathers are small businessmen, better-off peasants, teachers, and so on.

The officers can therefore be quite hostile to the big monopolies, while supporting the capitalism of the myriad of small firms in Portugal.

They did not benefit from the African wars and so opposed Caetano and then Spinola when it looked as if he might prolong the wars. But they also have cause to fear the effects of the growing workers' movement on the property-owning middle classes. After all, the worst wages are usually paid by small firms, not big ones. And they cling to the ideas of military discipline and rank that provide them with their own privileges. That is why the first economic plan of the MFA leaders (February 1975) did not propose any nationalisation at all—although it called for economic reforms which proposed limited state intervention into key industries.

In general the army officers have a hierarchical concept of society. Only in very few cases are officers of the Portuguese army elected. One soldier told an IS member visiting Portugal in August this year:

> There are no elections in my barracks. I can only give cases of very left-wing officers who were sure of support from their men, and therefore probably submitted themselves for election before accepting a post they had already been appointed to.

The soldiers' commissions have a preponderance of officers, as members of the commissions are elected according to rank: officers elect officers, sergeants sergeants, other ranks other ranks.

In the 240-strong Assembly of the Armed Forces Movement there are very few soldiers, as opposed to officers. And of the 28 members of the Supreme Revolutionary Council of the MFA not one is a private.

In their material conditions the officers are far apart from their men. Thus a soldier told a couple of IS members that a private earned 500 escudos a month, a sergeant 6,000 to 7,000, a captain 10,000. As regards accommodation, he said:

> The sleeping quarters of ranks are separate. We sleep 24 to a dormitory (200 in training), while officers sleep three to four to a room (I'm not sure because I've never been there).

To identify officers with soldiers is to harbour illusions.

A worker from TAP put it in a nutshell:

> It seems to me important to stress our mistake in looking at the MFA as a whole, when it is certain that within it a class struggle is also developing. The MFA does not exist in isolation from a national context, from the society in which we live. In the MFA there genuinely exists a progressive faction of petty-bourgeois revolutionaries, but it is not capable of heading the revolution. This is because the only true revolutionary class is the working class, and it alone can therefore take command of operations. Besides, the MFA reflects the contradictions of the petty bourgeoisie as a class, inasmuch as it is unable to really break the hold of dependence on imperialism. In these conditions the question that is already being posed, the question of workers' control, has decisive importance in the direction of the revolution.[62]

The question is not whether one should have complete trust in the officers or not. In politics, blind credulity is stupid; never to trust is no better. One must simply learn to compare words with deeds. By putting clear demands on the officers, while keeping the independence of the rank and file, one can attract the honest, revolutionary officers and expose the others.

In this respect, the programme of demands put by the second CRTSM Conference of 2-3 August 1975 is a big step forward from what exists, but not enough:

> **Armed Forces:**
> (1) Election of Unit delegates in a general assembly of the unit, representation being by rank (privates, sergeants and officers) in proportion to their respective numbers.

(2) Frequent convocation of general assemblies of the unit to discuss all political and military problems.
(3) Convocation of assemblies of privates without sergeants and officers present.
(4) Convocation of assemblies of members of the Armed Forces and workers for discussion of common problems.
(5) Management of human, physical and technical resources in the service of the collective.
(6) Abolition of privileges and subsidies that benefit sergeants and officers (separate messes, expense subsidies (ajudas de custo), various subsidies, canteens, etc).
(7) Free transport to privates.
(8) Establishment of a minimum salary for privates of 1,250 escudos a month.
(9) Contraction of the hierarchical spread.[63]

But this programme does not go far enough, as can be seen clearly if one compares it with the programme put forward by Lenin in 1917.

To point to a few items:

Lenin demanded equal pay for soldiers and officers. The CRTSM programme demands pay of 1,250 escudos for soldiers. At present captains get 10,000! And generals?...

Then again, the CRTSM programme does not say a word about the election of officers.

Army committees should be elected without difference of rank, argues Lenin; not so the CRTSM programme.

The role of the army committee is not clearly defined by the CRTSM. 'Order Number 1', issued by the Petrograd Soviet on 1 March 1917, made it clear, as we have seen, that the Army Committee should have the supreme political power in every army unit, and that all weapons should be in its control.

It is quite important that army committees should have the right and the duty to meet rank and file delegates from the factories, to plan joint training and joint guard patrols; that all army committees should have the right and duty to link up with rank and file soldiers outside their own unit.

Finally, the CRTSM document failed to raise the basic demand of the right of all members of the armed forces to belong to political parties. This is an extremely important demand. At present, as an inheritance from the Salazar era, members of the armed forces are banned from belonging to political parties. This situation is very dangerous for the revolution: it prevents revolutionaries from organising openly, while at the same time it allows the reactionary officers to hide their political views until a time when they will find it convenient to declare themselves. The revolution needs the truth, needs to throw light over all corners of life.

During a revolution half-measures, lacking precision or failing into equivocation are very dangerous. The weapons of the revolutionary army—above all its political ones—must be ship-shape.

Peruvian solution

Very few of the MFA officers would like a Chilean solution to the Portuguese crisis. Many may be attracted to a Peruvian solution.

In Peru the military government took certain measures benefiting the local middle class while breaking strikes and shooting trade unionists. The regime is highly nationalist, and to some extent has popular support.

But a Peruvian solution is not on in Portugal. The working class is far too strong, too assertive, to be put in its place except through very extreme measures.

That some officers in Portugal—however, not in the MFA—would not abhor the Chilean way is quite obvious. One must remember that the President of Portugal is none other than Costa Gomes, who was Secretary of State for the Army under Salazar, commander of the National Republican Guard (one of the pillars of the Salazar and Caetano regimes) and Commander-in-Chief of Caetano's forces in Mozambique. The strength of the MFA lies largely in the key positions its members occupy. The *saneamento* in the armed forces was very shallow indeed. Only in the navy, traditionally the most radical of the forces, did any significant *saneamento* take place. On 29 April 1974 a meeting of 700 naval officers voted for the programme of the MFA, and sacked over 80 admirals and vice-admirals. The purge was supported by mass meetings held throughout the fleet, and since then councils including career and conscript officers have been formed on a number of ships.

After the coup the MFA had a list of at least 400 senior officers of known fascist sympathies, but under pressure from the right wing it decided not to sack them.[64]

The majority of the 10,000 career officers can lie low for a time, but the 'silent majority' waits for an opportunity to raise its ugly head.

Then again there are two paramilitary police forces which remain strongly right wing: the PSP (riot police) and the GNR (the National Guard).

Revolution deflected from soviets

The activities of members of the army and especially of COPCON, when they come to the aid of workers, tenants, schoolchildren, etc, are very similar to many activities of workers' councils in previous revolutions.

First of all the central role of the councils in a revolution is the generalisation of the struggle of the workers.

Workers' councils have in fact developed in almost all cases in this century where a revolutionary situation in which the working class has played a big part has developed.

In Russia in 1905-06 the soviets (the word means council) sprang up for the first time. In 1917, after the overthrow of the Tsar in February, they reappeared on a vastly greater scale and soon there were also soldiers' soviets, peasant soviets and, most important of all, workers' and soldiers' soviets. As everybody knows, the October Revolution was made under the slogan 'All power to the Soviets.'

These soviets were made up of elected delegates from workplaces, regiments, and so on, and also representatives of those political parties that were based on the working class and the peasants. They represented the active force of the working class and, to a lesser degree, the peasantry. Because they were created from below by workers and by peasant soldiers, and not from above by bureaucratic decree, no two soviets were exactly alike in their composition and structure. They were living, changing organisations evolving to meet particular needs and under the influence of different political ideas.

They were not, however, a response to peculiarly Russian conditions. Germany in 1918 was, in some ways, almost the opposite of Russia. It was a heavily industrialised country as opposed to largely agricultural Russia. It had had, for a long time, a powerful labour movement operating under legal conditions, conditions quite different from those of workers under the Tsar. Yet the German equivalent of the Russian soviets—Arbeiter and Soldatenräte—came quickly into being as the Kaiser's regime cracked. 'During the first days of the November [1918] revolution workers' and soldiers' councils were elected in all workshops, mines, docks and barracks', explains a history of the time.[65]

In Spain in July 1936 workers' and peasants' committees were created as the military and fascist forces under Franco tried to overthrow the Popular Front government and smash the workers' and peasants' movements:

> In all the towns and most of the villages in Spain, similar committees were operating under various names... They had been appointed in an infinite number of ways. In the villages, the factories, and on the worksites, time had sometimes been taken to elect them, at least summarily, at a general meeting. At all events, care had been taken to see that all parties and unions were represented on them...because the committees represented, at one and the same time, the workers as a whole and the sum total of their organisation.[66]

In the quite different conditions of the Hungarian Revolution of 1956, workers' councils again played a central part.

> By the third day of the revolution, 26 October, people everywhere were establishing institutions to give expression to their new power. They formed 'Revolutionary Councils' in the towns, the villages and the quarters of the cities, in newspaper offices and government ministries, in colleges, on collective farms and, above all, in the factories.[67]

These examples, which are not of course exhaustive, show that workers' councils (and workers' and soldiers' councils, workers' and peasants' councils, etc) have been created in widely different conditions which have, however, one thing in common—a revolutionary situation. Clearly they meet some need in a revolutionary situation which is not met by other forms of working-class organisation.

It is not difficult to see that one aspect of this is the need that is felt to create representative, class-wide organisations that can, in some measure, unite the workers as a whole and the sum total of their organisations. Workers' councils can indeed overcome the isolation between workers in different workplaces, different industries, different trades and occupations.

As the workers' councils have to generalise the struggle, and as in a revolutionary situation there is no abyss between economic struggles and political ones, the workers' council of necessity impinges on every aspect of the workers' struggles, be it small or big.

To give only a couple of examples from the working of the Soviet of Petersburg during the 1905 Revolution:

A few years after the events, its former chairman, Trotsky, wrote, 'The Soviet was the axis of all events, every thread ran towards it, every call to action emanated from it'.[68]

The Soviet acted first of all as the general strike committee of Petersburg both in October and December. It organised the arming of the workers. It organised food supplies for the city. It organised mass demonstrations. It led the campaign for amnesty for political prisoners. It organised a campaign in defence of freedom of the press. It led the struggle for the eight-hour day. It 'intervened in disputes between individual workers and their employers'.[69]

Even the smallest issues affecting working people were taken up by the Soviet:

> The Soviet's premises were always crowded with petitioners and plaintiffs of all kinds-mostly workers, domestic servants—shop assistants, peasants, soldiers, and sailors... An old cossack from Poltava province complained of unjust treatment by the Princes Repnin who had exploited him as a clerk for 28 years and then dismissed him without cause; the old man was asking the Soviet to negotiate with the Princes on his behalf. The envelope containing the curious petition was addressed simply to The Workers' Government, Petersburg, yet it was promptly delivered by the revolutionary postal system.[70]

Obviously the mass of the working class can only be won to the idea of a council in a very practical way: the council has to be seen as an essential means of solving all the immediate problems of the class as well as the great political issues of the day.

The MFA, obviously, is not as consistent, effective, directly rooted in the masses, as a workers' or soldiers' council. But acting as a surrogate, as a substitute, the MFA prevented the workers (and soldiers) from making the effort to build a real council for quite a long time.

In the last 18 months the working class has thrown up very strong local organisations, the workers' commissions, in each factory. Up until now these commissions have been able to win most of the simple economic battles that workers have faced, particularly because the bosses have in many cases fled the country, and the state, for other reasons, has not been able to intervene on the bosses' side. In one sense, the Portuguese workers thought they did not yet need soviets.

The fact that the state, and in particular the army, has not been powerful enough to intervene against workers has further added to the confusion. The state is so weak that the workers have, in practice, been able to force major concessions from the state, eg *Republica*.

The fact that the MFA has been forced into concessions has fostered the belief in the minds of many workers that it is somehow on their side, and that they can rely on the army to solve their problems for them rather than seeing the need to rely on themselves.

So although Portuguese workers see themselves as a class, with interests of their own to defend, they do not all see these interests as sufficiently different from those of other classes to demand the creation of their own class organs.

An example of that is the coup of 11 March. When the news reached the factories, workers rushed to the barracks and demanded arms to defend themselves. However, the attempt petered out, and it was possible to believe that the left-wing officers in the army had been responsible for the defeat of the coup. Had the fighting lasted a few hours longer, then conditions would have forced the workers in Lisbon to begin to organise themselves on a class basis.

Because issues have not yet been posed starkly in class terms, many of the most active militants in the working class, in particular the members of the PS and PC, have seen political problems in the light of the interests of their parties, both of which have managed to combine the interests of different classes. Thus inside the unions and factories militants have argued over the respective merits of their parties rather than over the needs of the working class.

The revolutionaries in Portugal, who see the need to build embryonic organisations of the proletariat, are not yet strong enough where it counts—in the key factories—to take the initiative in building soviets.

In the army too, although the soldiers in some units have a very strong voice, the left moves of the officers have meant that the issue of democratic elections of delegates and officers has seemed unnecessary to the mass of less politicised soldiers.

Not an act of god

The central importance of the MFA for so many weeks and months was not an inevitable phenomenon, supra-historically ordained.

It was the product of defects in consciousness and organisation of the working class. Above all it was the product of the activities of the CP [Communist Party] and SP [Socialist Party] leaders, who prevented the rise of an authentic, independent proletarian movement.

The working class of Portugal, without doubt, has the power to build a mass rank and file movement capable of overthrowing capitalism and shaping the future. The Communist Party leaders, with their heightened prestige through years of struggle against fascism, certainly had the trust necessary to build such a movement if they so wished. But they did not. Instead they manipulated the masses, injuring the self-activity, self-confidence and self-consciousness of the masses. The Communist Party leaders wanted the combination of Bonapartism at the top with centrism on the ground.

The predominant role of the MFA in the political life of the country created an impasse in which politicians of the predominant parties can play with politics without being forced to a real test in meaningful struggle. Manoeuvring and intriguing came to the fore. This disenchanted the mass of the workers, including the vanguard.

Such a situation, of course, can strengthen the bid of leaders of the MFA to try a Bonapartist solution in order to solve the crisis: to raise the army above society and control it with guns. However, no social stabilisation along this road is open in Portugal in the foreseeable future. The government of Portugal today is as unstable as that of Kerensky in Russia in 1917. When Lenin called the Kerensky government a Bonapartist government, he made it quite clear that it was very different from that of Napoleon I (1799) or his nephew, Napoleon III (1849). Kerensky's Bonapartism was much less stable and enduring:

> The Russian Bonapartism of 1917 differs from the beginnings of French Bonapartism in 1799 and 1849 in several respects, such as the fact that not a single important task of the revolution has been accomplished here. The struggle to settle the agrarian and the national questions is only just gathering momentum.[71]

Kerensky's Bonapartism was very unstable as it did not solve any of the fundamental social problems facing the country, and as the power of the proletariat was far from exhausted. The same applies to Portuguese Bonapartism.

The Socialist Party leaders had had an even more disastrous effect upon the MFA. If the Communist Party leaders are reformist, aiming to strengthen the mild left wing of the MFA, the Socialist Party do their best to strengthen the Right of the MFA. This is the meaning of Antunes's document.

The slogan 'Unity of the people and the MFA' can be double edged: it is not only that the army can influence the people, but that it can also be affected by them. Hence a mass right-wing movement must have a deleterious effect on the officers and men in the army. This is the thinking behind the fascist-inspired attacks on Communist Party offices in the North over recent weeks. Hence the dangers in the Socialist Party's nursing of reaction, and the Communist Party manipulation and maneouvring that plays into the hands of reaction. It seems that, as at present in the North, a considerable number of officers and soldiers are influenced by right-wing ideas, and stand aside when violent attacks are made on offices of the Communist Party and other left-wing organisations.

Neither the Communist Party nor the Socialist Party leaders understand the real dangers in their concentration of all their efforts on officers while saying little about soldiers. Both groups of leaders seek illusory strength by identifying themselves with one group or another of army officers. Military reformism accompanies Parliamentary reformism. The leaders of the Communist Party and Socialist Party forget that their Chilean counterparts, for three long years, preached 'the unity of the army and the people'.

The duty of revolutionaries is to subordinate all to the collective will of the rank and file of the workers, soldiers and sailors. This can be best expressed through the autonomous organisations of the working class—the councils.

The process of disintegration of the MFA will aid the revolutionaries if they are clear about the need for proletarian independence and sensitive to the changing situation. The MFA is less and less able to control the officer corps, so that its control over the rank and file of the army is slipping. Military discipline has become more and more difficult to enforce, as troops have been joining demonstrations, refusing to take action against workers, and often, when sent against workers, joined the crowd, giving the clenched fist salute.

The options before the MFA officers are wide open. Some can be integrated into the workers'-soldiers' councils, Others, unfortunately, will move to the right,

As a matter of fact the paper unity of the MFA is no more. The MFA has always been split—even in the immediate period after 11 March. However, a radical change took place recently. Until the last couple of months the MFA was, by and large, divided into the following four groups: (1) Right, (2) Bonapartist, (3) Communist Party and (4) Revolutionary. As the Bonapartist and Communist Party roads proved illusory, the MFA has been polarised between Right and Left, the majority of officers joining the Right.

As class conflict sharpens, the armed forces will be drawn more and more into it. The MFA will increasingly be pushed out on a limb, as it mirrors the divisions in society. The working class will realise more and more that 'Unity of the people with the movement of the armed forces' is not an adequate slogan; that the only alliance that can win and defend the revolution is the revolutionary alliance of workers and soldiers, organised in democratic councils, that the dictatorship of the proletariat is the weapon of real freedom and socialism.

The economy in impasse

The crisis

Portugal is virtually a neo-colonial country of the advanced capitalist states of the West, and was suffering the effects of the world crisis even before the coup of 25 April 1974. The oil crisis aggravated Portugal's difficulties.

The growth of the gross national product in 1974 fell to 2 to 3 percent from 8.1 percent in the previous year. New investment has dropped sharply, productivity is down, credit is very difficult to obtain, and inflation has remained generally high. Unemployment has reached a level of 8 to 10 percent. Income from tourism fell by 30 percent. The income from the 2 million Portuguese workers abroad has been slashed as a result of increasing unemployment because of the world recession, fears of instability at home and financial fiddles by the rich. At the same time the trade deficit almost doubled. As a result a balance of payments surplus in 1973 of $255 million became a $647 million deficit in 1974.

BALANCE OF PAYMENTS AND TRADE (in million US $)			
	1973	**1974**	**1973/74** % change
Gold and foreign exchange reserves	2,715.1	2,102.0	-22.6
Balance of payments	+255.6	-647.7	-
Balance of trade	-857.8	-1684	+96.3
Exports	1,780.8	2,253.6	+26.5
Imports	2,932.4	4,443.6	+51.5

Gold and foreign exchange reserves fell 22.6 percent to a level of $2.1 billion at the end of 1974, and fell another $440 million in the first four months of 1975. Of the reserves, $1.2 billion is in gold still valued at $35 an ounce, so that the country's reserves remain relatively strong.

But this cannot go on for very long. If in the coming few months the foreign exchange reserves dwindle at the same speed as in January-April 1975 then nothing will remain in the reserves at the end of September except the gold, and even this treasure cannot hold for too long.

The crisis gripped a country where in any case living standards were always very low. As one writer put it:

> Through any index used to evaluate the standard of living—consumption of essential food, education, public health, per capita income—Portugal was at the end of the list of the European countries, with Spain and Greece alternating the second last place. So the per capita income was evaluated in 1970 at $2,698 and $2,606 respectively, for West Gerniany and France, $889 for Spain, $891 for Greece and only $610 for Portugal, a bit less than Mexico with $632 and Panama with $629.[72]

The twin afflictions of inflation and unemployment scourged the people. The cost of food for an average Portuguese family increased 25 percent between May 1974 and May 1975. The number of unemployed, around 90,000 at the end of 1973, was 177,000 by the end of 1974, and about 270,000 in the middle of 1975.[73] And this before the mass emigration from Angola—some 4,000 a day—300,000 altogether!

Halfway plan

Everyone in authority in Portugal talks about the need to plan the economy, and in this way to overcome the crisis. But planning cannot work if key sectors of the economy are not under state control, but still in the hands of the multinational monopolies.

After the abortive coup of 11 March there was a great expansion of state ownership. Until then, in the ten months since 25 April 1974, the structure of the economy remained completely unchanged. The only nationalisations which took place were of the banks of issue—which were already governmental arms under the former regime. Even Decree 660/74, which authorised government assistance to, and intervention in, companies 'not contributing normally' to the economy, was originally inspired by the need to save the Torralta and Banco Intercontinental Portuguese groups from bankruptcy.

Calls for strong measures to counteract growing economic difficulties and to transform the country's economic structure were finally answered in February 1975, by promulgation of the transitional (three year) Economic and Social Programme. Besides incorporating measures to combat Portugal's economic problems, the Programme was to define those fields to be left open to the private sector and to establish the 'rules of the game' by which it would operate. However, the Programme was made obsolete within three weeks by the events which followed the abortive coup of 11 March 1975.

The Economic and Social Programme had not called for nationalisation of the banking or insurance sectors. But following the attempted coup all Portuguese-owned banks and insurance companies were nationalised. Because of the central role of these credit institutions as sources of loans and holders of stock in the large economic groups, the government by this stroke alone took control of approximately 30 percent of the country's industry.

This action was followed in April by Decree 203-C/75, giving the government broad powers to control the 'commanding heights' of the economy. At the same time the national airline (TAP), the railways, Portugal's only integrated steel mill, the Portuguese-owned oil refining and distribution companies, and the electric power, petrochemical and shipping sectors were nationalised. This was followed in May by nationalisation of the tobacco, cement, wood pulp and public transit sectors.

On the face of it such far-reaching nationalisation of industry and banking should create a sufficient basis for planning. But this is not so. First of all the predominant role of foreign capital prevents any effective planning.

When Abe Lincoln said, 'You can't have a society half-free, half-slave,' he was certainly right. No more can you have socialist planning, when key positions in the economy are in the hands of the multinationals.

We have already shown on how massive a scale foreign capital invaded Portugal in the 15 years before the fall of fascism, till during the 1969-71 period foreign capital made up 66.9 percent of the total capital invested in new enterprises.

The role of foreign capital was particularly crucial in key branches of industry:

	%
Oil refineries	100
Electric machinery	81
Rubber products	72
Transport equipment	62
Chemical industry	48
Paper and wood pulp	43

	%
Non-ferrous metals treatment	43
Metallurgy and building machinery	38
Mining industry	32
Manufacturing	30

Foreign companies owned 30 percent of all capital invested in companies active in Portugal; in addition foreign capital is invested in companies that are nominally Portuguese.[74]

Since the foreign banks were not taken over by the state, how can any control over the movement of money from Portugal be exercised?

As a matter of fact, the economy falls between two stools. Subordinated to the workings of world capitalism it needs the profits spur. But the working-class struggle is not conducive to this. Under fascism wages were extremely low. At the end of the fascist era the daily wage of a textile worker was only 60 escudos, as against 180 escudos in Italy, 220 escudos in France and 400 escudos in West Germany.[75] In general, wages in Portuguese industry were one third of those in Austria, a sixth of those in Norway, a fifth of those in Britain, and a seventh of those in Sweden.[76] Now the workers are fighting back, and with the social and political upheavals capital flight is not surprisingly intensifying the continuous decline of the economy.

Foreign capital's sabotage

To overcome the reluctance of foreign capital to invest in Portugal, not only did the government not nationalise any foreign enterprise, but it also tried to entice foreign capital. Thus, for instance, in his inaugural address as Prime Minister on 18 July 1974, Vasco Gonçalves defined the attitude of the government in the following words: 'We are interested in foreign investments that have a real stimulating effect on the economy which the government will give guarantees for'.[77] But words did not stop big business's economic sabotage.

Portuguese capitalists began to send their money abroad by all sorts of devious means, despite the strict exchange controls. One of the methods most commonly used was for the banks with foreign branches to retain money abroad deposited by Portuguese emigrants for transfer to their accounts in Portugal. The rich Portuguese would then deposit their money into the emigrants' accounts, and the foreign branch of the bank would then simultaneously transfer an equivalent amount out of the emigrants' account into its own account. In this way no foreign exchange entered Portugal but the emigrant would still receive his money. Considering that the remittances of emigrants to Portugal are enough to turn into a surplus what would otherwise be a heavy deficit in the balance of payments, the extent of this sabotage can be clearly seen.

Multinational companies in Portugal also began to move capital out of Portugal. They did this by moving work, and also by paying excessive prices for imported materials from the parent company, and exporting at artificially low prices to the parent company.

During April and May 1974 approximately 10 billion escudos was sent abroad.[78]

At the same time the World Bank and the IMF have refused credit to Portugal. British banks also withdrew credit facilities from Portugal at the same time as Britain was attempting to get money for the Chilean junta.

Big business resorted to other methods of economic sabotage. Orders from parent companies would be cancelled for no apparent reason, forcing contractions and closures. Lisnave shipyard workers were able to prove that the administration was diverting tankers due for repair to other shipyards abroad.

Again and again multinationals sabotaged economic effort in Portugal by stopping the supply of spares. This was one of the stories repeatedly told to IS comrades who recently visited Portugal. Workers in the bus garage in Alcantara, employing some 2,000 workers, told how supplies from Gardners, CAV and Leyland dried up. Workers in UTIC, part of Leyland, also complained that their plant was starved of parts by the parent company. The workers of the large Carnionagem Esteves haulage company, employing some 500 workers, reported difficulties in getting spares, especially of hydraulic pistons and oil seals.

Threatening catastrophe

On 30 August 1975, the paper *Expresso* published an article entitled 'The Deterioration Of The Portuguese Economic Situation'. It summed up the position with the words, 'The Portuguese economic situation as a whole is tending to degenerate with alarming rapidity.

The balance of payments situation is very grave indeed:

> The financial situation in June 1975 shows a rise in imports of around 30 per cent in comparison to the same month last year, having reached 10,853,000 contos. In the same period exports rose to 4,627,000 contos showing a more modest rise of 17.5 percent. Thus the ratio of exports to imports worsened, exports forming only 42.6 percent.

Months	Ratio of exports to imports %	Change in comparison to the same month last year
January	47.3	- 56.5
February	53.8	- 16.8
March	59.1	- 6.8
April	64.9	+ 20.6
May	55.6	+ 0.04
June	42.6	- 9.7

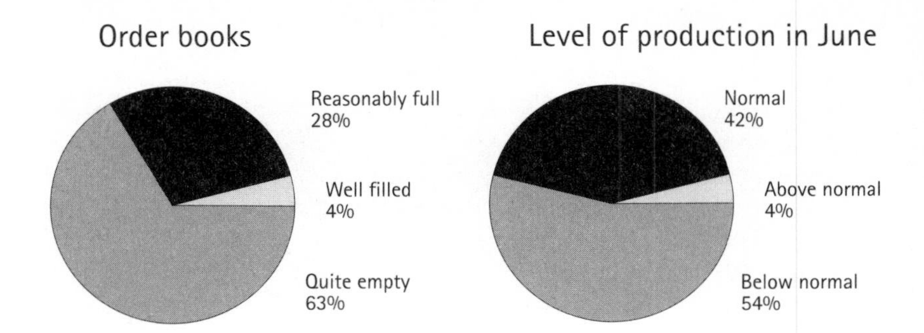

Investment plans in manufacturing industry have declined catastrophically, as can be seen from the following graph:

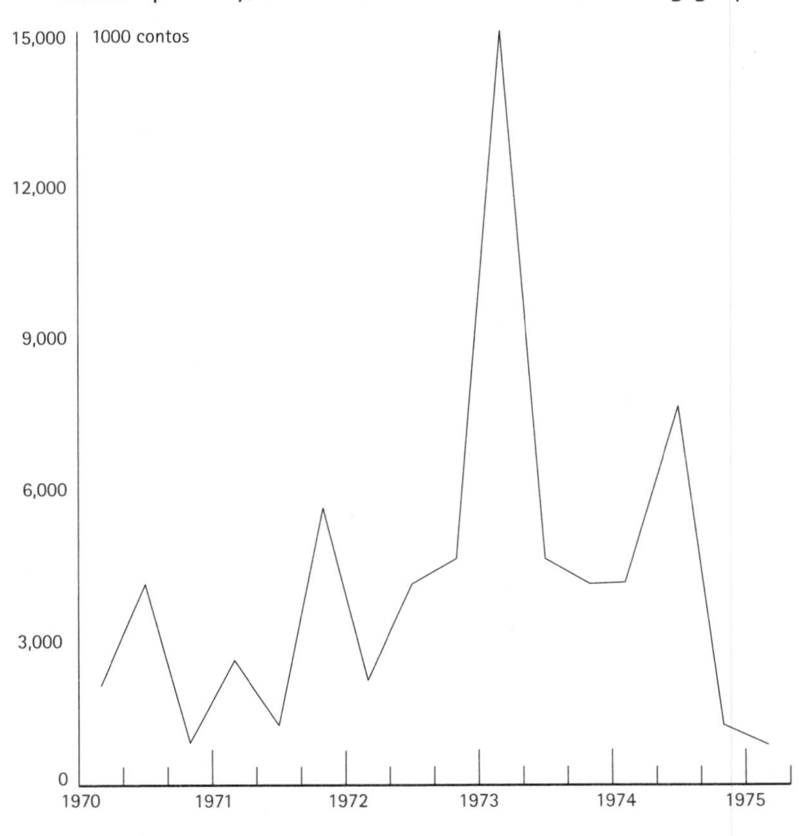

The situation in industry is deteriorating very rapidly: the number of firms with order books that are quite empty has reached 68 percent, while no more than 4 percent have full order books, and 28 percent reasonable ones. Only 42 percent of firms work to normal capacity.

Textiles, printing, chemicals, non-metallic minerals, and electronic equipment and machinery are principally responsible for this situation: in these fields there has been a decline of over 80 percent in investment plans.

The same article goes on to say that unemployment will probably reach, in the coming few months, the fantastic figure of 500,000. For a country of about 3 million earners, this is a rate of 17.5 percent—three and a half times worse than in Britain at present.

The battle of production

In face of the threat of economic collapse, the government, the Communist Party leaders and the Intersindical put forward the slogan of the 'Battle of Production': 'Let us all work harder and better. The more I work, the greater is the wealth to be justly distributed.' The Portuguese leaders, it seems, are no better than King Canute. Imagine raised productivity in the midst of rising unemployment to stop the crisis!

Militant workers quite quickly saw through this. To quote a few of them, one worker from TAP said:

> The call for a 'battle of production' at this time, when the productive class still does not hold power, when the workers are still exploited, will mean, in fact, not a 'battle for production', but a battle for exploitation.
>
> What the working class has to do now is not be dragged into campaigns that do not serve its own emancipation, but do all it can to drive the crisis of capitalism deep and make it succumb to this crisis.

A worker from Lisnave said, 'Now, all this talk of the "battle of production"—should not a better battle be to find work for the 250,000 unemployed in the country today?'

Another worker said:

> In the concrete Portuguese situation, the battle for production—that anyway is already a complete failure—seems to have two fundamental objectives: in the first place, to hold back economic demands; and secondly, to speed up the pace of work. Now, when the work speeds up, the time needed to produce commodities is shorter—and that means the rate of exploitation is higher.

Another worker compared the battle for production with a similar campaign in France after the Second World War. He said that one should compare the current campaign:

> ...to the methods used in the past and with their results. I refer, in particular, to the events in France after the Liberation when the Minister (in the PCF, I believe) who occupied a basically similar position and held the same Ministerial brief as

the one in Portugal, promoted this slogan: 'Produce, produce, produce'. Now, a couple of dozen years after the Second World War, we see the concrete result of this slogan. The UDR, which is the organised right, holds power in France.

In a society that desires change but in which the same structures still persist—in the organisation of labour and the productive forces—to call for a 'battle of production', does it not mean, objectively, an attempt to save what remains of the declining capitalist system?

Clearly the promoters of the battle of production put arguments and give reasons. They say, for example, that the country must produce so as to avoid economic chaos. Now, that is equivalent to hiding fundamental truths, to hiding who really owns the means of production, what is the real area of the class struggle. On the other hand, when they talk of cutting consumption of luxury goods, they do not define who profits from these privileges. We must define what is to be produced—who will actively and decisively intervene in this orientation. Produce more? But what? and produce for what, for whom?

To use one more quote from another worker: 'The objective role of the "battle of production" is to divert the attention of the workers in general from the vital problems that lead naturally to the taking of political power'.[79]

Workers who have been awakened to revolutionary ideas, who have the urge to shape society, to impose their own kind of order, cannot be convinced of the need to save capitalism by extra effort in the midst of massive and rising unemployment.

The crisis in agriculture

One of the most intractable problems facing Portugal is that of agriculture. Here the dead hand of the past threatens to choke any progress.

Portuguese agriculture, exploited very harshly and badly neglected over many generations, is very primitive indeed. A comparison of the productivity of Portuguese agriculture with that of other, even relatively backward, European countries, reveals this clearly. Thus, according to the OECD's 1974 report, the yield in quintals per hectare was:

	Portugal 1972	Italy 1973		Spain 1972
			Irrigated land	Non-irrigated
Wheat	12.0	24.7	14.1	27.5
Maize	13.3	53.9	21.9	48.9
Rice	37.7	41.0	-	59.1
Rye	7.3	20.1	9.2	20.8
Potatoes	101.8	146.5	100.2	151.4

Agriculture has been systematically neglected, and its share in the national product declined catastrophically throughout the years. Thus in 1950 an agricultural population of 48 percent of the total population produced 33 percent of the national product. The corresponding figures for 1971 were 31 percent and 13 percent.[80]

The share of agriculture in the total investment in fixed capital was even smaller: in 1972 it was only 5.5 percent.

One fundamental result of the position of agriculture was the extremely low living standard of the masses in the villages:

> Look at one agricultural area: Tras-os-Montes. This area covers about 10,000 square kilometres with about 400,000 inhabitants; in Lisbon there is a doctor for each 400 inhabitants, while in Tras-os-Montes there is one for every 3,000. In Lisbon...70 percent of the houses have running water. Here the percentage is less than 10 percent. In Lisbon the per capita consumption of electricity is 800 kilowatts—here 60.[81]

The twin of poverty—ignorance—is rampant in the countryside. Thus about 43.4 percent of the population in the countryside are illiterate.[82]

In trying to understand the agrarian problem in Portugal, one must remember the crucial fact that agriculture in Portugal falls into two very distinct zones—the North and the South. The border between them is the River Tagus.

In the South approximately 444,000 people work on the land as a rural proletariat. They sell their labour to the *latifundistas*, the absentee landlords of the vast estates that dominate agriculture in this region, where the main products are wheat, corn and olives. They suffer poverty and filthy living conditions—many are seasonal and migrant workers, forced to follow the harvest from estate to estate. But they have a long tradition of struggle. In 1962, 200,000 agricultural workers staged a national strike to demand an eight-hour day and won.

In the North approximately 300,000 peasants scratch a miserable existence out of small plots of land which they own themselves, or lease from the large estate owners—this is the wine growing region, and is one of the most barren and backward areas of Western Europe.

In the South the agricultural workers, following the 25 April 1974 coup, began to struggle for better conditions and decent wages. Though excluded from the national minimum wage they were not ready to wait with folded arms. Rampant inflation and growing unemployment together with the general militant mood of the country as a whole led them to take action. They put forward demands for better wages, a shorter working week and job security. The government was forced to act. And a national agreement was signed between the unions and the landowners' association which satisfied their basic demands: a daily wage of over 100 escudos on average (it varied according to the type of work), a 44-hour week and permanent employment. At the same time new legislation was introduced on the conditions governing the leasing of land which gave increased security to the tenants.

Although short (it lasted only one day), the struggle of the rural workers in Salvaterra de Magos is a good example of the action they took. On 9 September 1974 about 3,000 workers began a strike. Very early in the morning they organised a sophisticated communications network which ensured that all concerned were duly informed of the decisions taken by the strike organisers, and then formed pickets of 80 to 100 men at all the workplaces. It was a 100 percent stoppage and the bosses gave in.

A factor that greatly contributed to the success of this strike (called in the middle of the harvest) was the involvement of the neighbouring rural community. Even the migrant labourers who were brought from different regions to help with the harvest, and to undermine the bargaining position of the local workers, were won over. Flying pickets were organised to maintain a continuous flow of information among the different groups, and their identities were only known to the workers' committees.

These struggles followed months of useless negotiation in which the landlords perfected the use of delaying tactics. When defeated, they resorted to new weapons: setting fire to ripe harvests, abandoning all kinds of agricultural work, refusing to comply with the terms of the agreement they themselves had signed. They refused to pay the established wages, and began to sack workers they had employed on a permanent basis. They refused to renew the leases and left the land uncultivated and their cattle unfed.[83]

In reply to the landlords' machinations, and especially after the abortive right-wing coup of 11 March, widespread occupations of large estates took place.

Thus an IS comrade visiting the cooperative farm Quebrada, some 40 miles north west of Lisbon, was told the following story:

> On 17 February 1975 all the members of the village (200 people) gathered on top of a hill overlooking the estate. They swarmed down and occupied it. They took over tractors, wine cellars, the house—everything. The landlord fled.
>
> 80 of the 100-odd workers joined the collective. The others mostly worked elsewhere—factories, etc. Some opposed the collective. The collective sought approval and help from the MFA. The MFA lent them a big tractor at no cost. They also have a tractor lent by the government and the two tractors expropriated from the farmer, making four in all. The MFA tractor sported two large guns—against 'rabbits and trespassers', ie the owner who threatened to return. There were also a number of armed peasants around.

The Small Peasants League estimates that the total area of uncultivated land occupied by the peasants in the Southern Province of Alentjo up to mid-April 1975 was about 40 square miles.[84]

The temptation to occupy the *latifundia* was especially great because a large proportion of them were uncultivated. Many of them were turned into game reserves for the use of the idle rich. In 1974 only 33 percent of the land was under cultivation. 25 percent was capable of cultivation but remained unused, and the bulk of the remainder was under forest.

The North

Here there was no improvement at all in the conditions of villagers after 25 April. Quite the contrary.

The property relations were in no way changed, although land reform would have greatly improved the position of the majority of country people.

Look for instance at the size of farms in a few of the Northern Provinces:[85]

DIVISION OF OWNERSHIP

	Bragança	Castelo Branco	Coimbra	Vila Real	Total
Less than 0.5 ha	1,961	9,424	26,804	10,914	49,103
Between 0.5 & 5 ha	15,270	28,127	40,884	25,249	109,530
Between 5 & 20 ha	11,074	4,442	1,326	3,915	21,757
Between 20 & 50 ha	1,601	737	80	234	2,652
Between 50 & 200 ha	289	356	19	36	700
Between 200 & 1000 ha	27	130	0	2	159
Between 1000 & 2500 ha	1	21	1	0	23
Over 2500 ha	0	5	0	0	5
Total	30,223	43,242	69,114	40,350	182,929

If a land reform law had limited the size of a farm to, let us say, five hectares, then the overwhelming majority of the village population would have benefited greatly. In the above four provinces—158,633 out of a total of 182,929 would have benefited.

As no statistics are available about the total amount of land in each category of farms we shall make a very rough estimate of how much a land reform law limiting the area to five hectares would have benefited the peasants with less than five hectares. We assume that the farmers who had less than 0.5 hectares had on average one quarter of a hectare, those between 0.5 and 5 hectares 2.75 hectares, and so on. Those with more than 2,500 hectares we shall assume held only 2,500 hectares. Then the lowest two groups, who make up 87 percent of all the peasants, have altogether 313,583 hectares, or 33 percent of the land, while the higher groups which make up only 13 percent of all the peasants own 600,432 hectares, or 67 percent of the land.

The government of Portugal enacted a land reform (not yet implemented) which limits holdings to 500 hectares of dry land, or 50 hectares of irrigated land with some upward adjustment possible.

Such 'land reform' would of course leave the land relations in the North practically untouched.

How can we explain the government's timidity?

First of all, most of the Army Officers, as we have already mentioned, are part and parcel of the middle class, including the well-to-do farmers.

Secondly, the main parties support the line of 'national unity', hence they find it incumbent upon themselves not to antagonise the middle classes.

Many of the peasants with tiny farms of their own are forced to work for wages for other farmers, or to rent land from them, or both. Here too nothing has been done for the poor farmer.

Where wages are concerned: the law fixed a minimum wage of 3,300 escudos, later raised to 4,000, but this does not apply to agricultural workers. The average monthly wage of a permanent agricultural male worker at the end of 1973 was 2,400 escudos, and of women 1,500 escudos.[86]

Nothing was done about cutting the rent paid by the poor peasants. Most importantly, the peasants are weighed down by debts. Nothing has been done to cancel these debts. When the banks were nationalised, the agricultural credit institutions were not even touched.

The peasants need cheap tractors. In the whole of Coimbra province, with its 69,114 farms, there were only 476 tractors. In Bragança, with 30,223 farms, there were only 109 combine harvesters. A revolutionary government would have turned car production over to produce agricultural machinery. After all, how many Portuguese workers can afford cars? But nothing of the sort happened.

The peasant needs fertilisers. Fertilisers have doubled in price this year. What would have been more effective than using army lorries to deliver cheap fertilisers to the poor peasants? But again this did not happen. Instead...talk and talk about 'dynamisation'.

The peasants need to sell their wine. A revolutionary government would have found the funds to buy their wine by seizing the wealth of the rich, their luxury cars, their houses, their bank balances. But again this did not happen.

The peasants are robbed by the middlemen—the merchants. Nothing was done to get rid of the middlemen by organising a network of cooperative buying and selling, and fixing an agreed price for agricultural produce.

No wonder the agricultural population in the North are in a rebellious and reactionary mood. Again and again they hear on the wireless the talk of a new life in Portugal. And what they find is that everything is the same as before, only worse. The markets for their goods are shrinking, the price of feed and fertiliser rocketing, the debts in no way alleviated, etc, etc.

The reactionary policy of the government in the area of agriculture played into the hands of the most reactionary forces active in the North, especially the Catholic Church.

The Catholic Church hierarchy in Portugal has a long history of association with fascism and reaction. Agostinho Laurenco—the top man in the hated Portuguese secret police, the PIDE—was a Commander of the Order of Saint Gregory. Cardinal Manuel Gonçalves Cerejeira, dictator Salazar's friend and later Cardinal Patriarch of Lisbon, showed where he stood on his return from a fundraising mission in Africa in 1974. 'The Portuguese people must work harder and know hunger to become humble,' he said.

The efforts of Prime Minister Gonçalves, the MFA, the Socialist Party and the Communist Party to curry favour with the Church with nice words were naturally ineffective. In his inaugural address as Prime Minister on 18 July 1974, General Gonçalves said, 'The Church has a fundamental role to play in this revolution and will follow us towards the future. We know this is about to happen'.[87]

Traditionally the North was the main base of fascism. The ANP, the national party under fascism, had its headquarters in the main northern city, Oporto, as does the extreme right-wing Christian Democratic Party (now outlawed). The fact that over 60 Communist Party offices have been burnt in the North by mobs, incited by priests and organised fascists, is evidence that the North is still largely under extreme reactionary influence. The policy of all the governments that existed since 25 April 1974 has strengthened this reactionary influence.

In conclusion

The economy is in an impasse. The crisis of capitalism will become even deeper in the coming weeks and months. The present regime is one of permanent crisis. When the thunder of revolution has awakened hundreds of thousands, procrastination has become, and will become, more and more intolerable. In a revolutionary period, more than at any other time, the masses cannot tolerate a cleavage between words and deeds. The present impasse can be overcome in two ways: either by a victorious proletarian revolution or by the victory of extreme reaction.

We can have either a general plan of production in the interests of the proletariat and the poor peasantry, or a new freedom for big business—both foreign and Portuguese—to rob the people. 'Planned economy' with the anarchy and waste of capitalism becomes more and more unacceptable to the two contending classes.

A complete collapse of discipline in the factories was a condition and a result of the revolutionary situation. But a situation in which there is neither clear discipline imposed from above by the capitalists nor a discipline imposed by the free and conscious collective of the proletariat cannot continue for long. For the capitalists to re-establish their order—with the high aspirations of the awakened, assertive proletariat—a bloodbath will be necessary. On the other hand, a consistent struggle for workers to defend their wages and conditions grows naturally into a purge of nasty factory owners and foremen, and the forcible keeping open of plants which the owners wish to close. And the struggle for workers' control is inevitably locked in with the struggle for workers' state power.

The way ahead

Prospects of future development

A revolutionary situation is very unstable by definition. There is not an unbridgeable gulf between a revolutionary and counter-revolutionary situation. In such a situation the moods of different groups in society, their energies and strengths, change very quickly. Real life experience in a revolutionary situation is very complicated, with so many factors criss-crossing, that an exact prognosis of events is impossible. However, there are quite clear basic delineations of developments.

Up to now the capitalists have not managed to get a clear grip on state power in Portugal, while the proletariat has not been ready to challenge them for it. The result has been an unstable balance whose centre of gravity has been the MFA. The Communist Party has been able to substitute the MFA for the vanguard of revolutionary workers (while it substituted itself for the vanguard in the factories). The right has also kowtowed to the MFA. The MFA has stood above the nation. Its mediation between the contending classes, together with the inherent weakness of the middle class, made the movement look larger than life. But the class struggle goes on, and it breaks the false unity of the MFA to pieces.

For a number of months many workers saw the revolutionary process as an attempt to impose their kind of law and order on a chaotic situation. The reactionaries were regarded as wreckers who have to be dealt with a little more firmly each time they step up their activities. Since there was no significant reactionary initiative since 11 March, the mass of the workers saw no need to move significantly to the left. The masses need big events to advance their revolutionary education.

The capitalist class also marked time for a space of months. But this cannot go on for very long. The economic and social crisis is deepening and breaking up the MFA—the main factor that has till now acted as buffer and mediator between the classes.

Adding to the threat from the right is the fact that international big business is causing economic chaos and then blaming it on the left, as in Chile two years ago.

The middle class, who were prepared to tolerate the revolution when it was just a matter of fine words, are moving rapidly to the right as they get squeezed between the economic crisis and the demands of the workers.

This is just as true of the middle class in the armed forces. The officers who supported the revolution when it was a question of ending unpopular wars in Africa now fear that their privileges and those of their relatives will be ended. They are backed by all the pro-western political forces, in particular the Socialist Party of Mario Soares. Despite its name, it is a middle-class party which may get workers' votes but does not depend on workers for its funds and its organisers.

The right-wing forces have enjoyed enormous successes in the north and centre of the country in the last few weeks, as Socialist Party rallies have been followed by attempts to drive left-wingers physically from the area.

The right has been aided and spurred on by another important factor-the Portuguese ex-settlers in Angola and the Portuguese army in Angola.

The national liberation movements of the Portuguese colonies in Africa played a central role in the collapse of fascism. Now the former privileged settlers in Angola and the Portuguese army there are intervening as counter-revolutionary forces. There is no doubt that the 300,000 Portuguese arriving at the rate of 4,000 a day from Angola will aid the extreme right. They are bound to accuse the revolution of driving them out of Angola. They will by and large be unemployed, so their bitterness and demoralisation will be quite dangerous.

In the last few days the news from Lisbon is that the fascist ELP has been very active among the Angolan refugees in their camps.

And what about the Portuguese army in Angola? On 2 September a meeting of the Assembly of the Army voted overwhelmingly against the former Prime Minister holding the post of Commander-in-Chief of the Armed Forces. According to comments in the Lisbon newspapers, the alleged 70 percent majority of the army's anti-Gonçalves vote was partly due to the presence of 30 officers representing the army in Angola, who had flown in specially to take part in the Assembly. In addition to their influence on the result of the vote, the commentators say, the army is trying to indicate that it can count on the support of the Angola force which still includes some 24,000 highly trained and well-equipped men.[88]

The right is bound to try and challenge the working class, so as to re-establish capitalist law and order. And it is only in struggle—especially in a situation with so many contradictory and unknown factors—that one can find what is the real balance of class forces. There is bound to be greater and greater pressure from the right—from the moderate right of Antunes and Soares to the extreme right of the CDS, Spinola and the ELP.

The workers, especially the best-organised ones in Lisbon and its environment, are bound to fight back in defence of the gains they made since fascism was overthrown on 25 April last year. They know these gains are now at stake, no matter now confused some may be by the manoeuvres, the wrangles, the splits and the shifting alliances at the top of society between professional career officers and professional politicians. And the workers have developed an enormous power.

The present regime—whether it is the first, second, third, fourth, fifth, sixth or whatever government, is the most unstable caricature of Bonapartism. It does not represent a new equilibrium but the ending of an old one. It is a short-lived transitory regime leading either to victory of the proletarian revolution or to the victory of fascism. It is a void between two dictatorships.

Different governmental combinations

Because of the divisions and indiscipline in the army and, as Marx and Engels taught us, the State is essentially nothing but armed men and their accessories—a number of government combinations are on the agenda.

Two parties play a key role in deciding the governmental combination: the Socialist Party and the Communist Party.

Mario Soares, in a letter to President Costa Gomes made public on 4 September, asked for a guarantee that elections for a Legislative Assembly would be held within 60 days, and that a new government based on voting results would be formed. He also demanded, among other things: that regional elections be held before February next year, the newspaper *Republica* be returned to its Socialist Party former editor, and that Portugal's bishops be given back control of the Roman Catholic radio station Radio Renascenca.

In the atmosphere of hysterical anti-communism, with the deepening economic crisis, and especially if at the same time workers are forced to retreat, and the Catholic hierarchy is given a boost through the return of Radio Renascenca, it is clear that a general election now must lead to a landslide electoral victory for the right.

Again, for the proletariat, the return of *Republica* and Radio Renascenca is bound to appear as a symbolic defeat, the thin end of the wedge of the complete destruction of all factory occupations and the restoration of the old owners.

The Right is also going to insist on the complete restoration of the old discipline in the armed forces. Two right-wing officers, Major Melo Antunes and Major Vito Alves, were restored to the Supreme Revolutionary Council after being kicked off it about a month before. The very same day a leading right-wing officer and a member of the Supreme Revolutionary Council, Captain Sausa e Castro, in an interview with *Le Quotidien de Paris*, said that the army should be purged of all elements linked with the Communist Party or extreme left-wing groups. The army should return to 'classic discipline and hierarchy. All those who play the parties' game in the army have no place in it. They must end all these assemblies in the army,' he said. If the Communists and certain extreme left-wing groups did not give up their influence in the barracks voluntarily they would be forced to do so.[89]

The Communist Party leaders have a very difficult choice. The Socialist Party is offering the Communist Party a new coalition. But it demands a very high price. Restoring *Republica* and Renascenca to the old owners means reconsolidation of bourgeois authority. The Communist Party does not want to lose its own bastions of power in the state and the media (like *Diaria de Noticias*, *O Seculo*), or its influence on the radio and TV.

And if it sacrifices Radio Renascenca and *Republica* (which it does not control but which are symbols for all the most advanced workers in Lisbon and Setubal), its militants will find themselves completely isolated in the factories. Under such conditions, some, if not many, would leave the Party.

The Communist Party leaders will naturally be extremely reluctant to accept Soares's terms. But the pressure on them from international Stalinism is extremely strong, and will continue to increase.

One need only study the Italian and Spanish Communist Parties who see in Cunhal an 'ultra-left' bogey. What better proof than the praises the Italian Communist Party got from Soares himself? At the press conference in Rome on 13 June Soares said:

> If the Portuguese Communists had the same line as the Italian Communist Party there would be no problem for the Portuguese Left nor for the European Left. The Communist Party of Italy is truly a democratic party, for which political freedoms are a great conquest for humanity.

While in Rome Soares met Berlinguer, General Secretary of the Italian Communist Party. When asked if Berlinguer had promised him solidarity, Soares replied, 'That follows from our conversation'.[90]

On 11 July the Spanish and Italian Communist Parties issued the following declaration, which no doubt is an indirect criticism of the Portuguese Communist Party:

> Socialism cannot be established in our countries without the development and complete achievement of democracy... [this is based on] the affirmation of personal and collective liberties; these are guaranteed by the principles of the lay state, its democratic articulation, the plurality of parties in a true dialectic, trade union autonomy, religious freedoms, freedom of expression, culture, art and science.[91]

At a rally on 12 July at Livorno, Berlinguer and Carillo, General Secretary of the Spanish Communist Party, criticised the MFA. Berlinguer deplored MFA policies for reducing 'the participation of all expression of the popular will—in the first place the parties, which are the only guarantee of the renewal of Portuguese society and of its defence against any attempt at a reactionary return'. Carrillo said:

> We must show concern and anxiety. If the breaking of the alliance formed on 25 April round the MFA is confirmed, if the democratic process were to be definitely interrupted, that would seriously compromise the fate of the revolution, and harm above all the Portuguese people and the cause of democracy throughout Europe.[92]

On 29 July Pavolini, editor of the Italian Communist Party daily *L'Unità*, attacked the Portuguese Communist Party for supporting MFA proposals to reduce the role of the parties: 'We believe that basic political liberties, liberty of meeting and association, freedom of the press, information and culture, ought not simply to be "tolerated" but supported and defended as the true banner of the movement of socialist workers'.[93]

The Portuguese Communist Party perhaps could have stood up to the pressure of international Stalinism if not for the fact that its own mass base—including the army—is very seriously shaken.

The Communist Party at the moment is still organisationally strong. But it is completely isolated politically. This has been shown by the relative failure of the Intersindical's half-hour strike of 19 August—some of the strongest sections of workers (*Republica*, A Capital, RCP radio, RR radio, the underground, TAP, TLP, etc) ignored it; by the ease with which the 5th Division was closed down; by its leaders feeling, however briefly, that they needed a united front with the revolutionary left; by its loss of union elections in the Journalists, Pharmaceutical, Clerical, and Bank workers' Unions (NB the Bank workers' Union used to be synonymous with the Communist Party, and was the launching pad used by the Communist Party to control the Intersindical).

Among the army units with guns the Communist Party seems much weaker than the revolutionary left.

The military police (the most radicalised section of the army besides the RAL) voted unanimously for a resolution on Angola last week which referred to 'social imperialism'.

There were more troops on the revolutionary demonstration on 20 August—

in which the Communist Party did not participate—than on the United Front demonstration of 27 August in which the Communist Party did participate.

Within the class there are certain key sections where the Communist Party seems to have lost out completely—*Republica*, the Post Office, telephones. In other sectors (Lisnave, Setenave) one gets the impression that there is continual competition between the Communist Party and the revolutionary left, with the balance of influence shifting from day to day. Even in places like CUF, where the Communist Party has been very strong, the revolutionary left has some influence.

But, of course, there are all sorts of factories, not deeply involved in the agitation of last summer (when the Communist Party controlled the Ministry of Labour and condemned all strikes), where the Communist Party's influence is unimpaired.

But the *isolation* of the Communist Party presents it with insuperable problems.

A coalition with the Socialist Party will threaten the Communist Party with, firstly, loss of much of its control over the state machine, media, etc, and, secondly, loss of control of many of its own rank and file militants to the revolutionary left.

It was partly in order to protect its left flank, partly in order to get a mobilisation in the streets that could defend its position in the state, that the Communist Party accepted the United Front on 25 August.

But the front was an embarrassment to international Stalinism and to the Communist Party allies in the officer corps.

So after the zig came the zag.

The zigzags in policy must be very demoralising for the Party members. Of course the history of Stalinism has been a history of zigzag—but every three to four years, not every three to four days.

Thus it was clear on the 27 August United Front demonstration that many of the Communist Party core were hardly adjusted to the notion of raising revolutionary sounding slogans. After all, only six weeks before, all the Communist Party demonstrations had been for the 'battle of production'. Now they were saying Portugal was still a capitalist country. But faced with the role of the Socialist Party and its agitation in the north, they (the hardest Stalinists) shouted Costa Gomes down when he suggested an 'opening to other political forces' (ie the Socialist Party).

Yet within 24 hours Cunhal was making friendly moves to the Socialist Party. Again *O Seculo* (a Communist Party controlled daily) produced a special midday edition on Monday 25 August to greet the Revolutionary Front as a 'historic occasion'. Yet a week later the Communist Party was pretending the Front had never really existed.

In the short term at least, their isolation would seem worse than ever. The centrist groups that used to provide them with a certain left cover (MES, LCI, possibly FSP) have been forced to join with the PRP in denouncing the Communist Party's treachery.

And unless Soares lowers his demands considerably, it is not impossible that the Communist Party will be forced once again to try a United Front with the revolutionaries. Despite the size of the Communist Party's apparatus and the strength of its cadres, it could easily fall between two stools and fail in its attempts to exist as an apparatus suspended in mid-air.

If the Communist Party collaborated with the Socialist Party, and they are both backed by the army generals, then the prospects for Portugal are of a right-wing offensive, of the type carried out in Germany in 1918-19. If the Communist Party remains outside the government, then the prospects are of a right-wing offensive similar to that seen in Spain in 1936-39. Of course there can be many permutations. For instance, the Communist Party might join the government for a time and then be pushed out by the right. Or it might resign from the government for fear of losing its popular base to the revolutionary organisations. It is also possible for the Communist Party, while being outside the government, to try and use the popular pressure merely in order to influence the people at the top. There is a wide variety of possibilities before the Communist Party leaders for manoeuvring and zigzagging. In all cases the leaders will keep the masses in the dark about their real intentions, believing in the clever manoeuvre. But manoeuvres and tricks in politics, especially in a revolution, are very dangerous: they fail to dupe the enemy but threaten to dupe the masses.

The urgent need to organise workers' and soldiers' councils

As the present governmental set-up is a passage towards one of two dictatorships, the working class urgently needs to build a representative democratic organisation that covers the whole of the working class, ie soviets (councils). Parties, even large ones, can only include a minority of the proletariat. This could remain an abstract statement if one did not show how such soviets can be created from the immediate struggles and, first of all, from the need of workers to defend themselves against reaction.

The councils must be widespread, organised across the whole working class and not only its vanguard. The PRP-BR deserves real credit for urging the formation of Revolutionary Councils of Workers, Soldiers and Sailors. The CRTSMs demonstration on 17 June of some 40,000 people was very fine. But this was only the vanguard—ie workers, soldiers and sailors who should be members of a revolutionary party. The real councils must organise far more people with far greater unevenness in their levels of consciousness.

The United Front

The collapse of the MFA as a unified force, and the sharp threats from reaction, will make it possible and urgent to raise the question of the united anti-fascist front—as a transition to the soviets.

The problem of the United Front—notwithstanding the deep differences between the political parties within it, and the inevitable split between them—is rooted in the need to defend workers' organisations against attack from reaction.

'To carry on a war for the overthrow of the international bourgeoisie,' Lenin wrote in *Left-Wing Communism: An Infantile Disorder*, 'and to renounce in advance any change of tack or any utilisation of a conflict of interests (even if temporarily) among one's enemies, or any conciliation or compromise with possible allies (even if they are temporary, unstable, vacillating or conditional allies)—is that not ridiculous in the extreme?' It is:

> ...necessity, the absolute necessity, for the Communist Party, the vanguard of the proletariat, its class-conscious section, to resort to changes of tack, to conciliation and compromises with the various groups of proletarians, with the various parties of the workers and small masters. It is entirely a matter of *knowing how* to apply these tactics in order to *raise*—not lower—the general level of proletarian class-consciousness, revolutionary spirit, and ability to fight and win.[94]

And Lenin showed in practice how one should carry the policy of the united front without falling into either unprincipled compromises or dogmatic sectarianism. The classic test was on 26 August 1917 when General Kornilov, Commander-in-Chief of the Russian Army, threw his army against Petrograd, aiming to smash the Kerensky government, the soviets and all its parties—not only the revolutionary Bolsheviks, but also the reformist Mensheviks and Socialist Revolutionaries. The Bolshevik Party was semi-legal, suppressed and persecuted by the Kerensky government. Its leaders were slandered viciously as German agents. But the Bolsheviks did not hesitate to form a practical alliance with their jailors and slanderers—Kerensky, Tsereteli and company—to fight Kornilov.

Lenin's writings during these crucial days are by far the clearest and sharpest. In a letter to the Central Committee of the Bolsheviks he wrote:

> The Kornilov revolt is a most unexpected (unexpected at such a moment and in such a form) and downright unbelievably sharp turn in events.
>
> Like every sharp turn, it calls for a revision and change of tactics. And as with every revision, we must be extra cautious not to become unprincipled.

There must be no concealment of principled disagreements, no weakening of the criticism of the position of the temporary ally, no covering up of differences:

> *Even now* we must not support Kerensky's government. This is unprincipled. We may be asked: aren't we going to fight against Kornilov? Of course we must! But this is not the same thing; there is a dividing line here...
>
> We shall fight, we are fighting against Koniflov, *just as* Kerensky's *troops do*, but we do not support Kerensky. *On the contrary*, we expose his weaknesses. There is the difference. It is rather a subtle difference, but it is highly essential and must not be forgotten.'

What then constituted the change in Bolshevik tactics brought about by the Kornilov revolt?

> We are changing the *form* of our struggle against Kerensky. Without in the least relaxing our hostility towards him, without taking back a single word said against him, without renouncing the task of overthrowing him, we say that we must *take into account* the present situation. We shall not overthrow Kerensky right now. We shall approach the task of fighting against him *in a different way*, namely, we shall point out to the people (who are fighting against Kornilov) Kerensky's *weakness* and *vacillation*. This has been done in the past as well. Now, however, it has become the *all-important* thing, and this constitutes the change.

The change in the tactics of the Bolsheviks in the face of the Kornilov revolt was expressed by putting at the centre of the party agitation a number:

> ...of 'partial demands' to be presented to Kerensky: arrest Milyukov, arm the Petrograd workers, summon the Kronstadt, Vyborg and Helsingfors troops to Petrograd, dissolve the Duma, arrest Rodziariko, legalise the transfer of the landed estates to the peasants, introduce workers' control over grain and factories, etc, etc. We must present these demands, not only to Kerensky, and *not so much* to Kerensky, as to the workers. soldiers and peasants who have been *carried away* by the course of the struggle against Kornilov. We must keep up their *enthusiasm*, encourage them to deal with the generals and officers who have declared for Kornilov, urge *them* to demand immediate transfer of land to the peasants, suggest to *them* that it is necessary to arrest Rodzianko and Milyukov, dissolve the Duma, close down *Rech* and other bourgeois papers, and institute investigations against them.

In all the tactical changes Lenin never forgot to emphasise that the central issue must never for a second be overlooked: the seizure of power by the proletariat:

> It would be wrong to think that we have moved further away from the task of the proletariat winning power. No. We have come very close to it, *not directly*, but from the side. *At the moment* we must campaign not so much directly against Kerensky, as *indirectly* against him, namely by demanding more and more active truly revolutionary war against Kornilov. The development of this war alone can lead us to power, but we must *speak* of this as little as possible in our propaganda.[95]

And so, facing the threat of Kornilov, committees for revolutionary defence were organised everywhere, into which the Bolsheviks entered as a minority. This did not hinder the Bolsheviks, being the most consistent, from assuming a leading role.

The united front against Kornilov gave a new lease of life to the soviets which had become dormant under the Menshevik and Socialist Revolutionary leadership, especially since the July days when a massive persecution of the Bolsheviks started.

And no doubt, in a revolutionary situation, a united front may well lead to the soviet. As Trotsky put it so clearly, 'Just as the trade union is the rudimentary form of the united front in the economic struggle, *so the soviet is the highest form of the united front*, under the conditions in which the proletariat enters the epoch of fighting for power'.[96]

What forms exactly, with what parties, the united front will be built in Portugal, we can never know in advance. Quick changes of tactics, including that of the united front, are needed in a swiftly changing situation. But one thing we can be absolutely sure of, if we study the historical experience of the international proletariat. One of the main issues connected intimately with that of a united front, and leading directly to it, is the question of arming the workers, the creation of workers' militias.

Workers' militia

Workers have to protect themselves. Already in the North the need arises to patrol the streets, to defend working-class centres from reactionary attacks. This need will also arise in Lisbon and Setubal. Why not demand from the factory management that a certain number of workers be freed from work to do patrol duty paid by management?

While building the workers' militia the propaganda for the general arming of the revolutionary workers must be carried out.

At the same time one cannot have a workers' militia side by side with the regular army for any length of time. So the demand for their amalgamation has to be raised. This entails the election of all officers in the armed forces, the democratic election of soldiers' committees in each unit, centralised in a national election of soldiers' delegates to a national council. As the proletariat cannot win State power without arms, the slogan of 'arming the workers' and the slogan 'Build the Councils of Workers, Soldiers and Sailors' are indissolubly bound together.

The central role of the revolutionary party

Revolutions do indeed start as spontaneous acts without the leadership of a party. The French Revolution started with the storming of the Bastille. Nobody organised that. Was there a party at the head of the people in rebellion? No. Even the future leaders of the Jacobins, for instance Robespierre, did not yet oppose the monarchy and were not yet organised into a party. The 14 July 1789 revolution was a spontaneous act of the masses.

The same was true of the Russian Revolution of 1905 and the February 1917 Revolution. The 1905 Revolution started through a bloody clash between the Tsar's army and police on the one hand and the mass of workers, men, women and children, on the other, led by the priest Gapon (who was actually an agent provocateur of the Tsar). Were the workers organised by a clear and decisive leadership with a socialist policy of its own? Certainly not. Carrying icons, they came begging their beloved 'Little Father'—the Tsar—to help them against their exploiters. This was the first step in a great revolution. Twelve years later, in February 1917, the masses, now more experienced, and with a greater number of revolutionaries among them than in the previous revolution, again rose spontaneously. No historian has been able to point at any organiser of the February Revolution, for it simply was not organised.

However, after being triggered off by a spontaneous uprising, revolutions move forward in a different manner. In France there was a transition from the semi-republican government of the Gironde to a revolutionary one, which completely annihilated feudal property relations. This was not carried out by unorganised masses without any party leadership, but under the decisive leadership of the Jacobin party. Without such a party at the helm, this important step, which demanded an all-out fight against the Girondists, would have been impossible. The people of Paris could spontaneously, leaderlessly, rise up against the king after decades of oppression. But the majority were too conservative, and lacking in historical experience and knowledge, to distinguish, after only two or three years of revolution, between those who wanted to drive the revolution to an extremity and those who aimed at some compromise. The historical situation required a struggle to the bitter end and against the party of compromise, the allies of yesterday. The conscious leadership of this undertaking was supplied by the Jacobin party, which fixed the date and organised the overthrow of the Gironde on 10 August 1792 down to the last detail. Similarly the October Revolution was not a spontaneous act, but was organised in practically all its important particulars, including the date, by the Bolsheviks. During the zigzags of the revolution—between February and October, the April demonstration, the June demonstration, the July days and subsequent orderly retreat, the rebuff of the Kornilov putsch—the workers and soldiers came more closely under the influence and guidance of the Bolshevik Party. Such a party was essential to raise the revolution from its initial stages to its final victory.

Spontaneity is inevitably irregular and uneven, and while all revolutions in history have begun spontaneously, none have ended so.

For the working class to take and hold power, a revolutionary workers' party is necessary. That is not to say that a revolution, an overthrow of the old order, cannot happen except under the leadership of a revolutionary party. Even the 25 April coup demonstrates this clearly. Without a party the overthrow of an old regime can certainly take place.

Nor is there any magic in parties as such. The traditional working-class parties, social-democratic and 'communist', have for decades been a brake on, not a motor of, socialist revolution. 'The proletariat may tolerate for a long time a [party] leadership that has already suffered a complete inner degeneration,' Trotsky once wrote, 'but has not as yet had the opportunity to express this degeneration amid great events. A great historic shock is necessary to reveal sharply the contradiction.'

The shock may produce scepticism about the whole notion of a revolutionary party. Various substitutes may be supposed to exist, whether left-wing officers, spontaneous working-class action or whatever. But there is no possible substitute. Many kinds of non-party institutions can play a part in the revolutionary process, workers' councils in particular can play an almost indispensable part, but without a revolutionary workers' party the working class, as a class, cannot rule.

A revolutionary party is different in nature, not simply in policy, from reformist parties. Reformist parties are always substitutionalist. Vote for us and we will do this or that for you is their invariable approach. In the case of social-democratic parties it is virtually the only political call they make to their supporters in 'normal' circumstances.

There is also such a thing as revolutionary substitutionism. A classic example is Blanquism. On 12 May 1839 Blanqui led his 1,200 or so armed followers in Paris into the streets to overthrow the monarchy. His proclamation read:

> To arms Citizens!
>
> The fatal hour has sounded for the oppressors...
>
> The Provisional Government has chosen military leaders to direct the struggle.
>
> These people have come from your ranks; follow them—they will lead you to victory.
>
> Forward! Long live the Republic.

This coup was quite successful at first. It had been very well prepared, in a technical sense. Key government buildings were occupied. But the whole operation had been prepared in the utmost secrecy. No *political* preparations had been carried out. The great mass of the working population of Paris knew nothing of Blanqui's plan. They were completely ignorant, not just of the *technical* plan, which has to be secret, but also of the political and social aims of the movement. They remained inactive. The government rallied, brought in reliable troops and the rising was crushed.

It was not that the Paris workers of that time were incapable of revolutionary action. Far from it. In 1830 and again in 1848 they overthrew the regime. But in both cases a political ferment among them preceded the insurrection.

Nowadays everyone pays at least lip service to the need for political preparation, but in fact substitutionalism is still rife on the revolutionary left. It needs to be emphasised and re-emphasised that, in Marx's words, 'the emancipation of the working class must be the act of the working class itself'. A revolutionary party can never substitute itself for the working class. Other kinds of parties can, do and must. Their aims, however various, *all* include keeping the workers politically passive—voting fodder at best or supporters of well-controlled demonstrations planned from above.

But the rejection of substitutionalism *in no way* involves rejecting the necessity for a revolutionary workers' party. The working class is the product of *capitalist* society. Its consciousness and militancy and understanding are necessarily extremely uneven. To act, even in sectional struggles, it requires organisation. For it to act *as a class* for the biggest aim of all, the taking of power and the socialist reconstruction of society, the most conscious and confident workers must be welded together. They are the actual or potential leaders of their fellows. United they can, under favourable circumstances, carry the whole mass with them. This union of these advanced workers is the revolutionary workers' party. In times of crisis workers, like other sections of society, respond to some leadership or other. Acute problems have to be solved and they *will* be solved—in a progressive way or in a reactionary one. In the absence of a revolutionary party led by the more advanced workers, the mass of the working class will follow or acquiesce in some other kind of lead. The vacuum has to be filled, and if the advanced workers lack the cohesion and confidence to lead, if they are not able to act as a *party*, then the vacuum is always filled by a substitutionist force which builds on apathy and confusion.

Of course the revolutionary party also needs tradition and theory. In other words its cadres need to have absorbed some of the lessons of past workers' struggles nationally and internationally. To weld together a broad layer of advanced workers this tradition must to some extent be taught. After all, the cadres of the bourgeois class, bureaucrats, army officers, managers, lawyers, and so on, are subjected to an intense education process which is as much ideological as technical.

But it is very dangerous to see the party's job as *mainly* that of teacher. The main job is to give a lead. To do this effectively the party militants must listen, must be sensitive to changing moods among their fellow workers, must know how to link the aspirations of workers to the central political aim. In short they have to learn from their fellow workers as much as—or more than—they have to teach. To repeat, the job is to *lead*, and to lead you have to thoroughly understand those you are leading. Leadership is a two-way process.

The same is true of the party leaders. Only impractical utopians can suppose that party leadership is unnecessary. Just as the working class as a whole is led by its most conscious and confident members, so inside the party a differentiation is inevitable. The job of party leadership is to generalise the experience of the party militants and to lead them as they lead their fellow workers. It is the same two-way relationship *inside* the party.

Many on the left see the party as a substitute for the class, or primarily as the teacher of the class. Equally, many see the party leadership as the repository of doctrine, of theory, of organisational skill and knowledge. Of course it has to be all these things to some degree. But mainly it has to be the most apt *learner*, the most sensitive ear and the firmest will.

Theory and tradition all too often become lifeless dogma. Indeed, they must become so unless they are always connected to the living struggle, to the creativity and initiative of the working class. Engels's oft-repeated but rarely understood saying, 'Our theory is not a dogma but *a guide to action*,' sums up the correct relation between theory and practice.

Lenin loved to repeat, 'Theory, my friend, is grey, but green is the eternal tree of life.' Living reality is always richer in developments, in probabilities, in complications, than any theoretical concept or prognosis, and Lenin therefore derided those who turned Marxism into an icon: 'An icon is something you pray to, something you cross yourself before, something you bow down to; but an icon has no effect on practical life and practical politics'.[97]

A revolutionary leadership needs both an understanding of the struggle as a whole, and the capacity to put forward the right slogans at every turning point. These do not derive simply from the party programme. They must fit the circumstances, above all the moods and feelings of the masses, so that they can be used to lead the workers forward. Slogans must be appropriate, not only to the general direction of the revolutionary movement, but also to the level of consciousness of the masses. Only through the *application* of the general line of the party does its real value become manifest.

The party and its leadership must keep in continuous touch with the masses. The only real revolutionary politics is the principled open politics that avoids falling for 'tricks' that dupe the masses. So the party press must play a central role in the party's work, by giving local committees, members of the party and the mass of its supporters a clear idea of the politics of the party. It was so with the Bolsheviks. At the beginning of July 1917, 41 newspapers and journals were published by the Bolshevik Party, 27 in Russian and the remainder in the languages of various minorities (five Latvian, one Lithuanian, two Armenian, two Estonian, one Polish, one Georgian, one Azerbaijani). Of these 17 were daily papers (14 in the Russian language), eight papers appeared three times a week, five twice weekly, seven weekly, three fortnightly and one monthly. The word—including the written word—is of such central importance in the revolution. There was no period in Lenin's life in which he wrote more or better than in the months of February to October 1917.

For the revolutionary party to utter the right words is not enough. The party must be able to translate words, into deeds. For this it must have wide and deep implantation in the proletariat—it must be a mass party. Such was the Bolshevik Party. In July 1917 in Petrograd the Bolsheviks had 36,000 members (Petrograd had about the same population as Lisbon). Of course, the PRP-BR on 25 April 1974 was only a tiny organisation and for it to become a mass party is not at all easy, especially as the PRP has to contend not only with the Communist Party (and to a lesser extent the Socialist Party) in working-class circles but also with other small extreme left organisations (above all the Maoists). However, here again the Bolshevik experience is quite useful. In the revolutionary months of 1917 the Bolshevik Party grew very swiftly indeed. Thus, for instance, in Saratov at the beginning of March there were 60 Party members at the end of July 3,000; in Kiev the corresponding figures were 200 and 4,000; in Ekaterinburg 40 and 2,800; in Moscow 600 and 15,000; in Petrograd 2,000 and 36,000.

Whether easy or difficult, in one way or another, the success of the revolution in Portugal demands the budding of a *mass revolutionary proletarian party*.

Building the mass party, making the party paper a central organiser, making the party and every one of its members an active interventionist in the class struggle are integral parts of leading the proletariat to victory. Politics and organisation can in no way be separated.

Unlike the sects who appropriate the mantle of leadership without paying attention at all to what the workers really think, feel and do, the revolutionary party, above all, must relate to the workers in struggle. The central role of the party is 'to give full scope to the revolutionary creative activity of the masses, who participate but little in this activity in a time of peace, but who come to the forefront in revolutionary epochs'.[98]

It is especially during revolutionary periods that workers show the tremendous creative abilities they have. As Lenin put it, 'The organising abilities of the people, particularly of the proletariat, but also of the peasantry, are revealed a million times more strongly, fully and productively in periods of revolutionary whirlwind than in periods of so-called calm [drayhorse] historical progress'.[99]

A victory for the proletarian revolution in Portugal will open a new chapter in world history. The impact on neighbouring Spain will be decisive. Even before the fall of fascism the working class in Spain shows fantastic militancy. Official figures for 1974 record 1,196 industrial disputes involving 669,861 workers, and these are the conservative figures put out by the Spanish government. If the multinationals lose their factories in Portugal there is a good chance they will lose them in Spain too.

Portugal, the weakest link in the capitalist chain in Europe, can become the launching pad for the socialist revolution in the whole of the continent.

The stakes are extremely high for both the working class and the capitalist class. NATO, CIA, MI6, EEC, the State Department and the Foreign Office, Tories and Social Democratic leaders have joined together in a holy alliance to defend 'democracy'. The international proletariat should close ranks behind their Portuguese brothers and sisters to see that Portugal does not turn into another Chile, and that the struggle culminates in workers' power and socialism.

Notes

* Many members of the International Socialists contributed to this work. Much of what they had to say appeared in International Socialism and Socialist Worker. I borrowed freely from them as well as from Our Common Struggle, the newsletter of the Portuguese Workers' Coordinating Committee. I also benefited very much from the 54 reports written by IS members who visited Portugal during August. I am very grateful to Duncan Hallas and Chris Harman for making contributions to this work, and to Colin Sparks who compiled the chronology and the glossary. Special thanks are owed to Ian Birchall, Alex Callinicos, Elana Dallas, Donny Gluckstein, Joanna Rollo and Colin Sparks who helped in research. Alvaro Miranda must be thanked for his very constructive criticisms of the manuscript. — Tony Cliff, 9 September 1975.

1 V I Lenin, *Collected Works*, vol 31, p232.

2 In writing this chapter liberal use has been made of the following: I Birchall, 'April Dream in Portugal', *International Socialism*, May 1974; C Harman, 'Portugal: The First Six Months', *International Socialism*, October 1974; J Rollo, 'Portugal: One Year after the Coup', *International Socialism*, April 1975; and W Burchett, *Portugal depois da Revolução dos Capitaes*; Lisbon 1975.

3 V I Lenin, *Collected Works*, vol 21, pp213-214.

4 W Burchett, *Portugal*, pp203-204.

5 *Economist*, 28 February 1972.

6 *Economist*, 26 February 1972.

7 K Marx, *The Class Struggles in France 1848-1850*, (Progress Publishers, Moscow), pp33, 38.

8 K Marx, *Class Struggles*, p50.

9 R Luxemburg, *Ausegewählte Reden und Schrifte* (Berlin, 1955), vol 1, pp201-202.

10 Antonio Martins dos Santos, an official of the Lisbon Metal Workers Union, interviewed in *Socialist Worker*, 27 July.

11 *Our Common Struggle* 1, 1974.
12 *Our Common Struggle* 8, June 1975.
13 *Our Common Struggle* 9, July-August 1975.
14 *Morning Star*, 21 August 1975.
15 *Our Common Struggle* 2, October 1974.
16 *Our Common Struggle* 7, April 1975.
17 *Our Common Struggle* 8, June 1975.
18 A Cunhal, *Pela Revolução Democratica c Nacional* (Lisbon, 1975), pp211-212.
19 A Cunhal, *Pela Revolução*, p210.
20 A Cunhal, *Pela Revolução*, p205.
21 A Cunhal, *Pela Revolução*, p213.
22 A Cunhal, *Pela Revolução*.
23 A Cunhal, *Pela Revolução*.
24 A Cunhal, *Pela Revolução*, pp210-211.
25 A Cunhal, *Pela Revolução*, p211.
26 *Our Common Struggle* 3, November 1974.
27 *Our Common Struggle* 3, November 1974.
28 *Our Common Struggle* 2, October 1974.
29 J Rollo, *International Socialism*, April 1975.
30 *Our Common Struggle* 2, October 1974.
31 *Our Common Struggle* 7, April 1975.
32 *Our Common Struggle* 1, September 1974.
33 *Socialist Worker*, 26 July 1975.
34 K Marx, 'Address to the Communist League, 1850', Appendix to Engels' *Revolution and Counter-Revolution in Germany* (London, 1933).
35 *Documents do Partido Revolucionario do Proletariado-Brigadas Revolucionarios*, 1971-1974 (Lisbon, 1975), pp173-176
36 More on this in 'The Way Ahead', subheading, 'Central Role of the Revolutionary Party'.
37 C Harman, *International Socialism*, October 1974.
38 *Le Monde*, 2 May 1974.
39 *Le Monde*, 7 May 1974.
40 See, for example, V Marchetti and J Marks, *The CIA and the Cult of Intelligence* (New York 1975).
41 The FNLA is also supported by China. In May 1974, 200 Chinese instructors arrived in Zaire to start training FNLA guerrillas. According to Roberto, all FNLA have now been trained by the Chinese. Interview in *Le Monde*, 6 June 1975.
42 A Munster, *Portugal: Jahr 1 der Revolution* (Berlin 1975), p64.
43 *Le Monde*, 12 September 1974.
44 J Rollo, *International Socialism*, April 1975.
45 *Socialist Worker*, 22 March 1975.
46 J Rollo, *International Socialism*, April 1975.
47 *Socialist Worker*, 22 March, 1975.
48 *Socialist Worker*, 22 March 1975.
49 B V Stankevich, *Vospominaniia 1914-1919* gg, (Berlin 1920), p72.
50 B V Stankevich, *Vospominaniia*, p77.
51 A Wildman, 'The February Revolution and the Russian Army', *Soviet Studies*, July 1970.
52 V I Lenin, *Collected Works*, vol 34, pp100-101.
53 *Socialist Worker*, 10 May 1975.
54 V Gonçalves, *Citaçãos* (Portugal 1975), p17.
55 V Gonçalves, *Citaçãos*, p72.
56 V Gonçalves, *Citaçãos*, p88; speech in Oporto, 5 October 1974.
57 V Gonçalves, *Citaçãos*, p74.
58 *Expresso*, 9 August 1975.
59 ADU—Assembly of Delegates, according to rank.
60 AGU—General Assembly of the Unit.

61 *Expresso*, 15 August 1975
62 *Expresso*, 23 August 1975.
63 *Revolução*, 22 April 1975.
64 J Rollo, *International Socialism*, April 1975.
65 E Anderson, *Hammer or Anvil* (London, 1945), p43.
66 P Broué and E Témime, *The Revolution and the Civil War in Spain* (London, 1971), p127.
67 C Harman, *Bureaucracy and Revolution in Eastern Europe* (London, 1974), p137.
68 L Trotsky, *1905* (New York, 1971), p104.
69 L Trotsky, *1905*, pp105-112, 155, 107, 109, 136-137, 124, 125, 140-146, 179-186, 252.
70 L Trotsky, *1905*, pp222-223.
71 V I Lenin, *Collected Works*, vol 25, p221.
72 W Burchett, *Portugal*, pp195-196.
73 *Expresso*, 19 July 1975.
74 W Burchett, *Portugal*, pp203-205.
75 W Burchett, *Portugal*, p208.
76 W Burchett, *Portugal*, p207.
77 *Textos Historicos da Revolução* (Lisbon, June 1975), p114.
78 *Quarterly Economic Review* 3, 1974.
79 *Expresso*, 23 August 1975.
80 *Expresso*, 14 December 1974.
81 W Burchett, *Portugal*, p230.
82 *Expresso*, 15 February 1975.
83 *Our Common Struggle* 5, February 1975.
84 *Our Common Struggle* 8, June 1975.
85 Vasco Corregedor da Fonseca, *Eleicoes para a Constituinte em Processo Revolucionario* (appendix).
86 *Quarterly Economic Review* 1, 1974.
87 V Gonçalves, *Citaçãos*, p.96.
88 *Guardian*, 5 September 1975.
89 *Guardian*, 9 September 1975.
90 *Le Monde*, 15/16 June 1975.
91 *Le Monde*, 13/14 July 1975.
92 *Le Monde*, 15 July 1975.
93 *L'Unità*, 28 July 1975.
94 V I Lenin, *Collected Works*, vol 31, pp70-74.
95 V I Lenin, *Collected Works*, vol 25, pp285-289.
96 L Trotsky, *Fascism, Stalinism and the United Front, International Socialism* (first series) 38/39, August/September 1969.
97 V I Lenin, *Collected Works*, vol 30, p356.
98 V I Lenin, *Collected Works*, vol 8, p563.
99 V I Lenin, *Collected Works*, vol 10, p259.

Revolution and counter-revolution: lessons for Indonesia

International Socialism (second series) 80, Autumn 1998

The outbreak of the revolution in Indonesia raises a number of crucial theoretical questions. What are the preconditions for a victorious conclusion to the revolution? In the balance between revolution and counter-revolution, what determines which will triumph? What is the relation between the revolutionary party and the working class? What role does the revolutionary party play in the trade unions? What attitude should the working class take towards the capitalist class and the bourgeois intelligentsia? This article seeks to bring the experience of the Marxist tradition to bear on these crucial questions.

Preconditions for a victorious outcome of the revolution

As Lenin repeatedly stated, we live in the epoch of wars and revolutions. History has proved him right. During the present century more than 100 wars, large and small, have broken out. To mention but a few, chosen at random: the First and Second World Wars, Japan's aggression against China, Italy's war on Abyssinia, the eight-year war between Iran and Iraq, US imperialism's attacks on Iraq and Vietnam, the three Arab-Israeli wars, the two India-Pakistan wars, the Falklands War. But many revolutions have also taken place. Again, to mention only some of them: the Russian revolutions of 1905 and 1917, Germany 1918-23, Spain 1936, Hungary in 1919 and 1956, China 1925-27, the Portuguese Revolution of 1974, the overthrow of the Shah of Iran in 1979.

What is the nature of a workers' revolution? It is when the mass of workers break from the routine of being victims and passive objects of oppression and exploitation, and enter the arena of history, striving to achieve their freedom and shape their destiny. The revolution is not a one-day affair. The workers, with new emotions and ideas, still carry with them the baggage of the past. In

Marx's words, 'The tradition of dead generations hangs like a nightmare on the mind of the living.' The contradiction at the heart of the revolution is between the new and the old, and only through a very difficult and rigorous process can this contradiction be overcome.

Let us look at some examples, the first being the Russian Revolution of 1917. On 18 February 1917 workers in the largest factory in Petrograd, the Putilov factory where 30,000 workers worked, went on strike demanding a 50 percent wage rise. Bread riots broke out because of the food scarcity. Bakeries and foodstores were stormed, a scene repeated again and again in the following days:

> On 23 February at 9am the workers of the plants and factories of Vyborg district went on strike in protest against the shortage of black bread in bakeries and groceries; the strike spread to some plants located in the Petrograd, Rozhdestvenskii, and Liteinyi districts, and in the course of the day 50 industrial enterprises ceased working, with 87,534 men going on strike.

The following day the workers' movement had not abated. Thus a memorandum from the secret police, the Okhrana, compiled later in the evening of 24 February, stated, 'The strike of the workers which took place yesterday in connection with the shortage of bread continued today; in the course of the day 131 enterprises with 158,583 workers shut down.'

> Next day, on 25 February, the Okhrana report expressed even greater alarm, pointing out that troops, and even Cossacks, were not ready to suppress the workers. On 26 February, for the first time, there appears in an Okhrana report a direct description of a soldiers' mutiny.
>
> According to N N Sukhanov, an honest eyewitness and excellent chronicler of the revolution, some 25,000 soldiers had left their barracks to mingle with the crowd while the rest of the garrison—altogether 160,000-strong—were not prepared to actually suppress the workers. According to another source as many as 70,000 soldiers joined the 385,000 workers on strike on 27 February.
>
> 28 February brought the final collapse of the Tsarist forces: the last remaining 'loyal' troops surrendered; the fortress of Peter and Paul capitulated without firing a single shot; and the Tsar's ministers were either arrested or else surrendered to the new authorities.
>
> The revolution was completely spontaneous and unplanned. As Trotsky correctly states: 'No one, positively no one—we can assert this categorically upon the basis of all the data—then thought that 23 February was to mark the beginning of a decisive drive against absolutism.'
>
> Sukhanov observes: *'Not one party was preparing for the great upheaval.'*
>
> Similarly a former director of the Okhrana stated that the revolution was 'a purely spontaneous phenomenon, and not at all the fruit of party agitation'.[1]

A new political power rose in Petrograd: the soviet. As a matter of fact it was the renewal of an institution that was born in the 1905 Revolution. It was made up of delegates of all workers in the factories on strike, but it went beyond being a unified strike committee. In 1906 Lenin, in retrospect, said the following about the soviet:

> Soviets of Workers' Deputies are *organs of direct mass struggle*. They originated as organs of the *strike* struggle. By force of circumstances they very quickly became the organs of the *general revolutionary* struggle against the government. The course of events and the transition from a strike to an uprising *irresistibly* transformed them *into organs of an uprising*.

The February 1917 Revolution created an exciting new situation: the Tsar abdicated; centuries of the monarchy ended. The police were disbanded. In every factory workers' committees were established. In many army units soldiers' committees came into being. Soviets of workers and soldiers arose everywhere. Already during the 1905 Revolution Trotsky, Chairman of the Petrograd Soviet, could write of these institutions:

> The soviet really was a workers' government in embryo... The soviet was, from the start, the organisation of the proletariat, and its aim was the struggle for revolutionary power... With the soviet we have the first appearance of democratic power in modern Russian history... It constitutes authentic democracy, without a lower and an upper chamber, without a professional bureaucracy, but with the voters' right to recall their deputies at any moment. Through its members—deputies directly elected by the workers—the soviet exercises direct leadership over all social manifestations of the proletariat as a whole and of its individual groups, organises its actions and provides them with a slogan and a banner.[2]

But after the revolution in February 1917, parallel to the soviets, the old institutions continued. In the factories the old owners and the old managers continued to hold on to their positions. In the army the generals were still in command: the Commander-in-Chief of the army was General Kornilov, who was appointed by the Tsar. Parallel to soviet power was a bourgeois government headed by a liberal politician from Tsarist times. This situation, which Lenin and Trotsky called 'dual power', was full of contradictions.

Notwithstanding the nature of the soviet as outlined by Trotsky above, its leaders begged the bourgeoisie to retain power. The majority of the soviet delegates were right-wing socialists, Mensheviks and Social Revolutionaries. Out of 1,500 to 1,600 delegates only 40 were Bolsheviks. This was not an accident. It was the inevitable outcome of a situation in which millions of people moved to the left but still carried a lot of the ideological baggage of a Tsarist past. For millions who had hitherto supported the Tsar and the war, a move to the left did not mean straight away joining the most extreme of the parties, the Bolsheviks. The strong man of the Mensheviks, I G Tseretelli, who became Minister of the Interior in the bourgeois Provisional Government, explained the necessity of a compromise with the bourgeoisie: 'There can be no other road for the revolution. It's true that we have all the power, and that the government would go if we lifted a finger, but that would mean disaster for the revolution.'

In a pamphlet entitled *The Tasks of the Proletariat in our Revolution*, Lenin wrote the following on dual power:

> This dual power is evident in the existence of *two governments*: one is the main, the real, the actual government of the bourgeoisie, the 'Provisional Government' of Lvov and Co, which holds in its hands all the organs of power; the other is a supplementary and parallel government, a 'controlling' government in the shape of the Petrograd Soviet of Workers' and Soldiers' Deputies, which holds no organs of state power, but directly rests on the support of an obvious and indisputable majority of the people, on the armed workers and soldiers.

This unstable set-up could not last long:

> The dual power merely expresses a *transitional* phase in the revolution's development, when it has gone farther than the ordinary bourgeois democratic revolution, *but has not yet reached* a 'pure' dictatorship of the proletariat and the peasantry.

It was only after days, weeks and months of stormy events that the Bolsheviks managed to win over the majority of workers. On 9 September the Petrograd Soviet went over to Bolshevism and Trotsky was elected as its president. On the same day the Bolsheviks won the majority of the Moscow Soviet. From this point it was only a small stride towards the attainment of workers' power on 7 November 1917.

The May 1968 events in France tell a completely different story with a different outcome. France in May-June 1968 was in a deep social and political crisis. On the night of 10-11 May bloody clashes took place in the Latin quarter of Paris between revolutionary students and the riot police, the CRS. Thousands of young workers joined the students. The next day the CGT, the main trade union federation, called for a protest demonstration. One million people turned up to the demonstration. The unions called for a one-day general strike on 13 May and 10 million came out, four times more than the number of workers organised in trade unions. The whole country was paralysed. The CGT and Communist Party leaders hoped that the one-day strike and demonstration would serve as an effective safety valve—that this would be the end of the struggle. But they did not reckon with the rank and file, who entered the arena on their own account.

On 14 May the workers of Sud Aviation in Nantes declared an unlimited strike. They occupied the factory and imprisoned the manager in his office. *L'Humanité*, the Communist Party newspaper, tried to ignore the event, giving it only seven lines on page nine. The next day the strike and occupation movement spread to all Renault factories. In their footsteps all the engineering factories, the car and aeroplane plants, went on strike and were occupied by the workers. On 19 May the trams stopped along with mail and telegraph services. The subway and bus services in Paris followed suit. The strike hit the mines, shipping, Air France and so on.

On 20 May the strike became a general strike. Some 10 million workers were now on strike. People who had never struck before were involved—Folies Bergère dancers, soccer players, journalists, saleswomen, technicians. Red flags fluttered from all places of work. Not a tricolore was to be seen, notwithstanding the statement of the CGT and CP leaders that 'our banner is both the tricolore and the Red Flag'.[3]

All this was very new, representing the future, but the old, 'the tradition of the dead generations', was still hanging on. It is true that 1 million people demonstrated in Paris on 13 May. This was new. But the union bureaucracy, frightened of the thought that the revolutionary students would mingle with the workers, insisted on separating the two groups by creating a cordon of 20,000 stewards holding arms to separate them. It is true that 10 million workers went on strike...*but* the strike committees were not elected but appointed by the trade union bureaucracy. It is true that millions of workers occupied the factories...*but* right from the beginning of the occupations the union bureaucracy insisted that only a small minority of the workers should stay in the factories while the majority were sent home. If all the workers had remained in the occupation the strike would have been active. Now it was passive.

Tragically there was not in existence a large revolutionary organisation that could overcome the bureaucracy. In Russia in March 1917 the Bolshevik Party had 23,600 members and this number increased by August to 250,000. The French industrial working class was significantly larger than the Russian working class in 1917. Had there existed a revolutionary organisation of some tens of thousands, it could have argued that the workers' contingents in the demonstration should not be separated from the students. It could have called for democratic elections of strike committees and could have convinced the millions occupying the factories to remain inside the factories, creating a collective force many times stronger than when these same workers were simply an aggregation of individuals. Alas, the total number of revolutionaries in France could be counted in hundreds.

Therefore it was not long before the government got the unions to agree to a compromise with the employers on a wage rise. The occupation of the factories ended, the strike was called off, and the ground was prepared for the return of the president, General de Gaulle. When the factories were occupied de Gaulle was so demoralised that he had flown out of the country to find refuge with the French troops in West Germany. But now he came back to rule once more. On 30 May a right-wing demonstration of half a million people took place in Paris. The police seized back the TV and radio stations, threw out occupying workers, attacked any continuing demonstrations, and even killed two workers and a school student. Again and again during 1968 the revolutionary potential, which could have gone so far, stopped well short of victory. And this has been the pattern in other revolutions.

In November 1918 the revolution in Germany got rid of the Kaiser and brought the First World War to an end. Alas, big employers like Krupps and Thyssen remained along with the generals and the reactionary army officers who set up right-wing units called Freikorps. As in Russia, dual power prevailed in Germany, for side by side with parliament were the workers' councils. Under the umbrella of the Social Democratic government, Freikorps officers murdered revolutionary leaders Rosa Luxemburg and Karl Liebknecht. The revolutionary events continued with ups and downs until 1923, but they ended with the victory of capitalism. The Nazi movement was born in 1919.

In 1923 it organised a 'failed' coup in Bavaria, but it was waiting in the wings. This was another lost opportunity for workers and they would pay for it dearly when Hitler came to power.

France in the 1930s saw a massive rise of working-class struggle which started in February 1934 and culminated in 1936 in a decisive victory of the Popular Front—an alliance of the Communist Party, Socialist Party and Liberals (who were mistakenly called Radical Socialists—they were neither radical nor socialist). Millions of workers said to themselves, 'Now we own the government, let's take over the factories.' And in June 1936 a wave of factory occupations took place. The leaders of the Communist Party and Socialist Party, however, led a retreat following a compromise with the employers. After this the CP was thrown out of the Popular Front. It was the Radical Socialist Daladier who signed the Munich agreement with Hitler in 1938, and it was the same parliament elected in the great Popular Front victory of 1936 which voted support for Marshal Pétain, head of the Vichy regime which collaborated with the Nazis from 1940 onwards.

The Middle East is another area which has seen great upheavals which shook the establishment but failed to win a fundamental breakthrough. In Iraq, King Feisal was overthrown in 1951 by a mass movement. The Communist Party of Iraq was a very strong party, indeed the strongest CP in the Arab world. It entered into an alliance with the bourgeois nationalist party, the Ba'ath. The Communist Party, under Stalinist control, believed that the coming revolution would be a democratic one, which demanded an alliance between the working class and the bourgeois parties. Such an alliance means in practice the subordination of the former to the latter. The Communist Party members and the workers paid a heavy price for this alliance. The Ba'ath, headed by General Saddam Hussein, with the aid of the CIA, carried out a mass slaughter of Communists.

In Iran a general strike led to the overthrow of the Shah in 1979. Shoras (workers' councils) mushroomed throughout the country. Tragically the leadership of these shoras, largely the pro-Moscow Tudeh Party and the Fedayeen, saw the revolution as a bourgeois democratic revolution instead of a proletarian one, and so gave support to the establishment of the Islamic republic. Ayatollah Khomeini thus came to power without showing any gratitude to the Tudeh or Fedayeen, and the left was subjected to bloody repression.

All the above events completely confirm the prophetic words of St Just, a leader of the French Revolution of 1789: 'Those who half make a revolution dig their own grave.' To complete the revolution and bring it to full victory, the proletariat has to be led by a revolutionary party. The working class, not the party, makes the revolution, but the party guides the working class. As Trotsky aptly wrote:

> Without a guiding organisation the energy of the masses would dissipate like steam not enclosed in a piston box. But nevertheless what moves things is not the piston or the box, but the steam.[4]

The difference between success and failure, between Russia in October 1917 and all these other examples, was that in the former case there was a mass revolutionary party providing effective leadership. While socialists cannot determine the moment when the revolutionary crisis breaks, they do determine the eventual outcome by the degree to which they build a strong revolutionary party.

The revolutionary party and the working class

The heart of Marxism is that the emancipation of the working class is the act of the working class. *The Communist Manifesto* states:

> All previous historical movements were movements of minorities, or in the interest of minorities. The proletarian movement is the self-conscious, independent movement of the immense majority, in the interest of the immense majority.

At the same time the *Manifesto* also stresses, 'The ruling ideas of each age have ever been the ideas of its ruling class.' There is a contradiction between the two statements. But the contradiction is not in Marx and Engels' heads. It exists in reality. If only one of the statements were correct, the victory of the working class would either be inevitable or impossible. If the workers were not imbued with capitalist ideas—selfishness, apathy towards other workers, racism, sexism, etc—socialism would be inevitable. It would come into being even if revolutionaries did not lift a finger. If workers completely accepted the ideas of the ruling class, socialism would be impossible and this would remain so forever. The balance between the two factors—self-activity of the working class and subordination to ruling-class ideas—is not static. It changes all the time. Sometimes the changes can be slow and imperceptible over a long period, but then they can change dramatically in a very short time.

The sharpening of the class struggle which leads to increasing confidence among workers undermines the hold of bourgeois ideas. Conversely, a downturn in workers' combativity following serious, continuous defeats, or mass unemployment over a long period (that erodes the self-confidence of the workers), makes them more ready to imbibe reactionary ideas.

However, a change in the balance between the two factors does not depend only on what happens in the workplace, on the economic front. Engels wrote that the class struggle takes place in three fields: the economic, the political and the ideological. The three fields are of course interconnected, with the economic serving as the base, and the political and ideological as the superstructure. But workers' combativity can rise, and even explode, not only because they are victorious in a struggle over wages or against sackings, but also because of events in the political field.

The Russian Revolution of February 1917 was not the result of a big rise in strikes, but was a direct reaction to the war. Four million Russian soldiers had perished. Hunger stalked the country. The riots and demonstrations in Petrograd at the beginning of February ignited the revolution, but these events had very little connection with a rise in the level of the industrial struggle.

The balance between the two factors—the new thinking that grows out of self-activity of workers and the burden of capitalist ideas—does not alter only with changes in the general situation, but also affects different workers differently. One can say that in any given situation one section of workers completely accepts bourgeois ideas—these are the conservative workers. Another section completely rejects bourgeois ideas—they are the revolutionary workers. Those two groups are represented by two separate parties—a conservative party and a revolutionary workers' party. Between these two there is another group of workers on whom a third type of workers' party is based—the reformist party. One example of such a party is the British Labour Party. In a speech to the Second Congress of the Communist International in 1920 Lenin defined the Labour Party as a 'capitalist workers' party'. He called it capitalist because its politics did not break with capitalism. Why did he call it a workers' party? It is not because the workers voted for it. At that time more workers voted for the Conservative Party, and this party was purely a capitalist party. Lenin called the Labour Party a workers' party because it reflected the urge of workers to defend themselves against capitalism.

Of course this is a very rough classification. Between the revolutionary parties and the reformist parties there can also be another kind of party—the centrist party. Its main characteristics are fudge and vacillation. It is neither one thing nor another. A centrist party sometimes moves from the right to the left, or from the left to the right. And the same centrist party can change direction over a very short space of time. The centrist party is like a chameleon, changing its colour but never remaining consistent.

A great danger for a revolutionary party is that it adapts itself to the centrists while in turn the centrist party tail-ends the reformists and the latter tail-ends the capitalist party. To give just one example: during the general strike of 1926 in Britain the leadership of the Communist Party softened and adapted their key policies, hoping by this method to attract the centrist trade union leaders. As a result they tail-ended the likes of A J Cook, George Hicks and Alfred Purcell, the left leaders of the general council of the TUC. For their part Cook, Hicks and Purcell tail-ended the right-wing leadership of the TUC—Jimmy Thomas, Arthur Pugh and Ben Turner. These three followed the leadership of Ramsay MacDonald, leader of the Labour Party, and ended up effectively supporting the policy of Stanley Baldwin, the Conservative prime minister of the day. The Communist Party's adaptation to the centrists led finally to a terrible defeat of the British working class. A revolutionary party facing vacillating centrist leaders must demonstrate clarity and steadfastness. One has to be firm to steady the unsteady.

History is made by the working class, and so the revolutionary party must avoid two dangers: the first is substitutionism, believing that the party can act for the class; the second is opportunism, adapting itself to views prevailing in the class. To give an example: a revolutionary can stand on a picket line, and find next to them a worker who makes racist comments. The revolutionary can do one of three things: say, 'I'm not standing with a racist on a picket line. I'm going home.' That is sectarianism, because if the emancipation of the working class is the act of the working class, one must side with the workers against the employers, however backward the individual worker. Another possibility is to avoid facing up to racism. When the worker makes a racist comment, one can pretend one hasn't heard, and say, 'The weather's quite nice today, isn't it?' This is opportunism. A third possibility is to argue with this person against racism. If they are convinced, excellent. If not, still, when the strikebreakers come, one links arms, because the emancipation of the working class *is* the act of the working class. A revolutionary cannot afford either substitutionism or tail-ending the workers.

A successful revolution also depends on the revolutionary party acting as the university of the working class. The situation of the working class *vis-à-vis* the bourgeoisie is radically different to the position of the early bourgeoisie when it was in rebellion against the feudal lords. The capitalists, even when their class was very young, were intellectually independent of the nobility. It is true the capitalists had to overthrow the nobility, as the working class today has to overthrow the capitalists. But the working class lacks the advantages enjoyed by the bourgeoisie when it sought to make a revolution. Its enemy, the nobility, did not own all the wealth as do the capitalists today. As a matter of fact, the nobility were not as rich as the capitalists. The capitalist could turn round to the nobility and say, 'All right, you own the land, but we own money—we own the banks. When you go bankrupt how do you try to save yourself? You try to mix your blue blood with my gold. You try to marry my daughter.' When it came to the intellectual battle, the capitalist could turn round and say, 'Alright, you have the church, but we have the university; you have priests but we have professors; you have the Bible, but we have the encyclopedia. Come on, move over.'

The capitalists influenced the nobility much more than the nobility influenced the capitalists. The French Revolution started with a meeting of Estates General (the Three Estates—the nobility, the priesthood and the middle classes). When it came to the vote many nobles and priests voted with the capitalists, not the other way round. Is the position of the workers today *vis-à-vis* the capitalists similar to this? Of course not. The workers cannot turn round to the capitalists and say, 'All right, you own Ford, General Motors, ICI, etc. We own...' In terms of ideas there are hardly any capitalists influenced by the socialist press, while there are millions of workers influenced by capitalist propaganda.

When we say that the revolutionary party is the university of the working class, it means we have to learn from the historical and international experience of the working class, both its triumphs as well as its defeats. The revolutionary party must be the memory of the working class. Thus in looking at Indonesia today one must also bear in mind the experience of the first workers' government in the world, the Paris Commune of 1871, where workers held power for 74 days. We have to learn from the 1905 Revolution, and even more so from the victory of the October Revolution. At the same time we have to learn from the defeat of the German Revolution of 1918-23; from the defeat of the general strike in Britain in 1926; from the murder by Stalin of all the leaders of the Bolshevik Party after Lenin's death, his annihilation of the soviets, and his replacement of the proletarian regime which stood for the beginning of socialism with a state capitalist order. One has to learn from the 1933 catastrophe in Germany, when the strongest, best organised workers' movement in the world capitulated to the Nazis without a fight, because it was led by two parties, one of which was a right-wing reformist party and the other a Stalinist party. One has to learn why in China society has developed in such a way that there are at the top a massive number of millionaires, while at the bottom there are hundreds of millions who live in abject poverty.

To give confidence to workers' struggle, the revolutionary party must have theoretical clarity. Its converse, theoretical scepticism, is incompatible with revolutionary action. As Lenin said, 'The important thing is to be confident that the path chosen is the right one, this confidence multiplying a hundredfold revolutionary energy and revolutionary enthusiasm, which can perform miracles'.[5] Without understanding the laws of historical development, one cannot maintain a persistent struggle. During the years of toil and disappointment, isolation and suffering, revolutionaries cannot survive without the conviction that their actions fit the requirements of historical advance. In order not to get lost on the twists and turns of the long road, one must stand firm ideologically. Theoretical scepticism and revolutionary relentlessness are not compatible. Lenin's strength was that he always related theory to the processes of human development. He judged the importance of every theoretical notion in relation to practical needs. Likewise he tested every practical step for its fit with Marxist theory. He combined theory and practice to perfection.

Lenin believed in improvisation. But in order for this not to degenerate into simply the shifting impressions of the day, it had to be blended into a *general perspective* based on well thought out theory. Practice without theory must lead to uncertainty and errors. On the other hand, to study Marxism apart from the struggle is to divorce it from its mainspring—action—and to create useless bookworms. Practice is clarified by revolutionary theory, and theory is verified by practice. The Marxist traditions are assimilated in the minds and blood of women and men only by struggle.

Building a revolutionary party

By far the greatest Marxist in his understanding of the role of the revolutionary party and its activity was Lenin. His experience in building the Bolshevik Party from 1903 onwards is very instructive. The embryo of the revolutionary party is the discussion group, the study circle. This is a necessary stage in the 'primitive accumulation of cadres'. But it is only a stage. The circle mentality has serious weaknesses. It is amateurish and can become an impediment to the development of a revolutionary party proper.

In 1902 in a brilliant pamphlet entitled *What is to be Done?* Lenin argued that the Russian revolutionaries had to put an end to the circle mentality. The revolutionaries, he argued, had to build a centralised, all-Russian organisation. To achieve this they had first of all to fight against what he called *Kustarichestvo*—

a primitive 'handicraft method of organisation'. They had to establish a strong organisation made up of professional revolutionaries; this was especially needed under the illegal, harsh conditions of Tsarism. But to prevent the organisation becoming a sect it had to establish strong ties with workers and their struggles. The key to this is the party paper. The paper must serve as a weapon for building a centralised all-Russian organisation. In an article called 'Where to Begin' he wrote that 'the role of a newspaper' should not be:

> ...limited solely to the dissemination of ideas, to political education, and to the enlistment of political allies. A newspaper is not only a collective propagandist and a collective agitator, it is also a collective organiser. In this last respect it may be likened to the scaffolding round a building under construction, which marks the contours of the structure and facilitates communication between the builders, enabling them to distribute the work and to view the common results achieved by their organised labour. With the aid of the newspaper, and through it, a permanent organisation will naturally take shape that will engage, not only in local activities, but in regular general work, and will train its members to follow political events carefully, appraise their significance and their effect on the various strata of the population, and develop effective means for the revolutionary party to influence those events. The mere technical task of regularly supplying the newspaper with copy and of promoting regular distribution will necessitate a network of local agents of the united party, who will maintain constant contact with one another, know the general state of affairs, get accustomed to performing regularly their detailed functions in the all-Russian work, and test their strength in the organisation of various revolutionary actions.
>
> This network of agents will form the skeleton of precisely the kind of organisation we need—one that is sufficiently broad and many-sided to effect a strict and detailed division of labour; sufficiently well tempered to be able to conduct steadily *its own work* under any circumstances, at all 'sudden turns', and in face of all contingencies; sufficiently flexible to be able, on the one hand, to avoid an open battle against an overwhelming enemy, when the enemy has concentrated all his forces at one spot, and yet, on the other, to take advantage of his unwieldiness and to attack him when and where he least expects it.[6]

The party paper is the *organiser of the party*.

But with the outbreak of the 1905 Revolution Lenin changed his argument: *the party should not be made up of professional revolutionaries but be based on mass recruitment*. In the spring of 1905, at the Russian party congress, Lenin proposed a resolution urging the party to open its gates wide to workers, who should be brought forward to take a leading role in it. The party should:

> ...make every effort to strengthen the ties between the party and the masses of the working class by raising still wider sections of proletarians and semi-proletarians to full [revolutionary socialist] consciousness, by developing their revolutionary...activity, by seeing to it that the greatest possible number of workers capable of leading the movement and the party organisations be advanced from among the mass of the working class to membership of the local centres and of

> the all-party centre through the creation of a maximum number of working class organisations adhering to our party, by seeing to it that working class organisations unwilling or unable to enter the party should at least be associated with it.[7]

In an article called 'The Reorganisation of the Party', written in November 1905, Lenin says bluntly, 'The working class is instinctively, spontaneously' revolutionary socialist.[8] As a result of this reorientation the party membership exploded. While in 1903 the membership was counted in hundreds, in October 1906 the Bolshevik Party had some 33,000 members.[9] Without Lenin's understanding that the development of the party requires very different tactics and forms of organisation tailored according to the size of the organisation, the composition of its membership, and the tasks required of it by the balance of forces in the wider society, such growth would not have been possible.

The revolutionary party and the trade unions

Revolutionaries are involved in every aspect of workers' struggle. Hence they are deeply involved in the struggle of the trade unions. The reformists regard the working-class movement as split into different, separate compartments: economic struggle, that is the task of the trade unions; politics, ie participation in parliamentary and local government elections, is the concern of the reformist parties. Against this the Marxist looks at the working class as a totality, as a class that uses two arms in the struggle—the economic and the political.

In general the dichotomy between economic and political struggle is foreign to Marx. An economic demand, if it is sectional, is defined as 'economic' in Marx's terms. But if the same demand is made of the state it is 'political':

> The attempt in a particular factory or even in a particular trade to force a shorter working day out of individual capitalists by strikes, etc, is a purely economic movement. On the other hand the movement to force through an eight-hour, etc, *law*, is a *political* movement, that is to say, a movement of the *class*, with the object of enforcing its interests in a general form, in a form possessing general, socially coercive force...every movement in which the working class comes out as a *class* against the ruling classes and tries to coerce them by pressure from without is a political movement.[10]

In many cases economic (sectional) struggles do not give rise to political (class-wide) struggles, but there is no absolute separation between the two, and many economic struggles *do* spill over into political ones. The experience of Russia in 1905, with mass strikes acting as the motor of revolution, gave new depth to the understanding of the close connection between the economic and political struggles. Rosa Luxemburg pointed out that in a revolutionary period the economic struggle grows into a political one, and vice versa:

> The movement does not go only in one direction, from an economic to a political struggle, but also in the opposite direction. Every important political mass action, after reaching its peak, results in a series of economic mass strikes. And this rule applies not only to the individual mass strike, but to the revolution as a

> whole. With the spread, clarification and intensification of the political struggle not only does the economic struggle not recede, but on the contrary it spreads and at the same time becomes more organised and intensified. There exists a reciprocal influence between the two struggles. Every fresh attack and victory of the political struggle has a powerful impact on the economic struggle, because as it widens the scope for the workers to improve their conditions and strengthens their impulse to do so, it enhances their fighting spirit. After every soaring wave of political action, there remains a fertile sediment from which sprout a thousand economic struggles. And the reverse also applies.

The logical and necessary climax of the mass strike is the 'open uprising which can only be realised as the culmination of a series of partial uprisings which prepare the ground, and therefore are liable to end for a time in what look like the partial "defeats", each of which may seem to be "premature".' And what a rise in class consciousness results from the mass strikes!

> The most precious thing, because it is the most enduring, in the sharp ebb and flow of the revolutionary wave, is the proletariat's spiritual growth. The advance by leaps and bounds of the intellectual stature of the proletariat affords an inviolable guarantee of its further progress in the inevitable economic and political struggles ahead.[11]

It would be a great mistake to conclude from the above that there is no important qualitative difference between the party and the unions. This is especially important for countries like Indonesia in which the unions are just at the beginning of their existence and the border between the two is quite often very unclear. The slogan of the unions was set down in Britain in the 19th century: 'A fair day's pay for a fair day's work.' The aim of the revolutionaries, the socialists, is to abolish the wages system, to get rid of a society in which some people have to sell their labour power and others buy it. Obviously so long as capitalism exists we prefer high wages to low ones, but the different goals remain.

The unions recruit members on a radically different basis to the revolutionary party. The revolutionary party recruits those who are in ideological agreement with its principles. The unions aim to recruit every worker, revolutionary, reformist or conservative. It strengthens the unions if conservative workers are involved and under the ideological pressure of all other workers. The revolutionary party, by contrast, should not dilute its membership by including people who do not agree with its politics. The trade union movement is a blunt axe but a large one. The revolutionary party is a sharp axe even if it is relatively small. Lenin contrasted the roles of the revolutionary Marxist with the trade union secretary:

> For the secretary of any, say English, trade union always helps the workers to carry on the economic struggle, he helps them to expose factory abuses, explains the injustice of the laws and of measures that hamper the freedom to strike and to picket (ie to warn all and sundry that a strike is proceeding at a certain factory), explains the partiality of arbitration court judges who belong to the bourgeois classes, etc, etc. In a word every trade union secretary conducts and helps to conduct 'the economic struggle against the employers and the government'... the Social Democrat's ideal should not be the trade union secretary,

> but *the tribune of the people*, who is able to react to every manifestation of tyranny and oppression, no matter where it appears, no matter what stratum or class of the people it affects; who is able to generalise all these manifestations and produce a single picture of police violence and capitalist exploitation; who is able to take advantage of every event, however small, in order to set forth *before all* his socialist convictions and his democratic demands, in order to clarify for *all* and everyone the world-historic significance of the struggle for the emancipation of the proletariat.[12]

The revolutionary party and the liberal factions in the democratic revolution

In a whole number of countries where the bourgeoisie is young and the political regime is either autocratic or only recently become democratic, such as Indonesia, there is a danger that the proletariat will tail the bourgeois democrats. The French bourgeoisie succeeded in carrying out their revolution of 1789-93, but since then the pattern has been different. For example, the German bourgeoisie of 1848 betrayed their revolution and capitulated to the landowning Junkers and the monarchy. The German bourgeoisie was fearful of the rising working class. Today the working class exists everywhere and is employed in much larger plants than existed in 1789 or 1848. Fear of the proletariat inevitably paralyses the bourgeoisie and the bourgeois intelligentsia. In March 1850 Marx argued that the German working class should not subordinate itself to the liberal bourgeoisie and petty bourgeois intelligentsia:

> The relation of the revolutionary workers' party to the petty-bourgeois democrats is this: it marches together with them against the faction which it aims at overthrowing, it opposes them in everything by which they seek to consolidate their position in their own interests.
>
> Far from desiring to transform the whole of society for the revolutionary proletarians, the democratic petty bourgeois strive for a change in social conditions by means of which the existing society will be made as tolerable and comfortable as possible for them...
>
> While the democratic petty bourgeois wish to bring the revolution to a conclusion as quickly as possible...it is our interest and our task to make the revolution permanent, until all more or less possessing classes have been forced out of their position of dominance, the proletariat has conquered state power... For us the issue cannot be the alteration of private property but only its annihilation, not the smoothing over of class antagonisms but the abolition of classes, not the improvement of the existing society but the foundation of a new one...
>
> It is self-evident that in the impending bloody conflicts, as in all earlier ones, it is the workers who, in the main, will have to win the victory by their courage, determination and self-sacrifice. As previously so also in this struggle, the mass of the petty bourgeois will as long as possible remain hesitant, undecided and inactive, and then, as soon as the issue has been decided, will seize the victory

for themselves, will call upon the workers to maintain tranquillity and return to their work, will guard against so-called excesses and bar the proletariat from the fruits of victory... they themselves must do the utmost for their final victory by making it clear to themselves what their class interests are, by taking up their position as an independent party as soon as possible and by not allowing themselves to be misled for a single moment by the hypocritical phrases of the democratic petty bourgeois into refraining from the independent organisation of the party of the proletariat. Their battle cry must be: The Revolution in Permanence.[13]

Some one and a half centuries later the bourgeoisie and bourgeois intelligentsia are even more cowardly and reactionary. The revolutionary party must keep its distance from them, even if they take on a reddish coloration. The most prominent leaders in Indonesia today are Megawati and Amien Rais. Megawati is the daughter of the first president of Indonesia, Ahmed Sukarno. When Indonesia won its independence from the Dutch in 1949 the country was led by this bourgeois nationalist. His ideology was based on the principles of pancasila whose main planks were belief in god and national unity. Tragically the Indonesian Communist Party did not challenge Sukarno but, on the contrary, agreed with him completely on the need for national unity. The result was that St Just's words came true: 'Those who half make a revolution dig their own graves.'

The Communist Party of Indonesia had far more members than the Bolshevik Party had at the time of the revolution: 3 million as against a quarter of a million. The working class of Indonesia was larger than the working class of Russia on the eve of the revolution. The peasantry was larger in Indonesia than in Russia. In 1965 a general appointed by Sukarno, one Suharto, organised a coup with the backing of the United States, the British Labour government and Australia. Somewhere between half a million and 1 million people were slaughtered. Megawati has not advanced one inch further than her father.

The other most prominent leader of bourgeois nationalism in Indonesia at present is Amien Rais. He does not stand to the left of Megawati. He is the chairman of the Muslim movement, Muhammadiya, which claims 28 million members. He has for years been engaged in the most disgusting racist agitation against the Chinese minority in Indonesia, which led to pogroms on a massive scale, the main victims of which were the very poor. Amien Rais was harsh on the Chinese but quite accommodating to President Suharto. On 19 May, two days before Suharto's abdication, Amien Rais appeared on radio and television calling on people not to demonstrate, to keep calm!

Megawati and Amien Rais are pygmies compared to Robespierre or Danton and in no way more militant than the cowardly bourgeoisie in Germany in 1848 that Marx so sharply castigated.

Indonesia, like many Third World countries, faces serious bourgeois democratic tasks—achieving political democracy, solving the agrarian question, overcoming the fragmentation of the country, and putting an end to the oppression of national and religious minorities as well as to the oppression of women and gays. Only after the proletariat achieves a victorious revolution can these democratic tasks be fully carried out. At the same time in the struggle for workers' power the revolutionary party must act as a tribune of the oppressed and mobilise the energy of the peasants, the national and religious minorities, women and gays.

Notes

1. T Cliff, *Lenin*, vol 2 (London, 1976), pp76-82.
2. L Trotsky, *1905* (New York, 1972), pp251, 253-254.
3. C Harman, *The Fire Last Time, 1968 and After* (London, 1998), pp2-6.
4. L Trotsky, *History of the Russian Revolution* (London, 1997), p19.
5. V I Lenin, *Collected Works*, vol IX (Moscow, 4th edn), p103.
6. V I Lenin, *Collected Works*, vol VII, p363.
7. V I Lenin, *Collected Works*, vol VIII, pp409-410.
8. V I Lenin, *Collected Works*, vol X, p334.
9. T Cliff, *Lenin*, vol I (London, 1975), p179.
10. K Marx, F Engels, V I Lenin, *Anarchism and Anarcho-Syndicalism* (Moscow, 1972), p57.
11. T Cliff, *Rosa Luxemburg* (London, 1980), p28.
12. V I Lenin, *Collected Works*, vol V, p423.
13. K Marx and F Engels, *Collected Works*, vol X (London, 1981), pp280-282, 287.

Index